Post–Cold War Revelations and the American Communist Party

Post–Cold War Revelations and the American Communist Party

Citizens, Revolutionaries, and Spies

Edited by
Vernon L. Pedersen, James G. Ryan,
and Katherine A. S. Sibley

BLOOMSBURY ACADEMIC
LONDON • NEW YORK • OXFORD • NEW DELHI • SYDNEY

BLOOMSBURY ACADEMIC
Bloomsbury Publishing Plc
50 Bedford Square, London, WC1B 3DP, UK
1385 Broadway, New York, NY 10018, USA
29 Earlsfort Terrace, Dublin 2, Ireland

BLOOMSBURY, BLOOMSBURY ACADEMIC and the Diana logo are
trademarks of Bloomsbury Publishing Plc

First published in Great Britain 2021
Paperback edition published 2022

Copyright © Vernon L. Pedersen, James G. Ryan, and Katherine A. S. Sibley, 2021

Vernon L. Pederson, James G. Ryan, and Katherine A. S. Sibley have asserted
their right under the Copyright, Designs and Patents Act, 1988, to be identified
as Editors of this work.

For legal purposes the Acknowledgments on p. x constitute an extension
of this copyright page.

Cover design: Terry Woodley

Cover Image: Communists get together, Washington, D.C., 2/12/38.
Library of Congress, Prints & Photographs Division, photograph by
Harris & Ewing, reproduction number LC-DIG-hec-24052.

All rights reserved. No part of this publication may be reproduced or
transmitted in any form or by any means, electronic or mechanical,
including photocopying, recording, or any information storage or retrieval
system, without prior permission in writing from the publishers.

Bloomsbury Publishing Plc does not have any control over, or responsibility
for, any third-party websites referred to or in this book. All internet addresses given in this
book were correct at the time of going to press. The author and publisher regret any
inconvenience caused if addresses have changed or sites have ceased to exist, but can accept
no responsibility for any such changes.

Every effort has been made to trace copyright holders and to obtain their
permissions for the use of copyright material. The publisher apologizes for any
errors or omissions and would be grateful if notified of any corrections that
should be incorporated in future reprints or editions of this book.

A catalogue record for this book is available from the British Library.

Library of Congress Cataloging-in-Publication Data
Names: Pedersen, Vernon L., 1955– editor. | Ryan, James G., editor. |
Sibley, Katherine A. S. (Katherine Amelia Siobhan), 1961– editor.
Title: Post-Cold War revelations and the American Communist Party :
citizens, revolutionaries, and spies / edited by Vernon L. Pedersen,
James G. Ryan, and Katherine A.S. Sibley.
Description: London ; New York : Bloomsbury Academic, 2021. |
Includes bibliographical references and index.
Identifiers: LCCN 2020035984 (print) | LCCN 2020035985 (ebook) |
ISBN 9781350135758 (hardback) | ISBN 9781350202504 (paperback) |
ISBN 9781350135765 (ebook) | ISBN 9781350135772 (epub)
Subjects: LCSH: Communist Party of the United States of America. |
Communism–United States–History–20th century.
Classification: LCC JK2391.C5 P67 2021 (print) | LCC JK2391.C5 (ebook) |
DDC 324.273/7509–dc23
LC record available at https://lccn.loc.gov/2020035984
LC ebook record available at https://lccn.loc.gov/2020035985

ISBN: HB: 978-1-3501-3575-8
PB: 978-1-3502-0250-4
epub: 978-1-3501-3577-2
epdf: 978-1-3501-3576-5

Typeset by Newgen KnowledgeWorks Pvt. Ltd., Chennai, India

To find out more about our authors and books visit www.bloomsbury.com
and sign up for our newsletters.

*In Memory of
Daniel J. Leab
1936–2016*

Contents

List of Figures	ix
Acknowledgments	x
Introduction: Citizens, Revolutionaries, and Spies *Vernon L. Pedersen*	1
1 The "Mental Comintern" and the Self-Destructive Tactics of the CPUSA, 1944–8 *John Earl Haynes and Harvey Klehr*	17
2 Earl Browder's Changing Conception of the Marxian Revolution *James G. Ryan*	41
3 From Haymarket to Mao? The Radicalism of William Z. Foster *Edward P. Johanningsmeier*	65
4 Communists and Farmers in American History *William C. Pratt*	89
5 Soviet Spies, Russian Trolls, and the US Security State: The Consequences of Russia's Hold on American Imagination, Politics, and Culture since 1919 *Katherine A. S. Sibley*	111
6 Friendship Reforged in Anticommunism: Herbert Solow, Whittaker Chambers, and the Juliet Stuart Poyntz Disappearance *Denise Lynn*	141
7 Myth, Memory, and the Spanish Civil War: The World the Veterans Made *Vernon L. Pedersen*	161
8 "For a New Antifascist, Anti-imperialist People's Coalition": Claudia Jones, Black Left Feminism, and the Politics of Possibility in the Era of Trump *Erik S. McDuffie*	185
9 American Communism in a Time of Détente *Beth Slutsky*	205

10 The Party's Over: Former Communist Party Members in the San Francisco Bay Area *Robert W. Cherny* 229

Conclusion *Vernon L. Pedersen and Katherine A. S. Sibley* 255

Notes on Contributors 257
Index 261

Figures

0.1	Russia State Archive of Social and Political History where FOND 515 is housed	10
2.1	Communist Party Standard Bearers	50
3.1	William Z. Foster and Mary G. Harris "Mother" Jones at the Great Steel Strike of 1919	72
5.1	J. Edgar Hoover	118
5.2	Representative Jerry Voorhis	120
5.3	Senator Millard Tydings and Senator Joseph McCarthy	124
5.4	Julius and Ethel Rosenberg, separated by heavy wire screen as they leave US Court House	126
5.5	Joseph McCarthy and Joseph Welch at the Army-McCarthy hearings, 1954	127
6.1	Photograph, allegedly of Juliet Stuart Poyntz with German and Soviet spies	153
7.1	Keeping the legend alive, Victoria DogTakingGun	168
7.2	William McCuistion with his mother Dollie Crawford	173
8.1	Claudia Jones, circa 1930s	187
9.1	Angela Davis urges "Declare your independence: Vote for Hall and Tyner"	217
10.1	Phyllis "Pele" De Lappe, a staff member for the *People's World*	232

Acknowledgments

This book would not be possible without the generous support of Williams College and the Stanley Kaplan Program in American Foreign Policy. The editors wish to extend special thanks to Carrie Greene, Director of Commencement and Academic Events, and James McAllister, the Fred Greene Third Century Professor in Political Science, who cohosted the 2018 conference, One Hundred Years of Communism in the USA, on which this volume is based. The editors also wish to thank each other for their hard work, humor, and comradeship in both organizing the conference and editing this volume.

    Vernon L. Pedersen, American University of Sharjah
    James A. Ryan, Texas A&M University, Galveston
    Katherine A. S. Sibley, Saint Joseph's University

Introduction: Citizens, Revolutionaries, and Spies

Vernon L. Pedersen

Of all of the "third party" movements in American history, none has generated more controversy than the Communist Party of the United States of America (CPUSA).[1] Opponents have denounced it as a nest of traitors and subversives, loyal only to the Soviet Union, and dedicated to the violent overthrow of the American government. Supporters have praised it as a champion of racial equality, social justice, and workers' rights. Others, although not necessarily supporting the party's goals, have strongly protested attempts to suppress the organization or restrict the rights of its members. The party has even inspired its share of popular humor. A coffee mug in this writer's kitchen reads "Communist jokes aren't funny, unless everybody gets them." In the 1941 Howard Hawks's movie, *Ball of Fire*, Barbara Stanwyck attempts to convince Gary Cooper to let her stay at his town house. Pretending to be sick, she points to her throat and says, "It's as red as the *Daily Worker* and twice as sore."[2]

The history of the CPUSA is so tangled because of the extreme reactions it generated, combined with a lack of reliable sources needed to construct an objective narrative. Reaction to the party depends largely on how Communists are seen, as citizens, revolutionaries, or spies. Opponents see Communists as spies, dangerous subversives loyal to the Soviet Union and willing to commit treason if called upon by their foreign masters. Supporters applaud them as revolutionaries, seeking to redress injustices in society that they too want alleviated. Defenders may or may not agree with specific goals or actions undertaken by Communists, but they are united in regarding party members as citizens deserving of all the rights guaranteed by the Constitution. The problem with picking any one of these alternatives is that the CPUSA was all three things at once. The party did take direction, and funding, from the Soviet Union, and it did whatever the Soviets asked it to do including engaging in espionage. The party also sought a revolution, because its members sincerely believed that revolution was the only way to achieve their goals of racial equality, social justice, and the end of fascism. Finally, except for its early years, the majority of Communists in the United States were citizens, though they were frequently treated otherwise. Assessing the party's impact on American life is further complicated by the party's practice of changing its goals and methods depending on the needs of the Soviet Union. Following Soviet advice, the party sometimes operated in the open; at other times it concealed itself within larger organizations. Its stance on international affairs was contingent on Soviet demands. All of this exacerbated suspicion from its American opponents and government authorities, and frequently distressed the party's most ardent supporters.

Sorting out the party's multiple identities long proved impossible because of the lack of reliable sources. Institutional records existed in fragments randomly preserved in government records, often gathered for hostile reasons, or residing in collections held by former party members. Accounts by former party members were of little help: some denounced the organization; others remembered their membership with pride; and a surprising number dismissed the party as secondary to the goals of social justice it pursued. Further complicating the situation were the emotions and passions generated by the ebb and flow of the Cold War. Everything changed in 1991, when the Soviet Union collapsed and formerly closed archives were opened in Moscow, Eastern Europe, and the United States. Suddenly a massive amount of primary source material became available making it possible to construct a complete and nuanced history of the CPUSA. Such a retelling was essential because the history of the party touched on important aspects of wider American history from politics and ideology to civil rights, labor relations, and foreign relations. The nearly thirty years since have seen an outpouring of work from scholars intent on rewriting the story of a dynamic and influential part of American history.

In November of 2018, inspired by the approaching centenary of the 1919 founding of the CPUSA and the just passed twenty-fifth anniversary of the opening of the Soviet archives, members of the Historians of American Communism (HOAC) hosted a conference commemorating the two milestones at Williams College. With keynote addresses by John Earl Haynes and Randi Storch, leading proponents respectively of the two major schools of thought in the field, the conference showcased a range of current scholarship in a most stimulating atmosphere. The majority of the conference participants had traveled to Moscow to see the archives firsthand and were fully cognizant of the transformation of the field caused by the cascade of new information. The authors of the essays in this volume were all involved in the conference at Williams College. Their essays represent a broad spectrum of perspectives and approaches showcasing the new revelations, asking new questions of old topics, and transcending the existing schools of thought. The essays draw on more complete, balanced and up-to-date scholarship and offer a complex analysis of the party's activities and attributes, all of which help untangle its members' roles as citizens, revolutionaries, and spies.

The CPUSA came into existence not because of domestic circumstances, but as a reaction to events in Russia. The October Revolution that propelled the Bolshevik Party to power also caused the Socialist Party of America (SPA) to split into a left-wing faction seeking to emulate the Bolsheviks and a much larger right-wing faction, whose members remained committed to a reformist program within the political system. The radicals split further into the Communist Labor Party (CLP), composed primarily of native-born Americans, and the Communist Party of America (CPA), created by the foreign language groups of the SPA. The two new parties arrived at a particularly volatile time in American history. The year 1919 brought the Spanish flu, anarchist bombings, steel strikes, race riots, and the "Black Sox" scandal when the Chicago White Sox threw the World Series. At least three of those catastrophes could be blamed on the Communists and other radical groups like the Union of Russian Workers. The US government arrested thousands of members of the twin parties in the Palmer Raids, a nationwide sweep of radical groups on January 2, 1920. In the end only a few hundred were deported (as detailed in Chapter 5), but the raids drove the two parties underground. Both the CLP and the CPA applied for membership in the Communist International (Comintern), the Moscow-based organization created to direct the worldwide Communist movement. The Comintern insisted that the two parties merge, which they did in 1921 by becoming the Workers Party.[3]

Two notable incidents stand out in the party's early years—the Communist-led Gastonia Textile strike and the attempted take over of the Farmer-Labor Party (FLP). Created by progressives in Minnesota in 1918 the FLP (discussed in Chapter 4) went national in 1920, running Parley P. Christensen for president. At the 1923 convention, the Workers Party succeeded in gaining control of the FLP, renamed it the Federated Farmer-Labor Party, but were unable to translate the organizational victory into mass support. Confused maneuvering around the 1924 presidential election and the denunciation of the organization by progressive senator, Robert Lafollette, caused the national level party to collapse. The incident illustrates the difficulty American Communists had in cooperating with other left-wing organizations. Their need to be in complete control alienated moderates, made unnecessary enemies and kept the radicals in the minority.[4]

In 1929 Fred Beal, a communist organizer for the National Textile Workers Union (NTWU), lead a strike at the Loray Mill in Gastonia, North Carolina. The workers at the mills, suffering from layoffs and increased workloads in the name of efficiency, responded enthusiastically, walking off the job and creating a tent city for those kicked out of company housing. The insistence of party organizers on injecting ideology into the strike and the controversy over the party's insistence on biracial strike committees, eroded support for the union. The strike ended in violence after barely a week, with the deaths of a police officer as well as the striker Ella May Wiggins. In a tactic the party would use many times in the future, it turned the death of Wiggins, the failure of the strike, and the subsequent trials of the strike leaders into an effective propaganda campaign.[5]

The Gastonia strike took place in the wake of a change of policy in the Soviet Union triggered by Joseph Stalin's elimination of his right-wing opponents. Domestically the Soviets abandoned the New Economic Policy, instituted by Vladimir Lenin to allow the country to recover from the Russian Civil War of 1918–21. In its place, Stalin imposed Socialism in One Country, a program of collectivization of agriculture, rapid industrialization, and increased diligence against class enemies and saboteurs. In 1928 Stalin announced the beginning of the "Third Period" in revolutionary history, the international complement to Socialism in One Country. The Russian Revolution, he declared, inaugurated the First Period of revolutionary upheaval, while the Second Period witnessed capitalist recovery, but the Third Period would be one of renewed revolutionary potential, which required the worldwide Communist parties to adopt resolutely radical stances. Jay Lovestone, the CPUSA leader, resisted the change in tactics as inappropriate to American conditions, but the Comintern disagreed and arranged for Lovestone and his followers to be expelled from the party (the incident is recounted in Chapter 3), and be replaced by William Z. Foster. The tactics of the Third Period made party leaders seem prescient when the world economy collapsed in 1929. High-profile activities, like those of the Unemployed Councils, introduced the Party to mainstream America. Organized in the spring of 1930, the Unemployed Councils staged "Hunger Marches" on city halls and state capitol buildings, including two national marches in 1931 and 1932, and specialized in resisting evictions by moving people back into their houses as fast as landlords could move them out.[6]

Emboldened by the global economic crisis, the Comintern, through its labor arm the Red International of Trade Unions (Profintern), instructed the Communists to shift from working with established labor unions to founding dual, red unions that would demonstrate to workers where their interest truly lay. Party leaders denounced other labor unions and non-Communist left-wing political parties as "social-fascists"; just as misguided and destructive as the real thing. The red unions never succeeded in attracting a mass following and party membership suffered from high levels of turnover. The one bright spot of the Third Period was emergence of a tight-knit cadre of dedicated members who would guide the CPUSA for decades. The destruction of the German Communist Party after Hitler's rise to power and the success of the French Communists, in defiance of Moscow's instructions, in making common cause with other left-wing parties inspired the Comintern to change tactics. At the Seventh World Congress of the Comintern in 1935, Georgi Dimitrov introduced the policies of the Popular Front, which abandoned the "social-fascist" campaign in favor of making common cause with as many groups as possible in the name of antifascism, racial equality, and social justice.[7]

The change in the party line proved wildly successful. The party, after 1932 under the guidance of Earl Browder, sponsored dozens of groups designed to attract non-Communists, such as the American League against War and Fascism, International Labor Defense, Workers International Relief, and the Friends of the Soviet Union. Cooperation with the Congress of Industrial Organizations (CIO) allowed party members to gain influential positions in the automotive, electrical, maritime, and mining unions. Previously hostile to the reforms of Franklin Roosevelt's administration, the Popular Front turned the party into a strong supporter of the president. Communists joined government agencies, participated in New Deal programs, and led a cultural movement that finally reached a mass audience. But success came at the price of duplicity. Communist union organizers and front group managers often concealed their party membership and hid the true nature of the group behind economic and social goals. When confronted about their allegiances, party members denied that they were anything other than honest progressives and denounced their opponents as red baiters and tools of reactionary forces. The greatest success of the Popular Front was the antifascist movement culminating in the global organization of the International Brigades. Thousands of Communists from all over the world volunteered to join the brigades and fight on the Republican side in the Spanish Civil War. Although little more than instruments of Soviet foreign policy (as discussed in Chapter 8), the CPUSA successfully portrayed the volunteers as selfless champions of democracy.[8]

The Nazi-Soviet pact of 1939 reversed some of the party's gains and inspired a small red scare that saw the House Un-American Activities Committee (HUAC) shift its attention from fascists to communists. But the party weathered the storm intact and the American entry into the Second World War propelled the CPUSA to its greatest success. Although exact figures are not available, historians estimate that the party had approximately one hundred thousand members at the height of its power. If Communist-controlled unions and front groups are counted, the total number of individuals involved in the "communist movement" may have reached as high as one million. The alliance with Stalin allowed the party to equate patriotism with the defense of the Soviet Union and the advancement of world revolution. Hundreds of party members joined the armed forces. Many others worked in defense plants and supported the no strike pledge made by all labor unions. Party leader Earl Browder was so encouraged that he liquidated the CPUSA in 1944, replacing it with the Communist Political Association (CPA), a more loosely organized activist group that supported the Democratic Party. Browder's dream of a mainstream movement lasted only a short time. In 1945, Stalin ordered the Americans to restore the CPUSA and adopt a hard line against American capitalism.[9]

Party leaders responded by expelling Browder (an incident detailed in Chapter 2), and accusing the Truman administration of betraying the principles of the New Deal at home and attempting to establish global American hegemony at the expense of the Soviet Union. Although returning to a militant anticapitalistic stance, the party kept alive the tactics of the Popular Front in its takeover of the Progressive Party. A coalition of labor and liberal groups created the Progressive Party to support the presidential campaign of Henry Wallace, whose strong advocacy of postwar cooperation with the Soviet Union suited the party agenda perfectly. Unfortunately, the party's heavy-handed tactics alienated their liberal allies, and eventually Wallace himself, and the Progressive Party collapsed. So did everything the party had built during its heyday (the party's contribution to its collapse is considered in Chapter 1). Formerly friendly labor unions ousted party members and the CIO expelled ten unions it considered to be party dominated. The party responded by becoming more secretive and by sending trusted comrades underground in the "unavailable" program, where they would wait in reserve, emerging to keep the party running in the case of widespread oppression. From the party's point of view (as discussed in Chapter 9), these responses made sense. In 1949 ten national level party leaders went on trial for violation of the Smith Act, a wartime statute that made it illegal to advocate the overthrow of the US government by force and violence or belong to an organization that advocated this idea. Trials of regional leaders, the "second string" reds, followed throughout the 1950s concluding with the trial of John Hellman, party leader in Montana. A staggering 144 Communists faced charges and over 100 were convicted.[10]

More devastating to the party's reputation than the Smith Act trials were the espionage trials of Alger Hiss and Julius and Ethel Rosenberg. Whittaker Chambers, a self-confessed former Communist and Comintern agent, accused Hiss, a prominent New Dealer, member of the State Department and chair of the conference that founded the United Nations, of providing the Soviets with a steady stream of documents for years beginning in the early 1930s. Hiss went to prison in 1950, the year the Korean War began, and the year that the Federal Bureau of Investigation (FBI) arrested Julius and Ethel Rosenberg. Although accused of espionage, the statute of limitations only allowed Hiss to be charged with perjury. No such limitation existed for the Rosenbergs who were accused of giving the secret of the atom bomb to the Soviets. Convicted of espionage, they were sentenced to death and executed in 1953. The Hiss and Rosenberg trials had an interesting dual effect. The trials inflamed the public opinion, tarred all communists as traitors, and contributed to the worse excesses of the McCarthy era. But others were horrified by the thin evidence presented at both trials and unimpressed by the dubious character of the witnesses, in particular Chambers (Chambers's transformation from Soviet agent to anticommunist is discussed in Chapter 7). After his release from prison, Alger Hiss spent the rest of his life declaring his innocence and denouncing anticommunism as an assault on progressivism and the legacy of the New Deal. Over time, assertions that Hiss and the Rosenbergs were innocent victims of a right-wing conspiracy came to dominate academic and public opinion.[11]

The transition from supporters of America's ally to allies of America's greatest enemy devastated the CPUSA. Party members lost their jobs, endured questioning and surveillance by FBI agents, and experienced social isolation from former friends and coworkers (as captured in Chapter 10). In 1956, Nikita Khrushchev denounced the crimes of Stalin at the 20th Party Congress, causing the CPUSA to implode. By the early 1960s, it had been reduced to irrelevance. The party staged a recovery in the 1970s and 1980s (discussed in Chapter 6) under Gus Hall, a former steel organizer, who got his start in the heady days of the Popular Front. The revival proved short lived and the party lost most of its membership after the fall of the Soviet Union. It exists today as a tiny remnant with a largely geriatric membership.[12]

The first academic inquiries into American communism began in the 1950s as the party began its long decline. The most important effort was the ten-volume *Communism in American Life* series published by the Fund for the

Republic. Edited by Clinton Rossiter of Cornell University, the series launched in 1957 with Theodore Draper's *The Roots of American Communism*. Subsequent volumes, like Clark Kerr's *Unions and Union Leaders of their Own Choosing* (1960), explored communist infiltration of labor, civil rights, and cultural groups. Draper's second book, *American Communism and Soviet Russia*, also published in 1960, was his most important. In it he declared that the CPUSA was controlled in all respects by the Soviet Union, accepted instructions and funding from Moscow, and faithfully served the needs of Soviet foreign policy. The volume set the tone for the traditionalist school of studies of the CPUSA. Members of this school accepted the guilt of Alger Hiss and the Rosenbergs and, if not necessarily believing that all party members were literal "spies," regarded them as loyal to a foreign power and a disruptive influence in American life.

By the 1970s younger academics who had grown up during the social upheavals of the Vietnam War and civil rights era began to challenge the traditional school. They were aided by members of the CPUSA who, after years of keeping low profiles, began opening up about their former lives, giving interviews, or publishing their memoirs. One of the earliest and best efforts was Al Richmond's, *A Long View from the Left: Memoirs of an American Revolutionary* (1973), which combined tales from his life as a communist organizer with essays about the problems of American radicalism. Far from rejecting the revolutionary ideals of the "Old Left," the young scholars of the "New Left" embraced them as the precursors of their own efforts to transform American life. The narrative these scholars crafted dismissed the Soviet connection as ephemeral to the party's role as an early champion for civil rights and social justice, and brushed aside claims that it had been involved with Soviet espionage. Known collectively as the revisionist school, these writers depicted the party as the vanguard of progressivism and credited it with significant advances for labor and social equality. Well-regarded revisionist publications included Roger Keeran's *The Communist Party and the Auto Workers Union* (1980), Maurice Isserman's *Which Side Were You On? The American Communist Party during the Second World War* (1982), and Mark Naison's *Communists in Harlem during the Depression* (1983).

Another school of thought, anti-anticommunism, predates both the traditional and revisionist approaches. It began as a reaction against the excesses of the Second Red Scare, in particular, the hearings conducted by HUAC and the antics of Senator Joseph McCarthy. An early example is Alistair Cooke's account of the Alger Hiss case, *A Generation on Trial: USA vs Alger Hiss* (1951). Although not an academic work, Arthur Miller's play *The Crucible* (1953) captures the spirit of anti-anticommunism perfectly by equating the colonial American hunt for nonexistent witches in Salem with the contemporary hunt for equally nonexistent communists. A quirk of anti-anticommunism was to reduce the role of the CPUSA to insignificance and accuse anticommunists of inventing the communist threat as an excuse to destroy American progressivism. Other anti-anticommunist works include Victor Navasky's *Naming Names* (1980) and Richard Fried's *Nightmare in Red: The McCarthy Era in Perspective* (1990). By the late 1980s the revisionist and anti-anticommunist schools dominated scholarship on the CPUSA in both numbers and academic respectability. Adherents of the traditional school were dismissed as out of touch at best, and reactionaries at worst.[13]

In 1991 the Soviet Union collapsed, transforming the field. The new Russian government opened previously closed archives; some, such as the archives of the Comintern, almost without restriction. The Comintern archive, housed at the Russian State Archive of Socio-Political History (RGASPI), holds the pre-1952 records of the Communist Party of the Soviet Union (CPSU). Within the Comintern archive are the files of the Profintern as well as the Anglo-American Secretariat, the organization charged with overseeing the activities of the English-speaking Communist parties and the collected papers of the CPUSA. The CPUSA had long maintained that it destroyed most of its records during the persecutions of the McCarthy era. Yet, from the early 1920s until it was disrupted by the Second World War, the party sent its records in yearly batches to the Soviet Union for safekeeping. Known as Fond 515, the records consist of 4,400 separate files covering all aspects of its activities from the party's founding to the 1940s, and are exceptionally good for the time of the Third Period (Figure 0.1).

American scholars Harvey Klehr of Emory University and John Earl Haynes of the Library of Congress discovered Fond 515 while visiting Moscow in the early 1990s. In the spring of 1993, the two scholars, accompanied by Vernon Pedersen, who had just received his doctorate from Georgetown University, made a thorough examination of the records for Yale University. Haynes and Klehr published their findings in *The Secret World of American Communism* (1995) and *The Soviet World of American Communism* (1998). Pedersen published the results of his work in *The Communist Party in Maryland, 1919–1957* (2001). Haynes arranged, with Library of Congress support, for Fond 515 to be microfilmed, making it available to scholars at the Library of Congress microfilm reading room. RGASPI later sold additional copies to other institutions including Yale, Princeton, Stanford, New York University, and the University of Cincinnati.

The most important revelation from the archives was that the traditional school was right about its long-held assertion that the CPUSA had extensive ties with the Soviet Union. Correspondence between party leaders and their

Figure 0.1 Russia State Archive of Social and Political History where FOND 515 is housed. Photo by William C. Pratt

Comintern counterparts proved that the CPUSA followed Soviet instructions regarding every major (and most minor) policy issues, was extensively funded by Moscow, and, most shockingly, was directly involved in Soviet espionage. Anti-anticommunism had long reserved particular venom for accusations of espionage by American Communists. Writers in the school, such as Walter and Miriam Schneir who published *Invitation to an Inquest* (1983), had been prominent among those declaring that Julius and Ethel Rosenberg were innocent of the charges that sent them both to the electric chair. Others, such as William Jowitt in *The Strange Case of Alger Hiss* (1953) and Meyer A. Zeligs in *Friendship and Fratricide: An Analysis of Whittaker Chambers and Alger Hiss* (1967) were equally convinced that Alger Hiss was the victim of a conspiracy to discredit the New Deal. The revelation came as a surprise to members of the traditional school as well. Although they believed both Alger Hiss and the Rosenbergs to be guilty of espionage, they felt that these cases were exceptions and the CPUSA in general had little to do with covert activities.

The Comintern files in Moscow held clear evidence that, contrary to accepted opinion, the CPUSA had been extensively involved in "special tasks," the Soviet term for a range of activities including illegal procurement of passports, trafficking in industrial secrets, providing courier services, and engaging in old-fashioned political espionage. Additional documents released from East European archives and American and British intelligence agencies confirmed widespread party involvement in covert activities. The most import documents were the VENONA transcripts, a secret military intelligence project to decipher telegrams sent from the Soviet consulate in New York City to Moscow. Begun in 1943, the project uncovered massive evidence of the party's complicity in Soviet espionage, but the findings were kept secret until 1995, when new revelations coming out of the Soviet archives convinced members of Congress to authorize the release of the decrypted cables. The opening of formerly closed intelligence files created an entire subfield devoted to exploring the personalities, techniques, and moral ambiguities involved in covert activities. Many members of the traditional school became contributors to the espionage subfield as it offered both new material to write about and dramatically supported their central thesis.[14]

The revelations proved harder for the revisionist school to digest and some of its members gave up writing about communism altogether. Maurice Isserman, famous for his article "Three Generations: Historians view American Communism," published in *Labor History* in 1985, took up a new career writing about mountaineering. Robin Kelly, author of *Hammer and Hoe: Alabama Communists during the Great Depression* (1990), changed his focus from communism to African American popular culture. Ellen Schrecker, while accepting that party members assisted with Soviet espionage, has changed her opinion very little. In *Many are the Crimes: McCarthyism in America*, she suggested that communist internationalism justified spying and remains convinced that whatever espionage did occur did little harm.[15]

A nuanced response came from Randi Storch in her book *Red Chicago: American Communism at Its Grassroots, 1928-35* (2007). Storch advanced the thesis that the party was divided between rank-and-file party members who joined out of idealism and a desire to reform American society and a leadership made up of long-term party members who had strong ties to Moscow. An audience member at the Williams College conference echoed Storch's thesis. After a panel emphasizing Soviet influence on the party the conference participant, a long-time union activist who had worked closely with party members, remarked that he did not remember much being said about the Soviet Union, he only recalled men and women devoted to the cause of unionism. Storch's work illuminates another aspect of the opening of the archives on the discipline—the revisionists were correct as well. The CPUSA had a significant impact on American society and the party was deeply involved in progressive causes and took the leadership on several, racial and unemployment issues in particular. Freed of the need to argue about who was a communist and who was not and freed of the partisan compulsion to find heroes or villains, the discipline can finally focus on how communism intersected with all areas of American life and why it generated such extreme passions in its supporters and opponents.[16]

In the chapters that follow, the contributors explore the history of the CPUSA in detail, highlighting party movements, leaders, and individual members—spies, revolutionaries, and citizens among them.

In Chapter 1, John Haynes and Harvey Klehr explore the dependency of the party on the Soviet Union in "The 'Mental Comintern' and the Self-Destructive Tactics of the CPUSA, 1944–8" by looking at a period in Party history when circumstances deprived party leaders of guidance from Moscow. The resulting bad decisions contributed to the party's collapse during the McCarthy era. James G. Ryan, in Chapter 2, "Earl Browder's Changing Conception of the Marxian Revolution," delves deeply into the personal life of party leader Earl Browder while exploring Browder's evolving ideas on how to best achieve the party's ultimate goal. After Browder, the most well-known party leader was William Z. Foster, a labor leader before joining the CPUSA and frequent presidential candidate afterwards. Edward Johanningsmeier, in Chapter 3, "From Haymarket to Mao?" draws upon Soviet and American sources to understand the ways Foster's personality and political beliefs interacted with American and international radicalism to give him an amazingly long career in the Communist movement. William Pratt in Chapter 4 considers a little-known aspect of party history, its work among American farmers in "Communists and Farmers." Pratt outlines four distinct eras in the party's agricultural work and highlights the prominent role played by Finnish Americans.

Katherine A. S. Sibley explores the long pattern of American reaction to Soviet influence and involvement in US politics and government in Chapter 5, "Soviet Spies, Russian Trolls, and the US Security State." She examines different levels of activities directed against America and the often inappropriate responses of the United States to real or perceived Soviet actions. Denise Lynn's contribution in Chapter 6, "Friendship Re-forged in Anti-Communism," traces the roots of anticommunism, not to a right-wing attempt to roll back the New Deal, but to disillusioned ex-communists. Her discussion of the Juliet Stuart Poyntz disappearance reveals a new aspect of the life of Whittaker Chambers and sheds light on his break with the CPUSA that led, eventually, to his testimony against Alger Hiss. Although frequently the subject of intense criticism, the party has always received respect, however grudging, for its resolute antifascism, in particular, its support for the American volunteers fighting in the International Brigades in defense of the Republican side in the Spanish Civil War. Vernon L. Pedersen, in Chapter 7, in "Myth and Memory and the Spanish Civil War: The World the Veterans Made," reveals that the story of the "Good Fight" against fascism was a fabrication based on the party line and reinforced by the returning veterans. Far from idealistically motivated progressives, Pedersen demonstrates that the members of the Abraham Lincoln Battalion were dedicated communists, knowingly fighting in support of Soviet foreign policy objectives.

The final three chapters focus on individual communists, although from different perspectives and different eras. Eric McDuffie looks at life and work of black Communist Claudia Jones. In Chapter 8, "'For a New Anti-fascist, Anti-imperialist People's Coalition': Claudia Jones, Black Left Feminism, and the Politics of Possibility in the Era of Trump," McDuffie demonstrates why, given her personal experiences of the early Cold War, Jones might sincerely, if mistakenly, have believed that the United States was about to become a fascist state. His analysis of Jones's writings highlights their continuing relevance in the ongoing quest for a world free from racial, gender, and class oppression. Beth Slutsky's look at the 1970s, "American Communism in a Time of Détente" in Chapter 9, reveals how the party used the trial of Angela Davis as an accessory to murder to restore its relevance on the left and to recover from its decline during the early Cold War. After her acquittal the party arranged for Davis to tour Eastern Europe, turning its Soviet ties to its advantage. Robert Cherny examines the careers of twelve California Communists who left the party in the 1950s, but continued to be active in progressive causes for the rest of their lives. His essay brings to life the appealing character of so many members of the party. Far from being faceless automatons or shadowy conspirators, most party members were dedicated, idealistic people who were easy to admire. Cherny brings out this salient fact in the last, and appropriately entitled, chapter, "The Party's Over: Former Communist Party Members in the San Francisco Bay Area."

Notes

1 The controversy starts with what to call the party. Not only did it change its name frequently, but the open and underground branches of the party often had different

names. It has been known as the Communist Party of America, the Communist Labor Party, the Workers Party of America, the Communist Party of the United States of America and the Communist Political Association to name just a few. For consistency and clarity the editors have chosen to use the name Communist Party of the United States of America (CPUSA) throughout the volume.
2. Howard Hawks, *Ball of Fire* (Samuel Goldwyn Productions, 1941), Stanwyk's line was written by the legendary Billy Wilder.
3. For more information on the Palmer Raids and the party's early years see, Theodore Draper, *American Communism and Soviet Russia* (New York: Vintage Books, 1986).
4. For a good summary of the tangled relationship between the Farmer-Labor Party and the party see chapters 2 through 5 in Draper, *American Communism*, pp. 29–126.
5. Two recent accounts of the Gastonia strike are John A. Salmond, *Gastonia 1929: The Story of the Loray Mill Strike* (Chapel Hill: University of North Carolina Press, 2009) and Kristina L. Horton, *Martyr of Loray Mill: Ella May and the 1929 Textile Workers' Strike in Gastonia, North Carolina* (Jefferson: McFarland, 2015).
6. Draper, "How to Win a Majority," *American Communism*, pp. 127–52; Daniel J. Leab, "'United We Eat': The Creation and Organization of the Unemployed Councils in 1930," *Labor History* 8, no. 3 (1967), pp. 300–15.
7. An excellent description of the shift from the Third Period to the Popular Front is found in Harvey Klehr, *The Heyday of American Communism: The Depression Decade* (New York: Basic Books, 1984), pp. 167–222.
8. The Popular Front is one of the most written about periods in communist history and the story of the International Brigades almost constitutes a subgenre of its own. Good places to start with both subjects are—Helen Graham and Paul Preston (eds.), *The Popular Front in Europe* (London: Palgrave MacMillan, 1987); Bill Mullen, *Popular Fronts: Chicago and African-American Cultural Politics, 1935–46* (Urbana and Chicago: University of Illinois Press, 1999); Sean McMeekin, *The Red Millionaire: A Political Biography of Willi Munzenberg, Moscow's Secret Propaganda Tsar in the West, 1917–1940* (New Haven, CT: Yale University Press, 2004); Peter N. Carroll, *The Odyssey of the Abraham Lincoln Brigade: Americans in the Spanish Civil War* (Palo Alto, CA: Stanford University Press, 1994); Cecil D. Eby, *Comrades and Commissars: The Lincoln Battalion in the Spanish Civil War* (University Park: Pennsylvania State University Press, 2007).
9. For more information on the party in the Second World War see Maurice Isserman, *Which Side Were You On?: The American Communist Party during the Second World War* (Middletown, CT: Wesleyan University Press, 1982) and James G. Ryan, *Earl Browder: The Failure of American Communism* (Tuscaloosa: University of Alabama Press, 1997).
10. The Second Red Scare has been the subject of hundreds of books these are just a few. Thomas W. Devine, *Henry Wallace's 1948 Presidential Campaign*

and the Future of Post-War Liberalism (Jefferson: University of North Carolina Press, 2013); Richard M. Fried, *Nightmare in Red: The McCarthy Era in Perspective* (Oxford: Oxford University Press, 1990); Ellen Schrecker, *Many Are the Crimes: McCarthyism in America* (Princeton: Princeton University Press, 1998); Ted Morgan, *Reds: McCarthyism in Twentieth Century America* (New York: Random House, 2003); M. Stanton Evans, *Blacklisted by History: The Untold Story of Senator Joe McCarthy and His Fight against America's Enemies* (New York: Crown Forum, 2007).

11 The literature on Alger Hiss and the Rosenberg's is large enough to qualify as a cottage industry. Here are some to the more important works. Whittaker Chambers, *Witness* (Washington, DC: Regnery Press, 1952); Meyer A. Zeligs, *Friendship and Fratricide: An Analysis of Whittaker Chambers and Alger Hiss* (New York: Viking, 1967); Ronald Radosh and Joyce Milton, *The Rosenberg File: A Search for the Truth* (New Haven, CT: Yale University Press, 1983); G. Edward White, *The Looking Glass War: The Covert Life of a Soviet Spy* (Oxford: Oxford University Press, 2004); Lori Clune, *Executing the Rosenbergs: Death and Diplomacy in a Cold War World* (Oxford: Oxford University Press, 2016).

12 Relatively few books have been written about the declining years of the CPUSA. These are among the most interesting. Joseph R. Starobin, *American Communism in Crises, 1943–1957* (Cambridge, MA: Harvard University Press, 1972); Harvey Klehr and John Earl Haynes, *The American Communist Movement: Storming Heaven Itself* (New York: Twayne, 1992); Ronald Radosh, *Commies: A Journey through the Old Left, the New Left and the Leftover Left* (New York: Encounter Books, 2001).

13 Arthur Miller, *The Crucible* (New York: Penguin Classics, Reprint Edition, 2016).

14 Among the best offerings in the subfield are John Earl Haynes and Harvey Klehr, *VENONA: Decoding Soviet Espionage in America* (Haven, CT: Yale University Press, 1999); Alan Weinstein and Alexander Vassiliev, *The Haunted Wood: Soviet Espionage in America* (New York: Modern Library, 2000); Kathryn S. Olmsted, *Red Spy Queen: A Biography of Elizabeth Bentley* (Chapel Hill: University of North Carolina Press, 2002); Katherine A. S. Sibley, *Red Spies in America: Stolen Secrets and the Dawn of the Cold War* (Lawrence: University of Kansas Press, 2004); and Steven T. Usdin, *Engineering Communism: How Two Americans Spied for Stalin and Founded the Soviet Silicon Valley* (New Haven, CT: Yale University Press, 2005).

15 Schrecker, *Many Are the Crimes*, pp. 178–9, 188; Ellen Schrecker, "Stealing Secrets: Communism and Soviet Espionage in the 1940s," *North Carolina Law Review* 82 (June 1, 2004), 1841–89.

16 Randi Storch, *Red Chicago: American Communism at Its Grassroots, 1928–1935* (Urbana and Chicago: University of Illinois Press, 2007); Vernon Pedersen, personal notes on Williams Conference, 2018.

1

The "Mental Comintern" and the Self-Destructive Tactics of the CPUSA, 1944–8

John Earl Haynes and Harvey Klehr

In 1972 Joseph Starobin published *American Communism in Crisis, 1943–1957*, which told the story of the emergence of the Communist Party of the United States of America (CPUSA) from the Second World War in a position of strength to its near extinction by 1957. Starobin, at that time, was a distinguished academic historian but earlier he had been a senior CPUSA official, foreign editor of the *Daily Worker* from 1945 to 1954. However, he became disaffected and drifted away from the party. He then entered academic life, gaining a PhD in political science. In *American Communism in Crisis* he wrote that although the physical Comintern had disappeared in 1943, American Communists continued to live "in what can only be called 'a mental Comintern', imagining themselves part of something which did not exist ... They resorted essentially to zodiac signs for guidance."[1] Starobin's concept of the "mental Comintern" helps to explain catastrophic decisions of the CPUSA that led to its political isolation and loss of its vital base in the American labor movement by the early 1950s.

The CPUSA emerged from the Second World War with significant strength. Its membership exceeded sixty thousand, close to its high of the late 1930s. The party also largely consisted of native-born citizens for whom English was their first language, unlike the prewar party that had a large noncitizen immigrant membership, many of whom spoke English only as a second language. The CPUSA had also achieved a base in the Congress of Industrial Organizations (CIO) with Communists leading unions with a quarter of CIO's membership. Communists achieved a significant role as part of the New Deal political coalition's left wing and were influential in mainstream politics in the states of New York, California, Michigan, Illinois, Wisconsin, Minnesota, Oregon, and Washington.

By 1958 membership had collapsed to about three thousand, and Communists had been expelled from the CIO. The CPUSA had become a political pariah and retained no significant influence in the Democratic Party or the Republican Party. Traditionally, the collapse has been attributed to government persecution and widespread public anticommunist sentiment brought on by the Cold War. Indeed, both factors played important roles. Less appreciated is the extent to which the CPUSA contributed to its own collapse by making disastrous political choices based on a misunderstanding of what Moscow wanted.

The Comintern Era

In 1919, radicals inspired by the Bolshevik Revolution founded the CPUSA and the Communist Labor Party (CLP). Both parties proclaimed their adherence to the newly organized Communist International (Comintern) and sent emissaries to Moscow seeking Comintern recognition. The differences between the two were chiefly over leadership, not ideology, and in Moscow the two parties competed with each proclaiming itself to be more loyal to the Comintern than the other.

The Comintern demanded a merger, and its representatives journeyed to the United States to arbitrate factional fights in the American movement, supervise conventions, and oversee party operations. In no case did the American Communist movement offer significant resistance to Comintern guidance. Those who resisted Moscow's guidance quickly became ex-Communists.[2]

In 1928, at the Comintern's urging, the American party expelled James Cannon, one of the movement's leading figures, as well as others thought to be infected with Trotskyism. In the aftermath of Cannon's expulsion, Jay Lovestone and Benjamin Gitlow led the party's dominant faction that controlled 95 of 104 delegates to the party's 1929 convention. But Lovestone had been associated with Soviet leader Nikolai Bukharin and, despite his disavowal of Bukharin when it was clear that Stalin intended to purge him, Joseph Stalin intervened to displace Lovestone. Stalin himself presided over a Comintern review of the American party. When Gitlow told the review committee that his faction was the majority of the American party, Stalin replied:

> You declare you have a certain majority in the American Communist Party and that you will retain that majority under all circumstances. This is untrue, comrades of the American delegation, absolutely untrue. You had a majority

because the American Communist Party until now regarded you as the determined supporters of the Communist International. And it was only because the Party regarded you as the friends of the Comintern that you had a majority in the ranks of the American Communist Party. But what will happen if the American workers learn that you intend to break the unity of the ranks of the Comintern and are thinking of conducting a fight against its executive bodies—that is the question, dear comrades? Do you think that the American workers will follow your lead against the Comintern, that they will prefer the interests of your factional group to the interests of the Comintern? ... A poor hope, comrades! At present you still have a formal majority. But tomorrow you will have no majority and you will find yourselves completely isolated.[3]

Stalin was right. Once American Communists heard that Lovestone and Gitlow had lost Moscow's mandate, the Lovestone majority vanished, and only few hundred loyalists followed Lovestone and Gitlow out of the party.

A thoroughly Stalinized CPUSA readily accepted a leadership slate approved by the Comintern, one that solidified in 1931 behind General Secretary Earl Browder. Browder's loyalty to Moscow was well established; he had spent several years on the staff of the Comintern's labor arm, the Red International of Labor Unions (RILU).

In the 1930s, the Great Depression caused a segment of Americans to question the justice of the capitalist economic system, and the rise of fascism and Nazism also called into question the will of the Western democracies to resist fascist aggression. In the circumstances, the CPUSA grew rapidly, particularly after 1936 when the Comintern's "Popular Front" stance allowed Communists to adopt patriotic rhetoric and use antifascism as a platform for alliances with the broad liberal coalition supporting President Franklin Roosevelt's (FDR) New Deal program. The CPUSA reached a peak membership registration of sixty-six thousand in January 1939, established a strong presence in the CIO, won prestige in cultural circles, and achieved significant influence in mainstream politics in eight states, including New York and California.

With the CPUSA under Browder's steady leadership, the Comintern reduced its micromanagement. Moscow continued to review CPUSA decisions and leadership slates, making changes when it wished. Overall, however, the Comintern afforded Browder and the CPUSA more initiative and latitude than in the 1920s. Gerhart Eisler, the last Comintern representative with plenipotentiary authority, left the United States in 1936. Comintern supervision, albeit less intrusive, continued through close communications. In addition to a constant flow of telegraphic cables and postal letters, all through the 1930s, the CPUSA sent a stream of American Communists to Moscow: official party "representatives" to the Comintern, "referents" who served apprenticeships with sections of the Comintern, cadre attending training sessions at the International Lenin School, and delegations of party activists attending Comintern-related conferences. High-level CPUSA officials also delivered lengthy written reports and were examined in person by the Comintern's supervisory Anglo-American Secretariat.[4]

Loyalty to the USSR continued to be a core value of American Communists. In the mid-1930s, new members of the CPUSA recited a pledge to "defend the Soviet Union, the land of victorious Socialism." The party's 1935 manual of organization declared that "the Soviet Union is the only fatherland of workers all over the world" and "therefore, the workers all over the world must help the Soviet Union in building socialism and must defend it with all their power."[5]

During the Popular Front era, party conferences mixed American flags with traditional red banners and portraits of Washington, Jefferson, and Lincoln hung beside those of Marx, Lenin, and Stalin. Browder announced that the American Declaration of Independence should be understood as a foreshadowing of Marx's *Communist Manifesto*, and had the patriotic "Yankee Doodle" played at party conventions. Party activists adapted American folk music as the musical format of agitational songs. "Communism Is Twentieth Century Americanism" became the quintessential party slogan of the Popular Front. Attractive to potential recruits and garnering approving attention from the mainstream media, the slogan encapsulated the party's public embrace of American values. The slogan's history, however, also demonstrates the limits of the CPUSA's commitment to those values. Moscow thought American flags at party conventions and pro-union lyrics set to banjo music were acceptable ways to promote the Popular Front. "Communism Is Twentieth Century Americanism," however, went too far with its implication that Marxism-Leninism should be understood as an expression of American political traditions. In early 1938, the Comintern ordered the CPUSA to drop the slogan, and it did so without hesitation.[6]

On August 23, 1939, Nazi Germany and the Soviet Union signed a treaty dividing Eastern Europe and guaranteeing Soviet fuel and raw materials for Germany's war machine. On September 1, the Wehrmacht smashed into Poland, and American Communists faced a political problem. Until this point, the CPUSA had been calling for an anti-Nazi alliance of Britain, France, the United States, and the USSR to hold Hitler in check, as well as a domestic center-left alliance behind Roosevelt and his New Deal program.

There was never any possibility that the CPUSA would not support the Nazi-Soviet Pact; there was, however, initial confusion about how the pact would be defended because the Comintern had not given advance warning or laid the groundwork for so abrupt a change. The first weeks after the pact produced confused statements by American Communists who did not know what Moscow wanted. Several attempted to reconcile the pact with the party's antifascist stance by presenting it as a clever anti-Hitler ruse that would restrain Nazi aggression. Browder told the *New York Times* that the pact made "a wonderful contribution to peace" and the *Daily Worker* proclaimed that "German fascism has suffered a serious blow."[7] Hitler's launching war a week later canceled that rhetoric. For a few days the CPUSA cheered on Polish resistance to the Nazi blitzkrieg. This, however, was not what Moscow wanted.

In 1938, the Comintern had instructed Browder to acquire a shortwave radio and to assign an aide to listen on a prescribed frequency during specified times for coded messages. After the pact, the CPUSA received a series of messages instructing it to make a sharp break with past policies. One chastised Browder for "continuing to hold positions which were correct until the start of the European war, but are now incorrect." The Comintern went on to tell American Communists that "the contrast between 'bourgeois-democracy' and fascism is disappearing. At the same time the conditions for a 'democratic front' [Popular Front] are being undermined." The CPUSA was also told it "should stop following Roosevelt."[8]

The CPUSA had invested heavily in an alliance with Roosevelt's New Deal, but it obeyed. Starting in the late fall of 1939, the CPUSA harshly attacked FDR's program of assisting those nations fighting Nazi Germany and opposed FDR's reelection in 1940, denouncing Roosevelt himself as an imperialist and fascist. Communists took a fierce antiwar stance, opposed any American intervention in the war, and opposed passage of Lend-Lease aid to Britain and steps toward America's own military mobilization.[9]

All of the Popular Front's faux-Americanism disappeared, and in 1940 young CPUSA organizers marked for future party leadership heard senior leaders lecture:

> The single country where the dictatorship of the proletariat has triumphed represents a wedge driven into world capitalism by the world proletariat. The USSR is the stronghold of the world proletariat; it cannot be looked on as merely a nation or a country; it is the most advanced position of the world proletariat in the struggle for a socialist world. When the Red Army marches,

it is the international proletariat marching to extend its sphere of operations in the struggle against world imperialism ... [I]t also builds up the strength of the USSR to provide the world working class with greater might. Stalin, the great genius of socialism, stands like a colossus of steel as the leader of the world proletariat.[10]

On June 22, 1941, Hitler invaded the USSR. American Communists knew they would be dropping their antiwar policy and shifting to defending the USSR. However, they were initially unsure as to what line Moscow wanted them to take toward those other nations fighting Nazi Germany. Consequently, the initial statements by the CPUSA, while calling for an all-out defense of the USSR, were cautious about offering any assistance toward those, such as the British, who had been fighting Hitler since 1939. The day after the invasion, the *Daily Worker* warned that the Nazi attack on the USSR set up the conditions for a new "Munich," a peace between Nazi Germany and Great Britain leaving the Soviets alone to face the Nazis.[11]

The Comintern, however, quickly provided different instructions, and on June 26 sent the outline of a more far-reaching change in policy. The message stated that "the aggression of German fascism against Soviet Union has basically changed whole international situation and character of the war itself." Georgi Dimitrov, head of the Comintern, told the CPUSA that the anticapitalist and anti-imperialist phraseology that had dominated communist rhetoric during the Nazi-Soviet Pact period no long applied, explaining that the war was now to be seen as "neither a class war nor a war for socialist revolution," but a "just war of defense."[12]

Another Comintern message reinforced the point that Marxist-Leninist concepts would be dropped for the time being. It told American Communists to "keep in mind that at the given stage the question is about defense of peoples against fascist enslavement and not about socialist revolution."[13] Dimitrov also explained that

> this basic change of situation and of character of the war requires also a change in tactics of the Party. The main task now is to exert every effort in order to secure the victory of Soviet people and to smash the fascist barbarians. Everything must be subordinated to this main task. From this follows; first that the Communists and the working-class in America ... with all forces and all means, must resolutely raise struggle against German fascism. Secondly, they must demand from the American government all aid to the Soviet people.

Dimitrov ordered the CPUSA to drop opposition to assisting Britain, explaining that Communists must "support all measures of the government which makes possible the continuation of the struggle of the Anglo-American bloc against fascist Germany; because this struggle itself is actually a help to the just war of the Soviet people."[14]

All foreign parties received similar instructions to pursue what evolved into a "National Front" policy that served Stalin's initial goal of a stance by which Communists around the world could rally broad support for assisting the USSR's defense. But as the war proceeded, it also served Stalin's need to deepen the wartime "Grand Alliance" with the United States and Britain by reassuring the latter that the USSR and communism no longer represented a revolutionary threat to democratic societies and free-market economies. As the historian Eduard Mark observed:

> From the Atlantic Charter onward the Soviet Union signed every agreement promising democratic self-determination to the occupied nations of Europe; it even tendered unilateral assurances of its own. Soviet diplomats routinely explained to Western colleagues that Moscow "did not want to sovietize the Eastern European states," though it "would insist on Governments whose policy was friendly to the Soviet Union, which did not preclude equally friendly relations with Britain and [the United States]." Stalin himself made light of world revolution at Teheran, saying "We won't worry about that. We have found it is not so easy to set up a Communist society."[15]

Once the Comintern's instructions on the proper response to the Nazi attack arrived, the CPUSA adjusted its position as ordered. On June 28, 1941, the party adopted a "People's Program of Struggle for the Defeat of Hitler and Hitlerism" that was in full accordance with Dimitrov's messages.[16] Rhetoric about opposition to aid to Britain vanished; instead, the new line demanded all possible aid to anyone fighting Hitler. The party then set about reviving its Popular Front policies and presenting itself as an ardent backer of President Roosevelt.

The Second World War, nonetheless, reduced the direct organization ties of CPUSA to Comintern as well as drastically reducing the volume of communications. Postal communications became unreliable and subject to government inspection. International cable traffic was routinely reviewed by wartime security officials. Travel to the USSR for anyone without government sponsorship became nearly impossible. In 1940, the US Congress passed and President Roosevelt signed the Voorhis Act that imposed regulatory requirements on organizations with foreign government ties, and to avoid possible Voorhis Act coverage the CPUSA (with Comintern's permission) severed its official membership in the Comintern, and the last officially designated CPUSA representative in Moscow left in 1941.[17] Additionally, the Comintern itself dissolved on Stalin's orders in 1943, as part of his "National Front" stance.

The "Mental Comintern"

The CPUSA's loyalty to Moscow was not diminished by the reduced communications. Inevitably, however, the CPUSA's understanding of what Moscow wanted became more indirect and uncertain. Joseph Starobin, both a scholar of communism and a veteran senior level communist during the period in question, wrote that although the physical Comintern had disappeared, American Communists

> lived in what can only be called "a mental Comintern," imagining themselves part of something which did not exist. Seen in the best light, they were a species of self-proclaimed guerrillas, operating in what they believed to be a world battle, but having no significant contact with any "main force" and without a perception of the battle plan. They resorted essentially to zodiac signs for guidance. Because they dared not analyze Soviet aims in terms of the hard realities of power, they could not appraise Soviet policy either pragmatically or cynically ... The American Communists not only were viewed by others as expendable, but they also expended themselves—in a noble or pathetic fashion, depending on one's point of view. Their international commitment was thus a species of drug, contracting the mind as it expanded the illusions of the mind.[18]

Party leaders still sought to do what Moscow wanted, but they could no longer rely on a constant flow of cables, direct conversations with Comintern officials, and information obtained by CPUSA cadre visiting Moscow to tell them what Moscow really wanted. (Regular direct communications between the CPUSA and the Communist Party of the Soviet Union (CPSU) were not reestablished until the late 1950s.) Instead, like later Cold War academic and government experts who came to be called "Kremlinologists," American Communists tried to "read between the lines" of stories in the Soviet press and they intensely parsed the speeches of Soviet officials. And, like later Kremlinologists, while they often got it right, sometimes they were only half-right, and sometimes disastrously wrong. On occasion in the 1920s and 1930s Comintern communications with the CPUSA had been blunt and even harsh, but it had been clear about what Moscow wanted. Understanding what Moscow wanted in the period of the "mental Comintern," however, was often distorted. The first to suffer from misreading the signals was Earl Browder.

Browder's Teheran Doctrine and the Duclos Article

In November 1943, Roosevelt, Churchill, and Stalin met in Teheran (spelled Tehran today), Iran, to map out a joint strategy for the defeat of Nazi Germany. They reached an agreement on immediate major issues and issued a statement affirming three-power unity not only about war issues, but suggesting in vague terms an agreement about postwar goals.

As head of the CPUSA, Earl Browder considered himself to be the leading Marxist-Leninist thinker in North America. He had been the object of a minor personality cult, regarded himself as America's Stalin, and possessed a large measure of Stalin's confidence in his own judgment. To Browder, the Teheran meeting signaled "the greatest, most important turning point in all history." The ruling classes in the United States and Britain, through their alliance with the Soviet Union, had accepted the USSR as a partner in a new postwar world. For its part, the Soviets had dissolved the Comintern in 1943 and no longer urged its allies in the West to foment revolution. To Browder, the Teheran meeting signaled that "capitalism and socialism had begun to find the way to peaceful co-existence and collaboration in the same world" and the duty of American Communists was "to work for such policies within the country that will lead toward, and give realistic promise of, the continuation of national unity into the post-war period for a long term of years." Acknowledging that "the American people are so ill-prepared, subjectively, for any deep-going change in the direction of socialism," Browder pledged that the CPUSA "will not raise the issue of socialism in such a form and manner as to endanger or weaken that national unity." Instead "the policy for Marxists in the United States is to face with all its consequences the perspective of a capitalist post-war reconstruction in the United States ... and not a perspective of the transition to socialism." Browder extended this analysis to liberated Europe as well: "Europe west of the Soviet Union probably will be reconstructed on a bourgeois-democratic, non-fascist capitalist basis, not upon a Soviet basis." If Browder had gone no further, he would have stayed within the boundaries of Stalin's National Front stance. But the wartime lack of exchanges between the CPUSA and Moscow led Browder to rely on his own judgment of where Stalin was headed. Browder declared that in the new era there was no political room for an independent Communist party in America. Instead, Communists would dissolve the CPUSA, reorganize as an ideological advocacy group, and take a place as an integral part of the broad New Deal coalition headed by the Democratic Party. The Popular Front of the 1930s was transformed from a tactical alliance to an institutional strategy that would permanently integrate Communists into mainstream American politics.[19]

Browder's domination of the CPUSA was such that most American Communists accepted the new line without demurrer. However, a few veteran leaders were discreetly upset with the unorthodox nature of Browder's analysis. Within the confines of the CPUSA's top leadership William Z. Foster criticized Browder's plans. Although a leading Communist since the early 1920s, he had clashed with Browder over the years and was isolated. Browder brushed aside Foster's criticism but did agree to forward it to Moscow.

The Comintern no longer existed in 1944, but there were remnants. Dimitrov was still in Moscow and headed Institute 205, a secret body that housed the residue of the Comintern's central staff. Although the CPUSA had officially disaffiliated from the Comintern in 1940 and the Comintern had officially dissolved in 1943, checking with Moscow was a fixed CPUSA habit. Browder, early in 1944, forwarded Foster's critique to Dimitrov along with his own report explaining his Teheran Doctrine and party reorganization plans via Soviet diplomatic channels. In March, Dimitrov sent a memo to Soviet Foreign Minister Molotov about the situation and cabled Browder with this reply:

> I am somewhat disturbed by the new theoretical, political and tactical positions you are developing. Are you not going too far in adapting to the altered international situation, even to the point denying the theory and practice of class struggle and the necessity for the working class to have its own political party? Please reconsider all this and report your thoughts.[20]

Confident that he knew where Stalin and history were headed, Browder did not reconsider. Meanwhile, he misled his American comrades, assuring them that his reforms had Moscow's approval. Believing Moscow had approved Browder's reforms, Foster backed down. In May 1944 a CPUSA convention, with Foster presiding, unanimously voted to dissolve the CPUSA and reorganize as the Communist Political Association (CPA).

Moscow noticed Browder's decision to proceed despite Dimitrov's warning and was not pleased. Browder's reorganization of the CPUSA and his revision of Marxist-Leninist political analysis would over time permanently transform the American Communist movement. But Stalin never intended the National Front policy to be a permanent stance. He emphasized that the goal was always the same: socialism (defined as the Soviet state Stalin had created). How to get there was a matter of tactics and changed when necessary. For example, Stalin, in a speech to German Communists in 1948, urged the avoidance of disruptive immediate Sovietization in East Germany, remarking that "you should advance toward socialism not by taking a straight road but by moving in zigzags."[21] The National Front policy that Browder had thought was permanent was a zigzag.

In the fall of 1944, an as yet unidentified senior Soviet official commissioned a critique of Browder's reforms that appeared in the January 1945 issue of the *Bulletin of the Information Bureau of the CC RCP(b): Issues of Foreign Policy*, a secret CPSU journal that circulated among leading officials. The article harshly denounced Browder's Teheran Doctrine, stating flatly that Browder's views were "erroneous conclusions in no wise flowing from a Marxist analysis of the situation" and that his "notorious revision of Marxism" had led to the "liquidation of the independent political party of the working class." The essay denied that the wartime Soviet-American agreements could be interpreted to lay the foundation for "a political platform of class peace in the postwar era" or that there was "the possibility of the suppression of the class struggle in the postwar period." Instead, the Teheran agreement of the USSR with Britain and the United States was only "a document of a diplomatic character." Appearing as it did in an authoritative CPSU ideological journal, it signaled profound Soviet dissatisfaction with Browder's ideas. Based on past loyalty to the Soviet cause, the Soviets had every reason to be confident that once American Communists learned of Moscow's displeasure, the problem would be solved.

But how to get the message to American Communists? The *Bulletin of the Information Bureau* was secret and American Communists had no access to it. The alternative of publishing in an open Soviet journal would certainly bring the matter to the attention of the CPUSA, but this method would risk the article being interpreted as a diplomatic signal that might upset official Soviet-American diplomatic relations. Stalin still held to his wartime National Front policy and did not wish to signal to the West that the wartime policy of Communists promoting national unity and alliance with non-communists was tactical and might be coming to an end. With no Comintern in existence to discretely but clearly deliver Moscow's message, a less direct mechanism was needed. The ad hoc solution was to translate the article into French and give it to Jacques Duclos, a senior official of the French Communist Party. The article was published with Duclos listed as the sole author in the April 1945 issue of *Les Cahiers du Communisme*, a French party journal that appeared publicly and to which Americans had easy access, and, by May, translations of Duclos's article were circulating in the United States.[22] The result was consternation. The Duclos article was immediately recognized not as the singular opinion of a French party official but as Moscow's unequivocal condemnation of Browder's reforms.

The physical Comintern was dead, but the "mental Comintern" lived. Earl Browder had been the supreme leader of the CPUSA since the early 1930s. Every major and many minor CPUSA officials owed their position subject to Browder's approval and, in many cases, had been personally picked by him. Most rank-and-file members had joined the party subsequent to his taking the leadership and had no memory of any party leader prior to Browder. None of this counted when Moscow, even by the indirect means of an article in a French Communist journal by a French party leader most American Communists had never heard of, indicated its disapproval. In June the CPA stripped Browder of his authority, and in July 1945 an emergency convention dissolved the CPA and reconstituted the CPUSA. The CPUSA expelled Browder in 1946 and denounced its former leader as "an unreconstructed revisionist ... a social-imperialist ... an enemy of the working class ... a renegade ... an apologist for American imperialism."[23]

The Mental Comintern and the 1948 Election

The reconstitution of the CPUSA in 1945 repudiated "Browderism," but the CPUSA did not repudiate the Popular Front strategy and remained fully in line with Stalin's still reigning National Front policy. American Communists continued to emphasize working with liberal and left allies in the Democratic Party and within the CIO.

The revived CPUSA, however, faced a political dilemma. The Duclos article had told American Communists what not to do: they were not to give up their independence by integrating into mainstream liberalism, and they were not to assume that the postwar world would see a continuation of the wartime alliance. It was unquestioned that the CPUSA would defend the interests of the Soviet Union in the postwar era. As American-Soviet tension began to develop in 1946, President Truman began to position the United States for what would become the Cold War. Instinctively, the CPUSA opposed Truman's policies and had no doubts that Moscow wanted American Communists to oppose Truman. But what was unclear was *how* the CPUSA should oppose Truman.

There were two paths. The first, and more cautious, was to oppose Truman from within the broad liberal-left movement and the Democratic Party. Such a path had some hope for success. Truman's leadership seemed pedestrian after that of the charismatic FDR, and the demobilization in 1946 had produced a great deal of confusion, waste, and resentment. Republicans won control of the Congress in the 1946 elections, and the union movement was feuding with the Truman administration's attempts to discourage postwar strikes that threatened the economic transition from a wartime to a peacetime economy. Truman's popularity sank so low in 1947 that Republicans were confident of defeating him in 1948. If Communists and their allies stayed within the Democratic Party, they could appeal to Democrats disenchanted with Truman's policies or concerned that the president was unelectable. And they had potentially viable replacement for Truman as the Democratic candidate: Henry Wallace, who had served under FDR as secretary of agriculture, vice president, and secretary of commerce before being fired by Truman for opposing the new president's Cold War policies. Wallace could challenge Truman in Democratic primaries and caucuses and possibly wrest the 1948 nomination from Truman.

The barriers to success, however, were large. The majority of Democratic Party national convention delegates were not chosen in primaries but by party caucuses and conventions controlled by party professionals unlikely to support a naive idealist like Henry Wallace. And, if Truman won the nomination at the Democratic National Convention in 1948, then Communists and their allies would face a frustrating situation. The American electoral system was such that if they waited until after the Democratic nomination was decided in the summer of 1948, there was as a practical matter no effective way to offer an alternative to Truman or the Republican nominee in the fall election. Essentially, if Communists and their allies stayed in the Democratic Party and failed to prevail at the Democratic National Convention, the most they could do would be to sit out the fall election and wait until 1950. However, this result also pointed to the safety of this path; even if Communists and their allies were defeated at the 1948 Democratic convention, they would survive to fight another day with their positions in the broad New Deal coalition and the labor movement intact. And if Truman lost the general election, as was expected, then the position of Communists and their allies in the liberal coalition would be strengthened.

The second path was bolder: to pull out of the Democratic Party and create a new third party that could offer an alternative to both Republican conservatism and Truman's combination of moderate liberalism and an increasingly anti-Soviet foreign policy. Although victory for a third party was unlikely, even a respectable third place would so divide the New Deal voting base that Truman would be defeated and it would force Democrats in 1950 to appease progressives by dropping Truman's Cold War policies for something more accommodating to Soviet needs. And, if Truman's popularity continued to drop in 1948 as it had in 1947, there was even a possibility that Democrats would fall into third place and the new party with concealed Communists in its leadership would become the primary political vehicle for New Deal voters.

This bold path, however, also had very grave risks. Once Communists and their allies pulled out of the Democratic Party, they were exposed, and if Truman won the election, their third party might be marginalized and their opportunity to get back into the Democratic Party would be limited. Further, to abandon the Democratic Party would risk the Communist position in the CIO. Despite feuding with Truman, most CIO leaders regarded the labor movement's protection under federal labor regulations as being tied to the fate of the Democratic Party. The Republican controlled Congress had passed the Taft-Hartley Act in 1947 that chipped away at labor union protections under the New Deal era's National Labor Relations Act. Truman had vetoed Taft-Hartley, but Congress had overridden his veto. Without Truman in the White House, labor leaders feared that the next Congress would pass, and a Republican president sign, a much more drastic dismantling of the National Labor Relations Act. Many CIO leaders would oppose any third party that threatened liberal and labor unity in 1948.

Which path to take? There was no longer a Comintern to consult in 1946. And with Dimitrov's departure to head the new Bulgarian Communist regime in the fall of 1945, there was no readily identifiable authoritative figure in Moscow for the CPUSA to consult. Temporarily the CPUSA put off a decision by proceeding on two parallel tracks in 1946 and early 1947, supporting both liberal allies who wanted to fight Truman within the Democratic Party and those who wanted to break with the Democratic Party and create an uncompromised progressive party. The CPUSA was desperate for detailed discussions with the Soviets but little opportunity existed. Soviet diplomats were not authorized to discuss domestic American politics with the CPUSA. And travel to Moscow by Americans was severely restricted by Soviet policy and lingering wartime disruptions in international travel.

The first opportunity to talk frankly with Soviet officials came in March 1947 when Moscow hosted a conference of the foreign ministers of the USSR, Britain, and the United States. The Soviets allowed a delegation of American journalists to cover the conference, including Morris Childs, editor of the CPUSA's *Daily Worker*. Childs, however, was not primarily a journalist. He was a senior CPUSA official who had served in numerous responsible party posts.

Once in Moscow, he sought out officials of the International Department of the CPSU and briefed them on all aspects of the CPUSA's activities. Memos on the meetings by a CPSU official, Boris Vronsky, suggests he had no guidance about how to respond to Childs's urgent request for Soviet advice on several matters, the most important of which was how to approach the 1948 American presidential election. Childs specifically asked: "What is the best use to which the growing progressive movement can be put in the upcoming U.S. presidential campaign?" and "What is [our, the CPSU] opinion on the creation of a third party if Wallace, Pepper, Murray and others refuse to participate in this at the present time?"[24]

In response to Vronsky's request for guidance, Alexander Panyushkin, a senior CPSU central committee advisor (to become Soviet Ambassador to the United States in October 1947) observed, "it seems to us that in the U.S. the conditions are not yet in place to create such a party at the present time." Panyushkin suggested that Childs be cautioned, "the apparent task of the CPUSA at the present time is to struggle for unity of action of all progressive forces and above all for unity of action in the workers' movement. And resolving the problem of creating a third party depends on that."[25]

Childs had asked for an audience with a prominent Soviet official so that he could carry back an authoritative answer to the CPUSA. He was allowed to meet with Solomon Lozovsky, once a deputy foreign minister and former chief of the RILU. While Lozovsky was known to the CPUSA from his RILU days, in 1947 he was director of the Soviet Information Bureau, an arm of the International Department. Lozovsky conveyed to Childs the essence of Panyushkin's cautious guidance: the key to the decision over creating a third party was achieving unity on the progressive left, and Lozovsky cautioned against jeopardizing the CPUSA's role in the CIO.

Lozovsky also spoke approvingly of Eugene S. Varga's *Changes in the Economics of Capitalism as a Result of the Second World War*, that had been published in Moscow in 1946. Varga headed Moscow's Institute of World Economy and World Politics and was a leading Soviet authority on economics and ideology. He argued that due to the destruction of European industry for a time the chief source of war, capitalist overproduction and competition for markets, was absent. America would face overproduction but with Europe suffering from underproduction, the obvious remedy was the export of American capital to Europe to support the rebuilding of European industry. Varga also suggested that the economies of Eastern European nations would remain capitalist in character and tied to Western European markets for a lengthy period.[26]

Childs dutifully carried this cautious advice on a third party back to his colleagues in the CPUSA leadership along with Lozovsky's recommendation of Varga's book. In the short run, this advice did little to resolve the CPUSA's dilemma. The Soviets had not flatly rejected the bold third-party path, but they had warned that progressive unity should be maintained and that the CPUSA should avoid severing ties with the CIO and its more cautious liberal allies. But how could one be sure that a third party would or would not break links with the CIO and liberal allies before one actually founded the third party and the political dynamic worked itself out? The CPUSA wanted clear guidance and got cautious ambiguity instead. For the moment that CPUSA continued on its two tracks.

The cautious advice that Childs delivered, however, was quickly undercut by the CPUSA's Kremlinologist-like interpretation of events in the USSR. During the war, Stalin desperately needed Britain and the United States as military allies in fighting Nazi as well as needing the massive economic and military aid of American Lend-Lease that sustained the Soviet military machine and even its ability to avoid starvation. Stalin's wartime National Front policy supported this vital alliance by reassuring the United States and Britain that the USSR and its Communist subordinates were no longer an existential threat to Western democracy. Victory over Germany, however, did not immediately end Stalin's desire to sustain the Grand Alliance.

Victorious though the USSR was, the war left it economically devastated and, without Lend-Lease, facing a difficult trade-off between sustaining its military machine and rebuilding its economy. Continuing the wartime alliance would reduce the threat to Soviet security and allow more resources to be transferred to economic rehabilitation. Additionally, continuation of the alliance might mean American aid in the form of credits to assist in economic rebuilding. As Eduard Mark noted, Stalin had "every reason to suspect that if he followed in Eastern Europe and the Balkans anything like the program he had applied to the Baltic states, Eastern Poland, Bessarabia, and Bukovina during 1939–41—immediate revolution through massacre and deportation—there would follow in the West so sharp a reaction" that all hope of maintaining the Grand Alliance as well as any prospect of American economic support would end.[27]

Stalin's alternative to the blood-soaked repression of 1939–41 was a continuation in the postwar period of the National Front policy as a transitional mechanism to full Sovietization. In the short run, this would reassure the West and at least partially meet the multiple promises the Soviets had made of respecting the national independence and supporting democratic institutions in the liberated states of Eastern Europe.

Stalin envisioned the postwar governments in Eastern Europe as regimes where the institutions of "bourgeois" democracy would be partially maintained and some space allowed for non-Communist political entities. In his view Communist parties would be the dominant political actors in broad ruling National Front coalitions with social democratic, socialist, liberal, and peasant political parties that deferred to Communist leadership. (Fascists, rightists, and monarchists, however, would be repressed.) Over time, the success of Communist leadership of the National Front coalitions would see the withering away of non-Communist entities and the eventual implementation of total Communist regimes.

And, in fact, from 1945 and for a few years thereafter, the regimes of Eastern Europe imposed under Soviet occupation were built on this vision with National Front coalition governments that allowed limited but real political space for non-Communist socialist, liberal, and peasant political formations.

However, Stalin's confidence that his National Front policy would lead eventually to Sovietization had been based on faulty premises. He assumed the postwar Communist parties of Eastern Europe would be popular and have electoral success. In fact, while certainly much stronger than their prewar status, the postwar Communist parties fell short of electorally dominating their rivals despite having the patronage of Soviet occupation authorities. Assumptions that the new National Front governments would achieve rapid economic success that would build popular support for Communist leadership also proved faulty as mismanagement was widespread and economic rehabilitation slow. The leaders of the Eastern European Communist parties, while voicing the pieties of National Front compromise and civil behavior, found it much harder to restrain their repressive instincts. Their thuggish behavior did little to increase Communist electoral appeal. Non-Communist political formations also failed to defer to Communist leadership and aggressively and often successfully competed for popular support.

Stalin soon realized that his postwar National Front policy was failing to work as he had anticipated. He also realized that ending the National Front policy likely meant forfeiting the postwar continuation of the wartime alliance. But it was a price he had become willing to pay. As Mark stated:

> From his Marxist–Leninist perspective, moreover, it was obviously more prudent that the military security of the USSR should ultimately be entrusted to a glacis of socialized states in Eastern Europe than to agreements with capitalist states that he viewed as intrinsically predatory potential enemies … The chief deterrent to Stalin's reordering of Eastern Europe unilaterally after the fashion

of 1940 was the expectation that significance advantages would accrue in the shorter term from continued association with the West. Two processes, which began to work almost simultaneously soon after the war, disabused him of this hope. The weakness of the national fronts became apparent, presenting him with a stark choice of either seeing Eastern Europe fall into the hands of non-communist political parties or else resorting to repression inimical to continued alliance with the United States and Britain. At the same time, Western positions at the meetings of the Council of Foreign Ministers and at the Paris Peace Conference increasingly showed Stalin that he had invested excessively in his hopes for continued alliance with the Western democracies. Washington soon decided that it would not extend economic aid or even credits to the USSR ... Stalin's reasons for maintaining the alliance gradually evaporated. That, in turn, removed the chief inhibition against the use of methods to consolidate the faltering "popular democracies" of Eastern Europe that were faster and cruder than Moscow had envisioned in its wartime instructions to the region's Communists.[28]

In 1947, 1948, or 1949, depending on the country, the political space provided non-Communist entities in Eastern Europe was erased and replaced by a far more repressive regime modeled directly on the Soviet police state example.

Varga's book, the one Lozovsky recommended to Childs, a recommendation Childs had duly reported to the CPUSA, with a theme that appeared to accept American economic predominance in Europe, did not fit well with Stalin's increasingly confrontational stance. In May 1947, Soviet leaders launched an ideological attack on Varga for having failed to take a Stalinist position on the world situation. The CPSU ordered Varga's institute to be merged into another Soviet agency, and once high-flying Varga sank into obscurity until after Stalin's death.[29]

The anti-Varga campaign had nothing to do with the cautious advice that Childs had received, but in the absence of adequate communications, many CPUSA leaders saw a connection. In their "mental Comintern," if Moscow could signal its disapproval of Browderism via an article authored by a Frenchman in a French journal, Varga's fall must call into question the advice that Childs had gotten from Lozovsky, who had spoken well of the newly disgraced Varga. His fall along with increasingly belligerent statements from Moscow on Cold War issues convinced CPUSA leaders that Morris Childs had talked to the wrong people in Moscow, gotten wrong advice, and misled the CPUSA on what Moscow wanted. He was ousted from the editorship of the *Daily Worker*. But if Child's report that Moscow counseled caution had been wrong, exactly what was right was still unclear. A June meeting of the CPUSA's leadership continued the party's simultaneous pursuit both paths to the 1948 election.

Then in September, 1947, Moscow organized the Communist Information Bureau (Cominform). Andrei Zhdanov, Stalin's chief ideologist, dominated the meeting and his speech gave the organization its policy line:

> the division of the political forces operating in the international arena into two main camps—the imperialist and anti-democratic camp on the one hand and the anti-imperialist and democratic camp on the other. The main, leading force of the imperialist camp is the U.S.A. ... The anti-imperialist and anti-fascist forces constitute the other camp. The U.S.S.R. and the countries of the new democracy [Eastern Europe] constitute the mainstay of that camp.[30]

This two camps thesis left little room for accommodation and compromise.

But the Cominform was not a new Comintern. The Comintern had supervised Communist movements everywhere on the globe and its mission was world revolution. The Cominform had a limited membership and a limited purpose. Only European Communist parties belonged, and not all of them. Essentially, the Cominform was an anti-Marshall plan agency, a mechanism for Soviet coordination of assaults by European Communist parties on Truman's plan to use American financial aid in a coordinated European economic recovery program that would rehabilitate Europe on a democratic and open market based on the American model.

The CPUSA was not a member of the Cominform (it hadn't been asked), and no CPUSA representatives were invited to or present at its founding, but once the news reached the United States of its formation and Zhdanov's harsh assaults on American policies, CPUSA leaders ended their two-track policy in the lead up toward the 1948 election. In their eyes, the long-awaited signal had arrived: no accommodation, no compromise, only bold steps were acceptable. In the fall of 1947, the CPUSA moved swiftly to establish a third party, no matter what the costs to its existing alliances.

Allies of the CPUSA persuaded Henry Wallace to abandon the Democratic Party and lead a third party, the Progressive Party, in the 1948 election. Communist activists in the CIO used all their influence to get their unions to support Wallace's Progressive Party and defied the CIO's national leadership decision to oppose the Progressive Party as a threat to liberal unity. Popular Front liberals and Democratic politicians allied with the CPUSA were encouraged, cajoled, persuaded and, in some cases, ordered on threat of political oblivion to break with the Democratic Party and join the new Progressive Party. Every magazine, newspaper, journal, front group, civil body, and organization where the CPUSA had influence was mobilized for the Progressive Party campaign that ran not only Wallace for the presidency but candidates for the US Congress, state governorships, and state legislatures as well.[31]

The result was disaster. Anti-Communist liberals, already growing stronger as the Cold War grew more intense, used the creation of the Progressive Party as an illustration of CPUSA manipulation of naive liberals and stressed that any association with Communists was a threat to liberal unity and a political liability with the public. Many liberals who had earlier been allied with Communists in the Democratic Party refused to make the jump to the Progressive Party and fled from association with what was perceived by much of the American public as a Communist front. As the election approached, in the fall of 1948, the Progressive Party, rather than being the broad progressive coalition it was intended to be, was little more than Henry Wallace, Communists pretending they were non-Communist progressives, a handful of genuine Popular Front liberals, and a few Communist CIO union officials. Compounding the weakness of the Progressive Party was the revival of President Truman's popularity as his forceful foreign policy and his criticism of Republican domestic policies struck a chord with the public.

Truman won with 24,045,052 votes; Thomas Dewey (Republican) was second with 21,896,927 votes; and Strom Thurmond (segregationist States Rights Democratic Party) was third with 1,168,687 votes. Wallace came in fourth with 1,137,957 votes, 2.3 percent of the total. Results for congressional elections were even more dismal. Only a single Progressive Party nominee won election to Congress while the revived Democrats regained control of both houses.

Earlier, Communists and their Popular Front allies had been part of the broad New Deal coalition. After 1948, the New Deal coalition was dominated by Truman's Cold War Democrats. By leaving the Democratic Party, Communists and their allies had exposed, tainted, and marginalized themselves. The most damaging result for the CPUSA, however, was in the union movement. Many union leaders had long mistrusted Communists, but had grudgingly tolerated their presence. And CIO Communists in positions of responsibility in a number of major unions had been able to lend considerable institutional support to Communist causes. But Communist defiance of CIO political decisions in 1948 enraged CIO leaders. In 1949 and 1950 CIO organizers identified as Communists were fired and anti-Communist caucuses in individual CIO unions drove most Communists from union offices. Those few unions that retained Communist leaders were expelled from the CIO, and both the CIO and

American Federation of Labor (AFL) sponsored competing unions that sought to take over their members. Within two years the once strong Communist presence in the trade union movement was reduced to a remnant of what it had been.

The 1948 Progressive Party adventure broke the back of communism in America by destroying its political position in the New Deal coalition and its institutional role in the union movement. In the years that followed, American Communists suffered other defeats and setbacks. The US government used the antisedition provisions of the Smith Act to prosecute CPUSA leaders, hostile congressional investigations exposed party activities, and fierce public anti-Communist sentiment delivered additional blows. But the CPUSA's own decision to create the Progressive Party resulted in the party's decisive defeat. What followed was a long dying.

The Progressive Party disaster was not the result of the CPUSA blindly following orders from Moscow. Moscow had issued no orders. The only guidance it had offered via Lozovsky had been cautious and imminently sensible. But the CPUSA was so concerned to do what Moscow wanted that it needed clarity. The one instance of sensible advice delivered via Lozovsky was quickly lost in the clutter of American Communists seeing signs and signals in Soviet actions where none existed. It is doubtful that anyone connected with the creation of the Cominform or that Andrei Zhdanov when preparing his speech thought that their actions would be seen as signals of what path the CPUSA should take toward the 1948 American election. But American Communists continued to live in a "mental Comintern." They wanted to do what Moscow wanted. Indeed, they not only wanted to know, they needed to know. The CPUSA's only mechanism for resolving disputes and dilemmas was to have Moscow decide. It needed to receive a signal to resolve its indecision about 1948. The creation of the Cominform was a relief to CPUSA, a sign from Moscow about what they should do, and so the CPUSA marched into folly.

Notes

1 Joseph R. Starobin, *American Communism in Crisis, 1943–1957* (Cambridge: Harvard University Press, 1972), 223.
2 On the early years of the American party and its relationship to the Comintern, see: Theodore Draper, *The Roots of American Communism* (New York: Viking Press, 1957); Theodore Draper, *American Communism and Soviet Russia* (New York: Viking Press, 1960); Harvey Klehr and John Earl Haynes, *The American*

Communist Movement: Storming Heaven Itself (New York: Twayne, 1992); Harvey Klehr, John Earl Haynes, and Kyrill M. Anderson, *The Soviet World of American Communism* (New Haven, CT: Yale University Press, 1998). For a more positive view of Comintern supervision see: Jacob A. Zumoff, *The Communist International and US Communism, 1919–1929* (Chicago, IL: Haymarket Books, 2015).

3 "First Speech Delivered in the Presidium of the E.C.C.I. on the American Question, May 14, 1929," in Joseph Stalin, *Stalin's Speeches on the American Communist Party, Delivered in the American Commission of the Presidium of the Executive Committee of the Communist International, May 6, 1929, and in the Presidium of the Executive Committee of the Communist International on the American Question, May 14th, 1929*, pamphlet (New York: Central Committee, Communist Party, USA, 1931).

4 Klehr, Haynes, and Anderson, *Soviet World*, pp. 48–71, 166–73.

5 J. Peters, *The Communist Party: A Manual on Organization* (New York: Workers Library, 1935), pp. 8, 16, 104–5.

6 Klehr, Haynes, and Anderson, *Soviet World*, pp. 36–40.

7 "Pacts Hurt Axis, Browder Asserts," *New York Times* (August 24, 1939), p. 9; Harry Gannes, "The Soviet Union and Non-Agression," *Daily Worker* (August 23, 1939), p. 1.

8 Philip J. Jaffe, *The Rise and Fall of American Communism* (New York: Horizon Press, 1975), p. 40; To Browder, "Despite the Fact …," RGASPI 495-74-469; Klehr, Haynes, and Anderson, *Soviet World*, pp. 81–3.

9 See also James Ryan, *Earl Browder: The Failure of American Communism* (Tuscaloosa: University of Alabama Press, 1997), pp. 159–68.

10 Junius Scales, *Cause at Heart: A Former Communist Remembers* (Athens: University of Georgia Press, 1987), pp. 93–84.

11 CPUSA Politburo statement, *Daily Worker* (June 23, 1941), p. 1.

12 Dimitrov to New York, "The aggression of …," June 26, 1941, Russian State Archive of Socio-Political History (RGASPI) 495-184-3 (1941 file).

13 "Perfidious attack against …" RGASPI 495-184-3 (1941 file).

14 Dimitrov to New York, "The aggression of …," June 26, 1941, RGASPI 495-184-3 (1941 file).

15 Eduard Mark, *Revolution by Degrees: Stalin's National-Front Strategy for Europe, 1941–1947*, Working Paper No. 31 (Washington, DC: Cold War International History Project, Woodrow Wilson International Center for Scholars, 2001), 16.

16 Plenary Meeting of the National Committee, Communist Party, USA, June 28–29, 1941, "People's Program of Struggle for the Defeat of Hitler and Hitlerism," *The Communist* 20, no. 8 (August 1941), pp. 678–82.

17 Klehr, Haynes, and Anderson, *Soviet World*, pp. 87–8.

18 Starobin, *American Communism in Crisis*, p. 223.

19 Earl Browder, "Teheran – History's Greatest Turning Point," *The Communist* 23, no. 1 (January 1944), pp. 3, 7; Earl Browder, *Teheran and America: Perspectives*

and Tasks, pamphlet (New York: Workers Library, 1944), in Bernard Johnpoll, *A Documentary History of the Communist Party of the United States*, vol. 5 (Westport, CT: Greenwood Press, 1994), pp. 294, 297, 299–300; Earl Browder, *Teheran: Our Path in War and Peace* (New York: International, 1944).

20 Georgi Dimitrov diary entry, Dimitrov to Molotov, March 8, 1944, RGASPI 495-74-482, reproduced in translation in Klehr, Haynes, and Anderson, *Soviet World*, pp. 105–6; Georgi Dimitrov, *The Diary of Georgi Dimitrov, 1933–1949*, ed. Ivo Banac (New Haven, CT: Yale University Press, 2003), pp. 305–7.

21 Quoted in Vladimir Volkov, *German Question as Stalin Saw It (1947–1952)*, "Stalin and the Cold War, 1945–1953" conference, Cold War International History Project, September 1999, quoted in Mark, *Revolution by Degrees*, pp. 17, 38.

22 The Russian original: "O Kommunisticheskoy Politicheskoy Assotsiatsii SShA [On the Communist Political Association of the USA]," *Byulleten' Byuro Informatsi Tsk VKP(b): Voproy Vneshney Politiki*, no. 2 (January 1945); manuscript translation into French, "Au sujet de l'Association Politique Communiste des Etats-Unis" attached to a printer's page proof of the Russian article and to a cover letter dated January 19, 1945 in RGASPI 17-128-754; Jacques Duclos, "A Propos de la Dissolution Du P.C.A.," *Cahiers Du Communisme* nouvelle série 6 (April 1945); Jacques Duclos, "On the Dissolution of the American Communist Party," *Political Affairs* 24 (July 1945).

23 "CP Raps Press Hubbub on Browder," *Daily Worker* (April 30, 1946), p. 2.

24 B. Vronsky, "Conversations with CPUSA Politburo Member Morris Childs," undated but attached to a April 10, 1947 memo, RGASPI 17-128-1128, in Klehr, Haynes, and Anderson, *Soviet World*, pp. 265–8. Claude Pepper was US Senator (Democrat, Florida). Philip Murray was chief of the CIO.

25 Panyushkin to A. A. Zhdanov and A. A. Kuznetsov, April 10, 1947, RGASPI 17-128-1128 in Klehr, Haynes, and Anderson, *Soviet World*, pp. 270–1.

26 An account of Childs's meeting with Lozovsky is in Jaffe, *Rise and Fall of American Communism*, pp. 87–135.

27 Mark, *Revolution by Degrees*, pp. 14–15. Here and below follows the argument Mark advanced.

28 Mark, *Revolution by Degrees*, pp. 45–6.

29 Philip J. Jaffe, "The Varga Controversy and the American Communist Party," *Survey [Great Britain]* 18, no. 3 (1972).

30 A. A. Zhdanov, "On the International Situation," *Political Affairs* (December 1947), pp. 1095–6.

31 On the role of Communists in the Progressive Party, see Thomas W. Devine, *Henry Wallace's 1948 Presidential Campaign and the Future of Postwar Liberalism* (Chapel Hill: University of North Carolina Press, 2013); Klehr and Haynes, *The American Communist Movement*, pp. 109–22.

Bibliography

Jaffe, Philip J. *The Rise and Fall of American Communism*. New York: Horizon Press, 1975.

Jaffe, Philip J. "The Varga Controversy and the American Communist Party." *Survey [Great Britain]* 18, no. 3 (1972), pp. 138–60.

Klehr, Harvey, John Earl Haynes, and Kyrill Anderson. *The Soviet World of American Communism*. New Haven, CT: Yale University Press, 1998.

Mark, Eduard. *Revolution by Degrees: Stalin's National-Front Strategy for Europe, 1941–1947*, Working Paper No. 31. Washington, DC: Cold War International History Project, Woodrow Wilson International Center for Scholars, 2001.

Ryan, James. *Earl Browder: The Failure of American Communism*. Tuscaloosa: University of Alabama Press, 1997.

Starobin, Joseph R. *American Communism in Crisis, 1943–1957*. Cambridge: Harvard University Press, 1972.

2

Earl Browder's Changing Conception of the Marxian Revolution

James G. Ryan

Most historians of twentieth-century America have heard the name Earl Browder, although the public quickly forgot it after the Cold War began. The Vietnam conflict, however, stimulated some opponents of the war to search for a usable American leftist past. That effort unearthed memories of Browder, the cause he had once ridden to global name recognition, and his subsequent, dramatic descent into obscurity.[1] Today many scholars know that he had headed the Communist Party of the United States of America (CPUSA) throughout its heyday, 1932–45. During these years, the party reached its modest zenith of about eighty thousand members, but exercised influence among many times that number. Under Browder, the CPUSA once played an important minor role in America's politics, labor movement, and cultural life. Browder's Communists attempted to use working-class Americanism, so ably described by historian Gary Gerstle, to build a mass radical movement.[2] In so doing, the CPUSA received unprecedented acceptance and nearly achieved respectability. Furthermore, according to historian and political scientist Harvey Klehr, the Communists even enjoyed a measure of prestige in some circles.[3] During the Great Depression they appeared throughout American life and displayed an ability to dominate organizations filled with non-Communists, such as the Minnesota Farmer-Labor Party (FLP) and numerous Congress of Industrial Organizations (CIO) unions. Indeed, Browder's achievements seem even more remarkable now than they did during the late 1930s. Public opinion in the present-day United States sits much farther to the right than it did nearly eighty years ago. After the Soviet Union collapsed, historians learned for certain that Browder had put his skills and energy toward darker matters as well. Modern historians, East and West, now know beyond doubt that the incredibly busy Browder had also acted as a talent scout seeking to create new Soviet spies. Indeed, he had directed the nonatomic espionage in the United States.[4]

If modern scholars have rediscovered many of Browder's ideas and actions, they have not probed deeply into his complex personality. Most leaders of national Communist parties during the Stalin era were gray figures, successful in following Moscow's orders but in little else. Indeed, Browder sought to appear dull as well. He would have enjoyed, and probably chuckled at, the way most journalistic accounts portray him. They describe a hardworking, overachieving, and typically silent man whom major US apparatchiks during the 1930s found gallingly aloof. Few colleagues and fewer non-Communists understood that beneath Browder's pedestrian exterior lay an intensely ambitious figure, possessing both enormous physical courage (as opposed to moral courage) and a steely determination to achieve whatever he happened to value most at the time. Many historical accounts briefly relate Browder's response to outside events. The time has come to show that Browder initiated many of the changes in his life—some carefully thought out and others dangerously reckless. His evolving concept of how best to achieve the much-desired Marxian revolution led him to meet—and often know well—the leaders of future Soviet puppet states. Communist International (Comintern) figures once respected him as a colleague with a seemingly brilliant future. At least two of its highest ranking figures considered Browder a close personal friend.

Browder, born in 1891, was the eighth of nine children , to William Browder and his second wife, Martha Jane. They lived in poverty in Wichita, Kansas, and William espoused first populism then socialism. For some reason Earl Browder always refused to mention his father's earlier family, which included wife Jennie and four children. They remained unknown to the public until 2007.[5] By 1900, William had suffered some type of breakdown and had become an invalid. Loss of William's income forced Earl to leave school at age 9 and never return to formal education. Like other children, he enjoyed sports and games. Yet he possessed a frail body and suffered frequent injuries that included broken bones. Sidelined, he had time to ponder on deeper things. At night "Paw" Browder helped inculcate an elementary school curriculum and his own radical politics. Unlike many boys, Earl never rebelled against his parents' values. Instead, he began a lifelong avocation of self-improvement projects. He eagerly joined the Socialist Party (SP) at age 15 in 1906. As did the entire Browder family, he believed that socialism would usher in a better society through evolution or revolution.

Somehow, the small, slender Browder learned to play the flute. By adulthood, he proved to be quite accomplished at it. Young women found his arresting light blue eyes very attractive and he married Gladys L. Groves during his early twenties. She was gentle and kind, with an endearing sense of humor, still evident fifty years later.[6]

Browder left the SP in 1913, when the membership recalled the charismatic "Big Bill" Haywood from its National Executive Committee. By then Browder had learned accounting through teenage jobs with different firms. Thereafter he earned a comfortable wage by day, and roamed Kansas's left-wing political haunts during the evenings. For several years, he possessed no clear vision of how to achieve a Marxian revolution. He joined a local affiliate of William Z. Foster's Syndicalist League of North America, later headed an American Federation of Labor (AFL) bookkeepers' union and, for a while, even managed a farmer's cooperative. Yet the one cause that most held his attention during his twenties was resistance to the First World War's Selective Service Act. Browder, his brother William, and a future brother-in-law, Thomas R. Sullivan, began urging young men to resist nonviolently.

On May 30, 1917, their actions resulted in being arrested; and that December juries convicted them. Judges handed each a year's imprisonment for nonregistration and two years for conspiracy. Because the antiwar movement caused overcrowding in the era's penitentiaries, the Browders spent ten months in a small Platte County, Missouri, jail for the first violation. Freed between October 1918 and the following July, pending the appeal of his conspiracy conviction, Earl Browder was mesmerized by Russia's revolutions. First, a bourgeois uprising in early 1917 had overthrown the czar's regime, arguably the most repressive in Europe. Then in November, the Bolshevik takeover ushered in the world's first proletarian government. Similar revolts temporarily toppled capitalism in Finland, Hungary, and Bavaria. Against such a backdrop in 1919, four million American laborers hit the streets. A work stoppage closed New York's harbor and a general strike in Seattle raised the specter of class warfare. William Z. Foster led some 367,000 laborers off their jobs at US Steel. Boston's police strike helped teach both radicals and government reactionaries that America might not be an exception to the era's revolutionary events.[7]

The Browders, after losing their conspiracy conviction appeals in July 1919, began serving sixteen months at Leavenworth Penitentiary. Earl received surprisingly mild treatment during both of his early incarcerations. He later referred to the Platte County jail as "Mr. Vestal's boarding house," after their jovial jailer who was happy to receive federal maintenance money. Vestal allowed numerous relatives to visit Earl and William with picnic baskets and home-cooked food. They probably never joked about Leavenworth, however. It offered a grim stone environment, packed more than two thousand inmates into an institution built to house five hundred, and enforced the strictest military regimentation. It held more than one hundred members of the Industrial Workers of the World (IWW), the war's fiercest opponents. They considered noncooperation a matter of honor. As a result, they toiled in rough labor gangs and endured backbreaking drudgery. By contrast, the Browders, skilled office workers, offered no resistance whatever. Earl played the flute in the prison band and orchestra. He also persuaded the chaplain, who controlled the library, to allow him to receive books on religion and economics. Browder later contended that friends sent him all the works of Marx available in English. Supposedly, he also received the few translations of Lenin then existing.[8]

Doing relatively soft time did not stop Browder from being embittered. He emerged from Leavenworth displaying a zealotry he had never shown previously. Once free, he sought to devote all his time to promoting the cause. Instinctively Browder now felt that the American Socialist Party (ASP) would never bring about the much-desired Marxist revolution.

Accordingly, he callously abandoned Gladys and their young son Jay, although she clearly suffered from epilepsy by then. Earl traveled to New York City and joined the CPUSA. He soothed his conscience by employing a Manhattan attorney to send her a relatively generous $50 per month for about twenty years thereafter. (Earl never bothered to obtain a divorce, though Gladys did in 1959, when she needed one to inherit her mother's property.[9]) Sometime after prison, he grew a mustache, perhaps because he remained youthful-looking well into his thirties.

Browder could hardly have chosen a more fortuitous time to become a professional Communist. By coincidence, three Moscow representatives were visiting the United States. They sought to recruit a working-class delegation to the first congress of the Red International of Labor Unions (RILU). Commonly known by its Russian abbreviation, Profintern, the RILU began operations in July 1921. On paper, it was subordinate to the Comintern, the objective of which was to destroy every capitalist government. Yet the Profintern also provided an alternate source of leaders during Soviet political crises. It already possessed its own staff, funds, and networks in foreign countries.

The visitors liked Browder's Midwestern and AFL backgrounds, and that he could help break the widespread stereotype that most ranking Communists were Jewish. They asked him to attend the congress as a delegate from Kansas's left-wing miners, an AFL union. Browder had found a well-paying job with an accounting firm in New York before locating the CPUSA. Immediately, however, he quit and began darting about the country enlisting delegates possessing union support. Significantly, all were genuine labor activists rather than professional revolutionaries. As such, they offered the movement a growth opportunity. Organizing this single overseas project did not make Browder America's top Communist, but it signaled his arrival to the second stratum of leaders.[10]

In Moscow, the Soviets whom Browder met overwhelmed him with their friendliness, education, and sharp intellects. Their respectful attention, despite his lack of formal schooling and modest achievements, intoxicated him. They had overthrown the government of a large, if backward, nation and were now winning the Russian Civil War that followed. Surely, the Comintern was the Marxian revolution Browder had dreamed of joining during his lonely months in Leavenworth. A mere five years earlier he had just risen above his poverty-stricken background. Now, by contrast, he faced an opportunity to help remake the world.

In a move he would soon regret, Browder had invited his old Syndicalist League associate, William Z. Foster, to join the Moscow trip as an observer.[11] Foster had since become America's top left-wing unionist. When he decided to become a communist, the Profintern made Foster's Chicago-based Trade Union Educational League (TUEL) its American section. Moscow gave Foster a generous budget and appointed Browder, ten years his junior, as assistant.

Browder and Foster participated in Comintern agent John Pepper's attempt to take over a native FLP in 1923. Failing, they sought to infiltrate Robert LaFollette's third-party, 1924 presidential campaign. This proved an even larger disaster, isolating the Communists from the labor movement for years to come.

Within the CPUSA, however, Browder performed his duties well during the early 1920s. Every source emphasizes his diligence and efficiency. Always an introvert, he became what a later generation would label a "workaholic"—a driven, seemingly tireless, compulsive overachiever. Throughout his life, this trait occasionally receded but always returned with new vigor. Eventually, he came to feel that Foster was taking credit for his achievements. James P. Cannon, a friend to neither, noted that Foster flattered those whom he needed and abused those who needed him. Browder resented being known as "Foster's boy."[12] Annual trips to the USSR, however, seemed worth the price he had to pay. Indeed, on his very first Moscow visit Browder started a long, auspicious friendship with Profintern boss Solomon A. Lozovsky. Yet, during this era, Browder displayed no hint of greater ambition, and perhaps no one in the CPUSA considered him capable of holding high rank. The early 1920s marked the nadir of Browder's career as a communist. He was doing the mundane, detailed work that Foster gladly delegated to him.

The wiry Browder compensated by becoming something of a Communist party playboy. His slender build and sharp facial features continued into his forties. Whereas many American Leninists donned leather jackets to project a proletarian image, Browder only appeared in Middle America's suit and tie. His clean-cut, if rumpled, appearance contrasted sharply with that of his rougher comrades. Women enjoyed Browder's company greatly, and he became the subject of many salacious rumors by jealous comrades. Had his life continued in this manner, it would hold little historical interest.

V. I. Lenin died in 1924, leaving behind a power struggle. Before his contemporaries did, Browder decided that Stalin would win. One day, during a January 1926 Moscow meeting, Stalin asked Browder, who had just arrived from the United States, to evaluate a proposed tactic. During the translation, Browder felt unsure which way Stalin would lean. Not daring to risk offending the USSR's rising strong man, he demurred. He contended that his recent, lengthy journey had left him unprepared to speak. Although Stalin had not yet killed millions of people, he clearly intimidated Browder. The USSR's new boss despised communists who hedged, and he never spoke to Browder again. Stalin rarely offered anyone a second chance. Browder nevertheless respected power, wanted to side with a winner, and thereafter entrusted his future to the Russian Communist Party's general secretary. To Browder, the Marxian revolution was now Joseph Stalin, who would industrialize the Soviet Union and later inspire his nation to repel Nazi German invaders. Comintern propaganda soon proclaimed Stalin a "brilliant heir" to Karl Marx and V. I. Lenin. The rising leader was "putting into practice" the aspirations of the "entire world's workers." Historian Jacob A. Zumoff has summarized the change's significance well: "Subservience to the Comintern apparatus and Stalinist dogma became paramount, instead of the revolutionary program that had animated the early Comintern."[13]

The year 1926 was important to Browder for another reason. In Moscow, his good looks and fondness for women paid a considerable dividend. While Browder mingled comfortably in high-level Soviet circles, he attracted notice from a Profintern bureaucrat, thirty-one-year-old Raissa Luganovskaya. A woman of mystery and wild rumors in the West before the Soviet Union's collapse, she was a flaxen-haired, hazel-eyed legal scholar. She had joined the Bolsheviks shortly before the monarchy's collapse. Thus, she had entered the party early, when it had contained few attorneys or women. During the short-lived Kerensky government, she had belonged to the Communists' Kharkov city committee. After the Bolshevik coup, she had organized sanitation detachments of women and men in different Red Guard companies. During the Russian Civil War that broke out shortly thereafter, she had found herself appointed local justice commissar. By 1919, she lived in Moscow as a member of the People's Commissariat of Justice. Here her youth and inexperience slowed her upward mobility greatly.[14]

When she met Browder at a government social function, she was a secretary to the Profintern's executive committee. She had been divorced for less than two years. They had an affair and she became pregnant quickly, but the two did not wed.

According to American Communist Samuel Adams Darcy, RILU circles considered Luganovskaya a climber. She pestered Profintern chief Lozovsky to give Browder a career-making assignment.[15] Lozovsky, who already liked him, quickly found a suitable challenge.

Noting Browder's organizing experience in Kansas and Chicago, Lozovsky sent Browder to civil-war torn China to head a permanent secretariat there. Its goal was to undermine the governing Kuomintang (KMT), a nationalist party. Browder's duties included creating Communist labor unions and politicizing workers. While avoiding KMT troops, Browder demonstrated his greatest character strength: the ability to overcome challenges for which he possessed neither training nor previous experience. In China, he risked his life virtually every day. Still, he found time to have an affair with an arresting young Canadian Comintern agent, almond-eyed Kitty Harris.[16] Meanwhile, in Moscow, Luganovskaya bore Browder a son, Felix, on July 31, 1927.

Typifying the CPUSA's overall history, the crisis that brought Browder to high party rank concerned events in the Soviet Union. At the Sixth Comintern Congress during mid-1928, Stalin opened the international movement's "Third Period." The first, 1919–21, had featured unsuccessful Communist uprisings in Bavaria and Hungary. The second, 1922–8, saw capitalist stabilization and Soviet diplomatic gestures toward the West. Stalin announced that the Third Period signified a new round of wars and revolutions, leading to international capitalism's inevitable demise. That doom meant that Europe's Social Democrats, as communism's chief remaining rival, had now become the chief enemy.

Browder returned home via Moscow in January 1929. Before the year was over, powers in the USSR put the loyal Comintern soldier Browder, labor leader William Z. Foster, and City College intellectual William W. Weinstone into a troika leading the faction-plagued CPUSA. Their dispositions virtually guaranteed strife. Each member felt contempt for the other two, and each quickly came to believe himself entitled to sole leadership.

The Great Depression hit that autumn, and the Communists were the first to organize massive public demonstrations and "hunger marches" on American city halls. The party, under its divided leadership, promoted integrated industrial unions, and struggled for African American rights when no other primarily white group bothered to do so.

On September 7, 1932, Foster, making the CPUSA's first vigorous campaign for America's presidency, suffered a devastating heart attack. Shortly thereafter Browder emerged as the sole party leader. Before the Soviet archives opened, most Western historians simply assumed that the Soviets had chosen Browder by default.

Since the late-1990s, however, we have known that Browder and Weinstone battled viciously before the CPUSA's Polburo and the Comintern's Anglo-American Secretariat.[17] Addressing the Polburo, Weinstone succeeded in showing that Browder had repeatedly resisted the troika's division of labor, "definitely sealed in Moscow." Furthermore, Browder would not replace ineffective functionaries loyal to him.[18]

The toughness and sophistication of Browder's rebuttal speeches presented a bold contrast. Weinstone's bickering, Browder insisted, undermined his work. Never again would he "retreat from disagreements." The present "impossible relations" demanded change "by whatever means necessary." He urged the Comintern's Executive Committee (ECCI) to reassign one of them to overseas work. Feigning magnanimity, he suggested that Weinstone plead his case in Moscow before the Comintern because he had not made a very coherent Polburo presentation.[19] Having lost the debate, Weinstone nevertheless offered prescient closing words. After slamming his opponent's "bureaucratic, presumptuous" attitude, he predicted that nobody who did not "kowtow" would be able to work with Browder, because he demanded only "yes-men."[20]

From Moscow, on November 13, 1932, came the Soviet verdict abolishing the American Communist Party's shared secretariat. Yet the decree misread the American situation, declaring that henceforth the CPUSA's leadership would be "built around Browder and Foster."[21] Actually, Foster had suffered a total nervous collapse that had left him "helpless as a child," according to biographer Edward P. Johanningsmeier. Not trusting capitalist physicians, Foster spent five months recovering at a sanitarium near the Black Sea. There the Soviets could see firsthand the precarious nature of Foster's health. He did not give another speech until 1935. Biographer James R. Barrett goes so far as to declare that Foster "never fully recover from the illness."[22]

Almost from the day Browder achieved unquestioned control, he began putting a more domestic face on the movement. He scrambled duties at party headquarters in New York. Historian Maurice Isserman has shown that shortly thereafter, younger cadres, many of whom were the descendants of Jewish immigrants, moved into secondary leadership positions and held them for two decades.[23] The party controlled the livelihoods of some six hundred employees, and Browder, like Stalin, demanded total loyalty. Quickly Browder laid the foundations for a personality cult by upgrading his title. The *Daily Worker's* June 24, 1933, edition employed the rubric "National Secretary" for the first time. That August former opponent Jack Stachel displayed proper fealty by resurrecting the 1920s term "General Secretary."[24]

Although Stalin despised Browder, he allowed him a virtual free hand during the 1930s and the Second World War. Browder, clearly an effective administrator, had created some of his own good fortune by anticipating communism's next change of international line. Throughout the Third Period Communists had denounced all reformers as "social fascists." Adolf Hitler's rise to power in January 1933 underscored vividly that approach's folly. German Communists were the first major group sent to concentration camps. Months before Hitler's takeover, the Comintern's Western European bureau leader, exiled Bulgarian Georgi Dimitrov, had implored comrades to create a working-class United Front without Communist domination. Browder had first met Dimitrov in 1921. They had worked together in the Profintern in 1926 and remained very close friends.

In 1935, Stalin finally endorsed a Popular Front: unity with virtually every group that opposed fascism. That year Moscow urged Communist parties everywhere to find links to indigenous roots. Browder, who often took other people's ideas to strange, unusual lengths, tapped into his Kansas populist background. Immediately, he launched an ambitious program that scoured US history, searching for a revolutionary heritage that Republicans and Democrats deliberately ignored. Heroes he found could be lauded as Communist party forerunners. Soon Browder was glorifying rebellious slaves, John Brown, and the abolitionists in *Daily Worker* newspaper articles. The party press sold longer versions as five-cent pamphlets. In this effort Browder found himself thirty years ahead of his time. Not until the 1960s did neo-Marxist historians reject the magnolia blossom school of southern history and culture (Figure 2.1). Browder was no scholar, but his oversimplified propaganda brought the CPUSA and his leadership unprecedented attention.[25]

Figure 2.1 Communist Party Standard Bearers, June 2, 1940, New York, NY: Earl R. Browder (right) and James W. Ford exchanging congratulations after they were nominated by the Communist National convention as the party's presidential and vice-presidential candidates, respectively. Credit: Bettman Archive/Getty Images.

There is no reason to doubt the sincerity of Browder's articles and speeches against Jim Crow. Eagerly he posed for photographs with the so-called Scottsboro Boys, Angelo Herndon, and other African American party members. He put blacks on every dais, even the American Friends of the Chinese People. Like millions of white citizens during the 1930s, however, Browder had no close African American friends.[26]

Unmindful of comrades overseas, Browder popularized the slogan "Communism Is Twentieth Century Americanism." He failed to understand that there was no place for US nationalism in the Russian-dominated world proletarian movement. Eventually Dimitrov telegraphed other leading Comintern figures to send Browder his "warm regards," but that "It would be helpful to explain" the necessity "concerning the gradual retiring of" this "popular but non-Marxist slogan."[27]

The Popular Front made communism seem less threatening to Western nations. Browder's financial angel, Philip J. Jaffe, termed the era 1936–9 "years of euphoria" for Browder. Carrying the CPUSA's revised message, he rapidly became a public figure, though rarely recognized on the street. Dimitrov labeled him the world's greatest English-speaking Marxist. The Soviets expected Browder to supervise Latin American Communist parties. Jaffe reminisced that no longer did Browder "have to call FDR a fascist" nor the National Recovery Administration and the National Labor Relations Board "enslavement programs." No more did he even have to malign Socialist party leader Norman Thomas a social fascist. Indeed, Browder sought accord with nearly all past antagonists. He considered the new Comintern policy a long-term strategy, not a temporary tactic.[28]

In 1936, Browder persuaded the Comintern to allow him to run for president against Franklin D. Roosevelt, so no one could honestly label FDR the "Communist candidate." That year Browder popularized the bewildering slogan "Defeat [Republican nominee Alfred] Landon At All Costs; Vote for Earl Browder." Such strange words drew attention even from circles that did not usually discuss politics at all. In 1938, possibly with Dimitrov's aid, Browder invented the "Democratic Front" and convinced the world movement to accept it as the Popular Front's peculiarly American form. In practice, it meant that the CPUSA would accept a junior, sometimes hidden role in other organizations. Browder believed, erroneously, that the American Communist Party had become the New Deal's left wing. He considered the favorable national attention the new default condition, and he felt that certainly only better things lay ahead. As his success had grown, so had his self-regard. Unfortunately, he could not stop his ego's continual swelling after the CPUSA had reached its zenith.

Browder's ecumenical attitude did not extend to intra-party rivals. After Foster finally returned from convalescing in the USSR, Browder humiliated him constantly. He overwhelmed Foster with what ranking Communists called the "genteel treatment." Feigning personal concern for Foster's well-being, Browder severely limited his former boss's work and public appearances. Ever so frequently, Browder warned against any activity that might cause another heart attack. Foster appealed repeatedly to Moscow, to no avail.

If the public might have questioned Browder's refusal to forgive an old comrade, had they known of it, Americans probably would have felt revulsion toward another Browder practice as well. Soviet and US government archives reveal that during the early 1930s he began to serve as a talent scout for Soviet espionage. He also began receiving indirect payments from the Comintern between 1934 and 1936. Funds for underground activity came through a shadowy figure, Solomon Mikhelson-Manuilov. At times Browder, following Comintern orders, destroyed receipts. The Russians strove to keep track of their largesse, but were adamant that no capitalist authorities ever find direct evidence of Soviet sub-rosa funding.[29]

Browder fortified his intra-party position by supporting all of Joseph Stalin's atrocities. Browder refused to discuss Stalin's 1936–8 purge of the "Old Bolsheviks," every living member who had helped make the revolution a reality back in 1917. Browder could not claim that he did not know what was going on in Moscow during the late 1930s. He visited there every year before 1939 and noticed that previous acquaintances had disappeared. Abruptly, no one mentioned them, and he knew not to ask dangerous questions.

Browder's era of elation ended with communism's most startling turnabout. In late August 1939, the USSR suddenly signed a nonaggression pact with Nazi Germany. Secret protocols therein divided Poland and gave the Soviets the Baltic states. Before the year had ended, the Russians had also invaded Finland.

The CPUSA received no advance notice whatever. On July 5, 1939, Browder had told a Charlottesville, Virginia, audience that a Ribbentrop-Molotov pact was as likely as Earl Browder's being elected Chamber of Commerce president.[30] Learning of the nonaggression pact through the capitalist press proved a rude and degrading shock. For the first time Browder felt afraid to field reporters' questions. In an August 23 office interview, journalists deluged him with sarcasm, ridicule, and outdated *Daily Worker* quotations. Attempting to affect confidence, Browder rocked uneasily in his swivel chair. His pseudo-scholarly pipe having vanished, he now smoked cigarette after cigarette, although he was an avowed nonsmoker. For the following six weeks, CPUSA heads quarreled over the party's next moves. Foster sought to unseat Browder, but proved equally befuddled, logic-challenged, and uninspiring. Browder, too vain to accept a diminished role, termed the treaty an eastern response to the 1938 Munich pact. He asserted that Stalin's latest move strengthened the peace, until Germany invaded Poland on September 1. Browder then praised the besieged Poles as heroic, until a secret Moscow cable denounced their government and termed the war "imperialistic." Through October, Browder feared that a direct rupture with President Roosevelt would bring political disaster. Accordingly, the CPUSA blamed presidential advisors for administration policies it disliked. Critics publicly predicted the party's imminent demise. Because Browder still considered Stalin the embodiment of the Marxist revolution, however, he neither possessed the desire nor the courage to defy Moscow openly.

Eventually Dimitrov sent clandestine shortwave radio directives ordering Browder to alter the CPUSA's official view of FDR and adjust party propaganda. Browder, summoning all his toughness, ignored those commands that affected the president and observed the remainder. He even hid the message's existence from other CPUSA figures, and in doing so, created considerable angst. Believing the Communists could support Roosevelt and the Nazi-Soviet pact simultaneously was irrational. FDR, of course, considered the treaty a threat to European democracies, American national security, and world peace.

On October 23 federal officials spared the party from its emergency, but devastated Browder. A deputy marshal seized him on ancient passport fraud charges. Never before had the national government jailed a Communist Party general secretary. For the next twenty-two months, the CPUSA attacked President Roosevelt in the wildest terms. The party even dropped its boycott of Nazi goods.

In an eerie preview of the Cold War, the Roosevelt administration brandished its anticommunism. A miniature Red Scare swept the country. Browder's trial opened on January 17, 1940, in New York's federal district court. John T. Cahill, US attorney in Manhattan, employed legal hairsplitting to circumvent a three-year statute of limitations. Browder had used bogus passports because the State Department had refused to supply travel papers to known Communists before 1934. Cahill argued that each renewal of an illegally obtained passport constituted a separate felony. Theatrically he employed anti-Communist hyperbole and took testimony from a parade of federal officials and ex-party figures.

Browder presented a surprisingly competent argument for someone lacking formal legal training. Relying on a correspondence-school law course taken decades earlier, he brushed his attorney aside and seized control of his case. This unusual maneuver enabled him to advance points without facing cross-examination, risking perjury, or invoking the Fifth Amendment. It did nothing, however, to enhance his credibility or overcome the negative impact of his appearance. For some reason, he had trimmed his mustache; now it covered only the area immediately below his nose. Employing fine understatement, the *New York Times* reported Browder's "slightly Hitleresque look."[31] Although resourceful, Browder proved no match for the US attorney. The jury found him guilty and the judge sentenced him to four years' imprisonment plus a $2,000 fine—a hefty sum in 1940.

As his case ground slowly through the appeals process, Browder launched a lecture tour of those prestigious colleges willing to invite him. He also ran for an unexpected congressional vacancy then, in November, the US presidency. He received more newspaper ink than he had in years. Under pressure from Republicans, the Roosevelt administration retaliated by launching deportation proceedings against Raissa Browder. From Canada, she had joined Earl in 1933. On October 30, 1940, Attorney General Robert H. Jackson ordered her expulsion, but time-consuming appeals eventually allowed civil libertarians to gravitate to her aid.

That same month Congress passed the Voorhis Act, forcing Justice Department registration upon organizations possessing international ties. Accordingly, on November 16 Browder told a special CPUSA convention, "We are not foreign agents" and cancelled the CPUSA's Comintern affiliation.[32] He did this to avoid the new statute's penalties, which included dissolution of those extrinsic bodies that the attorney general considered national security threats. Browder's action constitutes first evidence that he had begun to consider independent paths to Stalinism. Indeed, the Comintern would specifically cite the CPUSA's action as precedent when it formally disbanded it altogether on May 15, 1943. Not coincidentally, when Stalin applauded the action two weeks later, he avoided quoting Browder.

On February 17, 1941, the Supreme Court upheld the passport conviction. The decision depressed Browder markedly and created a gripping tension. Two decades earlier, as an anonymous young radical, he had secured relatively easy time at Leavenworth. Now, however, he proved a most reluctant prisoner. He neared age 50, was known around the world, had a wife plus three dependent sons, and headed an organization whose loyalty he might well lose to Foster.

As prisoner 60140 in Atlanta Penitentiary, Browder suffered the worst days of his life. Serving as a humble storeroom clerk proved difficult for a proud workaholic used to speaking before thousands in Madison Square Garden. Years of recruiting and supervising spies had swollen his ego, but he could not brag to anyone. He had written a half-dozen books and almost one hundred articles, but that would not impress inmates who read at the fifth-grade level, if they read at all. Fewer than three months after his arrival, Nazi Germany invaded the USSR without warning. Browder compounded his misery by shunning other convicts and brooding over every Soviet battlefield defeat. The CPUSA's new patriotic, antifascist line fit his personality and leadership style so well, yet he remained a political prisoner.

Browder's mind became an issue at Atlanta. Most reluctantly he suffered through interviews with both a psychologist and a psychiatrist. Fielding their probing questions, he felt a fear that is unknown today. Browder was aware that officials might use the era's existing, unreformed mental health laws to incarcerate him for life. Indeed, one can read their Bureau of Prisons diagnoses as suggesting they may already have started building a case against him.[33] Browder's despair deepened daily, and he developed stomach troubles. Indeed, in the early 1940s mainstream mental health officials may have sincerely considered any loyalty to Hitler's or Stalin's dictatorships as abnormal.

Then suddenly on May 16, 1942, President Roosevelt commuted Browder's sentence. The USSR's Foreign Minister Vyacheslav Molotov was about to arrive for a White House visit. This sop to the Soviets was far more easily delivered than a second European Front.

The Comintern's demise and the Roosevelt administration's subsequent actions led to Browder's final redefinition of the Marxian revolution. Browder's depression rapidly metamorphosed into a euphoria that clouded his thinking and which previous historians have not recognized as pathological. Never modest, Browder now began receiving enough attention to generate grandiose illusions. That year and in 1943, undersecretary of state Sumner Welles sent Browder three invitations to discuss American foreign policy in his Washington office. The two corresponded frequently. A Federal Bureau of Investigation (FBI) informer reported Browder's boasting that the conferences would lead eventually to the CPUSA's representation in governmental circles. Surrounded by sycophants, Browder heard no chastening feedback. The only discordant notes in his American Communist Party symphony came from the despised William Z. Foster, whose solo Browder would never permit.

World events hastened Browder's departure from reality. In late November 1943 Roosevelt, Stalin, and Winston Churchill met and deliberated in Teheran, Iran. There they set a date for invading Western Europe, agreed to execute Nazi leaders, and published a vague statement pledging postwar tranquility. The communique pointedly ignored all divisive issues.

Browder took this optimism too literally. His gullibility led to a full-blown egomania. He spent months writing two lengthy speeches and a book proclaiming that the Teheran Declaration proved that the capitalist West now accepted the USSR as both legitimate and permanent. The class struggle had yielded to a long-lasting peaceful coexistence. Moreover, to prevent a return to the Great Depression at home, now that world war had doubled the American economy's size, big capitalists faced no choice except to voluntarily double workers' purchasing power.

At the CPUSA's next National Committee meeting in January 1944, Browder made what he considered his greatest political contribution. He announced that the CPUSA could never overcome America's iron two-party system. Instead, his followers could have a greater impact on postwar America as a left-wing lobbying group. Thus, after a ceremonial vote, the CPUSA became the Communist Political Association (CPA). It would thenceforth lobby both Democrats and Republicans in support of progressive causes. Quietly Browder calculated that the change would also build his reputation as a world Marxist theoretician.

Barely concealing his hubris, Browder proclaimed that he and his followers were standing on their own feet "for the first time."[34] To him, the Marxian revolution was now Earl Browder's leadership. He was so proud of himself that he did no contingency planning. Although the wartime Grand Alliance contradicted all previous history, Browder refused to even consider that once victory had eliminated the common Nazi enemy, East-West unity might vanish as well.

Of course, William Z. Foster felt no commitment to Browder's Teheran Thesis, nor did Sam Darcy. Indeed, they saw their opportunity to wound Browder gravely. During the week following Browder's National Committee speeches, they plotted together despite distance and discomfort. Darcy drove through the primitive, maddeningly congested roads from his Philadelphia home to Foster's cluttered Bronx apartment several times. Together they produced a ponderous seven-thousand-word critique of Browder's program over Foster's signature alone, lest they be accused of factionalism. The tract did not question the CPUSA's uncritical support for the Roosevelt administration, its antistrike policy, or even the CPUSA's scheduled transformation into the CPA. Instead, it ripped Browder's Teheran Thesis. Under its formulation, American imperialism had virtually disappeared and socialism played "practically no role whatever." The concept of enlightened capitalism was a "dangerous illusion." Entrepreneurs would not support the Teheran decisions, much less lead the nation in carrying them out. Finance capital remained "strong, greedy and aggressive," and only Social Democrats believed it otherwise. Labor courted disaster when it assumed capitalists were farsighted.[35] Not inaccurately, Foster and Darcy implied that the upbeat Browder was naïve to expect employers to understand the wisdom of doubling workers' wages.

At long last, Browder believed his opportunity to crush intra-party opposition had arrived. On February 8, 1944, Browder figuratively seized his antagonists by their throats and wrung both men viciously. He did this before the entire Political Committee, to which he had added extra personal supporters for good measure. He could treat Darcy, who was not a hero to left-wing labor, especially roughly. Attacking Foster, however, required greater finesse, as he remained a venerated working-class icon. Still Browder relished the task, and Foster suffered in silence. A few weeks later, Foster handed Browder a single-page synopsis of his views and requested its transmission to Georgi Dimitrov, who still directed the supposedly defunct Comintern. Browder coded it and cabled it to Moscow. By more secure methods, he also sent Foster's seven-thousand-word treatise and transcripts of January's and February's proceedings. Despite his prized autonomy, Browder always took all the foreign help he could get. In April, he ordered Darcy expelled. At his meanest, Browder chose Foster to preside over the official ostracism.

Before Darcy's departure, Dimitrov had received Browder's documents, including Foster's telegram. Few if any other comrades had ever presented Dimitrov with a fait accompli, and he sought advice on handling Browder's activities from Stalin's closest associate, Vyacheslav Molotov. As a result, Dimitrov sent his friend Browder a cipher that constituted a mild reprimand with a clear order to rethink all his recent actions. When Browder responded that Foster "had gone over to" the Political Committee's "opposition," Dimitrov indicated that Browder's innovations would soon receive a Soviet review: "Please report in greater detail the grounds of your disagreement. Have Foster himself formulate his point of view for me."[36] Here, Browder received what proved his final opportunity to abandon his grandiose illusions of independent communism.

Instead, Browder made a blunder so colossal as to suggest that his suffering in the Atlanta Penitentiary may have left intellectual as well as emotional damage. Previously, he had exercised extreme caution. For nearly twenty years, he had safely traveled overseas illegally. For a decade, he had recruited spies despite nearly constant FBI telephone taps and physical surveillance. Yet now he recklessly ignored Dimitrov's advice as if both men were political equals. Browder also deceived Foster, confidently contending that he possessed Dimitrov's support.

Browder's fabrications kept Foster silent for many months. The year 1944 proved one of the most ecstatic times of Browder's life. He campaigned openly for the president's election to a fourth term. Roosevelt rejected the CPA's endorsement, but urged Attorney General Francis Biddle to arrange a new Immigration Appeals Board hearing for Raissa Browder. That body permitted her voluntary departure to Canada. There she applied for an American visa and reentered legally, to the FBI's chagrin.[37] Exhilarated, Browder appeared before the House Committee on UnAmerican Activities (HUAC). Knowing the full extent of Communist doings in the United States, he cheerfully minimized them. His beaming confidence so angered some HUAC members that their behavior became churlish.

Browder, while yearning for the sort of public influence that European Communist Party leaders enjoyed, received his most flattering invitation that year. Former Republican presidential nominee Wendell Willkie invited him to his New York area home. Willkie voiced interest in Teheran and sought primarily to listen. The catalyzed Browder obliged, talking most of the evening. He returned to his Yonkers apartment convinced he would soon be a celebrity.

Rumors from ranking foreign Communists and international visitors warned that a major confrontation awaited Browder. He deemed himself too important to address them and vainly anticipated a larger personal role in the New Deal coalition. In April 1945 a French Communist journal printed a Moscow-written article. It had been translated into French and allegedly penned by Jacques Duclos, the number two Gallic comrade. It denounced Browder's Teheran Thesis as a "notorious revision of Marxism" and quoted at length internal CPA documents that only the Soviet news agency Tass could have supplied to Duclos, because the Nazis still held Paris. The article breached Communist discipline, portraying Foster as Leninism's heroic American defender and Darcy as its martyr. Clearly, the disquisition sought to humiliate Browder before the entire world. The unforgiving Joseph Stalin could have sent precisely the same message via private messenger, cable, or shortwave radio. Unsubtly the "Duclos article" suggested Browder's complete removal, terming him the CPA's "former secretary."[38] Browder's top followers knew not to question any commands from Moscow, but they were unsure of what to do with him. As Browder's financial angel, Philip J. Jaffe later noted, no Russian Communist Party organ criticized Browder until December 1945.[39]

Foster was determined to destroy his adversary. Eugene Dennis, previously Browder's staunchest loyalist, immediately switched sides and treated the Duclos article as the holy writ. The three quarreled over how to present it to the membership. On May 21, 1945, *New York World-Telegram* reporter Nelson Frank, who had access to governmental eavesdropping, printed an account of the Duclos article that informed the entire English-speaking world. That night the CPA's Political Committee began an emergency meeting that lasted nearly twenty-four hours. The prewar Browder might have ridden out the storm. More modest and pliable before his stint in the Atlanta Penitentiary, he had always steered the CPUSA within the international movement's narrow tideway. Now, however, Browder remained convinced he was so important that he could debate Duclos or whoever else had penned the essay. His shortwave's continued silence reinforced his belief that the message did not come from Stalin. Furthermore, Browder could never again work beside Foster. The two Communists had come to hate each other more than they did the capitalists.

Browder retained a number of followers until the National Committee's three-day mid-June meeting. Foster, red-faced with rage, opened on June 18. Skillfully he fused his message with US Communist war veterans' demands for recognition. Browder gave only one hectoring speech, taunting his departing followers as if they were intractable children. He then retreated to his ninth-floor office. Like an attorney planning an appeal to a higher court, he had stated his case, with modest concessions, merely for the record. The listeners replaced Browder with a new secretariat of Foster, Dennis, and John Williamson. In July, an emergency convention reestablished the CPUSA.

Browder remained a party member with no specific duties and no paycheck after his previously scheduled August vacation. At age 55 he was still robust enough to work. Yet the only offers he received came from the CPUSA's National Board, textile importer Alfred Kohlberg, and right-wing zealot Gerald L. K. Smith. Browder was unwilling to knuckle under to Foster, toil for capitalists, or crusade for anticommunist fanatics. Workaholics do not handle idleness well, and Browder began publishing *Distributors Guide*, a newsletter on economics, politics, and world markets. Even admirer Philip J. Jaffe later characterized it as "an amateurish piece of analysis with absolutely no influence."[40] The bulletin, costing an outrageous $100 per year, reached few people, but obviously violated party discipline. Accordingly, on February 5, 1946, the CPUSA expelled him.

Browder's twenty-seven post-Communist years were triply difficult. He could have made a deal with the FBI to save himself. Yet the bureau was unlikely to also overlook the treason of close relatives who knew less than Earl did. Browder also was aware he could never be safe from KGB (Soviet Secret Police) or GRU (Russian Military Intelligence) assassins if he revealed secrets. And his ego made things still worse for him. He simply refused to believe that he was no longer a world-class Marxist, and did everything he could to regain the CPUSA's leadership.

Isolation brought him agony. Even his dentist and insurance agent asked him to find replacements.[41] Browder's physical courage remained. He applied for a US passport and a Soviet visa. By April he had both and paid for the expensive trip to the USSR himself. When he arrived in Moscow and was received as an old friend, CPUSA leaders trembled. None of Browder's Russian comrades would discuss politics except Solomon Lozovsky, now Soviet Information Bureau chief. He talked with Browder for ten days and had him write a memorandum. Lozovsky knew there was no chance of Browder's ever talking directly with Stalin, so he sent the papers to Foreign Minister Molotov, then in Paris. Molotov, upon his return, quickly summoned Browder to his Kremlin office for a late-night meeting. They spent two-and-a-half hours together. Too eager to please his famous host, Browder did almost all of the talking, yet failed to mention the Duclos affair. Such treatment for a deposed Communist leader was unprecedented, and Browder knew not to push too hard.

He met no physical harm in Moscow, perhaps because of his American passport. Molotov cold-bloodedly offered him a token post distributing Soviet nonfiction in the United States, primarily to keep him quiet. Browder had hoped to visit his old friend Dimitrov in Bulgaria on the way home. Both Lozovsky and Molotov cruelly vetoed his plans. The Russian nonfiction job squandered Browder's meager life savings in a few short years.

Even as "Browderism" became a capital crime in Eastern Europe during the 1950s, and the FBI hounded family members for espionage information, Browder waited in vain for reinstatement. He refused to denounce Stalin until seven years after the dictator's death. Near his own life's end, he even wrote a book repudiating Karl Marx.[42] In 1972, with a pacemaker in his heart, Browder reminded a graduate student interviewer repeatedly about his abandonment of Marxism, as if this were earth-shattering news.[43]

Into his final year, the lonely Browder still believed in himself. He probably would have accepted a vindicating call from the CPUSA. Yet he waited in vain. His heart stopped on June 27, 1973. Not one Communist newspaper in the world printed his obituary, and a mere handful attended his memorial service. Today the CPUSA's failure, and Browder's, stand as preludes to the collapse of Soviet communism.

Notes

1 James Gilbert Ryan, "The Making of a Native Marxist: The Early Career of Earl Browder," *Review of Politics* 39, no. 3 (July 1977), pp. 332–63.
2 Gary Gerstle, *Working-Class Americanism* (New York: Cambridge University Press, 1989). One measure of the CPUSA's acceptance during the 1930s was the appearance of Earl Browder's photograph on the cover of *Time* magazine's May 30, 1938, cover.
3 Harvey Kehr, *The Heyday of American Communism: The Depression Decade* (New York: Basic Books, 1984); Maurice Isserman, *Which Side Were You On? The American Communist Party during the Second World War* (Middletown, CT: Wesleyan University Press, 1982).
4 Archives opened during the 1990s include CPUSA papers held secretly in Moscow since before the Second World War (fond 515) Russian State Archive of Social and Political History (RGASPI); papers of the Communist International (containing a vast English-language section) fond 495, RGASPI; and the "Venona" project (decryptions of Soviet cables sent from New York and Washington, DC to Moscow, intercepted and translated by the National Security Agency and the Central intelligence Agency). Secondary sources include John Earl Haynes and

Harvey Klehr, *Venona: Decoding Soviet Espionage in America* (New Haven, CT: Yale University Press, 1999); Katherine A. S. Sibley, *Red Spies in America: Stolen Secrets and the Dawn of the Cold War* (Lawrence: University Press of Kansas, 2004); and James G. Ryan, "Socialist Triumph as a Family Value: Earl Browder and Soviet Espionage," *American Communist History* 1, no. 2 (December 2002), pp. 125–42.

5   See John Earl Haynes, James G. Ryan, and Harvey Klehr, "Helen Lowry and Earl Browder: The Genealogy of a KGB Agent and Her Relationship to the Chief of the CPUSA," *American Communist History* 6, no. 2 (December 2007), pp. 229–38 and John Earl Haynes, Harvey Klehr, and James G. Ryan, "Correction to 'Helen Lowry and Earl Browder,'" *American Communist History* 8, no. 1 (June 2009), pp. 135–6.

6   Gladys Groves to James G. Ryan, December 21, 1976.

7   William Preston Jr., *Aliens and Dissenters: Federal Suppression of Radicals, 1903–1933* (Cambridge: Harvard University Press, 1963); Robert K. Murray, *Red Scare: A Study in National Hysteria, 1919–1920* (Minneapolis: University of Minnesota Press, 1955); Charles H. McCormick, *Seeing Reds: Federal Surveillance of Radicals in the Pittsburgh Mill District* (Pittsburgh: University of Pittsburgh Press, 1977).

8   Browder, unpublished autobiography, Earl Browder Papers, Syracuse University; James Ryan, telephone interview with John W. Roberts, Bureau of Prisons archivist, March 4, 1993; Office of the Pardon Attorney file on Browder, 3-3c, National Archives.

9   Gladys Groves to James G. Ryan, December 21, 1976.

10 Browder, Soviet autobiography (fewer than three hundred words in length) fond 495, opis 261, delo 16 (1) RGASPI; Theodore Draper, *The Roots of American Communism* (New York: Viking Press, 1957), p. 146.

11 On Foster, see Edward P. Johanningsmeier, *Forging American Communism: The Life of William Z. Foster* (Princeton, NJ: Princeton University Press, 1994) and James R. Barrett, *William Z. Foster and the Tragedy of American Radicalism* (Urbana: University of Illinois Press, 1999).

12 James P. Cannon, *The First Ten Years of American Communism* (New York: Lyle Stuart, 1962), p. 111; *Current History* (December 1944), pp. 10–14. Earl Browder, autobiographical manuscript, 168, Earl Browder Papers, Syracuse University.

13 Jacob A. Zumoff, *The Communist International and U.S. Communism, 1919–1929* (Leiden: Brill, 2014), p. 188. See also Dimitri Volkogonov, *Stalin: Triumph and Tragedy*, trans. Harold Shukman (Rocklin, CA: Prima, 1992).

14 Raissa Browder, Soviet autobiography, fond 495, opis 261, delo 3264 RGASPI, trans. Leon Luxemburg. For some reason Luganovska spelled her first name in this idiosyncratic manner on Roman alphabet documents.

15 Samuel Adams Darcy to James G. Ryan March 4, 1994.

16 Igor Damaskin with Geoffrey Elliott, *Kitty Harris: The Spy with Seventeen Names* (London: St. Ermin's Press, 2001).

17 James G. Ryan, *Earl Browder: The Failure of American Communism* (Tuscaloosa: University of Alabama Press, 1997), pp. 47–55.
18 Weinstone speech to Polburo, September 19, 1932, fond 515, opis 1, delo 2683, RGASPI.
19 Browder speech to Polburo, September 20, 1932, fond 515, opis 1, delo 2683, RGASPI.
20 Weinstone speech to Polburo, September 20, 1932, fond 515, opis 1, delo 2683, RGASPI.
21 "Report on the 12th Plenum of the ECCI by Gebert," November 13, 1932, fond 495, opis 1, delo 2679, RGASPI.
22 Johanningsmeier, *Forging American Communism*, p. 266; Barrett, *Tragedy of American Radicalism*, 186.
23 Isserman, *Which Side Were You On?*
24 Philip J. Jaffe to James G. Ryan, January 24, 1977.
25 James G. Ryan, "'Communism Is Twentieth Century Americanism': The Communist Party's Americanization Campaign," in J. Bret Bennington, Zenia Sacks DaSilva, Michael D'Innocenzo, and Stanislao G. Pugliese (eds.), *The 1930s: The Reality and the Promise* (Newcastle upon Tyne: Cambridge Scholars, 2016), pp. 111–19.
26 James G. Ryan interview with Philip J. Jaffe, January 3–4, 1977.
27 Ivo Banac (ed.), *The Diary of Georgi Dimitrov, 1933–1949*, trans. Jane T. Hedges, Timothy D. Sergay, and Irina Faion (New Haven, CT: Yale University Press, 2003), pp. 80–1.
28 Philip J. Jaffe to James G. Ryan, January 24, 1977.
29 Fridrikh I. Firsov, Harvey Klehr, and John Earl Haynes, *Secret Cables of the Comintern, 1933–1943* (New Haven, CT: Yale University Press, 2014), p. 46.
30 *Daily Worker*, July 6, 1939.
31 *New York Times*, January 23, 1940.
32 Browder speech, fond 495, opis 20, delo 540, RGASPI.
33 Reports by Dr. Zbranek and the psychologist, April 18, 1941, 4b and the following page (also numbered 4b). The Bureau of Prisons deleted their names but H. Park Tucker in "A History of the Atlanta Federal Penitentiary, 1901–1956" (unpublished manuscript), United States Bureau of Prisons file on Browder, reports Zbranek as the only psychiatrist during the era, 427.
34 Earl Browder, *Teheran and America: Perspectives and Tasks* (New York: Workers' Library, 1944), p. 28.
35 Foster letter to the National Committee, January 20, 1944, pp. 1–8, Earl Browder papers.
36 Dimitrov to Molotov, March 8, 1944, trans. Harry Walsh, fond 495, opis 74, delo 482 RGASPI; Banac, *Diary of Georgi Dimitrov*, p. 299.

37 "Memorandum for the Attorney General," January 14, 1944, Franklin D. Roosevelt Library; a departmental memo to J. Edgar Hoover declared that Assistant Secretary of State Adolph A. Berle insisted he had telephone orders from the president to approve the application 38. (Edward A. Tamm to Hoover, June 30, FBI file 39-878-31X), Raissa Browder FBI file.

38 The article, carrying the title "On the Communist Political Association of the United States of America," is reprinted both in the original Russian and in French in Harvey Klehr, John Earl Haynes, and Kyrill M. Anderson, *The Soviet World of American Communism* (New Haven, CT: Yale University Press, 1998), pp. 100–3.

39 Philip J. Jaffe, *The Rise and Fall of American Communism* (New York: Horizon Press, 1975), p. 84.

40 Ibid., p. 138.

41 Browder papers, Series 1–7, 1–32; Klehr, *Heyday of American Communism*, p. 486.

42 Earl Browder, *Marx and America: A Study of the Doctrine of Impoverishment* (Westport, CT: Greenwood Press, 1958).

43 James G. Ryan interview with Earl Browder, March 13, 1972.

Bibliography

Barrett, James R. *William Z. Foster and the Tragedy of American Radicalism*. Urbana: University of Illinois Press, 1999.

Haynes, John Earl, Harvey Klehr, and Alexander Vassiliev. *Spies: The Rise and Fall of the KGB in America*, trans. By Philip Redko and Steven Shabad. New Haven, CT: Yale University Press, 2009.

Isserman, Maurice. *Which Side Were You On? The American Communist Party during the Second World War*. Middletown, CT: Wesleyan University Press, 1982.

Johanningsmeier, Edward P. *Forging American Communism: The Life of William Z. Foster*. Princeton, NJ: Princeton University Press, 1994.

Klehr, Harvey. *The Heyday of American Communism: The Depression Decade*. New York: Basic Books, 1984.

Klehr, Harvey, John Earl Haynes, and Fridrikh Igorevich Firsov. *The Secret World of American Communism*. New Haven, CT: Yale University Press, 1995.

3

From Haymarket to Mao? The Radicalism of William Z. Foster

Edward P. Johanningsmeier

One crucial feature of the historiography of American communism that has remained prominent in the decades following the "opening" of certain Soviet archives in 1991 has been in-depth biographical inquiry. Biographical studies have continued to provide insight into important features of Communist party operations, ideology, and influence. Historical biographies of American Communists have generally portrayed a striking diversity of motives, interests, and abilities in their subjects, all asserted amid complex and powerfully conflicting political and social environments. These include: intense belief and paralyzing factionalism; energetic commitment and solidarity alternating with cynicism and decline into sullen obedience and principled dissent as well as determinist inertia. Overall, however, the predominant "logic" of these studies is of Communist organizational degeneracy and isolation: for instance, Earl Browder's biography is subtitled "The failure of American Communism." According to historian Bryan Palmer, the complex career of James P. Cannon exemplifies resistance to a Communist movement that gave itself wholly to Stalinism in the 1920s.[1]

In the years of the founding and establishment of the Communist movement in the United States, William Z. Foster remains an interesting and highly relevant figure for biographical study. Theodore Draper, in his 1957 study of the early Communist movement, identified Jay Lovestone and Earl Browder consecutively as the "dominant figures" in its first decade, and Louis Fraina as the "man who did more than anyone else" to make possible the formation of the American Communist movement in 1919. Yet, despite Fraina's prominent role in the establishment of ties between the left wing of the American Socialist Party (ASP) and the revolutionary regime in the Soviet Union from 1918–20, his early career as a communist was dogged by allegations that he was an informant, and his influence waned following his appointment as a Communist International (Comintern) agent in Mexico in 1921. Jay Lovestone was certainly a major figure, especially in the period from 1926 to 1929 as he led factional struggles on behalf of the former Charles Ruthenberg group in the party, but his influence lay primarily in the back rooms of the party and in Comintern conclaves until his dramatic expulsion from the party in 1929 in favor of William Foster. Earl Browder played an influential but clearly subordinate role largely as Foster's assistant in the party during its formative years, and obviously played a prominent public leadership role subsequently, following his appointment as General Secretary of the party in 1930.[2]

If one were to specify a leadership figure who perhaps best represented the American party's unique character, as well as its conflicting and changing ideological and tactical orientations from the years of its emergence from the underground in 1922 through to the period of its demise as an effective voice for left politics in America in the 1950s, it would be William Foster. As a public figure, Foster ran for president on the Party ticket three times, in 1924, 1928, and 1932. At the organizational level, Foster ranked first in terms of his total years of service on the party's Central Committee and involvement in various party administrative committees as Harvey Klehr notes in his careful study of Communist cadre as a historical cohort. James Ryan, the biographer of Earl Browder, concluded that if American Communists had chosen their leaders democratically in the period Browder was active, they certainly would have chosen Foster.[3] Important new information has come to light since the publication of Klehr's study, yet much that has been revealed since 1992 reinforces Foster's importance in representing major themes in the party's history. Foster was the only individual among the party's leadership to remain in the movement from the first years of its development through its decline in the aftermath of the McCarthy era. This is often attributed to Foster's agility in conforming to the shifting political requirements of the Comintern; in certain party circles this earned him the nickname "zig-zag." However, there were more enduring and consistent aspects of Foster's individual personality and outlook as a Communist that were inextricably related to powerful and multidirectional currents of early twentieth-century American and international labor radicalism. These characteristics remain crucial to explaining his remarkable persistence and adaptability in the Communist movement.

By the time he joined the American Communist movement in 1921, Foster was 40 years old. An examination of Foster's pre-Communist years reveals a rich and varied early life and range of experiences—most strikingly as a member of a fluid and transient working-class diaspora that knew few national boundaries. His father, James, emigrated to the United States as a Fenian political refugee in 1868, and his mother had been a worker at the English textile mills in Carlisle, England, before meeting her husband in Taunton, Massachusetts. William grew up in Philadelphia in the 1880s and 1890s in a gang-governed neighborhood close by the Seventh Ward, which W. E. B. DuBois studied intensively between 1896 and 1897 for his foundational work *The Philadelphia Negro*. His family's neighbors included many immigrants from Germany, Scotland, Italy, France, and Cuba. In this milieu, he was exposed to a wide variety of American radical dissent. A notorious Irish revolutionary, William Carroll, lived two blocks from the Foster residence. Growing up in a poverty-ridden neighborhood known as Skittereen, not far from the prosperous commercial downtown of the city but also within a mile radius of the main station of the Pennsylvania Railroad and only about a mile from the enormous manufacturing complex of the Baldwin Locomotive Works, Foster held vivid personal memories not only related to his father's militant Fenianism, but also to encounters with William Jennings Bryan, Coxey's Army, Socialist soapboxers, and quite likely also to the Knights of Labor. Foster began his industrial employment at age 13 at the giant MacKellar, Smiths and Jordan typeworks near his home. It was during a violent, paralyzing street railwaymen's strike in 1895, when he was 14 years old, that Foster gained his "introduction to the class struggle" as he put it; he participated in violent street fighting in his neighborhood in support of the American Federation of Labor's (AFL's) attempts to unionize conductors and was clubbed during one melee by a mounted policeman. In 1910 yet another AFL street railwaymen's strike paralyzed the city, once again vividly demonstrating the ability of the AFL to inspire militant organizing campaigns and energetic solidarity among the incredibly diverse working class of the city. The successes (and failures) of these strikes can be seen as offering a rough paradigm mapping the range of possibilities Foster envisioned for the American working class during his life as a radical labor activist and Communist.

The origins of William Foster's radicalism can also be glimpsed in his astonishing world travelling confidence and "unticketed" wanderings as a young man. Leaving Philadelphia at age 17, Foster found work in Cuba, Florida, New York, Texas, and Portland, Oregon.[4] In 1901, he left Portland and journeyed around the globe as a paid "ordinary seaman," and participated in a refusal of duty on an English bark. He travelled to France in 1910 to report on the radical French labor movement at the behest of Vincent St. John of the Industrial Workers of the World (IWW). There he met prominent radical syndicalists

Gustave Hervé, Pierre Monatte, and Alfred Rossmer and witnessed firsthand an astonishing general railroad strike organized by the Confédération Génerale du Travail (CGT). He witnessed giant Socialist Democratic Party of Germany (SPD) demonstrations in Berlin and attended a 1911 international trades union congress in Budapest, where he gained prominence contesting the credentials of the AFL delegation in favor of the IWW. As a young man Foster was a particularly close follower of the international syndicalist movement. A first syndicalist international was organized in London in 1913, some seven years before the founding of the Communist/syndicalist dominated Red International of Labor Unions (Profintern) which Foster ended up joining in 1921. As a peripatetic labor activist and agitator beginning in the 1910s, Foster was a familiar figure to Socialists, anarchists, Wobblies, European syndicalists, and American trade unionists. His activism and writings in the 1910s, "the age of industrial violence" in America, were well-known by figures as diverse as Samuel Gompers and Vladimir Lenin.

Working briefly as a lumber worker in 1911, he became closely associated with a group of anarchists at Home Colony on Puget Sound. Indeed, in his travels in the United States, Foster worked wherever he could, but his first relatively stable employment was as a railway shop and yard worker in Chicago. In noting Foster's close relations with the anarcho-syndicalist radicals of Home Colony and Chicago in the 1910s, Melvyn Dubofsky concluded that "much of the history of twentieth-century American radicalism can be written in terms of the life and times of William Z. Foster."[5] During this period, Foster developed close relationships with anarcho-syndicalists who would work with him in the Chicago labor movement, the Great Steel Strike of 1919, and later the CPUSA, including Jay Fox, Joseph Manley, and Esther Abramowitz, his future life partner. He worked closely with figures liked Sam Hammersmark, Anton Johannsen, and Jack Jones, Elizabeth Gurley Flynn's first husband and proprietor of the radical Dil Pickle Club in Chicago.[6] Fox and Hammersmark, as well as others in this circle, had been seared by their direct experiences of the Haymarket upheaval in Chicago in 1886. The anarchist "Chicago Idea" advocated by Haymarket defendants Albert Parsons and August Spies affirmed the futility of Socialist politics and the ballot, and saw trade unionism as the basis for overthrowing the existing order. "Theirs was militant, a revolutionary unionism … trade union as they viewed it, was an instrument of social revolution … to be satisfied with nothing less than the elimination of capitalism and its replacement by a cooperative commonwealth" as Paul Avrich has put it.[7] Foster and Esther Abramowitz lived for a time at Lucy Parson's boarding house in Chicago. Foster collaborated with Jack Jones in writing a widely circulated pamphlet, *Syndicalism* in 1912.[8] Working as an AFL organizer associated with the Chicago Federation of Labor, Foster witnessed firsthand the great IC-Harriman shopmen's strike and helped promote a powerful movement for associations of railway workers' unions centering in the Chicago railyards. It was from this milieu that Foster brought together a small group of anarcho-syndicalist associates who ended up providing leadership and impetus for two of the most significant labor organizing campaigns of the early twentieth century in the meatpacking and steel industries of 1918–19.[9]

Foster's *Syndicalism* is a fascinating document in which he draws upon the wide variety of social and intellectual trends to which he had been exposed in his wanderings, including not only French syndicalism but social Darwinism, neo-Malthusianism, the writings of Bakunin and Kropotkin, Bellamyite visions of collectivized industrial monopoly, and even the Modern School movement to justify class war and the revolutionary elitism of the syndicalist "militant minority." Because the militant syndicalist is fighting against an utterly unscrupulous enemy, "whether his tactics are 'legal' or 'moral' or not does not concern him, so long as they are effective."[10] Moreover, since "every forward pace humanity has taken has been gained at the cost of untold suffering and loss of life … the accomplishment of the revolution will probably be no exception."[11] The true syndicalist is antidemocratic in the industrial, social, and political senses of the term; bourgeois notions of natural rights are merely illusions to deceive workingmen into stupefied complacency. The syndicalist bases his tactics on the idea that might is right, and has "placed his relations with the capitalists upon a basis of naked power."[12] It is important to acknowledge that, as James Barrett has put it, the "brutal worldview" of this pamphlet reflects in part Foster's lived experiences with insecurity, transience, hard work, and brushes with death as a railway worker.[13] Although Foster later took pains to repudiate his early syndicalism in various articles for official Communist publications, the 1912 *Syndicalism* pamphlet represents above all Foster's persistent revolutionary empiricism or his "eclecticism" as some Communists derisively called it. Despite the fact that *Syndicalism* is itself an ideological construction, he portrayed the ideal revolutionary as unwilling, given the immediate circumstances of the class war, to be constrained by abstract ideology, whether in the form of systemic morality or the futile metaphysics of socialist or progressive politics.

Foster became closely involved, yet not formally affiliated with the Communist movement when he attended the first congress of the Profintern in Moscow in July of 1921, in the company of many other syndicalists from labor movements around the globe. For the purposes of understanding the career of William

Foster in the CPUSA, perhaps most important of all was his reading of Lenin's *Left-Wing Communism: An Infantile Disorder*, available in the United States in 1921. Crucially from Foster's standpoint, Lenin wrote that the primary task of Communists in the United States and elsewhere was to win the majority of the working class through aggressive activism in the established union movement on behalf of workers' control rather than by attempting to organize a separate industrial union movement based on grandiose "left wing" political objectives.[14]

In considering the question of the "Americanization" of the CPUSA in the early 1920s, the entrance of Foster with his great web of connections in the American labor movement is often cited as a large step in adapting the Communist movement to so-called native conditions. Paul Buhle has noted that by the 1910s under the original formulation of Daniel DeLeon, one of Foster's early intellectual influences, revolutionary syndicalism had marked a "fascinating shift in American Marxist logic. ... [it] proved the most internationally recognized strategic or theoretical perspective developed in the USA."[15] Foster's internationalism certainly reflected this "fascinating shift"; radicals well-known to Foster in the Chicago Federation of Labor had endorsed the Bolshevik Revolution in 1917, and in 1920 called for a general strike if the Soviet Union was invaded. Its leader, John Fitzpatrick, had boasted during the height of the unprecedented 1919 strike wave that "we are going to socialize the basic industries of the United States."[16] Yet, taken as he was by the still unformed possibilities of the Russian Revolution, Foster remained beholden to his exceptionalist ideas about moving American labor toward revolution through militant organizing work by adaptive minority organizations, shop-steward networks, and amalgamation leagues in the early 1920s.[17]

Foster was the only Communist leader to have once met the president of the United States in the White House in the midst of a national industrial emergency, the Great Steel Strike of 1919, that he himself had played a primary role in developing.[18] Earl Browder, future General Secretary of the Communist Party, wrote to Vladimir Lenin in May of 1921 from the Hotel Continental in Moscow, "I know you are interested in the problem of the American working masses organized in the AFL, and the possibilities of giving them a revolutionary direction. The man most qualified to give you information on this point is William Z. Foster, who is now in Moscow."[19] Foster never met with Lenin, but Lenin was aware of the 1919 Steel Strike and had a copy of Foster's *The Great Steel Strike and Its Lessons* (1920) in his library.[20] Browder, writing to Leon Trotsky in February 1922 in reply to Trotsky's query about whether there had ever been a revolutionary movement in the United States, replied that "the events of 1919 provided American workers with more fundamental education by one hundred percent than was accomplished by the Communist parties." According to Browder, reporting on behalf of Foster's non-Communist Trade Union Educational League (TUEL), the 1919 Steel Strike suggested that with Communist organization of militants in the trade union movement under the leadership of Foster (Figure 3.1), "the masses could be thrown into direct conflict with the state."[21]

In at least partial affirmation of this perspective, by October 1922, Foster's TUEL, now affiliated with but working largely independently of the developing CPUSA political apparatus in the United States, had gained the endorsement of hundreds of labor groups throughout the nation, including sixteen state federations and fourteen national unions, and dozens of central labor bodies. Its program of endorsing incremental amalgamation of craft unions into larger federations had a wide appeal during the postwar period of the "American Plan" open-shop movement and a sharp decline in bargaining power by unions; Eugene Debs endorsed Foster's aims and tactics. Both Earl Browder and James Cannon perceived the entrance of Foster, representing a modern and compelling syndicalist analysis of American labor politics circa 1921, as crucial to the CPUSA's early development.

Significantly, the highest ranking Soviet official whom Foster met in Moscow in 1921, Solomon Lozovsky, head of the Profintern, wrote that with regard to Communist and TUEL work within the established labor movement, "Everything changes in accordance with time, place and circumstances," and Communists working within the Profintern's ambit must rely always on a "relativity of methods and means of struggle." Moreover, he averred in 1924 that because of this, the success of Communists in the labor movement depends not on political control or resolutions by the party, but by day-to-day work in the unions "which by its very nature the party can neither carry on nor accomplish."[22]

At the Communist movement's Bridgman convention in early 1923, it appeared that only 5 percent of party cadre were involved in trade union work.[23] However, by the early 1930s, regardless of debilitating factional conflict and Stalinization, the party's membership had undergone a significant transformation, and its main source of real political and industrial influence lay within the American organized labor movement. Foster, because of his tireless work to maintain Communist influence in the trade-union movement through the TUEL and the Trade Union Unity League, may still be credibly ranked as one of the founders of the realistic and progressive industrial union movement that emerged in the United States in the 1930s and 1940s. Communist organizers were indispensable

Figure 3.1 William Z. Foster and Mary G. Harris "Mother" Jones at the Great Steel Strike of 1919.

to the building of the Congress of Industrial Organizations (CIO) and industrial unionism, which Michael Kazin has characterized as "the largest social movement of the 1930s." The historian William Denning has identified Foster as the radical left's key spokesman for the "laboring" of American Popular Front culture during the 1930s. No other American labor leader worked so tirelessly and effectively in carrying forward and embedding this "exceptionalist" tradition into the character of the American Communist movement.[24]

Yet Foster's early syndicalism also helps explain his role in what would come to be known as the Stalinization of American Communism. The syndicalist concept of the militant minority, which inspired much of Foster's pre-Communist radicalism, can easily be linked to Bolshevism and Lenin's conception of revolutionary elitism, which Foster celebrated in his writings in the early 1920s. Foster's class-war moral skepticism, disdain for democracy, and even his vision of an authoritarian future workers' society are all outlined quite starkly in his *Syndicalism*, and certainly help explain his early attraction to the Communist movement.

However, to move somewhat more tangentially to a different level of analysis, one may begin with an encounter Foster had with an Armour meatpacking executive in 1917 when Foster was escorted into his office to discuss the steamfitters' grievance. The workers' delegates were outraged to find that the company's representative would only discuss the weather with them. At the conclusion of the brief meeting, the executive exclaimed "go back to your trade union friends and tell them that Organized Labor will never get anything from this company that it hasn't the power to take!"[25]

In considering Foster and his career in the CPUSA, it is important to acknowledge that his early radicalism developed in synergy with certain features of American labor progressivism at the turn of the century, with its emphasis on organization, integration, and efficiency as a solution to what was then called "the labor problem." It was a time when the world seemed to endow men like Herbert Hoover, men with outstanding organizational skills, with the greatest powers of social and economic transformation. This is what led Foster to the offices of the Armour meatpacking executives to negotiate reasonable expectations for workers' power and integration in their firm, and ultimately to the Oval Office with Woodrow Wilson and Samuel Gompers in 1919 to discuss possible recognition of a new and more inclusive steelworkers' organization.

The unraveling of the packinghouse and steel workers organizing campaigns ultimately confirmed for Foster the fraudulence of Wilsonian promises of industrial democracy. Gompers's quid pro quo with Wilson during the war as well was ultimately inconsistent with Foster's particular brand of class-war syndicalism. AFL membership doubled during the war, yet twenty-three states also passed "criminal syndicalism" laws, and Eugene Debs was imprisoned for giving a speech in which he advocated industrial unionism.

According to Foster, real power for the working class would come first through organization, and not the idle "talk" of industrial democracy. According to Foster, "the Socialist Party in this country collapsed because it was built upon talk, instead of the solid foundation" of radical organizing in the trade union movement.[26] In Foster's world, power and "talk" were oppositional categories, not related to each other in any stable way. For him, the true power of the CPUSA came through its organizational strength, which in turn originated with the skill and energy of the elite militants of the Leninist vanguard. Throughout Foster's career as a communist, there is a profound tension between his class-war syndicalism and his organizational ethos—his profound respect for working-class organizational power and labor discipline could never be precisely or lucidly distinguished from his combustible anger at capitalist control at the point of production.

In tracing Foster's incipient Stalinism in the 1920s, his close factional ally and former syndicalist James P. Cannon perhaps came nearest to understanding Foster's contempt for the words and mere "talk" of Communist politics. Cannon understood that Foster in the 1920s finally came to apotheosize the principle of organizational power above all else. Cannon reflected in his correspondence with Theodore Draper that he "had the highest regard for Foster's ability in general, and for his feel and skill as a mass worker in particular-a most essential quality which the other leaders of the other faction seemed to lack." Foster, according to Cannon, "was the party's outstanding mass leader and most popular figure, and he carried himself well in that role. ... He symbolized the proletarian-American orientation, which the party needed and wanted, and I thought he was justly entitled to first place as party leader and public spokesman."[27]

Cannon believed that Foster's "Stalinization" could be ultimately attributed to personal ambition and dedication to "career." Yet, elsewhere, Cannon's analysis is more interesting and historical: he noted that Foster's tactics were partly forged by the syndicalist "cult of action" of the prewar years—Foster's "American pragmatism" was especially empowering, enabling him to "get things done" as a brilliant labor organizer. According to Cannon, Foster had learned too much from what Cannon characterized as the trade-unionist "school of Gompers" and operated on "the theory that nobody reads, or remembers what he reads." Foster, as Cannon discusses in relation to Foster's seeming acceptance of the CPUSA's dual-union line that emerged after 1928, was "master in the art of leaving the door open so that his words can be interpreted to mean one thing or the direct opposite—depending on the way the cat jumps." Significantly, Cannon believed that Foster had "[come] to Stalinism with tongue-in-cheek."[28]

Most people who knew Foster described him as a mostly quiet man with an intense, workaholic demeanor, mostly lacking in personal charisma. He possessed a simmering temper that occasionally surfaced with subordinates and factional opponents. Cannon himself allows that Foster, despite his apparent lack of principles, was at heart an organizer, specifically a trade-union organizer without peer, who was completely dedicated to "radicalizing and expanding the labor movement."[29] As E. J. Hobsbawm has noted, the Leninist Communist Party "was the most formidable political invention of the 20th century."[30] Foster's sacramental attachment to the unprecedented revolutionary power and efficiency of Lenin's and Stalin's Communist Party would enable radicals working within the American labor movement to at least match the power of the modern corporations that he believed ruled and degraded his world.

However, the irony of Foster's career as a self-described "expert in organization" in the CPUSA was that he was in some senses the most unruly and noncompliant of those in primary leadership positions. In 1924 he bitterly attacked the change in line that seriously jeopardized the party's relations with the Chicago labor movement and led a factional campaign for the removal of putative Comintern representative John Pepper. In 1925 he led a short-lived but nonetheless entirely unprecedented revolt of his majority faction against a Comintern cable that awarded leadership of the party to the Lovestone group.[31] Lovestone observed pointedly to Nikolai Bukharin that, following the decision, Foster had expressed "serious skepticism towards the Comintern" in his factional meetings.[32] Because of his opposition to various labor party schemes, as well as dual unionism experimentation during the Passaic Strike of 1926, his factional opponent John Ruthenberg could declare that "Comrade Foster is not yet a Communist and has not basic Marxian conceptions to guide his policies."[33] In 1928–9, Foster openly clashed with his powerful liaison and protector in the Soviet apparatus, Solomon Lozovsky, over the Profintern's call for the establishment of dual unions and abandonment of the "save the union" slogan during the United Mine Workers Union (UMW) bituminous strike of 1928. Crucially, in each of these cases, despite changes in "slogans," he was able to emerge with significant concessions from the Comintern, which he believed enabled him to continue to exercise primary control over the party's day-to-day trade union work.[34] Even Lovestone, in recounting to his factional allies a personal meeting with Stalin in 1928, acknowledged that Stalin had been respectful of Foster's extensive trade union connections and had cautioned Lovestone not to "press him too hard." Foster is "connected with the worker but the danger in him is that he is detached from the general political questions. He does not grasp political questions," according to Lovestone's description of Stalin's comments.[35]

Nonetheless, in 1929, presiding over a special "American Commission" called in Moscow to resolve a bitter dispute between Foster and a party faction led by Jay Lovestone, Stalin accused Foster of "rotten diplomacy" and "disgraceful conduct in his relations with the Comintern." Foster's speech in reply is significant. He reaffirmed his ultimate loyalty to the Comintern: "I came to the Comintern, I joined the Communist Party of the CI at a time when the Russian revolution was at its lowest, in 1921. I came here and found the Russian workers starving and I said: This is my fight." He reminded those present that "one of the first things that attracted me to the CP was the position of Comrade Lenin on the trade union question," and that it was ironic that he was now being corrected "in a Communist sense" about his (and Lenin's) commitment to the boring from within perspective of the TUEL. He said that despite having been offered "rich positions" in the AFL, "I came to the CI and I stayed with the Comintern and I shall be with the Comintern when many of those comrades who have got the guts to stand up and criticize me will be on the other sides of the barricades." He confronted those present with what he may have thought was an ultimatum: the campaign of the Lovestone faction (and presumably others who questioned his "true" communism) against him must be stopped, he said, because "it doesn't enable me to work effectively in the Party."[36]

As has been carefully chronicled by historians of the CPUSA, the "American Commission" of 1929 did indeed decisively put an end to Lovestone's factionalism, and put Foster in a position of shared leadership with secondary figures he most likely believed he could manipulate: Earl Browder, Max Bedacht, and William Weinstone. Yet, Stalin may have created such an unusual structure because he suspected that Foster's individual leadership might develop too independently. Even so, as had been the outcome of previous debates within the party/Comintern in 1923 and 1925, Foster was assured control over the trade union activities of the party. Despite his overt claims of solidarity with the new Comintern arrangement, one high-level cadre as early as 1931 noted that "extreme, sharp" conflict between Foster and Browder was in evidence in party meetings.[37]

Perhaps not coincidentally, the most significant example of Foster's personality and ability as a Communist organizer came in the spring and summer of 1931, when tens of thousands of coal miners, abandoned by the UMW, struck against unilateral wage cuts by the Carnegie mines in western Pennsylvania, as well as against operators in coal fields in Ohio, eastern Kentucky, and West Virginia. This was an area where Foster had worked more or less continuously since the Communists had committed to a "Save the Union" rebellion against John L. Lewis in the late 1920s. In 1931, Foster devoted himself entirely to the miners' strike; he was familiar figure in the Pittsburgh area because of his leadership of the 1919 Steel Strike. As Melvyn Dubofsky described, the Communists "organized mass marches by unemployed miners, their wives, and children; challenged local and state law enforcement officials; and, for over a year, kept the three coalfields in a state of turmoil. By late summer of 1931, the Communists had won a larger following among the regions' coal miners than Lewis."[38] The strike gained national attention, and was the subject of powerful writings by Theodore Dreiser, John Dos Passos, and Sherwood Anderson.

The strike was viciously repressed by local authorities and the UMW recruited strike breakers in key mines. In June, Foster addressed a crowd of approximately five thousand miners in the small town of Wildwood; the following day a demonstration and march resulted in the shooting of nine miners, one fatally.[39] As the strike faltered, Foster came under pressure from the party hierarchy to abandon his efforts—Foster in turn accused the national office, then under the control of Earl Browder, of not devoting enough organizers and resources to the struggle. Foster, too, was once again sharply questioned by Comintern authority, for what was termed his "trade-unionist, syndicalist" attitude in the organizing of the strike primarily around immediate demands of the strikers rather than the political objectives of the official Communist union. At one point a Comintern representative reported that, listening to Foster and others in their meetings with the miners, "I have never heard ... these comrades mention the Party with a single word." Moreover in party meetings Foster and his associates organized what he called an "open drive" against the rep's attempts to reframe the objectives of the strike in favor of a more Communist political line.[40] The causes of the failure of this strike were complexly related to conditions in the field; nonetheless, the strike demonstrated the continuing mobilizing capacity of Communist unionists in the coal fields on the eve of the passage of the National Industrial Recovery Act (NRA) with its unprecedented Section 7a prohibiting employers from interfering with the right of workers to collective bargaining. Lewis threatened in 1933 that it was his union and American organized labor more generally that stand between the rapacity of the robber barons ... and the lustful rage of the communists."[41] Foster himself was deeply demoralized by the outcome of the strike itself, and it perhaps was one factor that led to a disabling nervous breakdown he suffered in June 1932.[42]

During a long interregnum of uncertainty and relative isolation, Foster fought to regain his health. In the crucial months following the successful conclusion of the United Auto Workers (UAW)-Flint sit-down strike in February 1937, Foster asserted his still-considerable influence to aggressively articulate a syndicalist perspective on the way that Communists were operating within the fledgling CIO. From March through November, a series of wildcat sit-down strikes in the automobile industry in Michigan raised fundamental questions relating to the Popular Front. Communist organizers, who had played a crucial role in developing and sustaining the Flint strike, were subsequently involved in numerous unauthorized sit-downs in dozens of strikes at a time when John L. Lewis sought to establish his credibility with General Motors (GM) in light of continuing shop-floor dissent and accusations of Communist influence in the new federation. Because of the so-called Roosevelt Recession, by November one-quarter of all GM workers had been laid off. To what extent would Communist organizers in the automobile industry assist the CIO and Lewis in establishing shop-floor discipline and regularized contract bargaining by helping to suppress the strikes? "Unity Caucus" radicals in the UAW like Wyndham Mortimer and Walter Reuther were ostensibly in favor of "legal" bargaining, but also believed that GM managers were provoking many of the strikes as a way of forcing showdowns over shop-floor authority.[43]

John L. Lewis and Earl Browder demanded an unconditional end to a bitter wildcat strike that broke out at GM's Fisher Body plant in Pontiac in November. The pro-New Deal governor of the state, Frank Murphy, facing a reelection and fearing a conservative backlash against the CIO, threatened to call the state militia to clear the plant of sit-downers. Just the previous year he had refused to use force to evict the GM-Flint sit-downers. Nonetheless, the historian Nelson Lichtenstein has concluded that the Pontiac strike "marked a high point in rank-and-file militancy during the formative years of the UMW," and "demonstrated the extent to which the left might yet capture the social terrain occupied by the right" in the conservative town of Pontiac. UAW authorization of the strike would represent "a huge gamble, a lunge toward union power and a syndicalist flavored industrial democracy at the nation's most powerful corporation."[44]

It is now clear that during the crucial period, Foster, while formally offering rationales for the ending of the strikes in party resolutions and minutes, accepted Communist involvement in the strikes at the level of the rank and file. Leading organizers in Detroit had from the beginning requested that Foster make frequent visits to Detroit and assume the initiative on questions of policy there, but according to Browder, Foster and district secretary William Weinstone refused to suppress the sit-downs, thereby threatening the position the party had established with Lewis. Browder demanded that Foster accept the removal of Weinstone, and Foster refused, calling for Weinstone's ouster only under unspecified conditions. According to Browder, "Com. Foster responded in an extremely subjective manner, such as we have not had in our party leadership for years."[45]

In yet another "American Commission" meeting in Moscow in January 1938, Foster sharply attacked Browder's leadership of the party, accusing him of failing to work to establish an identity for the party independent of Lewis and Franklin D. Roosevelt (FDR). In 1936, he had complained vociferously that Lewis was making organizing a steel organizing campaign contingent on FDR's election.[46] Now, his primary example had to do with the Steel Workers' Organizing Committee (SWOC) strike against "Little Steel" in May of 1937, precisely during the period of the upheaval in Detroit. Communists did not strongly support the strikers around an aggressive agenda of immediate organizing demands, according to Foster, because the leadership was depending on FDR and Lewis to somehow pressure the owners to settle the strike. He felt that CIO officials increasingly neglected the rank and file, and as well: "Party workers, instead of assuming responsibility for these tasks themselves, rely upon the CIO officials to do so. The result is that the Party's line is often indistinguishable in such matters from that of the officials."[47]

In response, Browder went so far as to characterize Foster's actions of the previous year as "a basic challenge to the conduct of our Party." He acknowledged that Foster was indispensable for his labor contacts, and noted that he "is generally known as the best organizer ever produced by the American labor movement." Foster, according to Browder, "was my teacher for many years, beginning 23 years ago ... when I began my active association with him in the labor movement, at a time when I was completely ignorant of organizational questions." However, in this particular meeting, Browder also implied that Foster and Weinstone shared a common purpose with Socialist and Trotskyist dissenters in the automobile union in encouraging or at least acquiescing in the illegal sit-downs.[48] It is notable that Browder was making such accusations against Foster in Moscow in early 1938, at the height of Stalinist purges in which "Trotskyist" dissenters were being executed at a rate of perhaps hundreds daily.

Georgi Dimitroff replied: "We have great respect for Comrade Foster and value him very much." Yet, he directly upbraided Foster for his persistent suspicion of FDR and the "remnants of sectarianism" this represented. Foster, according to Dimitroff, gives expression "to those tendencies which existed among comrades who had a definite fear of going to the masses, particularly of going into the petty bourgeois masses, of going forward together with the Democratic and Republican progressive elements." Roosevelt "is the leader of the democratic movement … he is the central figure upon whom the working masses can rely … the same is true with regard to Lewis."[49] Once again Foster's syndicalism, in both its positive and negative manifestations, was brought forth as his defining characteristic as a Communist. Despite his serious challenge to Browder and the Democratic Front, ultimately he was less disposable and more independent than other leaders of the party because of his experience with and deep knowledge of the American labor movement.

Foster returned from Moscow chastened. Foster was not politically naïve; he must have journeyed to Moscow knowing that Dimitroff would refuse to endorse the sit-downs and job actions that had been carried out by the UAW dissenters, as well as the critique of Browder's leadership they represented. Weinstone was demoted after negotiating, with Foster, an alliance with UAW moderate Richard Frankensteen that alienated Walter Reuther, who had been a supporter of the sit-downs. Foster himself accepted the turn, he "agreed without one word of dissent" to Weinstone's demotion because Weinstone had at first gone along with the outlaw strikes.[50] The compromises that concluded the episode failed to halt the continued strengthening of currents of anti-communism in the unions and national politics in 1939.

Foster held tenaciously to his dwindling status in the party hierarchy. What is particularly striking, however, is Foster's continuing enmeshment with what might be called the "laboring" of the party at the level of the rank and file. As one Communist recalled, "what Foster did [in the 1930s] was to maintain contact with comrades in the field, in the industries."

> Comrade after comrade would tell the same story, and that was that Foster was one of the few Communist leaders who, when he came to town, would sit with a group of people, comrades, workers, and would spend hours drawing out every detail of the work process where they worked, every detail of the labor movement, every detail of the trends going on in that particular factory or union. He wasn't given to making big lectures to them, he would listen … that was what impressed every comrade I knew in the labor movement … this sensitivity to the workers' moods and his persistence in getting every detail.

Moreover, Foster's reservations about the official centrism were well known and respected by mid-level party personnel throughout the Popular Front era, especially his assertions that while "we want unity, we must always have our own independent policy as well ... he didn't just mean the Party, he was talking about the labor movement, the CIO must have an independent policy, that yes, Roosevelt was doing important things but he was not going to liberate anybody." Foster's writings and statements in unit meetings, Party Activist Dorothy Healey remembered, "had more weight on us than anything ... that Party resolutions or Browder was saying in regard to what our policy was."[51]

As James Ryan has concluded, throughout the crucial 1930s "Foster represented a coherent, principled opposition. Because of party loyalty and discipline, he could seldom display it openly. ... Yet Foster consistently maintained his left-wing perspective. And by 1939, if not earlier, he had to worry about the danger of expulsion, which Browder had not-so-subtly threatened." In January 1939, Foster raised yet another objection to the party's policies, this time opposing the Politburo's decision—because of perceived common interests between the United States and the USSR following the Munich agreement—to endorse increases in US defense spending. A subsequent Politburo meeting in March was consumed with anti-Foster polemics.[52] Foster's continuing attacks on the Popular and Democratic Fronts gained some momentum and legitimacy following the Molotov-Ribbentrop Pact of August 1939, and partly as a result of what one historian has termed a "syndicalist" turn in the party that was manifested by a series of "defense strikes" in crucial manufacturing centers.[53] Regardless, it is clear that by the decade ending in 1939, "a rigid adherence to the Party line" was not "Foster's most striking characteristic."[54]

Leon Trotsky, writing at the beginning of the decade, wrote that on the basis of what he termed "extensive" contact with Foster, he judged Foster to be above all an "empiricist" who inevitably adjusted his positions to fit circumstances. Trotsky, expanding upon the "zig-zag," opportunist view of Foster's Communist career, concluded that Foster was made of what he termed "more trustworthy material" than Lovestone or Joseph Pogány ("Pepper"), and wrote in 1929 that there has "always [been] much that was true and acute in Foster's recurring criticisms of the Party leadership."[55]

Significantly, J. Peters, an influential Hungarian underground operative who worked extensively in the United States, wrote in Foster's Comintern personnel file in the 1930s that he was a hard worker, but without a distinct Marxist political outlook. As Peters noted, Foster as a comrade was "good, straightforward, and honest," but many in the Communist movement believed that Foster joined the party primarily to benefit his TUEL. If this analysis is to be credited, "we could come to the conclusion that he is rather a syndicalist than a Communist."

According to Peters's judgment, Foster the "eclectic" was unstable in his political views and "unlikely to be able to lead the party."[56] It should be noted as well that Foster was never trusted with an overseas Comintern assignment, and there is no extant indication of Foster's involvement in the extensive espionage apparatus operating within the party, despite his intensive involvement with party organization at other levels.

It is tempting to see Foster's career as representing "the triumph of dogmatism on the American left," with Foster succumbing tragically to Soviet and Comintern political authority in helping to forge an inflexible, doctrinaire character for American communism.[57]

However, such a perspective tends to minimize the extent to which any of Foster's positions could be seen as consistent with particular elements of his vast experiences in the American and international labor movements. Moreover, it is inconsistent with the observations of many who worked most closely with him that Foster was essentially an "empiricist," as Trotsky termed him with respect to political matters, and that, as James Cannon characterized him, Foster "came to Stalinism with tongue-in-cheek."[58] In 1945, surely everyone who knew Foster understood what Earl Browder meant when he stated repeatedly that Foster's final triumph, assisted undoubtedly by Duclos and Stalin, over the Democratic Front and a return to a militant perspective for the CP was motivated primarily by his class-war syndicalism.[59]

In the Cold War era, elements of this radical style were manifest in Foster's endorsement of, or acquiescence in the complex and fateful decisions leading to the Henry Wallace candidacy, the formation of an underground apparatus, and the squelching of party reform in the 1950s. Foster was complicit in decisions which contributed to the party's isolation from the labor movement after 1945, regardless of the powerful external forces at work as well in the party's repression and expulsions during the Cold War era. Foster told one of his most trusted associates in 1957 that even if the party was reduced to a few thousand members, he believed that the militant minority would still retain its revolutionary potential.[60] Tragically, Foster's intense skepticism about the possibilities of "going to the masses" in a broad political sense as Dimitroff had characterized it, transmogrified into a kind of militant isolationism by the time of his final decade in the party. It is certainly relevant that the "exceptionalist" perspective Foster brought to the American Communist Party was increasingly rendered moot by both the increasing influence of legislative politics in the labor movement in the mid-twentieth century as well as organized labor's decline as an effective voice for worker representation at a number of levels.

Foster died in Moscow in 1961, but not before voicing his disapproval of the Sino-Soviet split to Nikita Khrushchev himself when the Soviet leader visited his hospital bedside. Like much of the rest of the world, Foster was astonished by Soviet achievements at the time of his death. He had, after all, witnessed firsthand the famine conditions of Moscow in 1921, and in 1961 was personally introduced to Yuri Gagarin. Foster received a full state funeral in Red Square, yet he was not to be interred in the Kremlin Wall along with American Communists Charles Ruthenberg, William D. Haywood, and John Reed. Instead, Foster's ashes were deposited in the Waldheim Cemetery in Chicago, not far from the anarchist martyrs who had inspired him in his earliest years as a labor agitator.[61]

William Foster's complex and unique formative role in the history of the American Communist Party in its most energetic and vital phases cannot be attributed primarily to rigid loyalty on his part to Soviet or Comintern authority. Foster's defining "eclecticism" and "empiricism" are at odds with the perspective that he was of essence a "disciplined Communist, an American counterpart to the Russian Bolshevist."[62] Foster was certainly drawn to Soviet power and what he and many others believed to be its world-revolutionary potential to the end of his days, but his was a radicalism that drew on a far more diverse and manifold set of working-class experiences for its primary inspiration and energy.

Notes

1 Paul Buhle, *A Dreamer's Paradise Lost: Louis C. Franina/Lewis Corey, 1892–1953* (Atlantic Highlands, NJ: Humanities Press, 1995); James G. Ryan, *Earl Browder: The Failure of American Communism* (Tuscaloosa: University of Alabama, 1997); Ted Morgan, *A Covert Life: Jay Lovestone: Communist, Anti-Communist and Spymaster* (New York: Random House, 1999); Thomas L. Sakmyster, *Red Conspirator: J. Peters and the American Communist Underground* (Urbana: University of Illinois, 2011); Thomas L. Sakmyster, *A Communist Odyssey: The Life of Jósef Pogany/John Pepper* (Budapest: Central European University, 2012); Bryan D. Palmer, *James P. Cannon and the Origins of the American Revolutionary Left, 1850–1928* (Urbana: University of Illinois Press, 2007); Helen C. Camp, *Iron in Her Soul: Elizabeth Gurley Flynn and the American Left* (Pullman, WA: Washington State University Press, 1995); Lara Vapnek, *Elizabeth Gurley Flynn: Modern American Revolutionary* (Boulder, CO: Westview Press, 2015); Alan M. Wald, *Exiles From a Future Time: The Forging of the Mid-Twentieth Century Literary Left* (Chapel Hill: University of North Carolina Press, 2002); Christoph Irmscher, *Max Eastman: A Life* (New Haven, CT: Yale University Press, 2017). This essay draws for general background

information on Edward P. Johanningsmeier, *Forging American Communism: The Life of William Z. Foster* (Princeton, NJ: Princeton University Press, 1994) and James R. Barrett, *William Z. Foster and the Tragedy of American Radicalism* (Urbana: University of Illinois Press, 1999).

2 Theodore Draper, *The Roots of American Communism* (New York: Viking, 1957), p. 7; see also Jacob Zumoff, *The Communist International and US Communism, 1919-1929* (Leiden: Brill, 2004), pp. 24-48.

3 Harvey Klehr, *Communist Cadre* (Stanford: Stanford University Press, 1978), pp. 110-11; Ryan, *Earl Browder*, p. 146.

4 Arthur Zipser, *Workingclass Giant: The Life of William Z. Foster* (New York: International, 1981), pp. 7-19.

5 Melvyn Dubofsky in Joseph R. Conlin (ed.), *The American Radical Press* (Westport, CT: Greenwood Press, 1974), p. 113.

6 For discussion of Fox, Hammersmark, Johannsen and others, see James P. Cannon, *First Ten Years of American Communism* (New York: Pathfinder, 1962), p. 98; James R. Barrett, "Introduction" to Hutchins Hapgood, *The Spirit of Labor* (Urbana: University of Illinois Press, [1907] 2004); Greg Hall, "Jay Fox: A Journey from Anarchism to Communism," *Left History* 16, no. 1 (Spring/Summer 2012), pp. 9-36; Randi Storch, *Red Chicago: American Communism at its Grassroots* (Urbana: University of Illinois Press, 2007), pp. 13-21.

7 Paul Avrich, *The Haymarket Tragedy* (Princeton, NJ: Princeton University Press, 1984), p. 72.

8 Jacqueline Jones, *Goddess of Anarchy: The Life and Times of Lucy Parsons, American Radical* (New York: Basic Books, 2017), pp. 320-1; Earl C. Ford and William Z. Foster, *Syndicalism* (Chicago: William Z. Foster, 1912), p. 6.

9 James R. Barrett, *Work and Community in the Jungle: Chicago's Packinghouse Workers, 1894-1922* (Urbana: University of Illinois Press, 1987); David Brody, *Labor in Crisis* (Urbana: University of Illinois Press, 1987).

10 Foster, *Syndicalism*, p. 9.

11 Ibid., p.13.

12 Ford and Foster, *Syndicalism*, pp. 9, 13. Similar themes are expressed in William Z. Foster, *Towards Soviet America* (New York: International, 1932), p. 212: quoting Lenin, "'there is no complete absence of a way out' for the bourgeoisie until it faces the revolutionary proletariat in arms."

13 Barrett, *William Z. Foster*, p. 58.

14 V. I. Lenin, *"Left-Wing" Communism: An Infantile Disorder* (New York: International, 1940), pp. 33, 37; Zumoff, *Communist International and US Communism*, pp. 83-6. On Foster and the Profintern see Edward P. Johanningsmeier, "The Profintern and the 'Syndicalist Current' in the United States," in Norman LaPorte, Kevin Morgan, and Matthew Worley (eds.),

Bolshevism and the Comintern: Perspectives on Stalinization, 1917–53 (Hampshire, UK: Palgrave, 2008).

15 Barrett, *William Z. Foster*, p. 31; Paul Buhle, *Marxism in the United States* (London: Verso, [1987] 2013), pp. 99–100.

16 Fitzpatrick quoted in Brody, *Labor in Crisis*, p. 13; see also Joseph A. McCartin, *Labor's Great War: The Struggle for Industrial Democracy and the Origins of Modern American Labor Relations, 1912–1921* (Chapel Hill: University of North Carolina Press, 1997), p. 119; David Brody, *Steelworkers in America: The Nonunion Era* (New York: Harper, 1960), pp. 241, 249.

17 William Z. Foster, *The Bankruptcy of the American Labor Movement* (Chicago: Trade Union Educational League, 1922), p. 54.

18 Brody, *Labor in Crisis*, pp. 102–3.

19 Browder to Lenin, May 27, 1921, RGASPI Comintern, op. 14, d. 97.

20 Johanningsmeier, *Forging American Communism*, p. 162.

21 Browder to Trotsky, May 9, 1921, CPUSA, d. 39, l. 35.

22 Lozovsky quoted in Johanningsmeier, "Profintern and the 'Syndicalist Current,'" p. 290.

23 Draper, *Roots of American Communism*, p. 373.

24 Trade union membership in the Party increased from 35 percent in 1932 to 80 percent in 1936. Ryan, *Earl Browder*, p. 99. Michael Kazin, *American Dreamers: How the Left Changed a Nation* (New York: Vintage, 2011), p. 172; William Denning, *The Cultural Front* (London: Verso, 1996), p. 97; on Foster as exceptionalist, see for instance Z. Leder, *International Press Correspondence*, March 1, 1923; Theodore Draper interview with Bertram Wolfe, September 25, 1953, Draper Papers, box 18, folder 20.

25 Johanningsmeier, *Forging American Communism*, p. 88.

26 Foster, *Bankruptcy*, p. 40.

27 Cannon, *First Ten Years*, pp. 120, 219.

28 Ibid., pp. 120, 123–4, 219; James Cannon, "Where Is the Left Going?," *The Militant*, August 15, 1929.

29 Cannon, *First Ten Years*, pp. 87–9; 123.

30 E. J. Hobsbawm, "Cadres," *London Review of Books* 29, no. 8 (April 2007), p. 23.

31 Barrett, *William Z. Foster*, pp. 150–1; Johanningsmeier, *Forging American Communism*, pp. 222–5; see also, *Communist International and US Communism*, pp. 164–8, and Sakmyster, *A Communist Odyssey*, pp. 125, 156–60, 175.

32 Lovestone to Bukharin, November 1, 1925, CPUSA, d. 423, l. 31.

33 Ruthenberg quoted in Zumoff, *Communist International and US Communism*, p. 194.

34 Here my interpretation differs from James Barrett, who concludes that "Foster's capitulation to dual unionism represented the final stage in his shift away from a

sort of syndicalist communism, what some in the Party called 'Fosterism', toward a more orthodox Stalinist position." Barrett, *William Z. Foster*, pp. 160-1. Foster, at presumably the most "Stalinist" stage in his career in 1946, frankly told Dorothy Healey, a high-ranking cadre, that "the biggest mistake he had ever made was agreeing" to the shift to dual unionism in the late 1920s under pressure from the Comintern. "Foster was a man of strong views ... and he was always very honest in expressing his views. He could be utterly ruthless in inner-Party battles, but you always knew what he believed and what he was up to." Dorothy Healey and Maurice Isserman, *Dorothy Healey Remembers: A Life in the American Communist Party* (Oxford: Oxford University Press, 1990), p. 159.

35 Lovestone faction letter, "Dear Comrades," August 6, 1928, CPUSA, d. 1248, l. 138, 146.
36 Foster speech, "American Commission," May 6, 1929, Comintern, op. 72, d. 66, l. 96-7.
37 Ryan, *Earl Browder*, pp. 47 and 51.
38 Melvyn Dubofsky and Warren Van Tine, *John L. Lewis: A Biography* (New York: Quadrangle, 1977), pp. 171-2.
39 Johanningsmeier, *Forging American Communism*, p. 260.
40 "Dear Alexander," signed "Pit," February 29, March 4, 1932, CPUSA, d. 2616, l. 39, 46, 76.
41 Barrett, *William Z. Foster*, p. 174; Lewis quoted in David M. Kennedy, *Freedom from Fear: The American People in Depression and War, 1929-1945* (Oxford: Oxford University Press, 2005), p. 299; Bert Cochran, *Labor and American Communism: The Conflict That Shaped American Unions* (Princeton, NJ: Princeton University Press, 1977), pp. 51-7 on the problems of "politicization" in this strike.
42 On Foster's health during this period, see Barrett, *William Z. Foster*, pp. 174-5, 182, 194-6.
43 This account drawn from Nelson Lichtenstein, *Walter Reuther: The Most Dangerous Man in Detroit* (Urbana: University of Illinois Press, 1995), pp. 106-28; Harvey Klehr, *The Heyday of American Communism* (New York: Basic, 1984), pp. 244-51; Harvey Klehr, "American Communism and the United Auto Workers: New Evidence on an Old Controversy," *Labor History* 24 (Summer 1983), pp. 404-13; Fraser M. Ottanelli, *The Communist Party of the United States from the Depression to World War II* (New Brunswick: Rutgers University, 1991), pp. 147-51.
44 Lichtenstein, *Walter Reuther*, pp. 119-20.
45 Earl Browder speech, "In American Commission," January 13, 1938, Comintern, op. 20, d. 530, l. 252-3.
46 "Minutes of Trade Union Commission," Comintern, op. 14, d. 80, l. 46.
47 William Z. Foster, "On the American Question," January 11, 1938, Comintern, op. 20, d. 530, l. 191.

48 Browder, "In American Commission"; l. 251–53, 255.
49 Georgi Dimitroff, speech, "Commission Meeting on American Question," January 21, 1938, Foster, "On the American Question," January 11, 1938, Comintern, op. 20, d. 528, l. 22–3.
50 Lichtenstein, *Walter Reuther*, p. 125; Klehr, "American Communism," pp. 408–11.
51 Dorothy Healey, interview with author, September 16, 1986, in author's possession.
52 Ryan, *Earl Browder*, pp. 147, 157–9.
53 Maurice Isserman, *Which Side Were You On? The American Communist Party during the Second World War* (Middletown, CT: Wesleyan University Press, 1982), pp. 94–5.
54 Barrett, *William Z. Foster*, p. 162.
55 Trotsky quoted in "Tasks of the American Opposition," *The Militant*, June 1, 1929, p. 2.
56 J. Peters, "Confidential Report," January 1938, Foster personnel file, Comintern, op. 261, d. 15, l. 69. James Barrett's translation has Peters citing Foster's "confused views" as disqualifying him from Party leadership, Barrett, *William Z. Foster*, p. 187. See also, Sakmyster, *Red Conspirator*, pp. 18–19, 27–8, 36.
57 Barrett, *William Z. Foster*, p. 3.
58 Cannon, *First Ten Years*, p. 219.
59 Ryan, *Earl Browder*, p. 260.
60 Healey and Isserman, *Dorothy Healey Remembers*, p. 164.
61 Johanningsmeier, *Forging American Communism*, pp. 349–52.
62 Barrett, *William Z. Foster*, p. 108.

Bibliography

Barrett, James R. *Work and Community in the Jungle: Chicago's Packinghouse Workers, 1894–1922*. Urbana: University of Illinois Press, 1987.
Brody, David. *Labor in Crisis: The Great Steel Strike of 1919*. Urbana: University of Illinois Press, 1987.
Draper, Theodore. *The Roots of American Communism*. New York: Viking, 1957.
Ford, Earl, and William Z. Foster. *Syndicalism*. Chicago: William Z. Foster, 1912.
Healey, Dorothy, and Maurice Isserman. *Dorothy Healey Remembers: A Life in the American Communist Party*. Oxford: Oxford University Press, 1990.
Palmer, Bryan D. *James P. Cannon and the Origins of the American Revolutionary Left, 1850–1928*. Urbana: University of Illinois Press, 2007.
Storch, Randi. *Red Chicago: American Communism at Its Grassroots*. Urbana: University of Illinois Press, 2007.

4

Communists and Farmers in American History

William C. Pratt

The topic of Communists and American farmers has received relatively little attention from historians or even Communists themselves. Yet for a fuller understanding of the American Communist experience it is important to acknowledge that Communists (or some of them) tried to organize farmers and that such efforts may have amounted to something at different times and in different places. Lowell K. Dyson's *Red Harvest: The Communist Party and American Farmers* is a good start on a serious study of this topic and is a solid contribution to what we now know of these efforts.[1] Dyson tracked down former participants, interviewed them, sometimes persuading them to share their correspondence and other items. His pioneering study on Communists and farmers covers a wide area of topics from the early 1920s into the 1950s, and his work is essential reading for students of American communism and farm movements in the United States.

Yet Lowell's book was published in 1982, almost forty years ago. Since that time, important new sources have become available that can provide additional detail, new perspectives, and corrections or at least clarifications of what we know of the history of American communism. Among the new sources that opened up was the massive Federal Bureau of Investigation (FBI) archives on God knows how many people and organizations. For more than three decades, a researcher could make a Freedom of Information Act (FOIA) request, and if carefully worded by the researcher and conscientiously complied with by the FBI, large amounts of useful information might be released. Yet I do not want to romanticize the "good old days" of FBI–FOIA compliance. My research benefitted enormously from FBI releases, but on one occasion it took more than ten years to obtain a particular file. Now, however, my impression is that the FBI does not comply with either the spirit or the plain meaning of the language of FOIA. My point here is that FBI releases *used to be* very helpful in studying Communist efforts in agriculture from the Second World War to well into the 1950s.[2]

But perhaps the most remarkable source for historians studying American communism was the opening up of the Communist Party records in Moscow in the 1990s. Materials sent from the United States for safekeeping decades earlier now became accessible to researchers willing to travel to Moscow.[3] Then, within a decade, the Communist Party of the United States of America (CPUSA) collection, some four thousand files, became available on microfilm at the Library of Congress and later at other research libraries. These materials have proved to be particularly useful for the study of Communist organizational efforts related to farmers from the 1920s into the mid-1930s.

These new sources—along with newspapers, interviews with former participants, and other archival materials—offer us another opportunity to evaluate Communist efforts in the countryside. My concern here is to answer the question: What did the topic of Communists and farmers amount to, or why is it worth studying?

To me, there are four things important or noteworthy about this topic: (1) What I call the farmer-labor era in essential to understanding what happened to the party in 1923–4 and its relations with the Robert La Follette presidential campaign; (2) Communist involvement in the farm revolt of the 1930s helps illuminate the history of that era's farm protest, as well as elaborating on ramifications of the Third Period in the party history; (3) the Popular Front in agriculture, especially in the 1940s, highlights Communist efforts to participate in a left-wing New Deal or left-liberal coalition up to the 1948 Henry Wallace presidential campaign and finally ending with the Korean War; and (4) the involvement of Finnish Americans in the Communist movement is essential to understanding their left-wing history, particularly with regard to farmers, as well as key developments in CPUSA history into the 1930s.

Farmer-Labor Era

The farmer-labor era was a crucial time in Communist history. Known as the Workers Party at the time, it established a national newspaper, the *Daily Worker*, and made a real effort to participate in domestic politics. Earlier divisions were superseded by a new one, a trade union grouping headed by

William Z. Foster and James Cannon, and a more overtly political grouping headed by Charles Ruthenberg and John Pepper. In 1923, Pepper engineered a takeover of a budding farmer-labor effort that had originated largely to promote a labor party by Chicago unionists. The same year, the CPUSA organized a very small farm group called the United Farmers Educational League (UFEL) and also recruited a few members and friends in small farmer-labor groups, who participated in the takeover of the convention, resulting in the formation of the Federated Farmer-Labor Party. Farmer-Laborism was in the air in 1923–4, and there was widespread interest to form a national party, with many people who wanted to run Robert La Follette as its presidential candidate. Ruthenberg and Pepper sought such a party as a vehicle to advance Communist efforts, but were not interested in La Follette's candidacy.[4] The Chicago takeover alienated mainstream Chicago trade unionists, putting Foster and Cannon in a difficult situation. Widespread publicity about the takeover identified the new party as Communist, causing many earlier supporters to drop out. In 1924, the La Follette candidacy gained steam, though the Wisconsin senator himself would not commit himself to a third-party race, initially hoping against hope to win the Republican nomination.

The divided leadership of the CPUSA appealed to the Communist International (Comintern) on whether or not to participate in a farmer-labor campaign, even if a new farmer-labor party nominated La Follette. In response, the Comintern decided against any participation in a larger farmer-labor effort, La Follette or no La Follette. At one point in the Moscow deliberations, Foster reportedly claimed that the Ruthenberg-Pepper group was more interested in organizing farmers than workers![5] The decision requiring the CPUSA to run its own campaign, despite earlier efforts to work with state farmer-labor groups, seriously damaged the party. This directive was the result of a controversy in the Russian party involving Trotsky, who said that farmers did not belong in a Communist party. In part, to avoid conceding a point to Trotsky, his opponents required the CPUSA to stay away from the farmer-labor movement.[6] Consequently, American Communists abandoned their farmer-labor strategy and ran their own ticket with Foster and Benjamin Gitlow in 1924. Foster may not have supported the original farmer-labor approach, but he was disgusted with the result here. Many years later, he wrote that it was a mistake, but did not point out that it was a mistake forced on them by Moscow. What happened in 1924 weakened the party and also helped to undercut major political developments outside the two-party system. The Communists were not responsible for all of what happened, as La Follette shared some of the responsibility. But regardless of the allocation of the blame, the fact remains that a significant effort to form a farmer-labor party did not get off the ground, and never again did such an opportunity present itself.[7] It also marks one of the most significant Soviet interventions into the operations of the CPUSA.

Involvement in the Farm Revolt of 1930s

Communist involvement in the farm revolt of the 1930s is crucial to understanding the overall topic of farm protest in that era. The best-known group in the insurgency was the Farmers Holiday.[8] But before the Holiday appeared, the Communist-led United Farmers League (UFL) stopped sheriff sales and organized demonstrations to pressure local authorities for relief in the Upper Peninsula of Michigan, northern Minnesota, and northeastern Montana. Aside from Montana, the UFL found most of its initial support in Finnish neighborhoods. In fact, for much of its history, it was often largely a Finnish operation, though it also had strong support in the extreme northeast corner of South Dakota in a non-Finnish area, as well as along the border area of North Dakota–Montana. The CPUSA had formed an agricultural department in 1930 and appointed Henry Puro as its head. A Finnish immigrant, he had been a fixture in left-wing Finnish affairs in the United States and was a member of the Polburo. Initially, the UFL had its headquarters in New York Mills, Minnesota, which was a section of the state with a significant Finnish population. The secretary of the UFL, then an editor of a local Finnish farm paper, also was assigned to edit the UFL organ, the *United Farmer* (which soon lost its postal privileges).[9] As a practical matter, the UFL never had adequate funding, and neither Puro nor whoever became the organization's chief functionary truly was able to direct the organization's activities. In 1932 and 1933, there was widespread farm protest, in which the UFL participated. Once the Farmers Holiday emerged, the Communist-led group was overshadowed, and Holiday people led protest marches to state capitols in the region in early 1933. These demonstrations had been preceded by a well-publicized farm strike, and penny auctions or Sears and Roebuck sales, seeking to stop forced sales by indebted farmers. Communists participated in the Holiday in many locales, sometimes assuming leadership roles. In fact, more Communists and their allies took part in the broader-based Holiday than in the UFL.

A key development took place in northeast Nebraska in the fall of 1932. There, a group of militant farmers, some of them former populists and

Nonpartisan Leaguers, organized a spin-off of the Holiday calling themselves the "Madison County Plan," which eschewed farm strikes and focused on stopping foreclosures.[10] At the core of the group were fourteen farmers who, according to Moscow records, had been recruited into the CPUSA by the party section leader in Omaha. The formulation of the Madison County Plan was the result of a consultation with Hal Ware, the oldest son of Mother Bloor and a veteran of earlier efforts to organize American farmers in the 1920s and also a key figure in introducing tractor farming in Soviet Russia.[11] The Madison County approach had widespread appeal, and groups as far away as eastern Wyoming and northeast South Dakota identified themselves with it rather than the Holiday mainstream headed by Iowa's Milo Reno. In early October, Madison County farmers "repossessed" two repossessed trucks and then conducted a penny auction on a farm near Elgin, Nebraska. Hundreds of farmers showed up, and a young widow's farm was saved.[12]

A key associate of Ware was Lem Harris, a Harvard graduate who also had worked in Russia in the 1920s.[13] Perhaps the highpoint of Communist farm activity in Nebraska occurred in February 1933 when a large-scale march on the state capitol occurred. An immediate demand was a moratorium law to stop farm foreclosures, but other demands were made as well. Perhaps as many as four thousand people participated in the protest. The march and subsequent demonstration received widespread publicity, and Ware and Harris claimed a major victory. But the Holiday movement in the state was divided between the mainstream group headed by Milo Reno and the Madison County group which was denounced as Communist. The initial leadership of the Madison County group soon lost the initiative and would be replaced by others close to the CPUSA.[14]

Ware and Harris developed an alternative to the UFL, not as a replacement for the Communist-led organization, but as a way of attracting farmers to address particular immediate issues with the hope that that such involvement would ultimately lead many of them to take up the party membership. This was to be done under the auspices of an umbrella group called the Farmers National Committee for Action (FNCA), which, in practice, would be pretty much directed by Harris. Theoretically, the UFL was closer to the party, while the FNCA was a looser grouping.. Perhaps we also need to be reminded that the farm revolt broke out during the Third Period era. The term "social fascist" routinely was thrown around in the direction of the Farmers Union, the Minnesota Farmer-Labor Party (FLP), and the mainstream of the Holiday in these years. That being the case, there were real challenges at the grassroots to build alliances. Articles in the party press and journals like *The Communist* also could complicate the situation, as well as perhaps misleading scholars years after the fact.[15]

At one level, there was a competition between the UFL which was under party control and the FNCP which seemingly was a loose grouping of different groups. While that lineup was the case at times, both elements were led by Communists and, to my mind, differences between the two approaches on the ground may have been more a reflection of differences among party functionaries than anything else. Each group had its own newspaper, the UFL utilizing *Producers News*, published in Plentywood, Montana, and the FNCA published the *Farmers National Weekly*, which was based at times in Washington, DC, Chicago, and Minneapolis. New Deal farm programs began to kick in in 1933 and would have the effect of undercutting farm protest across the Upper Midwest, Northern Plains, and elsewhere, whether it was orchestrated by the Reno-led Holiday, or the UFL, or other groups influenced by Communists.

Party objectives were seriously hindered by the administrative muddle of its farm efforts. In some respects nobody seemed to be in charge, and people in the field sometimes directed what happened according to their own ideas. Until 1935, the UFL and FNCA operated out of separate cities and the *Farmers National Weekly* was published in still another location. Puro, who theoretically oversaw the party's farm activities (and as a member of the Polburo) was in New York much of the time, and the Farm Research office was based in Washington, DC. It was no wonder that one insider observed early in 1935: "One of the chief weaknesses of our farm movement today is that we have several national centers sometimes working at cross purposes, with the result that the ag. commission is frequently in the role of arbitrator between the different national centers. Until we change this situation, we will continue to have disagreements on basic questions which remain unclarified."[16] Others made similar comments, and by mid-1935 several changes were made. The UFL, the FNCA and the *Farmers National Weekly* were moved to Minneapolis, and a more concerted effort was made to allot financial support on a coordinated basis.[17]

By now, however, the momentum of the insurgency protest had dissipated, and it was too late to regroup as a protest movement. Key functionaries left farm work, including Rob Hall, who had served stints as an editor of *Producers News* and the *Farmers National Weekly*, as he would later become district organizer of District 17 (which consisted of Alabama, Georgia, and Mississippi).[18] The biggest loss to the Communist farm effort probably was the death of Hal Ware, killed in an automobile accident in mid-1935. Since the early 1920s, he had been a key party person in agriculture. As a practical matter, however, much of his attention had shifted by 1934 from farm organization work to clandestine efforts among government employees in Washington, DC. Later, in the post–World War II years, participants in the "Ware group" would be identified with Soviet espionage activities.[19] (Perhaps Ware's involvement in this activity is yet another example of Soviet interests superseding those of the CPUSA.)

The New Deal, which undercut left-wing efforts in the United States across the board, played a major role in reducing farm protest. (A former party functionary recalled the comment of a South Dakota comrade: "What the hell do we need the Communist Party for? We have the Democratic Party now.")[20] By late 1935, UFL leaders urged its supporters to join the Holiday or the Farmers Union. Such a move paralleled what happened in left-wing labor circles, as the Popular Front was espoused by party leaders. The UFL in some places already had merged into or had been absorbed by the Holiday. And it was only a matter of time that the Holiday itself was absorbed by the Farmers Union.[21] The farm revolt of the 1930s had been over for some time, and Communists and their allies had to adjust to the challenges of a new era. Whatever else can be said about this episode, the party had a greater following in the countryside then it had prior to the Depression and, despite numerous setbacks and false starts, some of its membership gains would persist into the post–World War II era.

Popular Front in Agriculture

The Popular Front in agriculture peaked in the 1940s with Communists and supporters (not always identified as such publicly) often working as part of a left-liberal coalition.[22] Such an informal arrangement was in place during the war years when Communists went all out for the war effort, tempering and even suppressing long-standing antipathies to basic capitalist institutions and enterprises, going so far as abolishing the party and replacing it with a Communist Political Association (CPA) in 1944.[23] This dramatic wartime shift probably had little consequences for Communist efforts among farmers. As a practical matter, when we talk about Communist involvement with American farmers during these years it is pretty much limited to the Farmers Union. Dyson quotes an internal party document from 1945:

> Since 1935 our farm work has been declining, and although there have been occasions during which some expansion has occurred, the trend has been steadily downward. ... [I]n fact, we can now look back and see that liquidatory

tendencies, stemming from a false, undialectical concept of unity, undermined our farm work even before they visibly weakened our work in basic industries. *With each new unity move and each new merger, our farm colleagues sooner or later noticed that the Communist Party seemed to be receding from the countryside and they found themselves cut off from their former base of support.*[24]

Yet, without denying insights in these comments, as it was apparent that rural support in many locales, including the South and across the Upper Midwest and Northern Plains, had declined, Communists now had influence in some areas and institutions beyond that they had previously. The Farmers Union now probably was more important and influential politically than in any other period in its history and was a key component of the left-liberal coalition or the Popular Front. National president James Patton and key state affiliates of the Farmers Union, including Minnesota, North Dakota, Montana, and Wisconsin, had leaders committed to the left-liberal alliance. Smaller state affiliates such as Iowa, New York, and the Eastern Division, which consisted of New Jersey and eastern Pennsylvania, also were part of this grouping. (At times in the 1940s, Communists probably served as presidents of two state unions.)[25]

Historians and other observers often have commented on the impact of the 1945 Duclos letter and how it resulted in a major shift in leadership and policy, but I am not convinced that it had much effect on Communist activities in agriculture, at least not in the short run. Lem Harris wrote an article in the *Daily Worker* soon after the Duclos letter was publicized and, while agreeing that Communists had gone too far in accommodating the existing order, cautiously warned not to go too far in the opposite direction.[26] In the immediate postwar years, Communists maintained their standing in a number of Farmers Union state organizations. In Minnesota, for example, Einar Kuivinen continued to get reelected president of the Farmers Union until 1949; Alvin Christman was elected president of the Eastern Division; and at the county level Communists or their allies often served as officers and sometimes as president.[27] Party membership clearly dropped below wartime numbers, but the CPUSA continued to hold meetings in private homes in many places in Farmers Union territory into the late 1940s.

The "red issue," however, became increasingly disruptive within the left-liberal coalition, as the Cold War developed and the party assumed a more assertive and antagonistic posture. AntiCommunist critics, liberal and conservative, became more vocal about Communists and their allies in liberal groups whether they were veterans organizations, trade unions, or the Farmers Union.[28] The

Wisconsin Farmers Union fired a husband and wife team from its staff, who had headed up the cooperative and education departments, and its president became a strong proponent of an anti-Communist membership provision in the wake of their firing. The national organization, however, opposed such a litmus test and would resist the Wisconsin initiative for years.[29]

The 1948, Henry Wallace campaign provided some of the final solvent for the left-liberal coalition, though its most definitive impact affected the Congress of Industrial Organizations (CIO).[30] Patton and the Farmers Union had been close to Wallace, but Patton was careful not to commit himself to a third-party campaign. He had been a public critic of Truman's "Get Tough with Russia" foreign policy, especially in 1947, and some of his domestic policies as well. That said, he was unwilling to break with the Democratic Party, worrying what a third-party effort would do to Congress. Bill Thatcher, head of the Farmers Union Grain Terminal Association, which controlled the Farmers Union cooperative elevator empire, also backed away from the Wallace insurgency. As a practical matter, few prominent Farmers Union figures ultimately announced their support for Wallace. Fred Stover, president of the Iowa affiliate, nominated the former vice president at the Progressive Party convention, and the Eastern Division endorsed his candidacy. But that was pretty much it. County presidents in Montana and other states took part in the campaign. Quentin Burdick, general counsel of the North Dakota organization, was a strong Wallace supporter and served on the platform committee at the Progressive Party convention. His boss, Glenn Talbott, president of the North Dakota affiliate, may have voted for Wallace, but did not publicly endorse him.[31]

Yet, it was the outbreak of fighting in Korea that truly ended the Popular Front in agriculture. Patton and the NFU board lined up with Truman's foreign policy with only one dissenting vote, that of Iowa's Fred Stover. Moving quickly to the center, Patton intervened in the Iowa's election, hoping to oust Stover as union president. That effort failed, resulting in severe criticism of Patton in some left-wing circles. Stover, despite suspicion and charges, never was a communist, and FBI records show that the CPUSA became very frustrated with his unwillingness to compromise in subsequent years and also with the fact that some Communist farmers outside Iowa seemed to follow his lead rather than that of the party.[32]

The party continued to have interest in farmers after the Korean War, but the prosecution of party leaders, the move of key cadre to underground status and a growing disillusionment on the part of rank-and file-members made it virtually impossible to regroup rural people into any coherent grouping, let alone organized activity. To be sure, there were remnants of support here and there among New Jersey egg farmers, or Dakota and Montana wheat farmers into the 1950s. But there was virtually no party activity aside from subscriptions to the *Daily Worker* or *Worker*, payment of dues and perhaps an occasional visit from a party functionary. By the time of the party upheavals of 1956–8 and certainly the early 1960s, the story of communism in the American countryside was over.

Finnish American Involvement in Farm Efforts

Finnish Americans played a crucial role in the history of Communist involvement with farmers. Finns helped form the Workers Party in late 1921 and made up approximately 40 percent of the party's membership into the mid-1920s.[33] One 1924 Moscow document shows that District 9 (consisting of Minnesota, northern Wisconsin, and the Upper Peninsula of Michigan) was overwhelmingly Finnish and continued to be so identified into the early 1930s.[34] Finnish party membership had declined significantly after the elimination of the foreign language federations, but as many as five thousand Finns remained within the Communist orbit through their local workers clubs and Finnish halls. Now they were affiliated with a Finnish Workers Federation, which was controlled by the party and often supported Communist-backed causes.[35]

The most important economic enterprise of left-wing Finns was a cooperative empire based largely in the western Great Lakes region. Most of the cooperative stores were located in small towns or villages like Mass, Michigan; or Cook, Minnesota; or Frederick, South Dakota.[36] While the number of party members in the cooperative movement was small, key leaders of the Central Co-operative Exchange (CCE) that supported the individual cooperative units often were Communists and, until late 1929, there was a close relationship between the CCE and the party. In the Third Period, following the purge of Jay Lovestone and his supporters, party leaders demanded significant financial contributions from the CCE. This situation resulted in a major fight within the Finnish cooperative movement. In some cases, it meant a struggle among Finnish Communists that led many of them to break with the party. By the spring of 1930, the party loyalists and individual cooperatives that supported them clearly were outvoted. Subsequently, the left-wing cooperatives formed a much smaller competitor to the CCE called the Workers and Farmers Cooperative Unity Alliance.[37]

Historians of American communism have pretty much ended the story of Finnish involvement in the party at this point. Such accounts focus on the fact that the vast majority of the cooperatives stayed with the CCE, while a much smaller number signed up with the Unity Alliance. Clearly, the party took a drubbing in the cooperative fight and never regained its earlier influence. But these scholars have not looked at what the Unity Alliance actually did. As a practical matter, the number of cooperatives affiliated with the Unity Alliance varied and perhaps as many as thirty or more stores may have been affiliated with or cooperated with it at times. One of the most successful Finnish cooperatives was in Mass, Michigan, on the Upper Peninsula. Organized in 1917, it seemingly thrived in the wake of the split. At its peak, it had five branch stores, two of them in neighboring counties.[38] For some, the cooperative movement was an ally of the working class, and it was not unusual for left-wing cooperatives to participate in protests and promote left-wing causes. In 1932, for example, the Frederick, South Dakota, cooperative store board voted to pay for a six-month subscription to *Producers News* for its members and customers.[39] And during the farm revolt, a number of the cooperatives used their trucks to take farmers to demonstrations and protests.

Finnish American involvement in the farm insurgency of the 1930s warrants attention. In some respects, the revolt began with Finns in 1931 on the Upper Peninsula, where the UFL was largely a Finnish operation, as was the case in many other locales in District 9. After the Farmers Holiday took off in late 1932, the UFL was overshadowed, and Finns participated in the new movement as well. Existing scholarship on the farm revolt tends to overlook the extent of Finnish involvement, but a close look at the Moscow records provides extensive details on this topic.[40] For some participants, this involvement may have been pretty much it, but for others it was simply one moment in a longer career of activism that would include the labor movement. And, for an even smaller group, it led to an extended career as a party functionary.

One episode, with tragic overtones, was "Karelian Fever." In the early 1930s, a number of Finns in the United States and Canada were recruited to go to Karelia, a Soviet republic bordering Finland. Their motivation in most cases was to improve their lives and build socialism in the Soviet Union. While the Karelian leaders had their own political reasons to attract North American Finns, the emigrants themselves often believed that they were going to a land where Finns were in charge and that ultimately there would be opportunities for them and their families which they did not have in the United States. Importantly, the CPUSA itself was not in favor of the emigration, concerned that its control of Finnish institutions here, including the left-wing cooperatives and the Finnish Workers Federation, could be threatened by the departure of so many committed Finns. Yet, at the same time, it did not openly oppose this effort because of its uncertainty over Moscow's intentions. It did, however, try to limit the number of party members who went.[41]

Ultimately, perhaps as many as six thousand and five hundred men, women, and children left the United States for Karelia, many of whom were from farms or rural communities, including active participants in the UFL and cooperatives. Their experience there proved to be very difficult, and many of the men were caught up in the purges of 1937–8. To this day, there is uncertainty over how many Finnish Americans were executed in those years, but it may have been as high as nine hundred or more. But whatever the actual number, this episode took its toll on many families, as well as left-wing Finnish causes in the United States.[42]

Finnish American communism did not survive the Popular Front of the 1930s. Initially, it offered new opportunities, as left-wing Finns found it easier to participate in more mainstream activities, such as the broader farm and labor movements. In 1938, the Unity Alliance was shut down, and some left-wing cooperatives rejoined the CCW, which now included a growing number of non-Finns.[43] A few cooperatives continued on their own, and there still were Communists in CCW affiliates, though greatly outnumbered. The Finnish worker clubs also declined by the end of the decade, as the first generation of members were dying, and the second generation was increasingly less interested in their activities.[44] But the Russo-Finnish War of 1939–40 had an immediate devastating effect on Finnish Communists in the United States, resulting in still further erosion of support for left-wing Finnish organizational life.[45]

Some individual Finns would assume important roles outside the confines of the Finnish community. In 1941, Einar Kuivinen was elected president of the Minnesota Farmers Union, a post that he held with the exception of one year until 1949, when he was defeated.[46] Other Finns, including Gus Hall, assumed leadership positions in the party, but their Finnish identity had no bearing on how they obtained these offices. Rather, it was more a sign that they had moved into a larger world outside the Finnish left.[47]

Conclusion

Communists in the United States seldom paid much attention to farmers, as Dyson observes: "Farm work was always the party's poor stepchild."[48] In fact, it may have taken a nudge from Moscow to get it to even think about farmers. While reading a report on the party's activities, Lenin reportedly asked: "Have you no farmers in America?"⁴⁹ Aside from what amounted to a false start in the 1920s, Communist efforts in the countryside did not amount to much until the Great Depression. To be sure, the party had had hundreds of farmers in its membership, but they were largely among Finnish Americans and pretty much isolated from the mainstream of the party by language, culture, and geography. In the 1930s, however, the party made a concerted effort to organize farmers. As early as 1931, Communists participated in protests and demonstrations under the auspices of the UFL, which in some locales was largely a Finnish enterprise. Once the Farmers Holiday appeared on the scene in 1932, Communists and their supporters also participated in this movement, and, in some locales, pretty much leading it. The farm protest of the 1930s dramatized the problems of the countryside, pressuring government at all levels, preventing foreclosures and perhaps, most of all, buying time until federal programs that ultimately provided benefits for many farmers. Communists had high hopes that the insurgency would continue in intensity, but the New Deal undercut the protest and deflated Communist expectations. The farm revolt of the 1930s was pretty much over by the middle of the decade.

From then into the post–World War II era, Communists shifted gears and took part in a Popular Front in agriculture which focused largely on the Farmers Union. Participants of earlier efforts like the UFL, the Sharecroppers Union and the Farmers Holiday was merged into the much larger Farmers Union, and Communists allied themselves with progressive elements in that organization seeking to tie it to the New Deal.⁵⁰ Key left-liberal figures such as Farmers Union president James Patton often sounded left wing, talking of the danger of fascism here at home and sometimes critical of Truman's foreign policy. But the Popular Front in agriculture pretty much ended with the 1948 Henry Wallace campaign and certainly with the outbreak of fighting in Korea. The Farmers Union, like the CIO and many other liberal groups moved to the center, ultimately expelling state affiliates in Iowa and the Eastern Division (which consisted of New Jersey and eastern Pennsylvania), because of their left-wing politics.

While there still would be some party members in the countryside and in a few predominantly Finnish cooperatives, they were isolated politically and subject to FBI inquiries from time to time. As late as 1959, six FBI agents drove across western Minnesota and the Dakotas, following a 67-year-old party functionary who was collecting dues and distributing Communist literature to a small number of people.⁵¹ But as a practical matter, Communist efforts in the countryside had played out years before. All that was left were memories, which historians have tapped from time to time over the past five decades.

Acknowledgments

I wish to acknowledge generous support from the Committee on Research and the Department of History of the University of Nebraska at Omaha over the years, as well as the Fulbright program who appointed me Distinguished Fulbright Lecturer in American History at Moscow State University in the spring of 2000. I also want to thank a number of individuals for their assistance, including Clarence H. Sharp (1891–1989), longtime Communist Party activist in the countryside; Toni Lewis, FBI documents examiner; Dasha Lotarev, Moscow translator and facilitator; and Vernon Pedersen for his encouragement to research in the Communist archives in Moscow and who twice shared a Moscow apartment with me in the 1990s.

Notes

1. Lowell K. Dyson, *Red Harvest: The Communist Party and American Farmers* (Lincoln: University of Nebraska Press, 1982).
2. A GoFundMe campaign was set up to digitize a large collection of FBI files already released through FOIA, saying that current developments have had the effect of making "historical research into FBI files virtually impossible for almost everyone." See "Digitizing Ernie Lazar's FOIA records," H-HOAC daily digest, September 24, 2018. The FBI also destroyed materials in the past that historians would have loved to examine. In 1942, it discovered a large amount of correspondence and records from the 1930s related to "the plans of the communist party in its infiltration into agrarian movements not only in Montana but the Dakotas, Minnesota and Nebraska." The assessment of the agents involved, however, was that the material was "so old it would have only historical value." H. B. Fletcher to Director, May 25, 1942, FBI File 100-55987-7. Subsequently these materials were destroyed. Frank LoTurco to author, December 19, 1985.
3. See Harvey Klehr, John Earl Haynes, and Fridrikh Igorevich Firsov, *The Secret World of American Communism* (New Haven: Yale University Press, 1995).
4. Virtually all serious research on American Communism in the 1920s begins with Theodore Draper, *American Communism and Soviet Russia* (New York: Vintage Books, 1986). This work and his earlier *The Roots of American Communism* (New York: Viking, 1963) set the standard for thorough research on the history of communism in the United States and remain required reading for all students of the topic. He located a sizeable amount of internal party records and interviewed large number of former participants in the Communist movement. Other important studies

on this topic in the 1920s include Dyson, *Red Harvest*, chapter 2; Jacob A. Zumoff, *The Communist International and US Communism, 1919-1929* (Chicago: Haymarket Books, 2015). For Pepper's role, see Thomas Saskmyster, *A Communist Odyssey: The Life of Jozsef Pogany/John Pepper* (Budapest: Central European University Press, 2012), chapter 6. For an essay focusing on the theme of farmer-laborism in the years 1920-4, see William Pratt, "Farmers, Farmer-Laborism and the 1924 La Follette Campaign," in *Experiencing American History: Viewpoints of American and Russian Historians* (Moscow: University of Moscow Press, 2005), pp. 198-212.

5 The party representative in Moscow, aligned with the Ruthenberg-Pepper faction, wrote back to the United States that the Foster-Pepper team told the Comintern "that the CEC [then controlled by his group] regards the farmers as more important than the situation of the workers and therefore is inclined to make it the center of its observations and policy." Grove [Israel Amter] to CEC, December 15, 1923, Communist Party USA Files, 515-1-174, 486, Russian State Archive of Social and Political History (RGASPI), Moscow, Russian Federation. Later, when Foster himself was in Moscow, he asserted again that the US Party placed too much emphasis on farmers. Foster, comment, May 6, 1924, 515-1-257, 272, RGASPI. For a recent survey of Communist efforts in agriculture in the 1920s, which covers this topic in greater depth than I have here, see William C. Pratt, "Communists and American Farmers in the 1920s," *American Communist History* 17 (June 2018), pp. 162-75.

6 Zumoff, *Communist International and US Communism*, p. 141.

7 David Brody, "On the Failure of U.S. Radical Politics: A Farmer-Labor Analysis," *Industrial Relations* 22 (Spring 1983), pp. 141-6; Pratt, "Farmers, Farmer-Laborism," pp. 207-8. See also Tom Foley, "The La Follette Campaign of 1924," *Political Affairs* 48 (September-October 1969), pp. 31-40.

8 John L. Shover, *Cornbelt Rebellion: The Farmers' Holiday Association* (Urbana: University of Illinois Press, 1965); Lowell K. Dyson, "The Farm Holiday Movement" (Ph.D. dissertation, Columbia University, 1968).

9 William Pratt, "The Finnish Farm Revolt of the 1930s: What Was It and Why Should We Still Be Interested in Its History?," Talk at FinnFest, Minneapolis, MN, August 8, 2014.

10 Shover, *Cornbelt Rebellion*, pp. 70-2.

11 (George) Stalker to C.P. Secretariat, October 28, 1932, 515-1-2900, 163-4, RGASPI. For Hal Ware's background, see Lement Harris, *Harold M. Ware (1890-1935): Agricultural Pioneer, U.S.A. and U.S.S. R.* (American Institute for Marxist Studies, Occasional Paper No. 30, 1978).

12 Shover, *Cornbelt Rebellion*, p. 72.

13 Lement Harris, *My Tale of Two Worlds* (New York: International, 1986).

14 Shover, *Cornbelt Rebellion*, pp. 83-5, 132-3; Dyson, *Red Harvest*, pp. 104-6, 113-14. Shover wrote: "The Communist farmers' movement passed high tide in the early months of 1933." Shover, *Cornbelt Rebellion*, p. 132.

15 Articles in *The Communist* dealing with CPUSA farm efforts usually were critical, arguing that organizers should have done more and done it better. Lem Harris told John Shover years later: "You see, there was a clash on a more amusing than serious level over the field workers and the Manhattan professors. I remember once one such made a formal complaint re one of my actions in Dakota. Unfortunately for him I had consulted with brother Puro first, whom the guy thought would agree with him, so the thing flattened. I recall that Browder, then head of the Party, never gave any encouragement to such criticisms. There was no running clash." Lem Harris, Memo re Chapter by John Shover on 1933 Farm Crisis and the Communist Party, John L. Shover Papers, University of Iowa, Iowa City, IA.

16 J. Martin to Agrarian Commission, January 14, 1935, 515-1-3756, 7, RGASPI.

17 Dyson, *Red Harvest*, p. 130.

18 Robin D. G. Kelley, *Hammer and Hoe: Alabama Communists during the Great Depression* (Chapel Hill: University of North Carolina Press, 1990), pp. 125–6. Another key figure worth noting, was Charley "Red Flag" Taylor, from Plentywood, Montana. He was expelled from the party for "Trotskyism" in mid-1935. Playing a big role in the UFL in 1931 and 1932, he had been appointed its chairman in the latter year. Party records, however, provide one complaint after another about his behavior, and he was a problem for party officials virtually everywhere he went. Although Taylor had shown Trotskyist sympathies earlier, that was not the basis of these complaints until 1935. Taylor and his Plentywood comrades have attracted recent scholarly attention, which was aided and abetted by Lowell Dyson's extensive 1965 interview with him, the transcript of which totals close to three hundred pages. Research in Moscow archives provides information that corrects or qualifies some of Taylor's remarks. For well-researched work that portrays Taylor more sympathetically than what I suggest here, see Gerald Zahavi, "'Who's Going to Dance with Somebody Who Calls You a Mainstreeter': Communism, Culture and Community in Sheridan County, Montana, 1918–1934," *Great Plains Quarterly* 16 (Fall 1996), pp. 251–86; Verlaine Stoner McDonald, *The Red Corner: The Rise and Fall of Communism in Northeastern Montana* (Helena: Montana Historical Society Press, 2010).

19 For Ware and the "Ware group," see Allen Weinstein, *Perjury: The Hiss-Chambers Case* (New York: Random House, 1997); Thomas Saskmyster, *Red Conspirator: J. Peters and the American Communist Underground* (Urbana: University of Illinois Press, 2011).

20 Interview with Clarence H. Sharp, March 26, 1988. Sharp was the party's key functionary in South Dakota when he heard this comment.

21 Dyson, *Red Harvest*, pp. 125–48.

22 On the use of the term "Popular Front," see Doug Rossinow, *Visions of Progress: The Left-Liberal Tradition in America* (Philadelphia: University of Pennsylvania Press,

2008). Interestingly enough, he does not refer to farmers or farm movements in this discussion. For Dyson's use of the term, see Dyson, *Red Harvest*, pp. 148-9, 190-7.

23 Maurice Isserman, *Which Side Were You On? The American Communist Party during the Second World War* (Middletown, CT: Wesleyan University Press, 1982); Joseph R. Starobin, *American Communism in Crisis, 1943-1957* (Cambridge, MA: Harvard University Press, 1972).

24 Dyson, *Red Harvest*, p. 187 (emphasis in the original).

25 Alonzo L. Hamby, *Beyond the New Deal: Harry S. Truman and American Liberalism* (New York: Columbia University Press, 1973), pp. 149-50; Dyson, *Red Harvest*, pp. 190-2. For the Montana Farmers Union, see William C. Pratt, "The Montana Farmers Union and the Cold War, 1945-1954," *Pacific Northwest Quarterly* 83 (April 1992), pp. 63-9.

26 Lem Harris, "Strengthen Labor-Farmer Coalition," *Daily Worker*, July 20, 1945. Unlike a number of scholars and many observers at the time, I do not see the Duclos letter as an order from Moscow to depose Browder as head of the American Communist movement. To me, it was more of a rebuke than a command to remove him, indicating Moscow's great displeasure with the direction Browder had taken the Party. But stubbornness or hubris on Browder's part not to admit mistakes enabled his longtime party enemies, most importantly Foster, to kick him out and reverse his wartime policies. See Isserman, *Which Side Were You On?*, pp. 216-34.

27 For the persistence of Communists in the countryside in the post-World War II era, see William C. Pratt, "Farmers, Communists, and the FBI in the Upper Midwest," *Agricultural History* 63 (Summer 1989), pp. 61-80.

28 Mary Sperling McAuliffe, *Crisis on the Left: Cold War Politics and American Liberals, 1947-1954* (Amherst: University of Massachusetts Press, 1978).

29 William C. Pratt, "The Farmers Union, McCarthyism, and the Demise of the Agrarian Left," *The Historian* 58 (Winter 1996), pp. 331-2. See also "Communists Brag of Victory at Nat'l F.U. Convention; Claim Wis. State Pres. Demoted for Anti-Communism," *Cooperative Builder*, April 20, 1950, clipping, Talbott Family Papers, Box 9, Folder 4, University of North Dakota, Grand Forks, ND. For a work that treats the Farmers Union in the Cold War years into the mid-1950s, see Bruce E. Field, *Harvest of Dissent: The National Farmers Union and the Early Cold War* (Lawrence: University Press of Kansas, 1998).

30 For the 1948 Wallace campaign, see Karl M. Schmidt, *Henry A. Wallace: Quixotic Crusade 1948* (Syracuse: Syracuse University Press, 1960); Curtis D. MacDougall, *Gideon's Army* (New York: Marzani and Munsell, 1965); Norman D. Markowitz, *The Rise and Fall of the People's Century: Henry A. Wallace and American Liberalism, 1941-1948* (New York: Free Press, 1973); Thomas W. Devine, *Henry Wallace's 1948 Campaign and the Future of Postwar Liberalism* (Chapel Hill: University of North Carolina Press, 2013).

31 William C. Pratt, "The Farmers Union and the 1948 Henry Wallace Campaign," *Annals of Iowa* 49 (Summer 1988), pp. 349–70. Stanley Moore, Talbott's nephew and later president of the North Dakota Farmers Union himself, told me that his uncle probably voted for Wallace. Interview with Stanley Moore, July 22, 1991.

32 Dyson, *Red Harvest*, pp. 197–9; Pratt, "Demise of the Agrarian Left," pp. 333–40. The Farmers Union expelled the Iowa and Eastern Division affiliates in 1954. Earlier in 1951, the left-wing Farmers Union of the New York Milk Shed was kicked out for non-payment of dues. CP efforts to get these groups readmitted to the Farmers Union were unsuccessful. Neither Stover in Iowa nor Archie Wright in New York were willing to make any effort to compromise their position in regard to the Farmers Union leadership, much to the disgust of party farm people. Wright, who had been close to the CPUSA, resisted "all pressure to apply for reaffiliation" to the Farmers Union. According to a FBI informant's report: "The differences have been so sharp that Wright has accused the Party of trying to undermine him in his own organization and has threatened to expel CP members because they plug for the Party viewpoint." Report attached to SAC, New York to Director, June 17, 1954, FBI File 100-3-79-312.

33 For Finnish American involvement in the Communist movement, see Auvo Kostianen, *The Forging of Finnish-American Communism, 1917–1924: A Study in Ethnic Radicalism* (Turku, Finland: Turin Ylipisto, 1978); Michael Gary Karni, "Yhteishyva—or, for the Common Good: Finnish Radicalism in the Western Great Lakes Region, 1900–1940" (PhD dissertation, University of Minnesota, 1975); David John Ahola, *Finnish-Americans and International Communism: A Study of Finnish-American Communism from Bolshevization to the Demise of the Third International* (Washington, DC: University Press of America, 1981). For a brief overview of this topic, which utilizes Moscow records, see William C. Pratt, "Finnish Americans in the Communist Party in the Upper Mid-Western United States," in Michel S. Beaulieu, Ronald N. Harpelle, and Jaimi Penney (eds.), *Labouring Finns: Transnational Politics in Finland, Canada, and the United States* (Turku, Finland: Institute of Migration, 2011), pp. 70–83.

34 C. A. Hathaway to C. E. Ruthenberg, November 19, 1924, 515-1-322, 11–15, RGASPI. He reported a total of sixty-one Party branches, of which forty-seven were identified as Finnish. Later, in 1931, a Party functionary there wrote: "[O]ur district which is composed largely of Finnish farmers ..." N. Bernick to Wm. Weiner, November 28, 1931, 515-1-2315, 170, RGASPI.

35 Auvo Kostiainen, "The Finns and the Crisis over 'Bolshevization' in the Workers Party, 1924–25," in Michael G. Karni, Matti E. Kaups and Douglas J. Ollila Jr. (eds.), *The Finnish Experience in the Western Great Lakes Region: New Perspectives* (Turku, Finland: Institute for Migration, 1975), pp. 171–85; Carl Ross, *The Finn Factor in*

American Labor, Culture and Society (New York Mills, MN: Parta Printers, 1977), p. 184.

36 Arnold Alanen, "The Development and Distribution of Finnish Consumers' Cooperatives in Michigan, Minnesota and Wisconsin, 1903–1973," in Michael G. Karni, Matti E. Kaups and Douglas J. Ollila Jr. (eds.), *The Finnish Experience in the Western Great Lakes Region* (Turku, Finland: Institute for Migration, 1975), pp. 103–30.

37 Michael Karni, "Struggle on the Cooperative Front: The Separation of Central Cooperative Wholesale from Communism, 1929–30," in Michael G. Karni, Matti E. Kaups and Douglas J. Ollila Jr. (eds.), *The Finnish Experience in the Western Great Lakes Region* (Turku, Finland: Institute for Migration, 1975), pp. 186–201.

38 William C. Pratt, "Radicalism in the Finnish Co-operatives in the 1920s and 1930s," Talk at FinnFest, Minneapolis, MN, September 22, 2017. For brief accounts on a number of left-wing co-ops, see *Farmers National Weekly*, September 27, 1935.

39 S. D. Frederick, "Co-operative Gets Behind Producers News in Drive," *Producers News*, February 26, 1932.

40 Pratt, "Finnish Farm Revolt."

41 For Karelian Fever, see Mayme Sevander with Laurie Hertzel, *They Took My Father: A Story of Idealism and Betrayal* (Duluth: Pfeifer-Hamilton, 1992); Alexey Golubev and Irina Takala, *The Search for a Socialist El Dorado: Finnish Immigration to Soviet Karelia from the United States and Canada in the 1930s* (East Lansing: Michigan State University Press, 2014); William C. Pratt, "Background on 'Karelia Fever', as Viewed from Communist Party USA Records," in Irina Takala and Ilya Solomeshch (eds.), *North American Finns in Soviet Karelia in the 1930s* (Petrozavodsk: Petrozavodsk State University Press, 2008), pp. 39–54.

42 A mass grave of purge victims in Karelia includes 141 Finnish Americans. For their names, see "Appendix," in John Earl Haynes and Harvey Klehr, *In Denial: Historians, Communism and Espionage* (San Francisco: Encounter Books, 2003), pp. 235–47.

43 "Communist Buying Group to Close," *Co-operative Builder*, July 2, 1938. The Cooperative Central Exchange (CCE) had changed its name to the Central Cooperative Wholesale (CCW) soon after the 1929–30 split. Alanen, "Development and Distribution," 118.

44 For a sociological study that showed the persistence of left-wing sentiment among first generation Finns in contrast with the second generation, see Harry Rickard Doby, "A Study of Social Change and Social Disorganization in a Finnish Rural Community" (PhD dissertation, University of California, 1960). The community was Waino, Wisconsin, near Superior.

45 The reaction to the Russo-Finnish War among Finnish Americans "isolated the Communist radical movement and reduced its numbers to hard core supporters." Ross, *The Finn Factor*, p. 177.
46 Phil Clark, "Roy Wiseth Defeats Einar Kuivinen as Liberals Out-vote Leftists," *Willmar Tribune*, November 14, 1949.
47 See Ross, *The Finn Factor*, p. 168.
48 Dyson, *Red Harvest*, p. 202.
49 Harris, *Harold M. Ware*, p. 30.
50 I have not discussed the Share Croppers Union (SCU), but it was an important effort to organize black sharecroppers in Alabama, beginning in 1931. It was met with extreme violence, and a number of its members were murdered. Communists played an active role in its organization and encouraged its merger with the Alabama Farmers Union, which occurred in 1935. See Kelley, *Hammer and Hoe*, chapters 2 and 9. See also Timothy V. Johnson, "'We Are Illegal Here': The Communist Party, Self-Determination and the Alabama Share Croppers Union," *Science and Society* 75 (October 2011), pp. 454–79. The SCU eventually was organized in Louisiana as well, and it merged into the Louisiana Farmers Union, which received its charter in 1937. See Greta de Jong, "'With the Aid of God and the F.S.A.': The Louisiana Farmers Union and the African American Freedom Struggle in the New Deal Era," *Journal of Social History* 34 (Autumn 2000), pp. 105–39.
51 Homer L. Ayres, May 19, 1956, FBI File 100-6280-238. This report is found in the FBI files of a number of individuals, but this particular one has the least amount of redactions among those that I have obtained.

Bibliography

Ahola, David John. *Finnish-Americans and International Communism: A Study of Finnish-American Communism from Bolshevization to the Demise of the Third International*. Washington, DC: University Press of America, 1981.

Draper, Theodore. *American Communism and Soviet Russia: The Formative Period*. New York: Vintage Books, 1986.

Dyson, Lowell K. *Red Harvest: The Communist Party and American Farmers*. Lincoln: University of Nebraska Press, 1982.

Karni, Michael G., Matti E. Kaups, and Douglas J. Ollila Jr., eds. *The Finnish Experience in the Western Great Lakes Region: New Perspectives*. Turku, Finland: Institute for Migration, 1975.

Klehr, Harvey, John Earl Haynes, and Fridrikh Igorevich Firsov. *The Secret World of American Communism*. New Haven, CT: Yale University Press, 1995.

Pratt, William C. "Farmers, Communists, and the FBI in the Upper Midwest." *Agricultural History* 63 (Summer 1989): 61–80.

Pratt, William C. "The Farmers Union, McCarthyism, and the Demise of the Agrarian Left." *The Historian* 58 (Winter 1996): 329–42.

Ross, Carl. *The Finn Factor in American Labor, Culture and Society*. New York Mills, MN: Parta Printers, 1977.

Shover, John L. *Cornbelt Rebellion: The Farmers' Holiday Association*. Urbana: University of Illinois Press, 1965.

Soviet Spies, Russian Trolls, and the US Security State: The Consequences of Russia's Hold on American Imagination, Politics, and Culture since 1919

Katherine A. S. Sibley

Introduction

Celebrating his acquittal on charges stemming from a congressional impeachment probe into attempts to have Ukrainian president Vladimir Zelensky investigate his Democratic opponent, former vice president Joe Biden, US president Donald J. Trump looked back on his presidency in February 2020: "We first went through Russia, Russia, Russia. It was all bullshit," he stated.[1]

This expletive was not a new allegation from the president. Not only were the impeachment charges a "hoax," he declared; claims of Russia's involvement in the 2016 election were "the greatest hoax, probably, in the history of our country."[2] This, despite the findings of Special Counsel Robert Mueller, the Federal Bureau of Investigation (FBI), the Central Intelligence Agency (CIA), the National Security Agency (NSA), a Republican-led US Senate Select Committee, and other watchdog groups, all of which found the allegations of Russian involvement credible.[3] Russia scholar Angela Stent affirms that what happened in 2016 was an "unprecedented attack on American democracy."[4] To the president, though, this "so-called Russian meddling" amounted to nothing more than a "Rigged Witch Hunt."[5]

As former undersecretary of state William Burns reminds us, "Trump stood alongside Putin, absolved him of election interference, and publicly doubted the conclusions of America's intelligence and law-enforcement services."[6] Like Trump, many of his supporters affirm that American security analysts who investigated the Russian interference were part of a "deep state" conspiracy, even more dangerous than Russia to this nation.[7] And after intelligence officials briefed Congress on Moscow's plans to interfere in the 2020 elections, Trump complained that this material could be "weaponized" against him, and quickly replaced the acting director of national intelligence.[8]

There is strong evidence that Russia did exploit the "glaring vulnerabilities" in the US electoral system and its social media market in 2016, and continues to do so, with "troll factories" disseminating disinformation and donations. Indeed, "chaos is the point," says Laura Rosenberger of the Alliance for Democracy.[9] Stent contends that the interference has been "toxic" for the relationship between the two countries, and has had more impact than anything that has "happened during or after the Cold War."[10] But as this chapter will suggest, this pattern is not new; instead, it picks up a recurrent theme in US relations with Russia. Since the Bolshevik Revolution, Moscow's influence and involvement in US politics and government—whether understood accurately or not—has regularly and effectively whittled away at American democracy. This is not just Russia's doing. It has been abetted by US officials and the American people themselves, who have regularly distorted this influence, either excessively enlarging it or too quickly minimizing it throughout the past century.

Sometimes, as in the Red Scare after the First World War or in the early 1950s, an American conspiratorial worldview inflated the extent of this influence, to the detriment of civil liberties and democratic values; other times, as during the Second World War or in our own age, US leaders have actively downplayed the existence of Russian misbehavior when it was quite real. Both patriotic pressures for unity in wartime as well as deep political divisions in more peaceful periods have fostered this warped response. This chapter will illuminate this pattern by exploring some of its key episodes and what they might tell us about the US-Russian relationship from the time that the American Communist Party was first emerging in 1919, just after Bolshevik leader Vladimir Lenin had announced in a letter to American workers that the US laboring class "will be with us … adopting communist, Bolshevik tactics," while "the corpse of capitalism is decaying."[11] We will look at four key periods: the Red Scare of 1919–20; the interwar years; the Second World War; and the Cold War. The chapter will conclude by highlighting again today's moment and how it reflects these patterns.

It is important to mention that there have been as well intervals of rapprochement and understanding between the two countries—one thinks of the improving relationship that led to the resumption of diplomatic ties in the

1930s; the wartime relationship of the 1940s (even while spies ran rampant); détente in the 1960s–1970s; glasnost in the 1980s; and the brief window of possibility after the fall of the Soviet Union in the early 1990s—all of them allowing for better relations and especially, in the 1990s, more transparency. These warming trends and episodes of openness do not belie the legacy of the troubled relationship, however, and sometimes these connections themselves were based on a distorted understanding, as they were in the Second World War.

There are any number of reasons for the problematic US-Russian relationship—but one overarching theme is the American people's propensity for conspiracy thinking. In the 1960s, Richard Hofstadter called it the "paranoid style"; more recently, Kathryn Olmsted pointed out that "Americans have a special relationship to conspiracy theory," an assessment that only seems even more compelling as this chapter goes to press, with the QAnon movement now drawing a growing number of believers. The tendency of Americans to traffic in conspiracies, of course, is not only oriented toward Russia. As a nation of immigrants with varied beliefs, traditions, and ethnic backgrounds, "Americans have worried that their country is especially open—and vulnerable—to alien subversion," Olmsted writes, and thus at various times, Catholics, Mormons, Jews, Chinese, and Muslims have all been targets of suspicion. While earlier a key concern was the safety and security of the government and the nation from such influences—we may think of George Washington's concerns about the pro-French schemes of diplomat Citizen Genet, or the Know-Nothing Party's fears of Catholic priests dividing voter loyalties—Olmsted argues that in the twentieth century, Americans became increasingly concerned that their government *itself* was the conspirator. They had reason to worry: beginning in the First World War, a powerful modern state began to arrest people for dissenting views, charge them under the Espionage Act, and control the press and public opinion.[12] In some of the better known conspiracy theories that have flourished since, the US government is often seen as a central actor, from Pearl Harbor to Area 51 to the Kennedy Assassination to 9/11, and these conspiracies have contributed to the deep state theories of today.[13] Of course, Senator Tom Cotton (R-AR)'s recent suggestion that China may have cooked up the coronavirus in a laboratory is evidence that not all conspiracy theories are about the US government.[14]

While conspiracies certainly abound in the United States, those around Russia have been particularly long-lasting and consequential for American society and culture, spurring much of the expanded national security state apparatus and its policies of secrecy, and leading as well to a more brittle domestic politics. We may consider that just as Joseph McCarthy exaggerated the idea of a Communist conspiracy against the United States, with great cost to American democracy, so too have Trump and his supporters cultivated the idea of a "deep state" conspiracy, minimizing the evidence of *actual* Russian influence and thus weakening protections for the US political system. From the Bolshevik Revolution a century ago to today, Russia's hold on American imagination, politics, and culture, including academic scholarship, has left a pattern of conspiracy-infused magnification and minimization of that nation's influence, creating concrete and long-lasting consequences for every American.

Early Responses to Bolshevik Russia: 1919–20

Although some experts, like Thomas Graham, have suggested that Russian-American relations became "fundamentally competitive" as soon as the United States became a global power in the late nineteenth century, the distorted, conspiratorial approach in US-Russian relations really began with the birth of the Communist party in the United States in 1919, less than two years after the Bolshevik Revolution.[15] This becomes clear when we explore how the United States faced the threat of subversion posed by radical political groups before the Bolsheviks came to power. In 1906, in the wake of the assassination of William McKinley by the American-born anarchist, Leon Czolgosz, Congress passed new naturalization laws that required prospective American citizens to state that they were "not a disbeliever in or opposed to organized government." But immigrants of extreme political stripes were safe from deportation if they had lived here more than three years—based on the notion that if they were still radical at that point, their views were presumably not so much tainted by foreign influences as by American ones. In 1918, however, with Europe in upheaval, and a wartime security state intent on dousing dissent through such measures as the 1917 Espionage Act, Congress passed immigration legislation that made deportations much more likely for all "alien anarchists, and those who advocated property destruction," no matter how long they'd been in the United States. With anarchist bombings taking place in 1919 on Wall Street and at the home of the Attorney General A. Mitchell Palmer as well, another law turned the screw tighter against those who believed in the "absence of government," even if they did so only by propaganda and not by force.[16] While communists and anarchists had different aims, their mutual belief in the destruction of the present US government was enough to tar them all with the same brush.

As the postwar Red Scare developed, greater scrutiny was applied to all radical groups, including the two Communist parties that emerged in 1919, the Communist Party of America (CPA) and the Communist Labor Party (CLP), both of which had broken off from the American Socialist Party (ASP); they would combine into one organization, later named the Communist Party of the United States of America (CPUSA), under Moscow's urging in 1921. Along with his deputy, J. Edgar Hoover, Attorney General Palmer (who had survived the bombing of his home when Carlo Valdinoci's explosive went off too early, killing the anarchist instead) carried out raids and deportations of not just communists and anarchists but others too, many of them members of groups like the Industrial Workers of the World (IWW). New York state officials, meanwhile, made plans to expel the newly arrived Soviet trade representative Ludwig Martens from the United States.

In the face of Russian propaganda like Lenin's Letter to American Workers, the authorities were increasingly nervous. The Bolshevik leader had warmly praised the American civil war in its efforts against "Negro slavery ... [and] the rule of the slaveowners" and its "immense, world-historic, progressive and revolutionary" significance; now, he suggested, just such a war, even bigger, was needed to end "wage slavery." Lenin was realistic that an American workers' revolution, as in other bourgeois nations, was still a "developing" prospect.[17] Nevertheless, US officials must have thought that American democracy was fragile. Certainly, they believed that some groups were especially vulnerable, as the *New York Times* reported, worrying about "Reds Inflaming Blacks."[18] Palmer himself made his views clear: one press report blared that he "WARNS NATION OF RED PERIL—U.S. Department of Justice Urges Americans to Guard Against Bolshevism Menace."[19]

This magnification of the Russian threat was evident in the deportation in December 1919 of 249 souls on the transit ship *Buford*, including most famously, Emma Goldman, an anarchist who had arrived in the United States as a teenager in 1885 from Lithuania. Despite never having been a communist, she was listed among the "hundreds of Reds" the *New York Times* reported on the ship.[20] Most of those on the *Buford* were actually members of the Union of Russian Workers, Russian-born immigrants who were tagged as Bolshevik propagandists, although they were not members of the party. Communists were certainly targeted as well; less than two weeks before the *Buford* sailed, the New York district attorney broke up a meeting of two thousand members of the party in the Bronx who had planned to gather in the London Casino on Third Avenue. Of course, not being at a large party gathering was no guarantee of safety, either. Those dining at the Tolstoy Vegetarian Restaurant in Chicago or singing with Philadelphia's Lithuanian Socialist Chorus were also nabbed in this sweep, as Adam Hochschild writes. In early 1920, Department of Justice agents were holding hundreds more in captivity in cities like Detroit, Boston, and New York, often under deplorable conditions; one group of 401 in January 1920 were sent to a "concentration camp" at Fort Upton, where the *Times* made the dubious claim that the quarters were "comfortable."[21] So eager were the Department agents to beef up their arrests that some accused them of "forming Communist organizations which could be raided," agents provocateur style.[22]

Fortunately, cooler heads soon prevailed. Although at the height of the Red Scare in 1919–20 more than three thousand were arrested, 2,200 of those ended up having their charges dropped, owing to the interventions of the acting secretary of labor, the aptly named Louis Freeland Post, who reviewed the cases and prevented the wholesale deportations.[23] Secretary of Labor William B. Wilson also declared that mere membership in the CLP was "not a deportable offense"—after all, the party had been careful to leave any mention of "violent overthrow" out of its constitution.[24] His views were echoed by others who considered such actions "contrary to American traditions," including the American Civil Liberties Union. While twenty thousand or more were deported annually in this era owing to their physical conditions, mental health, or criminal proclivities, historian Robert Murray notes that only an additional 591 radicals beyond the famous *Buford* group were deported in 1919–20.[25]

Thus, 1920 was both a peak year of arrests for such activists and a year when this entirely turned around, as William Preston Jr. writes: "deportation as a method of dealing with radicals fell into disrepute."[26] Yet this "return to normalcy" was accompanied by another restriction on immigrants, a far worse one, in fact, that codified a long-simmering xenophobia. If fewer people were being deported now, far less of them were being allowed in in the first place. The Red Scare and its record of anarchist bombings and flourishing Communist parties provided justification for the National Origins Act, which in 1924 sharply limited Southern and Eastern Europeans, including of course, Russians, and allowed in less than 165,000 people in total each year; Japanese applicants were completely excluded. By contrast, 1.3 million immigrants had arrived in 1907, the year of the highest immigration to the United States until 1990, and nearly 20 percent of those people were Russian.[27]

The Interwar Years

The policies established in the Red Scare era and immediately after it, including the deportations, Woodrow Wilson's refusal to recognize the Soviet Union (exemplified in the 1920 Colby Note),[28] and the National Origins Act, all underline the first period in the distorted US-Russian relationship. Even so, the 1920s and 1930s also included more realistic approaches between the two, when a number of groups in the United States called for quelling fears and expanding contacts with the Soviets. American businessmen, for example, had been trying to make deals with Soviet representatives since the moment when Ludwig Martens opened his Soviet Bureau in New York City in 1919; though Martens was soon deported, Soviet-American commerce grew significantly in the ensuing decade, as the Soviet Union became the largest foreign purchaser for US industrial machinery, and overall its seventh largest international customer by 1931.[29] American firms eagerly signed contracts and set up concessions in Russia aided by the State Department's liberalization of credit policies with Moscow.[30]

J. Edgar Hoover (Figure 5.1) may have worried that men who claimed to be buying American "automobiles and other machinery" were actually lobbyists for recognition, but Josef Stalin reassured US officials that "no representative of the USSR has the right to meddle in the internal affairs of countries in which he is directed ... [they] are not the least bit connected with propaganda in any way." That, however, did not prevent the Communist International (Comintern) from pressing American Communists to lend their efforts outside the United States, and "energetically help national-revolutionary movements in countries which are now colonies," including the Philippines, Cuba, and Puerto Rico.[31]

While businessmen pursued Soviet opportunities regardless of Moscow's propaganda, former diplomats and other leading statesmen at the Institute of Politics in Williamstown, Massachusetts, also urged a different path for the United States: "America should show some visible interest in Russia's great experiment [with] ... frank and open contact ... A conference with Russia would help remove distrust on both sides, and ... pave the way for the establishment of more friendly relations," was the assessment of members like Paul D. Cravath and Colonel William Haskell in 1930.[32] Such even-handed attitudes, along with the growing trade and a clear assessment of the expanding geopolitical ambitions of the Soviet Union's neighbor, Japan, helped spur President Franklin D. Roosevelt (FDR) at last to open diplomatic relations with the Soviet Union in 1933. Certainly, it seemed that the earlier pattern of magnifying the Russian threat had by now abated. Nevertheless, despite—or perhaps because of— extremely few Communists being deported in the late 1920s (just fifteen in four years), some Congressmen remained concerned. Hamilton Fish (R-NY) set up a Special Committee to Investigate Communist Activities, known as the Fish Committee, in 1930. The committee was not without its critics, including Iowa

Figure 5.1 J. Edgar Hoover, Director of F.B.I., in his office, April 1940. Credit: Library of Congress, Reproduction Number: LC-DIG-hec-28439 (digital file from original negative).

Republican Congressman C. William Ramseyer, who accused it of conducting "witch hunts."³³

Fish was not mistaken to be concerned about the threat posed by some Communists and their Soviet contacts, who were certainly taking advantage of their growing presence in the United States with passport forgery and secret intelligence gathering, but his effort was more bombastic than effective.

While focused on a largely fruitless investigation of the subversive activities of Amtorg, the Soviet trading agency, Fish missed Soviet "illegals" like Alfred Tilton, who operated without benefit of diplomatic cover, using bootlegged passports obtained from purloined birth certificates and other documentation.[34] Tilton assisted the Russians from 1928 to 1939, and along with obtaining false identification papers for Soviet agents like himself, did his share of espionage and recruitment of others to the cause, like party member Nicholas Dozenberg.[35] Meanwhile, Paul Crouch, another party organizer from 1925 to 1942 who had helped edit the *Daily Worker* with Whittaker Chambers, was instructed in 1928 to penetrate the US Army.[36] Harry Gold, later infamous in the Rosenberg ring, was also first recruited in the early 1930s.

Fish's committee expired in 1931, during a period when the FBI caught only a small number of agents, and the Army's Signals Intelligence Service abandoned a small-scale effort to decode Russian codes and ciphers.[37] This less than vigorous response reflected the sentiments of American public opinion, just as Ramseyer's retort to the Fish Committee did. In a reaction to the overzealous practices of the Red Scare era, as Frank J. Rafalko has noted, government agents were "severely handicapped" by "powerful influences which were constantly trying to limit activities along such lines."[38] Overall, an undeveloped counterintelligence apparatus in the 1930s made effective coordination in countering Soviet espionage well-nigh impossible, and serves as another example of the underestimation of the threat posed by Russia that this chapter seeks to highlight.

The rise of Hitler, however, prompted a new congressional probe in 1935, now with the title of Special Committee to Investigate Un-American Activities, and initially dedicated more to Nazi sympathizers than Communists. It became permanent in 1938, under Chair Martin Dies (D-Tex.), who soon renewed its focus on the topic of Russian influence: "The Communist Party's highly synchronized and highly disciplined organization has been permitted to entrench itself deeply into our body politic," Dies declared (Figure 5.2).[39]

Certainly the party's secret organization was busy, including its continuing campaign of generating fake passports for its operatives, and Dies's committee began to grapple with this issue. However, Soviet coordination with the work of American spies like Franklin Victor Reno and Harry Gold, gathering material on such items as aircraft bombsights at the Aberdeen Proving Ground and chemical processes at the Pennsylvania Sugar company, remained unknown to the congressman and his colleagues.[40] Even so, another congressional committee urged legislators to "revise and codify the nationality laws" specifically to "insert proper language to shut out communists," in the words

Figure 5.2 Representative Jerry Voorhis, Chairman Martin Dies, and Representative Joseph Casey holding a Communist Party recruitment flag seized in a raid on a Baltimore, Maryland office, March 20, 1940. Credit: Library of Congress, Washington, DC. Reproduction Number: LC-DIG-hec-28399 (digital file from original negative).

of Noah M. Mason (R-Ill.).[41] In 1941, as the war was taking over much of the world, Dies and his committee, too, would call for laws to permit "the immediate mandatory deportation of alien spies and saboteurs" as well as to prohibit "every political organization which is shown to be under the control of a foreign government."[42]

The CPUSA was of course financed and heavily influenced by a foreign government, the Soviet Union, which supported the work of those above-named agents; at that moment Moscow's allegiance to its nonaggression pact with Nazi Germany raised some questions as to who else the party might be loyal to. This stance had already cost the party a number of adherents; perhaps 8,500 of its 66,000 members left between 1939 and 1941 for that reason. Yet the vast majority stayed, understanding the geopolitical realities that Stalin was facing in Europe and drawn to the party's domestic initiatives, including its support of unions and its active defense of victims of racist justice like the Scottsboro boys.[43]

Second World War

Just like the previous war had, the Second World War accelerated fears of subversion in Washington. The FBI had taken on new emergency powers, and Congressman Dies would demand that leading Communists like Earl Browder testify; Browder would be jailed for just the kind passport fraud noted earlier, as James Ryan discusses in Chapter 2. Dies went as well after pro-Nazi groups like the Silver Shirts. At this tense time, even Jehovah's Witnesses who didn't salute the flag faced persecution.[44]

Despite the increasing scrutiny of individual Communists like Browder, the authorities still missed much of the work that Soviet spies and their American contacts were doing in gathering industrial and diplomatic intelligence. Certainly, the FBI's new responsibilities allowed for agents to deploy techniques such as wiretapping and microphone surveillance; its agents learned about Soviet espionage against the atomic bomb with their Communist Infiltration of the Radiation Laboratories, University of California, Berkeley (CINRAD) investigation, for example, when they identified Communist leader Steve Nelson's contacts with scientists there.[45] FBI initiatives drew a compelling picture of US vulnerability to Soviet espionage practices in the war. The bureau noted ominously in 1944: "Investigations have proved the continuous use of the Communists in the United States by Soviet agents and have confirmed the operation of an illegal and underground apparatus … The implications of this activity in this time of vital war effort … and in the trying period of post-war readjustment to come warrant the closest attention and consideration."[46] Even with its investigative apparatus, the FBI didn't know the half of it. Along with Klaus Fuchs and David Greenglass's pilfering of atomic technology at the Los Alamos's nuclear installation, in part facilitated by the courier services of Harry Gold, programs like Lend-Lease facilitated the entry of numerous Soviet agents into the United States, who used the opportunity to steal as much military-industrial information as possible.

President Roosevelt had strongly supported the enhanced role of the FBI beginning in 1939, in return for Hoover's provision of secret intelligence on domestic dissenters such as the America First Committee.[47] But FDR was not greatly interested in the records of Soviet espionage that Hoover brought him.[48] As Bradley F. Smith has noted, "Washington was firmly, and perhaps rather blindly, committed to making the partnership with the USSR work."[49] Roosevelt's own naïveté about the scope of Russian intentions—and his unwillingness, moreover, to consider them—is reflected in his earlier refusal to entertain Whittaker Chambers's allegations about Soviet espionage in the State Department, along with his limited response to the FBI reports on wartime Soviet spying.[50] This approach serves as another example of the distorted perceptions typical of the US-Russian relationship. While it is certainly understandable that the president saw the Soviet-American alliance in the Second World War as the chief priority, FDR's refusal to acknowledge discoveries of Soviet espionage prevented much serious response to the efforts of Communist spies who had infiltrated the atomic project. Such espionage, of course, assisted the Soviets to develop a nuclear weapon within a few years after the war ended and would greatly increase tensions and an arms race thereafter.[51]

During the war, the FBI also launched the Comintern Apparatus (COMRAP) probe and developed a "Security Index" of "dangerous" individuals, relying on countless informants. Through such diligent methods, by 1944 agents had identified one million people with Communist-front associations—largely through blanket infiltration of groups like the National Association for the Advancement of Colored People (NAACP).[52] Of course, these were mostly *not* Communists or spies. Both of these responses to Russian involvement, the *overreaction* that was the Security Index and FDR's *underreaction* to genuine Soviet activity in the United States, show how the Second World War gives perhaps the best example of both extremes in the distorted Russian-American relationship: *magnification* of certain kinds of party influence which enabled the rise of a large security apparatus, thus mislabeling many innocent people, as well as *marginalization* of reports of active Soviet espionage by President Roosevelt and others in his circle. The FBI and other counterintelligence institutions, of course, would trumpet their alarm of Soviet malfeasance at full volume in the Cold War, when the climate of Soviet-American relations had changed drastically, and their message found more receptive ears.

Cold War Conspiracy Thinking

After the Soviet Union emerged as a superpower in 1945, a Second Red Scare (and a much-expanded security state) would develop with the investigations of Communists in the US government, in industry, in Hollywood, in the American labor movement, and in other groups. Browder may have been freed from prison as a goodwill measure in 1943, but his return as a communist leader was relatively short-lived—Moscow no longer considered him a fitting leader, and he was sacked as a "right deviationist" and removed from the party in 1946. A year later, in what was perhaps one of the last bold proclamations by a Communist leader, Steve Nelson would tell a group of striking Pennsylvania miners, "The Communist Party won't overthrow the US Government by force and violence, but we will oust that Government by mass pressure."[53] Instead, of course, the federal government and the state of Pennsylvania spent much of the next decade hounding Nelson in investigations for contempt of Congress and sedition, among other charges; he finally left the party after Khrushchev's "Secret speech" of 1956.

As authorities learned of Nelson's work, and heard the confessions of Soviet spies such as Whittaker Chambers, Elizabeth Bentley, and by 1950, Harry Gold, who became an important informant about the Rosenberg atomic and industrial espionage ring, they did so against a backdrop of growing Communist influence over Eastern Europe, China, and Korea. In 1949, as well, eleven CPUSA leaders were found guilty of violating the Smith Act's provisions against advocating the overthrow of the US government and sent to prison. There were numerous other investigations by the FBI and Congress, but Senator Joseph McCarthy (R-Wis.) was determined to find his own spies, and this led to the most notorious episode of anticommunist overreaction in the era that bears his name. Many Americans, including public officials, teachers, broadcasters, and filmmakers lost their livelihoods in his crusade, with devastating effects on American democracy and discourse.

The McCarthy era was perhaps the last time before our own when terms like "witch hunt" and "fraud and a hoax" were used in such a high-profile way. These were the very words that Senator Millard Tydings (D-Md.) hurled at Joe McCarthy in response to the Wisconsin senator's charges of 205 (or was it 57? Or 81?) Communists in the State Department (Figure 5.3). McCarthy really *did* conduct a witch hunt, of course, one that did not uncover any new Communist threats to the nation. Defending McCarthy, Senator William Jenner (R-Ind.) accused Tydings of "the most scandalous and brazen whitewash of a treasonable conspiracy in our history."[54] Tydings was defeated in his reelection bid in 1950 in part because of "fake news": a doctored photo of himself supposedly seated with Earl Browder that some of McCarthy's supporters distributed. Such supporters included academics at prestigious universities, like the founder of Georgetown University's School of Foreign Service, Father Edmund Walsh, SJ, who had been frustrated earlier by his efforts to set up an office for the Holy See in Moscow; Walsh would urge the senator to pursue a campaign against "Soviet imperialism's threat to the U.S.," although McCarthy likely didn't need any encouragement.[55]

Figure 5.3 Senator Millard Tydings and Senator Joseph McCarthy. Credit: U.S. Senate Historical Office.

Despite his bombast and targeted use of the "big lie," there was really very little for McCarthy to find; by the early 1950s, Russian spies who had conspired to commit espionage in the Second World War had either confessed, been jailed, were in hiding, had insufficient evidence against them to be charged, or—in the case of one famous couple—were already waiting to be executed and hoping for a reprieve.[56] As John Earl Haynes and Harvey Klehr note in Chapter 1, the CPUSA itself soon shrank to all but a remnant, though undercover FBI agents valiantly filled in its ranks. Like Trump today, Tydings was pointing out that Russia did not have the influence that many claimed in the US political system. Unlike Trump, though, Tydings was accurate.

During the McCarthy era with its great distortion of imputed Russian power, not even Dwight D. Eisenhower would stand up for one of his wartime compatriots in the face of the Wisconsin senator's blistering attacks in 1952. Where Roosevelt had earlier downplayed Russian malfeasance, Eisenhower was only too willing to accept the most grandiose claims for it, including McCarthy's outrageous attack on General George C. Marshall for walking "'side-by-side' with Stalin" in a "monstrous perversion of sound and understandable national policy."[57] Eisenhower refused to speak in support of Marshall, despite having written a stirring defense of him into a Milwaukee speech one month before the election: "I knew him as a man and a soldier, to be dedicated with singular selflessness and the profoundest patriotism to the service of America. Here we have a sobering lesson of the way freedom must *not* defend itself." But Eisenhower scratched out this stalwart statement for fear of offending Wisconsin voters.[58]

Elected president that November, the general soon faced another crisis of conscience—what to do with Julius and Ethel Rosenberg, who had been consigned to the electric chair in a sentence meted out in 1951. But as calls for clemency came from around the world, and even as J. Edgar Hoover pressed for leniency—at least for Ethel—at the eleventh hour, Eisenhower remained unmoved. Hoover's plea to send her to prison rather than the chair drew, predictably, on her gender: "This woman is the mother of two small children," Hoover wrote to the president. "As the wife of Julius Rosenberg, she would, in a sense, be presumed to be acting under the influence of her husband."[59] The hero of D-Day disagreed. In his mind, "the more strong-minded and the apparent leader of the two—is a woman." He wondered, "if the Executive should interfere because of this fact, would we ... [be] encouraging the Communists to use only women in the spying process?"[60] Indeed, Eisenhower went even further than Judge Irving Kaufman, who blamed the Rosenbergs for fifty thousand deaths in Korea; the president believed instead that the couple's actions "may have condemned to death tens of millions of innocent people all over the world."[61]

As Lori Clune has noted, however, the case instead "tarnished the image of the United States" among millions of people worldwide (Figure 5.4).[62] It also contributed to the distorted view of the threat from Russia, with the twin effects of hardening the security state—this was of course the same time that the Subversive Activities Control Act of 1950 directed the building of camps for subversives—and weakening American liberties. Poignantly, at the end of his second term Eisenhower would rue this "garrison state" that the Cold War was creating in the name of fighting communism and eschew the "military-industrial complex" that sacrificed liberties for military power and expenditure.[63]

The tide had turned for McCarthy by then, of course; his reputation began to crumble after he was publicly shamed by Joseph Welch in the Senate Army-McCarthy hearings for his lack of "decency," on June 9, 1954 (Figure 5.5).

Eisenhower was himself furious at the senator's attack on the US Army after its refusal to give the senator's aide, G. David Schein, dispensation from military service. The president had now come to recognize McCarthy for who he was, and enthusiastically anticipated an opportunity "to let him have it."[64]

Figure 5.4 Julius and Ethel Rosenberg, separated by heavy wire screen as they leave US Court House after being found guilty by jury. Credit: Library of Congress, Washington, DC. Reproduction Number: LC-USZ62-117772.

Just as in the 1919 Red Scare, in the McCarthy era an American overreaction destroyed peoples' livelihoods and ruined lives; as Hofstadter noted, McCarthy and the forces he unleashed were "powerful enough to set the tone of our political life" for years to come.[65] And the senator was not the only damaging, conspiratorially minded crusader to go after suspected Communists in his time.

Figure 5.5 Joseph McCarthy and Joseph Welch at the Army-McCarthy hearings, 1954. Credit: U.S. Senate Historical Office.

FBI director J. Edgar Hoover and his informants, like Herb Philbrick, went after many innocents, as well. One of many sources in the Smith Trial, Philbrick's testimony, as Veronica Wilson notes, "helped discredit the CPUSA and pave the way" for the excesses of the early 1950s.[66] Philbrick became a household name to many with his book and his popular TV series, *I Led Three Lives*, about his life as an undercover informant in the party; the show ran until 1956, well after McCarthy was disgraced.[67] Hoover himself never stopped believing in the problem of Communist threats, either. Along with his wiretapping of Martin Luther King, whose putative Communist leanings obsessed the FBI director, there was also the bureau's surveillance of "student agitators" at Swarthmore and Bryn Mawr Colleges, the Black Panthers, women's liberation groups, and suspected pacifist organizations like the Women's International League for Peace and Freedom.[68]

The bureau's work went well beyond the purview of authorized FBI activities. After the Citizens' Commission to Investigate the FBI broke into the Media, Pennsylvania field office on March 8, 1971, in the dead of night, ransacking its files on students and other activists, the burglars aptly noted: "The FBI sees the Communist conspiracy everywhere: in colleges and universities ... The conspiracy is also behind ... the civil rights movement, black militant groups and the anti-war forces."⁶⁹ The Citizens' Commission also uncovered the FBI's COINTELPRO investigations, and when these methods, including its domestic surveillance campaign, were revealed in full detail in the Senator Frank Church (D-Idaho)'s hearings of 1975, a Senate investigation which also brought to light the CIA's own assassination attempts of Communists like Fidel Castro, and the NSA's widescale interception of Americans' phone calls, such practices were roundly denounced and deplored.⁷⁰ All of this vast overreaching by government agencies in the name of fighting communism, drawing on a distorted view of Russian influence, underlies the persistent threat to American democracy this particular preoccupation had engendered.

The Church Committee hearings, coming in the wake of President Richard Nixon's resignation amid the Watergate scandal and the end of the agonizing Vietnam War, met a receptive audience. Many Americans were highly critical by then of the notion of a Communist threat to the US government with all of its problematic associations, and the FBI, NSA, and CIA methods only further underlined the contrasting heavy-handedness of Washington agencies against the innocence of those they had targeted.

This reaction can be seen even more clearly in the rapid turnaround of fortunes for Soviet spy Alger Hiss among scholars. Fresh out of prison in 1956, Hiss was met with stunned silence by a Princeton faculty who disapproved of students' invitation of this "convicted traitor." (Hiss had actually been convicted of perjury.) Yet within a decade, the former State Department official was warmly welcomed by professors at colleges like Brandeis, Kenyon, Harvard, and the New School, although he produced no new evidence demonstrating his innocence. As his biographer G. Edward White noted: "Many found qualities in Hiss they could identify with or admire," whereas they "found qualities in [his] antagonists that ... they found distasteful."⁷¹ For academics, this roster of distasteful men, including Hoover, McCarthy, and of course, Nixon, would be joined by another, the adamantly anticommunist President Ronald Reagan, when he became president. An FBI informer on his fellow Hollywood stars in the 1950s, in the 1980s Reagan was once again magnifying Communist influence with terms like "the Evil Empire," and promoting anticommunist interventions from Grenada to Nicaragua.⁷² Meanwhile, his 1982 Executive Order, which extended even longer the period for classification of intelligence documents, led the US State Department to brush over the anticommunist interventions of the past. The department's highly respected historical compilation, the *Foreign Relations of the United States* series, published two volumes in this era that left out the US role in the overthrow of Muhammed Mossadegh in Iran and Jacobo Arbenz in Guatemala, to the further outrage of scholars.[73]

Given this antagonistic approach, perhaps it is not surprising that as late as 1991, with the Soviet Union crumbling, historians like Richard Fried continued to cast doubt on claims by J. Edgar Hoover that there had been "'an enormous Soviet espionage ring in Washington' seeking to acquire information about atomic energy ... this was half-baked and wrong," Fried wrote.[74] Hoover had been correct, of course, yet even after the end of the Soviet Union in the early 1990s, when its archives began to open, American academics instead insisted upon the definition of a Communist party made up of activists who focused on race discrimination and on improving conditions of the working poor, as its members surely did—but that was only part of the picture.[75] Scholars, it seemed, reacted against the excesses of characters like McCarthy, Hoover, and Reagan by denying the reality of the 1930s and 1940s. As John Earl Haynes and Harvey Klehr contend, such was the skepticism and desire of many historians to minimize Russian secret involvement in the United States that they refused even to "smell ... the cordite of the smoking gun" of the newly released evidence of the Party's work to promote Soviet espionage.[76]

Conclusion

That evidence came out fully in the mid-1990s, when the US government began at last to open its sources on Soviet espionage, including the Venona cables, flinging open a window on the story of Soviet spying during the 1930s, the Second World War, and the early Cold War that most Americans had known little about. Venona definitively confirmed the involvement of spies like Julius Rosenberg, Morton Sobell, David Greenglass, Elizabeth Bentley, Alger Hiss, Harry Gold, and many others. The Cold War's end also ushered in a new openness in the Soviet archives, which those in this book have been able to take advantage of in their research, although the accessibility has since been curtailed. These new materials have included both the Soviet official government archives like the Russian State Archive of Socio-Political History (RGASPI) and the records of the CPUSA from Moscow, as well as materials from defectors, like Alexander Vassiliev's Notebooks, all of which have shed new light on any number of topics, not just espionage.[77] At the same time, a revamped Historical Advisory Committee was created at the State Department in 1991, with congressional oversight, to ensure that *Foreign Relations of the United States* consistently provides a "thorough, accurate, and reliable" picture of historic US foreign relations, including CIA and Department of Defense (DOD) involvement, with coverage of past covert actions in its volumes.[78]

Academics' skepticism about US government actions in the Cold War was understandable, and often justified. Yet unfortunately, too often it led to a reaction that minimized Russian involvement and prevented scholars from seeing the whole picture about Soviet spying in the government and in the military industry during the first half of the twentieth century. It is ironic that the current US president seems to share a perception in common with liberal academics of thirty years ago: their skepticism of Russian malfeasance, and distrust of US intelligence agencies. Trump's recent dismissal of Moscow's political interference amid very clear evidence of it, just like scholars' skepticism about Soviet espionage up to, and sometimes after, the moment archives revealed it, underlines once again this historic pattern of *overreaction to minimal threats* and *underreaction to genuine dangers* in the Russian-American relationship.

As the Tydings/McCarthy and Mueller/Trump episodes show some seventy years apart, the American view of Russian power and its agents has long been a distorted one. As a result, we live today under the influence of the greater national security state that developed from these fears, *and* a more vulnerable political system. As Joseph Biden and Michael Carpenter noted in *Foreign Affairs* in 2017, "since the Trump administration has shown that it does not take the Russian threat seriously, the responsibility for protecting Western democracy will rest more than ever on Congress, the private sector, civil society, and ordinary Americans."[79] Indeed it will, but as this chapter has suggested, conspiracy-thinking and distrust around Russian influence, such as that demonstrated by A. Mitchell Palmer, Joseph McCarthy, J. Edgar Hoover, Cold War academics, or Donald Trump, has been widely shared among the American people for a very long time.

Notes

1 Steven Nelson and Bob Fredericks, "Trump Calls Russia Probe 'Bullsh—' in Post-Impeachment Remarks," *New York Post*, February 6, 2020, https://nypost.com/2020/02/06/trump-calls-russia-probe-bullshit-in-post-impeachment-remarks/ (accessed March 27, 2020).

2 Trump's twitter account, February 5, 2020, https://twitter.com/realDonaldTrump/status/1225179058000089090 (accessed March 27, 2020).
3 Trump quoted in Melissa Davey and Australian Associated Press, "Donald Trump wants investigation into Australia's role in 'Russian hoax,'" *The Guardian*, May 25, 2019, https://www.theguardian.com/us-news/2019/may/25/donald-trump-wants-investigation-into-australias-role-in-russian-hoax (accessed March 27, 2020); see *Report of the Select Committee on Intelligence United States Senate on Russian Active Measures Campaigns and Interference in the 2016 U.S. Election*, Volume 1: Russian Efforts against Election Infrastructure with Additional Views, 6, and Volume 5: Counterintelligence Threats and Vulnerabilities, 5, 116th Congress, first session, https://www.intelligence.senate.gov/sites/default/files/documents/Report_Volume1.pdf and https://www.intelligence.senate.gov/sites/default/files/documents/Report_Volume5.pdf (accessed March 27, 2020, and August 20, 2020); Annenberg Public Policy Center, February 6, 2020, https://www.factcheck.org/issue/russia-investigation/ (accessed March 27, 2020).
4 Angela Stent, *Putin's World: Russia against the West and with the Rest* (New York: Hatchette, 2019), p. 321.
5 Matt Flegenheimer, "After Putin Meeting, Trump Voters Mostly Dig in, But Cracks Are Showing," *New York Times*, July 17, 2018, https://www.nytimes.com/2018/07/17/us/politics/republican-voters-trump-putin.html (accessed March 27, 2020).
6 William J. Burns, "How the US-Russian Relationship Went Bad," *Atlantic*, March 8, 2019, https://carnegieendowment.org/2019/03/08/how-u.s.-russian-relationship-went-bad-pub-78543 (accessed March 27, 2020).
7 Zeke Miller, "Trump Tries to Cast Fresh Doubt on Mueller's 'Witch Hunt,'" *U.S. News and World Report*, July 22, 2018, https://www.usnews.com/news/politics/articles/2018-07-22/trump-claims-illegal-spying-after-warrant-papers-unveiled (accessed March 28, 2020); Peter Baker, Lara Jakes, Julian E. Barnes, Sharon LaFraniere, and Edward Wong, "Trump's War on the Deep State Turns against Him," *New York Times*, October 23, 2019, https://www.nytimes.com/2019/10/23/us/politics/trump-deep-state-impeachment.html (accessed March 28, 2020).
8 Adam Goldman, Julian E. Barnes, Maggie Haberman, and Nicholas Fandos, "Lawmakers Are Warned That Russia Is Meddling to Re-Elect Trump," *New York Times*, February 20, 2020, https://www.nytimes.com/2020/02/20/us/politics/russian-interference-trump-democrats.html (assessed March 27, 2020).
9 Matthew Rosenberg, Nicole Perlroth, and David E. Sanger, "'Chaos Is the Point': Russian Trolls and Hackers Grow Stealthier in 2020," *New York Times*, January 10, 2020, https://www.nytimes.com/2020/01/10/us/politics/russia-hacking-disinformation-election.html (accessed March 28, 2020); Neil McFarquhar, "Inside the Russian Troll Factory: Zombies and a Breakneck Pace," *New York Times*, February 18, 2018, https://www.nytimes.com/2018/02/18/world/europe/

russia-troll-factory.html (accessed March 31, 2020). Also see Kathleen Hall Jamieson, *Cyberwar: How Russian Hackers and Trolls Helped Elect a President: What We Don't, Can't, and Do Know* (New York: Oxford University Press, 2018).

10   Stent, *Putin's World*, pp. 310, 314.

11   Lenin's Letter to American Workers, August 20, 1918. Originally published in *Pravda* No. 178, August 22, 1918; from *Lenin's Collected Works* (Moscow: Progress Publishers, 1965), pp. 62–75, https://www.marxists.org/archive/lenin/works/1918/aug/20.htm (accessed March 28, 2020). Discussion of Martens in Katherine A. S. Siegel, *Loans and Legitimacy: The Evolution of Soviet-American Relations, 1919–1933* (Lexington: University Press of Kentucky, 1996), p. 20.

12   Richard Hofstadter, "The Paranoid Style in American Politics," *Harper's Magazine*, November 1964; Kathryn Olmsted, *Real Enemies: Conspiracy Theories and American Democracy, World War I to 9/11* (New York: Oxford University Press, 2011), pp. 3–4.

13   Glenn Kessler, "What's the Evidence for 'Spying' on Trump's Campaign? Here's Your Guide," *Washington Post*, May 6, 2019, https://www.washingtonpost.com/politics/2019/05/06/whats-evidence-spying-trumps-campaign-heres-your-guide/ (accessed March 28, 2020).

14   Yanzhong Huang, "US-Chinese Distrust Is Inviting Dangerous Coronavirus Conspiracy Theories and Undermining Efforts to Contain the Epidemic," *Foreign Affairs*, March 5, 2020, https://www.foreignaffairs.com/articles/united-states/2020-03-05/us-chinese-distrust-inviting-dangerous-coronavirus-conspiracy (accessed March 28, 2020).

15   Thomas Graham, "Let Russia Be Russia: The Case for a More Pragmatic Approach to Moscow," *Foreign Affairs*, November/December 2019, https://www.foreignaffairs.com/articles/russia-fsu/2019-10-15/let-russia-be-russia (accessed March 28, 2020).

16   Naturalization Act, June 29, 1906, https://www.historycentral.com/HistoricalDocuments/NaturalizationAct.html (accessed March 28, 2020). *U.S. vs. Stuppiello*, September 10, 1919, U.S. District Court for the Western District of NY, 260 Fed., 483, cited in *The Daily Washington Law Reporter*, volume 47, p. 831; on the Wall Street bombings especially, see Beverly Gage, *The Day Wall Street Exploded: A Story of America in Its First Age of Terror* (New York: Oxford University Press, 2010).

17   Lenin's Letter to American Workers, August 20, 1918. Originally published in *Pravda* No. 178, August 22, 1918; from *Lenin's Collected Works* (Moscow: Progress Publishers, 1965), pp. 62–75, https://www.marxists.org/archive/lenin/works/1918/aug/20.htm (accessed March 28, 2020).

18   See "For Action on Race Riot Peril," *New York Times*, October 5, 1919.

19   "Begin Procedure to Deport Reds," *New York Times*, January 6, 1920; Adam Hochschild, "When America Tried to Deport Its Radicals," *New Yorker*, November

11, 2019, https://www.newyorker.com/magazine/2019/11/11/when-america-tried-to-deport-its-radicals (accessed March 28, 2020).

20 "Hundreds of Reds on Soviet 'Ark' Sail Soon for Russia," *New York Times*, December 13, 1919.

21 "Begin Procedure to Deport Reds"; Hochschild, "When America Tried to Deport Its Radicals."

22 Frank Moore Colby (ed.), *The New International Yearbook: A Compendium of the Year's Progress for the Year 1920* (New York: Dodd, Mead, 1921), p. 698. I am grateful to John B. Fox, FBI Historian, for locating this and other hard-to-find sources for me.

23 Hearing before Subcommittee of House Committee on Appropriations, "Sundry Civil Appropriation Bill," 1921, 66th Congress, second session (1920), p. 1589; also see Constantine M. Panunzio, "The Deportation Cases of 1919–1920" (New York: Federal Council of the Churches, 1921), p. 95, who notes that of the 2,777 aliens deported in 1920, 314 were anti-anarchists.

24 Constitution of the Communist Labor Party of America, adopted September 5, 1919, http://www.marxisthistory.org/history/usa/parties/cpusa/1919/0905-clp-constitution.pdf (accessed March 31, 2020).

25 John Fox email to author, February 28, 2020. This was also a period when the total number of immigrants into the country expanded rapidly, amounting to nearly 15 million total persons between 1900 and 1920, increasing the total US population in 1900 by 20 percent. See Nicholas Nowrasteh, "Deportation Rates in Historical Perspective," September 2019, https://www.cato.org/blog/deportation-rates-historical-perspective (accessed March 28, 2020); Robert K. Murray, *Red Scare: A Study in National Hysteria, 1919–1920* (Minneapolis: University of Minnesota Press, 1951), p. 251.

26 William Preston Jr., *Aliens and Dissenters: Federal Suppression of Radicals, 1903–1933* (New York: Harper Torchbooks, 1963), p. 229.

27 United States Holocaust Memorial Museum, "United States Immigration and Refugee Law, 1921–1980," https://encyclopedia.ushmm.org/content/en/article/united-states-immigration-and-refugee-law-1921-1980 (accessed March 28, 2020).

28 In his infamous Note, Wilson's Secretary of State Bainbridge Colby stated, "We cannot recognize, hold official relations with, or give friendly reception to the agents of a government which is determined and bound to conspire against our institutions; whose diplomats will be the agitators of dangerous revolt." See Secretary of State Bainbridge Colby, August 10, 1920, https://nsarchive2.gwu.edu//coldwar/documents/episode-1/colby.htm (accessed June 5, 2020).

29 See Siegel, *Loans and Legitimacy*, p. 133.

30 On Armand Hammer's asbestos mine concessions, for instance, see "Project of Concession Agreement in Cultivation of Asbestos Production in Urals in the

Wording of Concession Committee of *Vesenkha*," RTsKhIDNI, fond 5, op. 1, del. 2697, quoted in Siegel, *Loans and Legitimacy*, p. 119; on credit extensions, see ibid., pp. 100–7.

31 Hoover to Col. Stanley H. Ford, November 21, 1928, Record Group 165, Records of the War Department General and Special Staffs, 10058-1257/4, Stalin, discussion with Mr. Campbell, January 28, 1929, cited in RTsKhIDNI, fond 558, op. 1, del. 2884; Resolution of the Colonial Commission of the Executive Committee of the Communist International on the work of the Workers Party in American Colonies and Possessions, 1929, RsKhIDNI, fond 558, op. 1, del. 3292, all cited in Siegel, *Loans and Legitimacy*, p. 100.

32 Arthur Howland Buffinton (ed.), *The Institute of Politics at Williamstown, Massachusetts: Its First Decade* (Williamstown, MA: Institute of Politics, 1931), p. 43.

33 William F. Buckley Jr. and the Editors of *National Review*, *The Committee and Its Critics: A Calm Review of the House Committee on Un-American Activities* (New York: G.P. Putnams, 1962), pp. 94–6.

34 US passports were very desirable, since Americans were so often immigrants and their names and accents could fit a Russian. As Whittaker Chambers wrote, without "boots," or passports, "a spy can get nowhere." See Chambers, "The Soviet Passport Racket," 1938, published by Herb Solow in "Stalin's American Passport Mill," *American Mercury*, July 1939, Sam Tanenhaus Papers, box 25, Hoover Institution, Stanford, CA; *New York Times*, April 24, 1934.

35 In 1929, when Tilton was recalled to Moscow, he brought Dozenberg with him. For the next few years, Dozenberg was employed in setting up Soviet military intelligence operations in such countries as Germany, Rumania, and China, until he broke with the Soviet Union in 1938. Dozenberg statement, November 8, 1949, *Hearings Regarding Communist Espionage in the U.S. Government*, U.S. Congress, House, Committee on Un-American Activities, 81st Congress, first and second sessions (Washington, DC: Government Printing Office, 1951), pp. 3540–1.

36 Hearings Regarding Steve Nelson, June 8, 1949, U.S. Congress, House, Hearings before the Committee on Un-American Activities, 81st Congress, first session, 186.

37 While occasionally picking up Russian intelligence in pursuit of Japanese and German traffic, these efforts "remained infrequent and unsystematic" until Second World War. See David Alvarez, *Secret Messages: Code Breaking and American Diplomacy, 1930–1945* (Lawrence: University Press of Kansas, 2000), p. 200. On Gold, see Harry Gold, "The Circumstances Surrounding My Work as a Soviet Agent—a Report," in Testimony in U.S. Congress, Senate, Subcommittee to Investigate the Administration of the Internal Security Act and Other Internal Security Laws, Committee of the Judiciary, *Scope of Soviet Activity in the United States*, 84th Congress, second session, April 26, 1956, pp. 1060–2.

38 Frank J. Rafalko (ed.), *A Counterintelligence Reader*, Volume I: *American Revolution to World War II* (Washington, DC: National Counterintelligence Center, 1996), p. 153.
39 Martin Dies, *The Trojan Horse in America* (New York: Dodd Mead, 1940), quoted in Katherine A. S. Sibley, *Red Spies in America: Stolen Secrets and the Dawn of the Cold War* (Lawrence: University Press of Kansas, 2004), p. 44.
40 Sibley, *Red Spies in America*, pp. 33–40.
41 U.S. Congress, Committee on Immigration and Naturalization, 76th Congress, first session, "A Bill to Revise and Codify the Nationality Laws of the United States into a Comprehensive Nationality Code," 1940, 305.
42 Congressional Record, Proceedings and Debates of the 77th Congress, first session, Vol. 87, Part I, January 3, 1941 to February 18, 1941, 215, 894.
43 John Haynes post on H-HOAC, April 17, 2019, https://networks.h-net.org/node/6077/discussions/4021026/cpusa-loss-membership-after-nazi-soviet-pact (accessed March 28, 2020).
44 The case was *Minersville School District v. Gobitis*. The decision was 8-1 in 1940, but the decision was overturned in a second case, *West Virginia State Board of Education v. Barnette* (1943), and is discussed in Mary L. Dudziak, *War Time: An Idea, Its History, Its Consequences* (New York: Oxford University Press), pp. 56–60.
45 On Nelson, see Sibley, *Red Spies in America*, pp. 136–47.
46 Federal Bureau of Investigation, COMRAP (Communist Apparatus) Summary Report, San Francisco, December 15, 1944, covering period March 29, 1943–August 1, 1944, FBI File 100-203581-3702, pp. 3–4.
47 See Douglas Charles, *J. Edgar Hoover and the Anti-Interventionists: FBI Political Surveillance and the Rise of the Domestic Security State, 1939–1945* (Columbus: Ohio State University Press, 2007), chapter 3.
48 On Hoover's efforts to alert the White House, see Memorandum for the Director, May 5, 1943, FBI File 100-16847-104; Hoover to White House, August 2, 1943, FBI File 100-16847-157.
49 See Bradley F. Smith, *Sharing Secrets with Stalin: How the Allies Traded Intelligence, 1941–1945* (Lawrence: University Press of Kansas, 1996), p. 186.
50 Chambers's allegations of Soviet espionage in the US State and Treasury departments, as well as other New Deal era agencies, first surfaced in a report he gave to A. A. Berle, head of State Department intelligence, in September 1939. See Sibley, *Red Spies in America*, p. 80.
51 David Holloway, *Stalin and the Bomb: The Soviet Union and Atomic Energy* (New Haven, CT: Yale University Press, 1994), p. 108.
52 "Intelligence Activities and the Rights of Americans," Book 2, Senate Select Committee to Study Government Operations with Respect to Intelligence Activities, 94th Congress, second session, April 14, 1976 (Washington,

DC: Government Printing Office, 1976), pp. 35-8; "Supplementary Detailed Staff Reports on Intelligence Activities and the Rights of Americans," Book 3, Senate Select Committee to Study Government Operations with Respect to Intelligence Activities, 94th Congress, second session (Washington, DC: Government Printing Office, 1976), p. 417. The NAACP investigation opened in 1941 after protests from African American mess attendants in the Navy. The Navy asked for the investigation which led to the FBI's spying on the NAACP to unearth its "connections with the Communist Party." The subsequent wartime investigation found "numerous contacts" between the NAACP and the CP, "but no evidence of CP control." See Rafalko, *A Counterintelligence Reader*, pp. 180-1.

53 Quoted in Sibley, *Red Spies in America*, p. 212.
54 Quoted in Richard M. Fried, *Nightmare in Red: The McCarthy Era in Perspective* (New York: Oxford University Press, 1991), p. 128.
55 Marisa Patulli Trythall, "The Little Known Side of Fr. Edmund Walsh: His Mission to Russia in the Service of the Holy See," *Studi sull'Oriente Cristiano* 14/1 (2010), 159-81, https://www.academia.edu/3274191/The_Little_Known_Side_of_Fr._Edmund_Walsh._His_Mission_to_Russia_in_the_Service_of_the_Holy_See (accessed March 28, 2020); Irmak Bademli, "Fr. Walsh Linked to McCarthyism," *The Hoya*, April 4, 2003, https://thehoya.com/fr-walsh-linked-to-mccarthyism/ (accessed March 28, 2020).
56 See, among other works on these spies, Eduard Mark, "Who Was 'Venona's' 'Ales'? Cryptanalysis and the Hiss Case," *Intelligence and National Security* 18 (Autumn 2003), pp. 45-72; John Earl Haynes and Harvey Klehr, *In Denial: Historians, Communism and Espionage* (San Francisco, CA: Encounter Books, 2003); Kathryn S. Olmsted, *Red Spy Queen: A Biography of Elizabeth Bentley* (Chapel Hill: University of North Carolina Press, 2002); Alexander Feklisov, *The Man Behind the Rosenbergs* (New York: Enigma Books, 2001); John Earl Haynes and Harvey Klehr, *Venona: Decoding Soviet Espionage in America* (New Haven, CT: Yale University Press, 1999); Allen Weinstein and Alexander Vassiliev, *The Haunted Wood: Soviet Espionage in America—the Stalin Era* (New York: Random House, 1999); Joseph Albright and Marcia Kunstel, *Bombshell: The Secret Story of America's Unknown Atomic Conspiracy* (New York: Times Books, 1997); Robert Louis Benson and Michael Warner (eds.), *Venona: Soviet Espionage and the American Response, 1939-1957* (Washington, DC: National Security Agency, 1996); Harvey Klehr, John Earl Haynes, and Fridrikh Igorevich Firsov, *The Secret World of American Communism* (New Haven, CT: Yale University Press, 1995. These assessments of espionage have not lacked detractors, including James M. Boughton and Roger J. Sandilands, "Politics and the Attack on FDR's Economists: From the Grand Alliance to the Cold War," *Intelligence and National Security* 18 (Autumn 2003), pp. 73-99; John Lowenthal, "Venona and Alger Hiss," *Intelligence and National Security*

15 (Autumn 2000), pp. 98–130; Ellen Schrecker and Maurice Isserman, "The Right's Cold War Revisionism: Current Espionage Fears Have Given New Life to Liberal Anti-Communism," *The Nation* (July 24/31, 2000), pp. 22–4; Walter Schneir and Miriam Schneir, "Cryptic Answers," *The Nation*, August 14–21, 1995, and Walter Schneir and Miriam Schneir, "Cables Coming in from the Cold," *The Nation*, July 5, 1999.

57 McCarthy quoted in David M. Oshinsky, *A Conspiracy So Immense: The World of Joe McCarthy* (New York: Simon and Schuster), p. 200.

58 Draft page, "Sixth Draft" of Eisenhower speech given on October 3, 1952 in Milwaukee, Wisconsin on "Communism and Freedom," in Stephen Benedict Papers, Box 4, October 3, 1952, Milwaukee, Wisconsin (1) (emphasis in original); NAID #16614761, Dwight D. Eisenhower Library, Abilene, Kansas. As the Library notes, "The deleted paragraph refers to accusations made by McCarthy against General George C. Marshall and was removed from the speech to avoid causing bad feelings in McCarthy's home state of Wisconsin." See https://www.eisenhowerlibrary.gov/research/online-documents/mccarthyism-red-scare (accessed March 28, 2020).

59 *The Washington Star*, "Hoover Urged Prison for Ethel Rosenberg," *New York Times*, November 16, 1975; also see Howard Blum, *In the Enemies' House: The Secret Saga of the FBI Agent and the Code Breaker Who Caught the Russian Spies* (New York: Harpers, 2018), p. 284.

60 See Eisenhower to Clyde Miller, June 10, 1953, https://www.eisenhowerlibrary.gov/sites/default/files/file/rosenbergs_Binder12.pdf (accessed March 28, 2020).

61 In Supreme Court of the United States, October Term, 1951, Transcript of Record, *Julius* Kaufman Statement in Doug Linder, "Trial of the Rosenbergs: An Account," 2011, http://law2.umkc.edu/faculty/projects/ftrials/rosenb/ROS_ACCT.HTM; Eisenhower quoted in "Enemies of Democracy," *The Guardian*, June 20, 1953. Also see Irving Saypol's testimony *Rosenberg and Ethel Rosenberg vs. The United States of America, Morton Sobell vs. The United States of America*, 1952, Volume 1, book 1, published by the Committee to Secure Justice for Morton Sobell, p. 183. Eisenhower is quoted in Dwight D. Eisenhower: "Statement by the President Declining to Intervene on Behalf of Julius and Ethel Rosenberg," June 19, 1953 in Gerhard Peters and John T. Woolley, *The American Presidency Project*, https://www.presidency.ucsb.edu/documents/statement-the-president-declining-intervene-behalf-julius-and-ethel-rosenberg.

62 Lori Clune, *Executing the Rosenbergs: Death and Diplomacy in a Cold War World* (New York: Oxford University Press, 2016), p. 166.

63 Jeffrey Engel, "Not Yet a Garrison State: Reconsidering Eisenhower's Military-Industrial Complex," *Enterprise and Society* 12 (March 2011), pp. 175–99; James

Ledbetter, *Unwarranted Influence: Dwight D. Eisenhower and the Military-Industrial Complex* (New Haven, CT: Yale University Press, 2011), p. 11.

64 Diary entry by James Hagerty, White House Press Secretary James C. Hagerty Papers, Box 1, June 8, 1954, NAID #16703041, Eisenhower Library, https://www.eisenhowerlibrary.gov/sites/default/files/research/online-documents/mccarthyism/1954-06-08-hagerty.pdf (accessed March 28, 2020).

65 Richard Hofstadter, *The Paranoid Style in American Politics and Other Essays* (New York: Vintage, [1954] 2008), p. 43; on McCarthyism's dangers, also see Landon R. Y. Storrs, *The Second Red Scare and the Unmaking of the New Deal Left* (Princeton: Princeton University Press, 2012).

66 An example of Philbrick's attacks is in "FBI Agent Says Student's Spouse Preached Communism," https://www.thecrimson.com/article/1949/4/13/fbi-agent-says-students-spouse-preached/ (accessed March 28, 2020); Veronica A. Wilson, "Anticommunism, Millenarianism and the Challenges of Cold War Patriarchy: The Many Lives of FBI Informant Herbert Philbrick," *American Communist History* 8 (June 2009), pp. 89–90. Russell Porter, "Red Trial Is Laid to Truman Order," *New York Times*, October 11, 1949.

67 Philbrick, *I Led Three Lives*, and Papers of Herbert Philbrick, Box 98, Library of Congress.

68 On King, see David Garrow, *The FBI and Martin Luther King, Jr.: From "Solo" to Memphis* (New York: Norton, 1981). This assessment is drawn from the files gathered by the Citizens Committee to Investigate the FBI in its 1971 break-in, contained in *WIN* Magazine's "The Complete Collection of the FBI Documents Ripped-Off from the FBI Office in Media, PA., March 8 1971" (March 1972), p. 38, https://www.swarthmore.edu/library/peace/DG051-099/DG077_WIN_magzine%20issues_pdfs/WIN_Magazine_V8_N4and5_19720301and15.pdf (accessed March 28, 2020); also see Women's International League for Peace and Freedom Investigation, "Communist Infiltration of the WILPF," October 20, 1968, Swarthmore College Peace Collection, WILPF Records, DG 043, SCPC, Part VII: US Section, Series I, Box 15.

69 "Complete Collection of the FBI," pp. 6–7.

70 "Alleged Assassination Plots Involving Foreign Leaders," An Interim Report of the Select Committee to Study Governmental Operations with Respect to Intelligence Activities, U.S. Senate, November 18, 1975, https://www.intelligence.senate.gov/sites/default/files/94465.pdf (accessed March 28, 1920).

71 John D. Fox, "The Hiss Hassle Revisited," *Princeton Alumni Weekly*, May 3, 1976; G. Edward White, *Alger Hiss's Looking-Glass Wars* (New York: Oxford University Press, 2004), pp. 123, 246.

72 Ronald Reagan, "Address to the National Association of Evangelicals," March 8, 1983, http://voicesofdemocracy.umd.edu/reagan-evil-empire-speech-text/ (accessed March 28, 2020).

73. Stephen G. Rabe, "The U.S. Intervention in Guatemala: The Documentary Record," *Diplomatic History* 28 (November 2004), pp. 785–90; Edward Brynn, "*The Foreign Relations of the United States* Series: An Orientation," September 29, 2011, https://history.state.gov/historicaldocuments/frus-history/research/brynn-on-frus-an-orientation (accessed March 28, 2020); https://history.state.gov/historicaldocuments/frus-history/research/to-the-1991-frus-statute (accessed March 28, 2020).
74. Quoted in Fried, *Nightmare in Red*, p. 19. Well into the 1990s, there was a striking neglect of the whole subject of Soviet espionage in surveys of US foreign relations. Robert Dallek's 670-page *Franklin Roosevelt and American Foreign Policy, 1932–1945* (New York: Oxford, 1995) manages to leave out the subject entirely, mentioning only German espionage; and a 1993 edition of Walter Lafeber's *America, Russia and the Cold War*, 7th ed. (New York: McGraw Hill, 1993) names Bentley only once and says nothing about her case.
75. Maurice Isserman, *Which Side Were You On: The American Communist Party in World War II* (Urbana-Champaign: University of Illinois Press, 1993), p. 141; Ellen Schrecker, *Many Are the Crimes: McCarthyism in America* (Princeton: Princeton University Press, 1999), p. 316.
76. Haynes and Klehr, *In Denial*, p. 81.
77. On these sources, see, for instance: "Index and Concordance to the Index and Concordance to Alexander Vassiliev's Notebooks and Soviet Cables Deciphered by the National Security Agency's Venona Project," November 1, 2014, https://www.wilsoncenter.org/sites/default/files/media/documents/article/Vassiliev-Notebooks-and-Venona-Index-Concordance_update-2014-11-01.pdf (accessed March 28, 2020).
78. See William B. McAllister et al., "Toward 'Thorough, Accurate, and Reliable': A History of the *Foreign Relations of the United States*," March 2015, https://history.state.gov/historicaldocuments/frus-history (accessed June 7, 2020).
79. Joseph R. Biden Jr. and Michael Carpenter, "How to Stand Up to the Kremlin," *Foreign Affairs*, January/February 2018, https://www.foreignaffairs.com/articles/russia-fsu/2017-12-05/how-stand-kremlin.

Bibliography

Burns, William J. "How the US-Russian Relationship Went Bad." *Atlantic*, March 8, 2019.
Holloway, David. *Stalin and the Bomb: The Soviet Union and Atomic Energy*. New Haven, CT: Yale University Press, 1994.
Jamieson, Kathleen Hall. *Cyberwar: How Russian Hackers and Trolls Helped Elect a President: What We Don't, Can't, and Do Know*. New York: Oxford University Press, 2018.

Olmsted, Kathryn. *Real Enemies: Conspiracy Theories and American Democracy, World War I to 9/11*. New York: Oxford University Press, 2011.

Sibley, Katherine A. S. *Red Spies in America: Stolen Secrets and the Dawn of the Cold War*. Lawrence: University Press of Kansas, 2004.

Siegel, Katherine A. S. *Loans and Legitimacy: The Evolution of Soviet-American Relations, 1919–1933*. Lexington: University Press of Kentucky, 1996.

Stent, Angela. *Putin's World: Russia against the West and with the Rest*. New York: Hatchette, 2019.

Wilson, Veronica A. "Anticommunism, Millenarianism and the Challenges of Cold War Patriarchy: The Many Lives of FBI Informant Herbert Philbrick." *American Communist History* 8 (June 2009): 89–90.

6

Friendship Reforged in Anticommunism: Herbert Solow, Whittaker Chambers, and the Juliet Stuart Poyntz Disappearance

Denise Lynn

By 1934, Herbert Solow was getting tired of his friend Whittaker Chambers's politics. Chambers was a committed communist and member of the Communist Party of the United States of America (CPUSA). Solow was an anti-Stalinist and vocal critic of the party and the Soviet Union. The two had regular arguments that eventually devolved into name-calling. Solow frequently called Chambers a Stalinist, an epithet party members disliked. It all came to a head in a hospital room in 1934. While visiting their mutual friend, Adelaide Walker, after the birth of her child, Solow and Chambers did what they always did, started discussing politics and exchanged "hot words." The argument intensified after they left the room to give the new mother some peace from their constant bickering, and became so heated that Solow called Chambers a "revolting cynic" and told him he wanted nothing to do with him. The old college friends parted ways and would not see each other again until 1938.[1]

When Solow and Chambers rekindled their friendship, Chambers was desperate to separate himself from the CPUSA because he feared for his life. Starting in 1936, the Moscow Show Trials put Bolshevik leaders on trial for so-called crimes against the revolution. Josef Stalin, the Soviet premier, used the trials to eradicate his political enemies and secure his position as unchallenged leader of the Soviet Union. The Great Purge, which occurred simultaneously with the show trials, impacted every level of Soviet society. Over seven hundred thousand people were liquidated and millions more were incarcerated in the Gulags. Less visibly, underground apparatchiks began to disappear, and some turned up dead. Although terrified, Chambers hesitated to act as he knew that leaving the underground could be as dangerous for him and his family as staying on.

Then in late 1937, a series of events brought the purges directly into Chambers's and Solow's lives. In early December, an American married couple went missing in Moscow. On December 2, Donald Robinson vanished after allegedly being taken to the hospital for pneumonia. His frantic wife Ruth was arrested on December 10. Mrs. Robinson reappeared a few days later in Lublanka Prison; Donald Robinson would never be seen again. On December 17, the disappearance of Juliet Stuart Poyntz, last seen in June 1937, was reported in the *New York World-Telegram*. It was Poyntz's disappearance that pushed Chambers to finally leave the underground and it was the combination of the Robinsons' and Poyntz's cases that would bring the two friends back together. Though Solow was only ever a background figure in American anticommunism, Whittaker Chambers would gain both fame and notoriety as an ex-Communist witness. Both were influential in framing anticommunist discourses and essential to that was Juliet Stuart Poyntz's disappearance. Solow's investigation into her disappearance and Chambers's knowledge of the underground revealed the terror people faced if they ran afoul of Stalin and confirmed for them that Stalin was merely a symptom and communism was the disease. For both men, her disappearance pushed them toward rejecting both the party and Marxism and embracing anticommunism. Their work in the Cold War, via newspaper articles, public testimony, and Chambers's book *Witness*, guaranteed that Poyntz's disappearance became a foundational story in American anticommunism.[2]

Juliet Stuart Poyntz was one of the original members of the CPUSA. She began her political career in suffrage after college and gradually moved toward socialism. For a time, she worked as the educational director of the International Ladies Garment Workers Union, but she was drawn further to the left after the Bolshevik Revolution and eventually joined the party. Her time in the party was not without controversy. When Soviet leader Vladimir Lenin's health was on the decline, a vicious competition emerged among leading Bolsheviks over leadership of the Soviet Union. Poyntz sided with Ludwig Lore, an American Communist who backed Leon Trotsky in the Bolshevik leadership conflict. When Trotsky was denounced and Josef Stalin eventually took power, those who backed Trotsky were forced to leave the party, including Poyntz's friend Lore. Poyntz recanted her former allegiances and returned to the party's good graces. She became a leader of its Women's Bureau and a CPUSA adjacent group, the International Labor Defense. In 1934, as fascism crept across the European

Continent, Poyntz agreed to work in the antifascist underground against German Nazism and Italian fascism. Friends alleged that she became disillusioned, however, after witnessing the interrogation of political enemies in Moscow. Sometime in early June 1937, Poyntz was seen leaving her boardinghouse in Manhattan, headed in the direction of Central Park two blocks away. She was never seen again. Her friends who knew about the disappearance and that she worked for the Soviets feared setting police on her, but when she failed to appear by December 1937, she was formally reported missing.

Chambers and Solow first met at Columbia College where they were "friendly" with one another and moved in the same circles that included other young radicals like Clifton Fadiman, Lionel Trilling, and Henry Rosenthal. After college, Solow estimated that the two only saw each other one time between 1924 and 1931. But around 1931, Solow was exploring communism, and it was his interest in that subject that brought them back together. Chambers claimed that it was Vladimir Lenin's text *The Soviets at Work* that inspired him originally to embrace communism and eventually join the party in 1925. Solow and Chambers would frequently get together to talk about politics in a "friendly manner."[3] Chambers became a member of the *New Masses* editorial board, a party magazine, and invited Solow to write some articles on student activism. Solow agreed but was not "wholly in agreement" with the party and asked to be published under the pseudonym Henry Storm. In the summer of 1932, Solow traveled to the Soviet Union and then to Turkey to visit the exiled Leon Trotsky. He claimed to be appalled at the conditions in the Soviet Union. After his meeting with Trotsky, he came back to the United States and began to steer American leftists away from the party and toward Trotskyism, though Solow himself remained independent of formal organizations. He continued his friendship and association with Communists like Chambers, and over the next few years the two became close political and social friends.[4]

Around this time, Chambers informed Solow that he was no longer a member of the CPUSA and was now in the Russian party. Solow also began to notice changes in his friend's behavior. On one occasion when the two were about to enter Chambers's apartment, Chambers asked Solow to enter first, he thought enemies might attack because he was doing counterespionage for the Soviets against the Japanese. Solow thought Chambers was being "rather silly."[5] Chambers's growing involvement with the party began to strain the friendship. Eventually, Solow became fed up with his "smug devotion to the Moscow regime" and by the fall of 1934, they saw less of each other. Solow was becoming "disgusted" with Stalinists and each time he met with Chambers, they would end up arguing about politics. By the time of the hospital visit to their friend Adelaide Walker, the two were ready to part ways. Communism drove them apart, but anticommunism would bring the friends back together.[6]

The intervening years between their split and reunification were definitive for the American Left. The rise of fascism in Europe and the party's antifascist commitments drew people into the party and party circles. The party especially appealed to women, immigrants, and black activists for its commitment to gender and race equality. Coupling the growth of fascism in Europe to the fear of racist violence and gender inequity in the United States, the party's message had a wide appeal. But there was also a growing number of those on the left that accused the party of blind obeisance to Soviet policy, which many linked to Stalin's dictatorial and increasingly paranoid rule.

The Great Purge and the Show Trials were an important turning point. As Stalin began to target political enemies and force them to confess to crimes against the state, the CPUSA began to lose its appeal. Judy Kutulas argues that instead of trying to rationalize the trials, the party attacked Stalin's favorite target, Leon Trotsky. The party's message became "managed confusion" which caused some liberals to distance themselves from the Left, and noncommunist leftists to attack the party. Kutulas emphasizes that it was this moment that split the Left and led to postwar anticommunism. Michael Kimmage agrees, arguing that there was continuity between the growing anti-Stalinist prewar Left and the postwar anticommunist right. One of the problems that anti-Stalinist leftists had was the CPUSA's rigidity. The party had an "innate disadvantage," and in its attempts to maintain discipline in "democratic, individualistic America" the and party pushed many radicals away from its ranks. These independent leftists were further disillusioned when the party failed to condemn the Show Trials, confirming their opposition to Stalin's rule.[7]

Anti-Stalinists, like Solow, sought independence from organizational discipline and saw their individuality as a "point of pride." This contributed to an intellectual fluidity that Kimmage argues gave the 1930s Left an "intellectual dynamism" and "self-confidence." Prewar conservatives were "confused and unpopular," but the Left was dynamic and intellectual. The anti-Stalinist education that many, like Solow, received in the 1930s was "invaluable" when the Cold War "transformed debates about theory into debates about policy." Solow and other anti-Stalinists were transformed into liberal anticommunists and "lent the fruits of their ideological training" to anticommunism. The left-wing conversions "strengthened the Right" and eventually led to the ascendancy of the Republican Party. While intellectual debates contributed to the defection of some leftists toward liberal anticommunism and conservatism, for Solow and Chambers the defection was deeply personal.[8]

The summer and fall of 1937 proved to be enormously consequential for both Solow and Chambers. Kimmage argues that Chambers's turn to the Right happened gradually around this time as he learned about individuals who were purged. By his own admission, he began his break from communism in 1937. Still in the underground, he was being ordered to Moscow, which many saw as a death sentence. Then he learned about the attempted defection and murder of Ignatz Reiss, a Soviet spy working in Paris, which moved him "deeply." But it was Poyntz's murder that "touched him closely" and sickened him in a "physical way." He decided to learn from Reiss's and Poyntz's mistakes and try to get himself and his family out of Soviet clutches.[9]

That fall, Solow learned through their old college friend Meyer Shapiro that Chambers was getting fed up with the party. Solow went to speak to Shapiro who offered up no additional information on Chambers and refused to even approach the topic. Then the Robinson case made headlines in December and shortly after that Poyntz's disappearance. By the end of December, authorities learned that Mr. and Mrs. Donald Robinson were Arnold and Ruth Rubens and both had suspected ties to the CPUSA; this linked the case to Poyntz's and some came to believe that there must have been a direct connection between them. Solow's friend Carlo Tresca became particularly animated in the press in accusing the CPUSA of killing an American woman and helping the Rubenses obtain false passports to travel to the Soviet Union. On Christmas Eve, the Federal Bureau of Investigation (FBI) received an anonymous tip that claimed that the three were dispatched by the "operations of the Russian Secret Service." The tipster also claimed that Arnold was linked to the Drama Travel Service, a party-linked organization that operated steamships. The tipster claimed that it was through this agency that Arnold obtained the false passports that he and his wife entered the USSR with and that the steamships could have been used to force Poyntz to Moscow. The CPUSA meanwhile disavowed Poyntz, claiming that she left the party in 1934. It also claimed that the Robinson-Rubenses were Trotskyite agents trying to spy on the Soviets.[10]

Solow suspected that the cases were linked and was collecting information on Poyntz's disappearance, working with Carlo Tresca and other contacts he still had in the party. He was having a harder time proving that Poyntz had any connection to the Robinson-Rubens, except that she was a known communist and had allegedly fallen afoul of Soviet authorities, according to Tresca who claimed that Poyntz had confessed as much to him. He was eager to get in touch with his old friend Chambers, but as it turned out, Chambers would be coming to him.

On a snowy night in early February 1938, after some of Solow's articles on the Robinson-Rubenses and Poyntz appeared in the *New York Sun*, and Carlo Tresca's accusations against the party were making headlines, two men appeared outside Solow's front door. Their faces were hidden behind collars and hats. Solow recognized them, despite the attempted concealment, as Chambers and Mike Intrator, a mutual friend who was forced out of the party in 1929. Solow refused to let the men come into his home, but he did agree to leave with them. Putting on his overcoat, he remembered a movie he had recently seen in which someone put a pipe in their pocket to mimic a gun. Solow grabbed his pipe, thrust it into his pocket, and walked out his front door with a "gun" pointed at the men. With it, he forced them down the street to a nearby restaurant. Once inside, Solow looked Chambers dead in the eye and asked, "Do you have anything to do with the liquidation of Poyntz?" Chambers said he did not, but also did not take issue with Solow describing her as liquidated. Solow thought this was "remarkable," and led him to believe he must have known something.[11]

Chambers claimed to know nothing about Poyntz's disappearance, though later in his memoirs, he would state that his handler, Boris Bykov, told him that Poyntz was "Gone with the Wind." He was concerned about her disappearance and even more so about Tresca and Solow's writings on the subject. Chambers knew that the New York City district attorney subpoenaed Carlo Tresca to appear before a Grand Jury investigating the Robinson-Rubenses' case. Tresca gave a press conference in which he claimed to have information about who kidnapped Poyntz and how the cases were linked, which led to the subpoena. Chambers wondered if Tresca intended to name him; he was worried about the attention because he intended to leave the party. Solow told him that Tresca was going to name everyone he believed was involved, though neither of them ever suspected Chambers and his name would not come up. In other accounts of this meeting, Solow stated that Chambers also wanted his help in securing contact to a high-level government official, preferably the president, so he could share information he had about the underground. After their meeting, the two would not see each other for several months.[12]

The two men revisited this moment several times in their writing and testimony, and though the details would vary, one thing that remained the same was the role Poyntz played in both their reunification and their move away from Marxism. Interestingly, both men used gendered language to describe this moment for themselves. They each described her as a victim of the Soviets, a construction of the pre–Cold War years. After the Cold War, female spies were coded as gender traitors and described as communist succubus. But before the Cold War, when Stalin was the enemy and not communism itself, it was still possible to forgive former communist spies. Forgotten in their accounts was that Poyntz, a leading party figure, and underground agent for several years, was part of the very communist apparatus that both would come to resist. She becomes in their view, a victim who was not responsible for her own actions.[13]

In Chambers's memoirs, he wrote that he knew of Poyntz as a party leader, but never knew that she was in the underground until her disappearance. He described her as an "intensely feminine woman," who was "heavy-set," and "dark," but also "softly feminine." This repetition of her femininity created a sympathetic image, though by all accounts, Poyntz was a forceful and sometimes abrasive personality. Chambers described her disillusionment as a physical affliction; she began to sag "self-consciously" from the weight of "secret authority and knowledge." He further suggested that it was Poyntz's inability to handle authority and knowledge, a specifically feminine affliction, that would lead to her liquidation. He also claimed that while he was leaving the party he could always see her in his "mind's eye." While Ignatz Reiss's murder bothered him, it was the disappearance of Poyntz that would affect Chambers both emotionally and physically. Solow used similarly gendered language when describing Poyntz. He repeatedly suggested that it was Poyntz's screams that influenced Chambers to finally leave the underground. And it was her screams that led Chambers back to Solow. Solow never described Poyntz as an active participant in the Soviet underground, rather that she was manipulated up to the last moments of her presumed death. Forgetting, like Chambers that she spent her entire adult life in radical politics, and was a highly intelligent and respected, sometimes feared, party member.[14]

These gender codes made her disappearance and arrest all the more troubling. That the party could so callously dispatch one of its valued leaders, a helpless woman, was a strong motivator for Chambers to make his break. After their first meeting, Solow claimed it was some months before Chambers was in touch again. Solow was writing about the Robinson case and Poyntz in the *New York Sun* and *New Leader* and decided that he would try to contact Chambers by writing under pseudonyms that might catch Chambers's attention. Publishing under both W. C. Hambers or Walter Hambers, Solow tried to reach out to Chambers and find out what he knew. In the interim period, law enforcement uncovered the Robinson-Rubenses' multiple passports and learned that both were linked to the party. In April 1938, Solow, writing as Walter Hambers, confirmed that Rubens was part of a crew that produced illegal passports and that Mrs. Rubens was a devoted Stalinist. The illegal passports did lead to a Grand Jury investigation and several indictments of the individuals involved. Solow was deep into an investigation of Poyntz's disappearance and the Robinson-Rubenses' arrests and doing his best to alert authorities to the party's likely role in both.[15]

That same month, Chambers made his final break by moving his family out of their current residence and moving into another. Chambers also stopped meeting with his handler Bykov. He wanted to speak to someone in authority and share whatever information he had about the underground, partly to locate enemies of the state, but primarily to protect himself and his family. Chambers, aware of Solow's articles on the spy cases, found Solow again in the hopes that he could connect Chambers to federal authorities. At this next meeting, Solow instructed him to make "a complete and detailed history" of his time in the party and then to let party leaders know of such a document so they knew that if he was killed the information would be leaked. Solow introduced Chambers to Carlo Tresca and later to Isaac Don Levine. He believed that either Tresca or Levine would have connections to officials that could get Chambers in touch with the authorities. It was to Levine that Chambers would relate much of his underground work, and Levine in turn would introduce Chambers to Assistant Secretary of State Adolf Berle. Chambers would provide Berle with information on a number of agents operating within the government, information that Berle would inexplicably sit on for five years.[16]

By this point, Solow had done a lot of legwork on the Poyntz case, and it was still unclear if there was any connection between her disappearance and the Robinson-Rubens case. Solow interviewed several of Poyntz's friends, particularly those that spoke to her in the days before her disappearance. Through these friends, he discovered some of what Poyntz had done in the underground.[17] Solow located a man named Mark Graubard, a former underground agent recruited by Poyntz. He learned that Poyntz's job in the underground was to recruit international students from Columbia College to return to their home countries and work as underground couriers. Graubard first met Poyntz in 1935 when she was using her married name, Juliet Glaser. In 1913, Poyntz married a German national named Frederick Franz Ludwig Glaser, which meant that she lost her American citizenship. Their relationship was rocky and the two only lived together for a short time. They finally broke off contact in 1924, though they never divorced and Poyntz was forced to apply for naturalization. By then she was deeply involved in communist politics and some suggest that she was being actively recruited for underground work. Poyntz used the sexist law that stripped American women of their citizenship if they married a foreign national, and applied for citizenship twice with two different spellings of her last name. No doubt this was intentional as Poyntz was always inconsistent with spellings of her name, which gave her several pseudonyms to work with in the underground.[18]

Graubard, a science postgraduate, was recruited to travel to Switzerland. He was instructed to find a job, and then contact some friends he had in Germany to try and convince them to become informants. Poyntz told him that she was in anti-Nazi opposition work and that his work would be to save Germany from Hitler's fascism. This was a shared commitment among American leftists who believed the Roosevelt administration was not doing enough to stop the spread of fascism. Graubard was a committed antifascist and therefore willing to become a Soviet spy. His contact, once in Europe, was a man named Phillips. Phillips intimidated Graubard, who later found out that he was a Russian general and a heavy drinker with a strong dislike for American Communists, including Poyntz. Phillips had a reputation for sexually assaulting the women Poyntz recruited, though Graubard was convinced Poyntz did not know.[19]

By February 1937 Graubard, living in Switzerland, was running out of money and had not heard from Poyntz or Phillips. He also began to hear news about the Soviet Show Trials and purges and worried that Poyntz might have been killed. Graubard decided to cut all ties with the underground and return to the United States. He was instructed first to travel to Paris, where he met a man named Danny who gave him some money and tried to convince him to stay. Danny was even more intimidating than Phillips and confirmed Graubard in his decision to leave. When he returned to New York, he avoided Poyntz, claiming he did not want to embarrass her, since he was her recruit. Some months later he read about her disappearance and when he asked fellow Communists what they knew, they claimed she was killed by Nazis. Solow asked Graubard to confirm this with his last remaining party contacts. When he confronted other party members, he was told that Poyntz was not dead and that she was doing "party work." Neither man believed that.[20]

Graubard gave Solow the name of a journalist, William Harlan Hale, who he tried to help Poyntz to recruit. Hale's family spent time in Germany and Hale himself praised the "quasi-Nazi writer" Oswald Spengler when he was younger, so he appeared to be a good candidate to send to Germany. But Hale was unimpressed by the recruitment attempts, because Poyntz could give him no real details about what he was expected to do. He did tell Solow that only days before Poyntz went missing, and months after she failed to recruit him, she contacted him and sounded rather nervous on the phone, insisting on a meeting. He reluctantly agreed to meet but never heard from her or saw her again and learned about her disappearance like others did, in the newspapers. Hale and Graubard both told Solow that Poyntz worked with an agent they knew as Lena or Miss West.[21]

Lena would be one of the more mysterious characters in the Poyntz disappearance, confirmed later by Chambers to be a dangerous and unpredictable underground agent, who did not get along with Poyntz and may in fact have been Poyntz's undoing. Her nationality was unconfirmed. Hale described her as a "beautiful blond" Russian; Graubard believed she was Slavic, and the FBI had an informant tell them she was a Polish dental student. She also went by several names including Tina, Mary Delmar, Rywka Brokowicz, and Ruth Brataslowsky. Lena lived in the American Women's Association Clubhouse where Poyntz lived; Solow speculated that this was so she could keep an eye on Poyntz. Lena had an unusual physical deformity that was used to identify her, a missing finger on one hand. Graubard met with Lena once, while living in Zurich in November 1936, after he decided to leave the underground. He described the meeting as "pointless," but she did inform him that Poyntz was in Moscow, which other eyewitnesses confirmed, and some came to believe that was when Poyntz had become disillusioned herself.[22]

Solow knew most of this information by the time he and Chambers reconnected, but he was still not clear on what, if any, connection there was between Poyntz and the Robinson-Rubenses, and what role the other cast of characters, including Phillips and Lena, had in Poyntz's disappearance. In the fall of 1938, he met with Chambers on three different occasions, and Chambers offered some new information that provided a tenuous link between the missing spies and confirmed that Poyntz was likely liquidated by the Soviets. Chambers told Solow that A. A. Rubens was in fact a Latvian named Ewald, later confirmed by Soviet spy and defector Walter Krivitsky, and that Rubens was an underground operative, whose job it was to produce fake passports. Danny, the man Graubard met in Paris, was seen days before Rubens left for the Soviet Union going to Rubens's place when he was specifically ordered not to. He may have been there to warn him, but later Danny went missing under similarly suspicious circumstances as Poyntz, suggesting that those working around Poyntz were also liquidated. Chambers also knew the woman Lena, known to him as Tina, who Poyntz worked with and believed it was the same woman introduced to William Harlan Hale as Miss West. He confirmed that Tina was dangerous and well-connected in the underground.[23]

Following Solow's advice, Chambers wrote a lengthy manuscript detailing the life and career of A. A. Rubens and suggesting how Rubens and Poyntz's underground work was connected and led to their liquidations. Solow refused to help Chambers find a publisher for it because, he claimed, there was no written evidence to substantiate Chambers's accusations, but he would use it as the basis for much of his investigation into Poyntz's disappearance and for several of his published articles. Chambers's manuscript, titled "The Faking of Americans," reflected the same gendered language he would use later in his book *Witness* to describe the women caught in the Soviets' clutches. Chambers referred to Ruth Rubens as an "American girl" or the "frightened girl," who had fallen prey to her husband's machinations. Solow was equally guilty. He referred to Ruth Rubens as a girl, an "American girl," and once a "Philadelphia and Long Island girl." Ruth Rubens was certainly not a girl; by the time of her arrest in Moscow she was 29 years old, the mother of a 7-year-old daughter, and on her second marriage. The press also described both women in sympathetic and vulnerable terms. Rubens was depicted as an attractive young woman who was used by her husband, while Poyntz was described as an elderly matron, who could not have known the danger she was in. In the pre–Cold War years, neither of these women were seen as gender traitors, or enemies trying to usurp appropriate gender or racial codes. They were unwitting victims, devoid of agency and culpability. This is a remarkably different gender representation of female spies than what evolved in the Cold War. At that time, female spies were seductive, untrustworthy, dangerous, and fully embedded in the Soviet conspiracy. In the prewar years, female spies could still be vulnerable and victimized by the Soviets, in other words, innocent.[24]

Chambers claimed that both A. A. Rubens and Poyntz were targeted for liquidation because they were linked to General Viovt Putna, a disgraced and disavowed Red Army general. He believed that both Rubens and Poyntz were associated with the general, and when Putna was executed, his associates became targets. Putna was a Soviet military attaché in London where Rubens was known to have traveled; Poyntz spent time there doing postgraduate work, and at least one person believed that Poyntz was Putna's lover. In August 1936, Putna was accused of plotting against Stalin and put on trial. At one time Putna participated in the Trotskyist Opposition against Stalin. Poyntz herself narrowly escaped expulsion in 1924, when she sided with Ludwig Lore against Stalin. This was one link between Putna and Poyntz, though not definitive.[25]

Putna's link to Rubens was equally as tenuous. Putna was a Latvian, like Rubens, and Chambers argued that Stalin wanted to loosen the grip the Latvians had in the Soviet Secret Police. Targeting a major Latvian figure and his allies was a natural means to discredit them and take control of the secret service.

Historian Robert Thurston has argued that Putna may have in fact been involved in an anti-Stalin plot, and this plot has been cited as the motivation for the Show Trials. Putna was tried, found guilty, and executed the same day as his sentence in June 1937, only a week after Poyntz went missing.[26]

Chambers suggested another link between Poyntz and Rubens, one that Solow and Carlo Tresca had hypothesized in their investigations of the disappearances—that there was a link between the Soviet and German military intelligence and that Poyntz was that link. An informant by the name of Turrou gave Solow a picture that allegedly depicted Poyntz and Phillips, along with notorious Soviet agent George Mink and a German agent named Griebl. Solow confirmed with Mark Graubard that Phillps was in the picture, and others identified Mink, but there was some doubt about whether Poytnz was the woman pictured because the woman in the picture was younger than Poyntz. Neither Graubard, nor Poyntz's old friend Ludwig Lore could identify her (Figure 6.1).[27]

In December 1938, Gunther Rumrich, a Nazi spy, helped American intelligence uncover a Nazi spy ring in the United States. Chambers and Solow believed that the Nazi spy ring was manufactured to draw attention away from the Robinson-Rubens and Poyntz cases. Chambers and Solow both thought that if American intelligence agencies did too much investigation into Poyntz's disappearance, they would uncover a link between the Soviet and German underground; thus the Nazi spy ring was a distraction. Both Chambers and Solow believed that the link between the two undergrounds was none other than Poyntz's estranged and now deceased husband Glaser. By the time of Poyntz's disappearance, Glaser had been dead for two years, but he worked in the German consulate in New York. Chambers and Solow contended that Glaser helped Poyntz link the two undergrounds and introduced her to Rubens, who would have gone to the German Consulate to secure passports. The photograph was proof of the link between the Soviets and the Nazis, and Chambers came to believe that Poyntz's liquidation was the "first step" in Stalin's regime of terror because she knew too much.[28] This is a remarkable claim; apparently, Chambers believed that Poyntz's disappearance was the beginning of the great purges. He also averred that the disappearance not only influenced his own defection, but that it was the beginning of the unraveling of communist influence on the American left and the growth of the anticommunism that would obsess the American government and public in the postwar years. The very terror that fed American anticommunism, according to Chambers, began with Poyntz.

But Chambers's and Solow's suspicion that the Nazi and Soviet undergrounds were linked was problematic from the beginning. First, the photograph was not

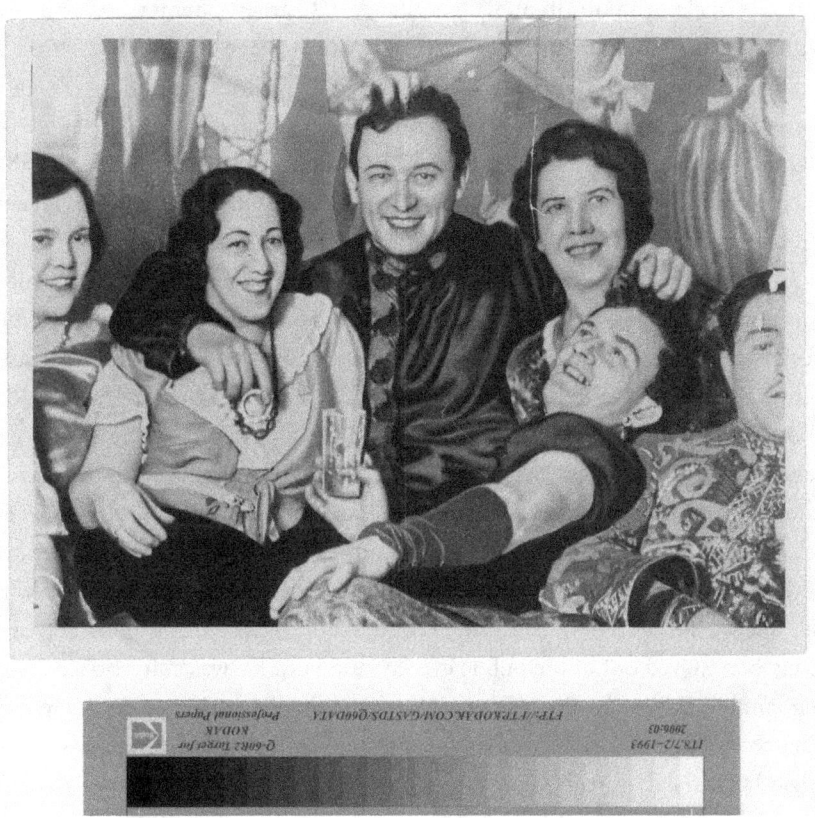

Figure 6.1 Photograph, allegedly of Juliet Stuart Poyntz with German and Soviet spies. Poyntz is sitting fourth from the left, George Mink is lying down. Credit: Photo in public domain.

definitive, partly because no one was certain it was Poyntz in the picture and others felt like it had been doctored. Second, the source of the photograph, Turrou, was a problematic character, who was once described by a State Department official as a "liar"; Solow claimed that he could never be a rebuttal witness because he would likely perjure himself. The largest problem with the theory is that Glaser would had to have been involved, but, by all accounts, Poyntz had no contact with Glaser after their split and neither Poyntz's friends nor Glaser's family and coworkers knew that the two had ever been married. Perhaps most importantly, while Glaser did work at the German Consulate, he was working as a freelance Associated Press reporter writing on the German steel industry for officials at the consulate, and thus not a consulate employee. Additionally, he was a known Socialist, raising the question why Nazi officials would trust him. Glaser's family was part of the IG Farben Chemical conglomerate and as his widow, Poyntz was able to claim a portion of his inheritance. IG Farben Chemical collaborated with the Nazi government and Glaser's socialism made him a black sheep in his family. Nevertheless, Poyntz tried to claim her widow's share. She was going through the legal process in the months before her disappearance and her lawyer claimed she was visibly uncomfortable in going to the consulate for fear that Nazi officials would identify her as a Soviet agent. Without tangible evidence, Chambers and Solow could not prove the Nazi-Soviet link.[29]

The more the two uncovered, the more they were convinced that communism was the real evil and that Stalin was corrupted by it. The evidence suggested to both men that Poyntz was murdered and that Stalin's purges reached American shores. In 1939, Ruth Rubens was released from Lublanka prison; she allegedly chose to stay in the Soviet Union and become a citizen and she would not return for her daughter. Her husband, A. A. Rubens or Ewald as Chambers knew him, was never heard from again, likely killed. The Soviets would not release any information about him to Ruth or the American press. Poyntz's whereabouts remained unknown when the United States became allies with her alleged murderers during the Second World War. During the war years, Chambers stayed out of the public eye intentionally. He was still worried about his family's safety. As postwar tensions between the superpowers increased, Chambers felt more comfortable going public with what he knew. It was the Alger Hiss trial that made Chambers a notorious public anti-Communist, while Solow remained in the background occasionally writing about anticommunism. Solow often defended Chambers against attacks that he fabricated his evidence, particularly in the Hiss case. He also, not very modestly, took credit for setting in motion the events that would lead to the Hiss conviction and for writing more on anticommunism, before it was fashionable, than others.[30]

Michael Kimmage argues that after the war, the prewar Left and conservatives both turned toward the political center. But anticommunism empowered the Right, granting it "intellectual respectability" and political influence. Meanwhile on the Left, advocating revolution became passé and moderation dominated liberalism.[31] While Solow retained a level of skepticism about the usefulness of anticommunism in defining American foreign and domestic policy, Whittaker Chambers became an outspoken conservative anticommunist and star witness in congressional hearings and trials. Through these years Poyntz remained a fixture for both men; Solow, in his dogged pursuit of the truth, and Chambers, in his testimony about the evils of communism.

In 1952, Chambers published his memoirs on his time in the underground. Titled *Witness*, the book described for its readers a godless, inhumane communism that left a body count to match the recent world war. Poyntz was at the center of the book; though only mentioned a handful of times, Chambers awarded Poyntz's disappearance pride of place in influencing his final defection from communism. It is here that he used his most gendered language to describe her as "intensely" and "softly" feminine. He also describes her as overwhelmed by the Soviet apparatus and fully incapable of making a break from it. In full masculine confidence, Chambers learned from her mistakes and planned a more intelligent exit from the underground, in which he was successful. Unusually, Chambers, who told Solow in 1938 that he did not know much about her disappearance, claimed that he was told she had been killed. Not only that she was dead, but Chambers intimated that Poyntz's alleged liquidation was used to scare other communists into following the party line. In 1952, he suggested that Poyntz's murder was an open secret used to extract loyalty, though years earlier he claimed to have little knowledge on the subject. This is not terribly remarkable considering that by the time his book was published, several other former Communists claimed that Poyntz had been murdered and that everyone in the party seemed to know. Chambers "revelations" about Poyntz in 1952 were no revelations at all, he was merely parroting what other former Communists said.[32]

Solow remained a reporter after the war and took a job at *Fortune* magazine in 1945. Despite his clear anticommunism, he never became as vehement as some of his conservative colleagues. During the war, his friend and confidante Carlo Tresca was gunned down in front of his newspaper offices. The murder was never officially solved, and Solow became a member of the Carlo Tresca Memorial Committee, a group that put pressure on law enforcement to solve the slaying. Unfortunately for the committee Tresca had a lot of enemies, including among them Communists. Solow and others on the committee believed that Communists were likely suspects because throughout 1938, Tresca was loudly accusing the party of participating in Poyntz's abduction and presumed murder. During the war years and beyond, Solow contacted law enforcement and elected officials in an attempt to resolve both mysteries. The Poyntz disappearance and Tresca murder became defining moments for Solow, forever linked because of the possibility of Communist involvement. Neither case was ever officially solved. Though the police had a suspect in Tresca's murder there was not enough evidence for conviction. Poyntz's whereabouts after June 1937 remain unknown, and with no body and no living witnesses, it is unlikely her case will ever be solved.

Solow and Chambers remained in correspondence for years and Solow continued to correspond with Chambers's widow Esther after he passed away in 1961 from a heart attack. Solow would not long outlive his friend, dying at 61 years of age in 1964. By the time both men died, many were questioning the legacy of the Cold War, and some were reflecting on Chambers's and Solow's roles within it. The Chambers-Solow friendship reveals two important things about the Cold War. First, that its roots lay deep within the American Left and not entirely within right-wing reactionism. Anticommunism has been an American fixture since the post–Civil War years, and progressives and leftists were important contributors to it. Centering this mystery in American Cold War history is a reminder that several leading anticommunist voices came out of the Marxist tradition, failed to find any middle ground, and moved to the political Right in what Gregory Taylor has described as a "Manichean perspective." By this, Taylor is describing a total political defection from one extreme to another. This political swing has had enormous political implications that have led to the rejection of the New Deal state and social justice initiatives, even to the present, for fear of some unseen communist menace.[33]

The second thing their friendship reveals is that Poyntz's disappearance and suspected murder was a framework for Cold War anticommunism and embedded within it is a gender script. Both Chambers and Solow spent years trying to unravel the mystery, and both went on the offensive against Communists after Poyntz was gone. They also deployed a gendered language that revealed the fear that communism sought to upend the heteronormative and white social order, fueling the hostility against calls for change. Though most Americans never knew her name, her abrupt disappearance and the alleged Soviet link influenced the American obsession with Communists during the Cold War and this was thanks in part to Solow's and Chamber's efforts. The anticommunist legacy is one that remains in American politics today as merely uttering Socialist or Communist against a political enemy can undermine their political efficacy. Poyntz's disappearance and the fear it stoked in her friends and contemporaries is foundational to American anticommunism and the political legacy it has left for contemporary politics; not likely the way that Poyntz, a social justice advocate her entire life, would have wanted to be remembered.

Notes

1 Herbert Solow, "Affidavit on Whittaker Chambers," 1938, p. 6, Herbert Solow Papers, Box 5, Folder "Whittaker Chambers," Hoover Institution Archives, Stanford University, Stanford, CA; Herbert Solow, "Untitled," 1938, pp. 1–5, Herbert

Solow Papers, Box 1, Folder 6, Hoover Institution Archives, Stanford University, Stanford, CA.
2 "Soviet Is Pressed to Find Robinsons," *New York Times*, December 11, 1937, p. 5; Arthur Irwin, "Woman Red Leader Vanishes Here: Had Lived in Fear Since Losing Sway in Party Councils," *New York World Telegram*, December 17, 1937, p. 1.
3 Whittaker Chambers, *Witness* (Washington, DC: Regnery Press, 1952), pp. 194–5; Solow, "Untitled," pp. 1–5.
4 Solow, "Untitled," pp. 1–5; Alan Wald, *The New York Intellectuals: The Rise and Decline of the Anti-Stalinist Left from the 1930s to the 1980s* (Chapel Hill: University of North Carolina Press, 1987), pp. 50–4.
5 Solow, "Untitled," p. 3.
6 Ibid., p. 6.
7 Judy Kutulas, *The Long War: The Intellectual People's Front and Anti-Stalinism, 1930–1940* (Durham: Duke University Press, 1995), pp. 14–17, 106–10, 112; Michael Kimmage, *The Conservative Turn: Lionel Trilling, Whittaker Chambers, and the Lessons of Anti-Communism* (Cambridge: Harvard University Press, 2009), p. 47.
8 Kimmage, *The Conservative Turn*, pp. 2–5; Terry Cooney, *The Rise of the New York Intellectuals: Partisan Review and Its Circle, 1934–1945* (Madison: University of Wisconsin Press, 1986), p. 112.
9 Kimmage, *The Conservative Turn*, pp. 88–9; Whittaker Chambers, *Witness* (Washington, DC: Regnery Press, 1980), pp. 36–7.
10 X to Mr. Edgar J. Hoover, December 24, 1937, and John Edgar Hoover to the Honorable, the Secretary of State, December 29, 1937, Record Group 59, Entry 205 C, National Archives and Records Administration, College Park, Maryland and "CP denies any knowledge of Juliet Poyntz," *Daily Worker*, December 18, 1937, p. 1; "Trotzkyite Tries to Shunt US Inquiry from 'Robinson' Trail," *Daily Worker*, February 18, 1937; "Soviet Press Points to Trotzkyite Link in Case of 'Robinson' Pair," *Daily Worker*, February 18, 1937, p. 1; Solow, "Untitled," pp. 6–7.
11 Solow, "Untitled," pp. 1, 4–5. Herbert Solow Papers, Box 5, Folder "Whittaker Chambers," Hoover Institution Archives, Stanford University, Stanford, CA. Solow wrote about this meeting in several places and in several ways, the above is the most dramatic by far. These accounts do raise a number of questions, Solow seems to remember that it was in early February when Chambers sought him out, but his articles with the names W. C. Hambers and Walter Hambers do not appear until later in the spring. It is likely that the period after Chambers made first contact was when Solow was trying to make contact with him again.
12 Chambers, *Witness*, p. 439.
13 Veronica Wilson, "Elizabeth Bentley and Cold War Representation: Some Masks Not Dropped," *Intelligence and National Security* 14, no. 2 (Summer 1999), pp. 49–69; Kathryn Olmstead, "Blond Queens, Red Spiders, and Neurotic Old

Maids: Gender and Espionage in the Early Cold War," *Intelligence and National Security* 19, no. 1 (Spring 2004), pp. 78–94.

14 Chambers, *Witness*, p. 36; Solow, "Untitled," p. 3.

15 Walter Hambers, "New Indictments Prove Rubens a Soviet Agent," *New Leader*, April 9, 1938, p. 1; Solow, "Untitled," p. 8.

16 "CONF WASH 37 BALT 3 FROM NEW YORK," 1952, Box 25, and Special Agent James R. Shinners, "Herbert Solow; Acquaintance of Whittaker Chambers," Box 56, Sam Tanenhaus Papers, Hoover Institution Archives, Stanford, CA; Chambers, *Witness*, pp. 463–9; John Earl Haynes and Harvey Klehr, *Venona: Decoding Soviet Espionage in America* (New Haven, CT: Yale University Press, 1999), pp. 89–90.

17 Sam Tanenhaus, *Whittaker Chambers: A Biography* (New York: Random House, 1997), p. 157.

18 Poyntz used several variations of her given name throughout her life. She was born Juliet Stewart Points, named after her maternal grandmother Juliet Stewart. She later changed the spelling of Stewart to Stuart, and even later Points to Poyntz. Her lawyer Elias Lieberman claimed she did it as a college student to sound more sophisticated, but it worked to her advantage as an older woman living in the underground. Elias Lieberman, "The Mysterious Disappearance of Juliet or a Lady Communist Vanishes (a True Story)," pp. 10–11, 26, Elias Lieberman Manuscript Collection, Kheel Center, Cornel University, Ithaca, New York, and "Juliet Stuert Glaser," vol. 628, p. 198, *New York, New York County Supreme Court Naturalization Petition Index, 1907–1924.*

19 Phillips would appear later in Elizabeth Bentley's account of her contact with Poyntz as the man who accompanied Poyntz while they tried to recruit Bentley and the same man that made Bentley feel uncomfortable. See: Elizabeth Bentley, *Out of Bondage: KGB Target: Washington, D.C.* (New York: Ivy Books, 1988). Herbert Solow, "Personal Memo – Graubard Interview," and Herbert Solow to Mark Graubard, November 10, 1939, Herbert Solow Papers, Box 10, Folder 8, Hoover Institution Archives, Stanford University, Stanford, CA.

20 Herbert Solow, "Personal Memo – Graubard Interview," and Mark Graubard to Herbert Solow, November 8, 1939, Herbert Solow Papers, Box 10, Folder 8, Hoover Institution Archives, Stanford University, Stanford, CA.

21 Carlo Tresca, "The Communazi Lady Vanishes," Herbert Solow, "Personal Memo – Graubard Interview," and "Memo – Worcester," Herbert Solow to Mark Graubard, November 10, 1939, Herbert Solow to William Harlan Hale (no date), and Mark Graubard to Herbert Solow, November 15, 1939, Herbert Solow Papers, Box 10, Folder 8, Hoover Institution Archives, Stanford University, Stanford, CA.

22 Herbert Solow, "Personal Memo – Graubard Interview," "Memo – Worcester," "Memo – Interview with Lore," and Mark Graubard to Herbert Solow, November

15, 1939, Herbert Solow Papers, Box 10, Folder 8, Hoover Institution Archives, Stanford University, Stanford, CA.
23 Herbert Solow, "Memo of Talk with Karl," Herbert Solow Papers, Box 10, Folder 8, Hoover Institution Archives, Stanford University, Stanford, CA.
24 Whittaker Chambers, "The Faking of Americans," p. 7, Herbert Solow Papers, Box 11, Folder "Spies-General," Hoover Institution Archives, Stanford University, Stanford, CA; Herbert Solow, "OGPU Plot Seen Involving US in Rubens case," *New York Sun*, February 8, 1938, pp. 1, 2; Chambers, "The Faking of Americans," p. 7; Certificate of Birth, Ruth Boerger, May 27, 1908, Commonwealth of Pennsylvania, Bureau of Vital Statistics.
25 Chambers, "The Faking of Americans," pp. 29, 35.
26 Robert W. Thurston, *Life and Terror in Stalin's Russia, 1937–1941* (New Haven, CT: Yale University Press, 1996), pp. 35, 50, 52, 57.
27 Hebert Solow, "Statement," and "Memo – Worchester," and "Interview – Hennessey," December 2, 1939, Herbert Solow Papers, Box 10, Folder 8, Hoover Institution Archives, Stanford University, Stanford, CA.
28 Chambers, "The Faking of Americans," pp. 31, 35; Herbert Solow to Professor Herbert L. Packer, July 11, 1962, Herbert Solow Papers, Box 5, Folder "Whittaker Chambers," Hoover Institution Archives, Stanford University, Stanford, CA.
29 Undated Memo, Herbert Solow Papers, Box 10, Folder 8, Hoover Institution Archives, Stanford University, Stanford, CA; Arnold B. Van Bergen, "Juliet Stuart Poyntz" file, 1 Federal Bureau of Investigation. Sam Tanenhaus Papers, Box 534, September 1944, Folder 1, Hoover Institution Archives, Stanford University, Stanford, CA.
30 Herbert Solow, "Untitled," Box 1, Herbert Solow Papers, Hoover Institution Archives, Stanford University, Stanford, CA.
31 Kimmage, *The Conservative Turn*, p. 3.
32 Chambers, *Witness*, pp. 36, 439.
33 Gregory S. Taylor, *The Life and Lies of Paul Crouch: Communist, Opportunist, Cold War Snitch* (Gainesville: University Press of Florida, 2014), pp. 1–7.

Bibliography

Cuordileone, K. A. *Manhood and American Political Culture in the Cold War.* New York: Routledge, 2005.
Fischer, Nick. *Spider Web: The Birth of American Anticommunism.* Urbana: University of Illinois Press, 2016.
Herzog, Jonathan P. *The Spiritual-Industrial Complex: America's Religious Battle against Communism in the Early Cold War.* New York: Oxford University Press, 2011.

Kimmage, Michael. *The Conservative Turn: Lionel Trilling, Whittaker Chambers, and the Lessons of Anti-Communism*. Cambridge: Harvard University Press, 2009.

Kutulas, Judy. *The Long War: The Intellectual People's Front and Anti-Stalinism, 1930–1940*. Durham: Duke University Press, 1995.

Lichtman, Robert. "Louis Budenz, the FBI, and the 'List of 400 Concealed Communists': an Extended Tale of McCarthy Era Informing." *American Communist History* 3, no. 1 (2004): 25–54.

Luff, Jennifer. *Commonsense Anticommunism: Labor and Civil Liberties between the World Wars*. Chapel Hill: University of North Carolina Press, 2012.

Olmstead, Kathryn. "Blond Queens, Red Spiders, and Neurotic Old Maids: Gender and Espionage in the Early Cold War." *Intelligence and National Security* 19, no. 1 (Spring 2004): 78–94.

Wald, Alan. *The New York Intellectuals: The Rise and Decline of the Anti-Stalinist Left from the 1930s to the 1980s*. Chapel Hill: University of North Carolina Press, 1987.

Wilson, Veronica. "Elizabeth Bentley and Cold War Representation: Some Masks Not Dropped." *Intelligence and National Security* 14, no. 2 (Summer 1999): 49–69.

7

Myth, Memory, and the Spanish Civil War: The World the Veterans Made

Vernon L. Pedersen

The Communist Party of the United States of America (CPUSA) never lacked critics. Congressional committees accused it of seeking to undermine American values and overthrow the government. Church leaders denounced it for promoting godlessness and immoral behavior. Labor leaders bitterly complained of its disruptive tactics and attempts to take control of major unions. Yet, even during the height of anticommunism in the McCarthy era, the party had its defenders who praised the organization for its dedication to social justice, its championing of civil rights and its resolute opposition to fascism. Nothing demonstrated the party's antifascism more than the Americans who volunteered to defend the Spanish Republic against the armies of Francisco Franco and the German and Italian interventionists. A contingent of 2,800 young Americans became the stuff of legend by traveling to Spain and fighting with the International Brigades.

The American volunteers created such an enduring legacy that the city of San Francisco erected an 80-foot-long, 40-foot-high monument to them on the Embarcadero. Dedicated on March 30, 2008, the monument was partially dismantled in 2018 because of its badly deteriorated condition. The reputation of the veterans themselves has suffered no similar collapse. Instead they continue to receive positive comments and praise whenever they are mentioned. This is particularly true in their obituaries, published with increasing frequency in the twenty-first century, as time has thinned their ranks. The obituaries of Charlie Kailin and Del Berg are typical. Kailin died in 2009 in Madison, Wisconsin, hailed as lifelong champion of social justice, who started his fight for progressivism on the battlefields of the Spanish Civil War. Kailin, according to his obituary in *The Nation*, said that he felt compelled to go, "if you were against totalitarianism, if you were against injustice, you had to care about what happened in Spain." The obituary praised Kailin for the work he had done over the years, first in the CPUSA and later as a Socialist to promote civil rights, organize labor unions, and integrate African American topics into the Wisconsin education system. His daughter recalled the difficulties his family faced from Federal Bureau of Investigation (FBI) inquiries and noted that J. Edgar Hoover himself had labeled her father a "premature anti-fascist."[1]

The Atlantic struck a similar note when it reported the death of Del Berg, who at the age of 100 was thought to be the last surviving American volunteer. A radical from an early age, thanks to growing up as the son of an impoverished tenant farmer in southern California, Berg volunteered for Spain after wandering into a branch of the Friends of the Abraham Lincoln Brigade in Hollywood and listening to their plea to go to Spain to oppose fascism. Berg claimed "political naiveté" about the conflict while in Spain, but apparently became very clear about politics on his return as he promptly joined the CPUSA, remaining an active member for the rest of his life. He devoted himself to antiracism, becoming the only white member of his chapter of the National Association for the Advancement of Colored People (NAACP). The FBI frequently questioned Berg's family members and the agency attempted to speak to him as well but never succeeded, because the agents were reluctant to enter the shabby majority black neighborhood where he lived in Modesto, California. David Graham, the author of Berg's obituary, lamented that with Berg's death it would become a little bit harder "to imagine the horror of the Spanish Civil War." Graham is correct in the sense that the loss of living participants in any historic event diminishes our ability to recapture its lived intensity. But, in another way Del Berg and his comrades spent their lives constructing such a powerful myth about their participation in the Spanish Civil War that it came to color both popular opinion as well as scholarly analysis. The real war with all its ambiguities, complexities and betrayals disappeared under the heroic narrative of the "Good Fight."[2]

The myth building started while the fighting in Spain was still on going on. An early initiative was to start calling the volunteers members of the Abraham Lincoln Brigade when the actual name of their unit was the Abraham Lincoln Battalion (popularly known as the Lincolns). The confusion of names may have begun as an honest mistake as the Lincoln Battalion was part of the XV International Brigade, one of seven brigades in the Republican army made up of foreign volunteers. But brigade also sounded better because it had the effect of making the contribution of the volunteers seem more significant. A brigade is a highly flexible military unit that can be easily divided or merged with other units to perform whatever task is required. Brigades range in size from 1,500 members to as many as 4,000 combatants, while battalions average only 500 soldiers each. The size of the Lincoln Battalion varied considerably. After the Battle of Teruel, which ended in February of 1938, it was down to 350 men, a number that included 125 replacements. In June the battalion was reinforced to 680, but only 150 of that number were Americans—the rest were Spanish conscripts. The name-change endured. Besides the memorial in San Francisco, there are three other monuments to the volunteers in the United States all dedicated to the Abraham Lincoln Brigade. Lost in the myth of the Lincoln Brigade is the George Washington Battalion. Created after the Battle of the Jarama Valley to accommodate the rising number of American volunteers, the Washington Battalion suffered so many causalities in the Battle of Brunete that it was merged with the Lincoln Battalion and its existence is largely forgotten.[3]

Another contribution to the myth came from no less a celebrity than Ernest Hemingway. Hemingway went to Spain to cover the civil war as a correspondent for the North American Newspaper Alliance (NANA), to revive his career and, to carry on a not very discreet affair with fellow journalist Martha Gelhorn. Hemingway was not a neutral observer, but a partisan for the Republican cause. Before leaving the United States, he joined with Archibald MacLeish, John Dos Passos, and Lillian Hellman to found the Contemporary Historians, an organization dedicated to making a film to educate the public about the Spanish crisis. Directed by Dutch documentarian Joris Ivens, and featuring voice-over commentary written and delivered by Hemingway, *The Spanish Earth* unabashedly praised the Republic, romanticized the Spanish people, and reduced the complexities of the war to a fight over land reforms. Hemingway summarized the theme of the film as the struggle of Spanish peasants to keep the right, gained "by democratic elections," to farm their own land in the face of opposition from "military cliques and absentee landlords." The film replaced the tragic complexities of the war in Spain with a heroic story of good versus evil. As a piece of cinematography it is regarded as one of Ivens's best and it generated considerable sympathy for the Republic. Franklin D. Roosevelt honored the film with a private screening in the White House, although it did nothing to alter his commitment to nonintervention.[4]

As *The Spanish Earth* made clear, an important aspect of the myth of the "Good Fight" is that it was not about communism. Robert Rosenstone, in his study of the make-up of the Lincoln Battalion, stated, "the activism [the American volunteers] showed in going to Spain did not spring from a desire to make the world safe for Joseph Stalin … but to defend what seemed to them to be the cause of western civilization itself." Rosenstone made his declaration in 1967, but the idea that communism was not a significant motivating factor goes back the early days of the Lincoln Battalion. CPUSA member Bill Baily, one of the first Americans to travel to Spain, wrote a letter to be given to his mother in the event of his death. Reproduced in his autobiography, *The Kid from Hoboken*, the letter states that he went to Spain because the poor citizens had elected a government that promised to improve their lives, but that a "group of bullies decided to crush and wipe out this wonderful thing the poor people had accomplished and drive them back to the old way of life." The letter elevates the defense of democracy over communist ideals and romanticizes the Spanish cause, while reducing the Spanish people to helpless victims in need of rescuing. Baily's letter masterfully, if sentimentally, captures the essence of the Communist position on the Spanish Civil War and demonstrates the degree to which Lincoln Battalion volunteers internalized it.[5]

The complete version of the myth of the "Good Fight" appeared in 1939, just as the Spanish Civil War ended in defeat for the Republic, with the publication of Alvah Bessie's *Men in Battle*, his fictionalized account of the eleven months he spent fighting in Spain. Bessie arrived in Spain in February 1938 and left in December after the Spanish Republic dissolved the International Brigades and sent the volunteers home. While in Spain , he kept a series of notebooks recording his experiences, which served as the basis for *Men in Battle*. They are very engaging, alternating between bare descriptions of events to detailed accounts of conversations among the volunteers. The novel expands dramatically on the source material. Bessie's first notebook describes his nocturnal march over the Pyrenees with a group of volunteers in two lines. *Men in Battle* gives the incident an entire chapter. The notebooks rarely mention names, but *Battle* is filled with them. The novel also adds lots of gritty detail to the sparer accounts of the notebooks. However, sometimes the notebooks are much better. In one entry Bessie describes "the edifying sight" of dung beetles rolling away pieces of the soldiers' feces commenting that in this way "we contribute (even on a hilltop in Spain) to the balance and economy of nature." He noted the size of the tiny balls of excrement and observed that the beetles without a ball of dung would try to steal one from other beetles. In the corresponding passage in *Battle* the incident loses its ironic and lighthearted quality, becoming instead a stilted metaphor of approaching death.[6]

Bessie also altered material from the notebooks for political purposes. Two examples stand out: one written to disconcert a critic; and the other to protect the CPUSA. In March 1938, Bessie and his group of trainees reinforced the

Lincoln-Washington Battalion (the term he uses in the notebooks) after it had been pulled from the front lines. Officers assigned the newcomers to Company Four, a machine gun company made up almost entirely of sailors. Bessie describes the battle-hardened men as "militant; hard as rock; … tough guys" who complained constantly, but seemed otherwise cheerful. They had lost all of their equipment in the retreat and spent their days remembering battles in Spain and union fights in the United States. In the novel, Bessie emphasizes the disillusionment of the mariners which gives one of his fellow replacements—a thinly disguised Irving Norman, who became an artist after returning from Spain—the chance to reprimand them for throwing away their weapons, calling it a cowardly act that would not advance the defeat of fascism. The sailors respond by cursing at Bessie and Norman and one of them, Joe Bianca, a legendary maritime organizer known as the best soldier in Spain, tells them to "move their ashes" meaning to get out. Bessie's notebook entry records no moralizing speech and does not identify Bianca. Peter Carroll, a prominent historian of the Lincoln Battalion, believes that Bessie added the passage as an insult to Norman who became disillusioned and critical of the International Brigades after his return from Spain.[7]

In his journal entry for June 6, 1938, Bessie described widespread dissatisfaction among the volunteers, who were badly demoralized and wanted to do nothing but go home. Even the party members were unhappy, directing much of their discontent at the CPUSA itself. Their resentments centered around three points. Point one was the refusal of the party to allow repatriation of long serving or physically unfit veterans. The Communists found this particularly galling, as the consensus among them was that the battalion had outlived any practical or even propaganda value. Point two was the mishandling of care packages from the United States and the fact that the funds collected by the Friends of the Abraham Lincoln Brigade to help "the American Boys in Spain" went to the entire Republican army and not just the American volunteers. Point three, the one that upset the Communists the most, was the constant misreporting of the conditions in Spain. The *New York Times* had truthfully reported that the battalion had been decimated in a series of engagements around Batea-Gandesa. Bessie estimated that only 120 Americans out of over 500 survived the battle. Joe North, who came to Spain as a reporter and stayed to fight with the Lincolns, countered with an article in the *Daily Worker*, the CPUSA newspaper, reporting that the battalion was intact, and morale was good. The Communists also deeply resented the fawning treatment given by the party press to "phonies," volunteers who had returned home and gone on speaking tours while everyone else remained on the front lines.[8]

All of this disappears in *Men in Battle*. Instead of a series of well-considered grievances Bessie's fictional account describes the battalion as suffering from the July heat, consumed by a sense of imagined injustice, and obsessed with the possibility of withdrawal. Long serving men received forty-eight-hour passes to Barcelona, but, the slow pace and seemingly arbitrary order in which they were given out only increased resentment. Tobacco was in constant short supply; the Spanish recruits were content to smoke dried Avellano leaves, but the Americans found them unpalatable. Rumors abounded that warehouses full of American cigarettes were being hoarded in Barcelona. The most serious problem was the constant talk of withdrawal which, in Bessie's words, "grew daily with an almost sinister insistence." Minor punishments for speaking out did nothing to control the situation so a battalion political meeting was called by John Gates, the XV Brigade Political Commissar. Gates, the future editor of the *Daily Worker*, gave a masterful speech, telling the men that they were critically needed by the Spanish government or they would have been sent home already. He dismissed rumors that the Non-Intervention Committee, an international group established to stop foreign involvement in the Spanish Civil War, was on the verge of success, stating instead that the Germans and Italians would never withdraw their armed units and condemning Britain as being a silent partner with the fascist powers. He sprinkled his speech with crudities, which Bessie reproduced as letters and dashes, and neatly sidestepped any attempts by the volunteers to bring up coherent grievances. The tactic worked. The men remembered that they "had come to Spain because they believed in Spain" and they still believed in the need to save it, and America, from fascism. Although criticizing Gates for his over-the-top delivery they realized, according to Bessie, that "had they deserted they would never have been able to look themselves in the face again."[9]

The passage is a brilliant morality tale of tough, exhausted men recovering their idealism, but has little resemblance to what actually happened. Gates did come to the battalion in late June to lay down the party line and speak harshly, probably with a lot of profanity, to the men demanding repatriation. His speech, however, did not revitalize morale. Bessie records in his journal that the talk settled nothing, because the men felt they had legitimate grievances and were being held in Spain against their will. Far from remembering their purpose Bessie speculates that, should the battalion return to the front, desertions would go up and there might be a rebellion. In the end he believed that most men would fight, but not with "the old-time zest." Instead, they would keep their heads down and avoid any risk.[10]

Bessie used *Men in Battle* to craft a narrative about the Lincolns and the cause they fought for, depicting them as idealistic and politically aware, alert to the menace of Nazi Germany before anyone else and determined to defend democracy. He effectively embeds his message in a gritty, realistic account of the impact of war on human beings. The book ends with "A Footnote," a political statement that makes it absolutely clear what it was about. He begins the section by declaring that the Spanish people, treated worse than American livestock, rose up against their oppressors and built a society modeled on American values, such as the separation of church and state, having access to public education, and democratic institutions. They were betrayed by the ruling classes of Great Britain, France, and the United States who overtly or covertly supported the ousted political classes and turned a blind eye to German and Italian intervention. Only the progressive, democratic, working class came to the aid of Spain by speaking out, fundraising and going to Spain to fight. Bessie admits that there were some communists in Spain, some in positions of command, and some of them the best men in the brigades. Yet they were only part of a much larger alliance of democratically minded progressives. No one, Bessie wrote, believed that the Republic could lose, but that was what happened. Fascism won. Spain was gone, Austria was gone, and Czechoslovakia was gone. But, Bessie insisted, all was not lost. France had been saved from fascism, and eventually the rest of the world would wake up. Bessie's timing was perfect. He dated "A Footnote," June 8, 1939; the Second World War began less than three months later.[11]

There is one more element to the myth, the concept of "premature antifascism." Bessie referenced the term in the preface to the 1954 edition of his book, declaring that the veterans were proud to wear the label. In the preface to the 1975 edition, he remarked that premature antifascists were honored in every country that had fought the Axis powers, except for the United States. The term supposedly originated with the FBI whose agents affixed it to the files they kept on the returning veterans. Widely seen as a code word for Communist, the term was used to keep Lincolns out of sensitive government jobs and, after the American entry into the Second World War, out of combat assignments and officers' training schools. Despite this, a number of Lincoln veterans, among them Milton Wolf, the last commander of the battalion, served in the army or with the Office of Strategic Services (OSS), the precursor of the Central Intelligence Agency (CIA). The Lincolns embraced the term as a point of pride. So did everyone else. Premature Antifascist and Abraham Lincoln Brigade T-shirts are easy to find for sale on the internet (Figure 7.1).[12]

Figure 7.1 Keeping the legend alive, Victoria DogTakingGun, the author's granddaughter, models a Tom Mooney Company sweatshirt. Note the use of the phase *Lincoln Battalion*, the correct unit designation. Photo by Katherine Pedersen.

However, the US Government did not invent the term. The veterans did. In the early 1990s scholars John Haynes and Harvey Klehr noticed, to their surprise, that none of the thousands of pages of FBI, OSS, and US Military documents they had examined made any mention of the term. Curious, they turned to the secondary literature and found that none of the numerous references to official uses of the term "premature anti-fascist" cited a government document, or any original document, as a source. Instead the monographs and essays invariably cited interviews, oral histories, or written sources composed decades after the end of the Second World War. The most promising lead was a 1942 letter from Milton Wolff. Supposedly, the letter described how he and fellow Lincoln, Gerald Cook, after volunteering for the army and not being deployed, broke into the company records office and discovered P.A. stamped on their files.

After considerable investigation, the letter turned out not to exist. Asked about the incident in 2000, Wolff recalled that only Cook had broken into the office, disavowing the original story altogether. However, the term can be found in dozens, if not hundreds of sources from the 1940s through the 1960s, as a self-reference by the Lincoln veterans. The term may have been invented as an ironic allusion to the fact that, after their return from Spain, Joseph Stalin signed a nonaggression pact with Adolph Hitler forcing them to abandon antifascism for two years until the German invasion of the Soviet Union. Some scholars suggest that rather than irony the term reflected their pride in being proven right all along after the United States declared war on Germany. But what the term really does, according to Harvey Klehr, is cover up the fact that they were treated with suspicion by the American government, not because of their opposition to Hitler, but, because of their membership in the CPUSA.[13]

Of course, according to the myth the volunteers were not communists. In 1967 Robert Rosenstone published "The Men of the Abraham Lincoln Battalion" in the *Journal of American History*. A distillation of his doctoral dissertation, the article analyzed data on 1,804 American volunteers that Rosenstone collected from a remarkable variety of sources to create a portrait of the "typical" volunteer. Rosenstone stated that part of the reason for his study was to demonstrate that communism was not an important motivating factor for the volunteers. Instead, Rosenstone posited they were inspired by a range of issues including the dire conditions of the Great Depression, the struggle to unionize, pacifism (an odd motive for someone volunteering to go to war), antifascism, and the ideals of the Popular Front which Rosenstone claimed were attuned "to the main themes of American society." Fifty years later Chris Brooks published "An Analysis of American and Canadian Volunteers Complied by the International Brigades in Spain," based on the Communist International's (Comintern's) own survey of 1,745 American volunteers in the summer of 1937. Rosenstone had claimed that the International Brigade recruiters did not record party affiliation, simply marking everyone as "anti-fascist." This was not true. As Brooks shows, the Comintern carefully recorded the political affiliation of all the volunteers noting that 72 percent of the Americans belonged to either the CPUSA or its affiliate, the Young Communist League, effectively demolishing the "communism was not important" aspect the myth.[14]

The Comintern also recorded the ethnicity of the volunteers, although the term "nationality" was used throughout the documents summarized by Brooks. Of the volunteers who were American citizens, twenty-three simply identified themselves as American, most likely indicating multigenerational presence in the United States. When the forty-one who self-identified as African American are added, the percentage of native stock volunteers rises to 25 percent. The other ethnic groups were Spanish, British, German, Greek, Finnish, and Cuban which made up another 23 percent of the total. The records of the International Brigades also list 235 Jews, all of whom were American citizens, as a distinct ethnic group making 13 percent of the total.[15]

Rosenstone was surprised to discover that mariners, who made up 20 percent of his sample, were the largest professional group among the volunteers followed by students at not quite 18 percent. He estimated that as many as six hundred sailors and one hundred longshoremen fought in Spain, making them far and away the largest single occupational group. Seafarers made up the largest occupational group in the Comintern survey as well, although the 139 sailors in their survey only made up 8 percent of the total. However, the Comintern survey lists 104 truck drivers, 6 percent of the total, as the second largest group. The forty-eight students surveyed make up only 3 percent of its sample. Rosenstone thought that the difficult and isolated lives led by mariners accounted for their overrepresentation. He is correct to ascribe the presence of a large number of sailors in Spain to their personal experiences, but mistaken in the attribution of experiences.[16]

A significant number of the seamen volunteers were former members of the Marine Workers Industrial Union (MWIU). Created by the Comintern to organize all waterfront workers, including seamen and longshoremen, the MWIU never attracted a mass following, but it did succeed in creating an energetic and tightly knit group of activists who cultivated a ferociously militant approach to organizing. MWIU cadres frequently participated in "special work" for the Comintern providing courier services, smuggling literature and recording the movement of munitions around the world's waterfronts. After 1933 such work increasingly targeted Nazi Germany putting the MWIU on the front lines of the Soviet opposition to fascism. In late 1934, in anticipation of the Popular Front, the Comintern ordered the liquidation of the MWIU, sending its members into the rival International Seamen's Union. The change from the rough and tumble dynamism of the of the early 1930s, when all organizations even slightly to the right of the CPUSA were derided as "social-fascists," to the coalition building, low-profile work of the Popular Front was too much of a shift for many of the waterfront radicals. When the Spanish Civil War began, they leaped at the chance to directly, and violently, confront their old enemies. Ironically the mariners supported the greatest project of the Popular Front out of dissatisfaction with the Popular Front.[17]

It is impressive how long the myth of the "Good Fight" has lasted. Eunice Lipton repeats it in her 2016 book, *A Distant Heartbeat: A War, a Disappearance, and a*

Family's Secrets, recounting her investigation into her Uncle David's death in Spain. In the introduction, she asks herself what drove her uncle and the thousands of others like him to travel to a "seething war-torn country." She answers that they sought to turn political outrage into concrete action to save Spain from the nightmare of fascism and to stop Adolf Hitler. Alvah Bessie couldn't have said it better. Accounts by or about individual veterans are one reason for the myth's persistence, but a more important reason was its careful promotion by an organized group, the Veterans of the Abraham Lincoln Brigade (VALB). Returning American veterans have always felt the need to join together for comradery and mutual support, beginning with the Society of the Cincinnati, founded after the American Revolution; the Grand Army of the Republic (GAR) created in 1866 similarly served members of the Union armies, and the Veterans of Foreign Wars (VFW) was organized by soldiers returning from the Spanish-American War. The Americans returning from Spain were no different and on January 10, 1940, they created the VALB open to anyone who had served in the Abraham Lincoln, George Washington, and Mackenzie-Papeneau battalions or with the North American sponsored medical services and, to prevent deserters from joining, had returned from Spain with the permission of the International Brigades. In addition to the usual mission of providing assistance to returning veterans in need of medical care or help in reintegrating into civilian life, the organization also declared its dedication to fostering and protecting "the principles of justice, liberty and democracy" and "to render voluntary aid and assistance to victims of oppression and injustice."[18]

What this pledge meant in practice was support for the foreign policy agenda of the Soviet Union, more or less what the volunteers had been doing in Spain in the first place. During the era of the Non-Aggression Pact VALB members protested against American intervention in the war, declaring "the Yanks aren't coming." When Germany invaded the Soviet Union, they did a precise about-face demanding that America intervene to "Smash Hitler." Milton Wolff, the president of VALB, cooperated with British intelligence to recruit former Lincolns for special operations behind German lines in the Balkans. After the end of the war, VALB members demonstrated against the Marshall Plan, which the Soviet Union opposed, and loudly protested American involvement in the Korean War. Despite the advancing age of its members, VALB was also prominent in protests against the war in Vietnam. In the 1980s a geriatric Wolff spearheaded a largely symbolic program to send tanks to Nicaragua, when Ronald Reagan sought the overthrow of President Daniel Ortega. The orientation of VALB was plain to see inspiring the Subversive Activities Control Board (SACB) to declare, in 1964 that VALB was a CPUSA controlled Front group.[19]

Besides crafting a narrative, the veterans actively attacked anyone who dared to differ with their version of the events in Spain, starting with one of their greatest supporters, Ernest Hemingway. Hemingway frequently encountered members of the Lincoln Battalion while in Spain; both Alvah Bessie and Harry Fisher mention him in their memoirs writing with a mixture of awe and skepticism. Awe because of Hemingway's towering reputation and skepticism because no matter how bluff and hearty Hemingway pretended to be, he was still a tourist while they lived in the war. That said, no one could doubt Hemingway's devotion to the Republican cause. When his longtime friend and companion in Spain, Jon Dos Passos, began trying to find out what happened to the writer Jose Roubles, who had been executed by the Spanish government, Hemingway demanded that he stop embarrassing the Republic and, when Dos Passos continued his quest, publicly ended their friendship. Along with his dispatches for NANA, Hemingway wrote a number of short stories based on his experiences in Spain. There is very little to distinguish between the stories and the dispatches, both are in Hemingway's distinctive style and conform closely to his personal experiences, so closely that a number of the stories take place in bars in Madrid, not on the front lines. Typical of Hemingway, the stories focus on the experiences of the characters and the essence of the moment with minimal political context. The same cannot be said of his signature work, *For Whom the Bell Tolls*.[20]

After the defeat of the Spanish Republic, which greatly embittered Hemingway, he remained close to the surviving Lincolns, paying the medical bills for one and helping Alvah Bessie publish *Men in Battle*. He provided review copy for the novel as well, calling it "a true, honest and fine book." In 1940 Hemingway published *For Whom the Bell Tolls*, which sharply criticized the Communist leadership of the Republic and heaped particular scorn on Andre Marty, the leader of the International Brigades, and Doelores Ibarruri (*La Pasionaria*), the public face of the Spanish Communist Party. Worse, Hemingway gruesomely depicted an atrocity committed by Republican loyalists, closely modeled on a real mass killing in the city of Ronda, but did not include similar outrages by the Nationalists. VALB issued a public statement declaring that Hemingway's novel so distorted the events it described that it amounted to "slander" of the cause that he and they had fought for in Spain. Hemingway, never one to take criticism well, called Milton Wolff a "prick" several times in a private letter defending himself.[21]

Hemingway was not the only person to be targeted by the veterans for deviating from the myth of the "Good Fight." A number of Lincolns found themselves denounced and shunned by their former comrades. Two such individuals were William C. McCuistion and William Herrick. McCuistion appears in Harry Fisher's *Comrades: Tales of a Brigadista in the Spanish Civil War* (1997), as a deserter and a coward. Although well regarded as a waterfront organizer and, for a time, considered as a possible future commander of the Lincoln Battalion, McCuistion wilted under fire and, according to Fisher, deserted during the Battle of Brunette. Born in Paris, Texas, McCuistion served in the army during the First World War, where he developed a strong dislike of authority. He joined the CPUSA in the 1920s, became a founding member of the MWIU and was prominent in the organizing of the party-dominated National Maritime Union. Although sincere in his devotion to Marxism, McCuistion had a rocky relationship with the party and was expelled at least twice for drinking and discipline problems. He went to Spain to make up his mind once and for all by seeing the party in action against its mortal enemy, fascism. Instead of affirming his beliefs, Spain horrified McCuistion (Figure 7.2). He witnessed summary executions of deserters and was appalled at the harsh discipline and poor leadership. After his return to the United States he started

Figure 7.2 William McCuistion with his mother Dollie Crawford after testifying about his experiences in Spain before the Dies Committee. Washington, DC, October 31, 1939. Credit: Library of Congress, Washington, DC.

an anticommunist faction in his union and served as a friendly witness for the House Committee on Un-American Activities (HUAC). Milton Wolff, called to testify (as an unfriendly witness) at the same 1939 HUAC hearing as McCuistion confronted the burly seaman outside the hearing room, shoved him and called him a "yellow bastard."[22]

William Herrick, the son of Belarusian immigrants, came by his radicalism in the nursery peering at portraits of Lenin and Trotsky from his bed. When he was older both were replaced by a portrait of Joseph Stalin. Herrick joined the CPUSA in the 1930s becoming an itinerant organizer wandering from Michigan to Georgia where he organized sharecroppers and, on one occasion, narrowly escaped a lynching party of white planters. Unlike McCuistion, Herrick was not a heavy drinker and did not have problems with authority. Yet, he had the same reaction to fighting in Spain as McCuistion, shock and horror at the suppression of dissent, in particular that of his friend Marvin Stern. Stern publicly announced he was keeping a journal of complaints that he planned to show to Earl Browder, the leader of the CPUSA, when he returned to the United States. Stern disappeared shortly afterwards and inquiries about him were firmly discouraged. Herrick believed he died in a penal battalion at the front. Herrick's greatest sin in the eyes of VALB was to besmirch the legend of Oliver Law. For four days, until he was killed in battle, Law was the commander of the Lincoln Battalion making him the first black American to command white troops. The CPUSA held Law up as a hero and example of the race-blind nature of communism. Herrick countered that Law was an incompetent officer promoted as a propaganda ploy, and suggested that he had been shot in the back by the Lincolns after leading them into one too many ambushes. The claim put Herrick permanently on VALB's blacklist and later inspired a lengthy essay by Grover Furr (2008), who investigated and discredited Herrick's sources for the story. Peter Carroll, Chair Emeritus of the Abraham Lincoln Brigade Archives, dismisses Herrick as so blinded by anger that he willingly mixed fact with fiction.[23]

Although the jury is still out on the case of Oliver Law, other elements of the myth of the "Good Fight" have been roundly refuted by the records of the International Brigades themselves. In 1991, the Soviet Union collapsed and once-secret archives were made available for study by scholars. The Soviet records of the Spanish Civil War were no exception. Ron Radosh published an annotated collection of hundreds of documents from the files in Moscow entitled *Spain Betrayed: The Soviet Union in the Spanish Civil War*. Published by Yale University Press as part of its Annals of Communism series, the records conclusively demonstrate that the International Brigades were created by the Comintern, organized by national level Communist parties and filled with party members. Far from being seen by the Spanish as the saviors of the Spanish Republic, many Republican military officers considered the volunteers to be little more than paid mercenaries. As a consequence, they received second-rate equipment and were often used as shock troops, which explains the 53 percent casualty rate among the Lincoln Battalion members. Far from a clear-cut crusade against fascism, Radosh produces documents demonstrating that the Soviets put almost as much effort into countering their perceived enemies on the Left as they did Franco's armies. It is also hard to reconcile political idealism and antifascism with the plundering of the Spanish gold reserves under the pretense of paying for Soviet defense of the republic.[24]

The myth survived the opening of the Moscow archives. In 1994 Peter Carroll published his definitive work the *Odyssey of the Abraham Lincoln Brigade: Americans in the Spanish Civil War*. Carroll spent much of his career interviewing veterans and collecting the oral histories and written accounts they left behind along with material from the *Daily Worker*, the *Volunteer for Liberty*, the veterans' publication, and a host of private collections. Just before completing *Odyssey* Carroll traveled to the Russian Federation to view the newly opened files of the Comintern at the Russian State Archive for Social and Political History (RGASPI). In *A Note on Sources* he praises the material at RGASPI calling it "a goldmine of previously unused source material about the International Brigades." However, Carroll made relatively little use of this goldmine. In 380 pages of text he only cites fourteen files from the Russian archives. Most of the material simply adds detail or color to well-known incidents. The best of these is a lengthy quote from the official statement of Paul White who was shot as a deserter. Another interesting document highlights the tension between Robert Minor, the American representative to the Comintern in Spain, and Andre Marty, overall commander of the International Brigades. Mildred Rackley, a doctor and CPUSA member, reported that a noncommunist physician "ought not to be trusted." Minor called Dr. Rackley and one of her colleagues on the carpet for not carrying out the United Front policy which advocated cooperation with non-party elements. Carroll believes the incident demonstrated American independence, but the fact that Marty condemned Minor's behavior in a letter to Earl Browder could just as easily be used as proof of Soviet control. Carroll also makes a reference to Soviet sources when discussing the average age of the Lincoln volunteers. Although the *Daily Worker* called the volunteers "boys" and remarked that they were younger than the volunteers from other countries, many of whom had seen service in the First World War, analysis of Comintern records indicated that the median age was 27.[25]

In Carroll's defense, he was seeking material to supplement a manuscript, that was already largely completed before he went to Russia. The same cannot be said of Adam Hochschild's *Spain in Our Hearts: Americans in the Spanish Civil War, 1936–1939*, which came out in 2016, after the new archival material had been widely available for more than two decades. Although Radish's *Spain Betrayed* is listed in the bibliography, Hochschild does not reference it, and in a 372-page book he refers to the RGASPI files only six times. Instead, Hochschild, like Carroll, relies heavily on memories from the volunteers, in particular, Alvah Bessie and Harry Fisher. To his credit, Hochschild takes a realistic view of the Spanish conflict, presenting the bloody reality and condemning the brutality of both sides. He concedes that, instead of being apolitical idealists, the Americans who took part in the civil war were overwhelmingly members of the CPUSA or close fellow travelers. Yet he denies that being communists made the Americans either cynics or unwitting dupes of the Soviet Union. Hochschild is right. The volunteers were not unwitting; quite the contrary, as communists they largely supported the Soviet Union. So does Hochschild, he too finds reasons to defend Soviet actions, such as their suppression of the Anarchist regime in Catalonia, arguing, correctly, that the social revolution undertaken by the anarchists was unsustainable and a threat to the survival of the Republic.[26]

It is time to retire the myth of the Good Fight, put communism back in the center of the story, critically examine veterans' accounts and acknowledge that the Lincolns fought to advance the interests of one authoritarian regime against the interests of another. Such an approach allows us to sort out the problems of rose-colored memories and construct much more nuanced narratives. An incident from Bill Baily's autobiography illustrates the first point while the legend of Joe Bianca, the best soldier in Spain, is an example of the second.

Baily was one of the first Americans to volunteer to go to Spain, motivated by a strong sense of antifascism gained by personal experience. In a famous incident in July 1935, Baily ripped the swastika banner from the ocean liner *Bremen* in a protest over the arrest by German authorities of fellow sailor Lawrence Simpson. The stunt earned Baily a beating from the crew of the *Bremen* and a night in jail from the New York police. Baily describes both the *Bremen* incident and his decision to go to Spain in his memoir *The Kid from Hoboken*. He devotes several pages to the amateur subterfuges his group of twenty-five volunteers went through to avoid detection by American and French authorities. These included posing as tourists and pretending they did not know each other on shipboard, a pretense undermined by the fact they all carried identical cardboard luggage given to them by the CPUSA. Baily does not write much about his experiences in Spain, jumping from the letter he wrote to his mother while in transit to his return to San Francisco. However, in the midst of a paragraph describing a woman he met on the bus ride home, he switches to an account of his fellow volunteer, Stanley Postek, one of the last Americans to arrive in Spain and one of the last to leave. Left behind in a hospital after the disbanding of the International Brigades, Postek had to flee across the Pyrenees with a horde of refugees after the Nationalist victory.[27]

Baily depicts Postek as a hard-luck case, a young kid who joined the Communist-led MWIU in its early days, showed promise as an amateur boxer, and came to Spain out of personal loyalty to his friends who had already volunteered. According to Baily, Postek appeared with a group of reinforcements clinging to the side of a food truck on a hot day just before the Lincolns went into action in the Ebro campaign. Baily recalled that Postek was sent to the rear for medical treatment in the midst of the campaign. He was returning to the battalion on top of Hill 666, once again balancing on the running board of a food truck, when a shell bounced off the mountain, blew up the truck and sent the hapless recruit back to the hospital. Word reached Baily in California that Postek had survived the war and was interned in France. Baily signed on board the *USS President Monroe* bound for the port of Marseilles intending to break Postek out of the camp and smuggle him on board. Upon arrival in France, he learned that Postek had already left the camp and made his way to Le Havre.[28]

Baily's account is stirring, romantic, and filled with errors. Although Baily notes that Postek was an organizer for the MWIU, he does not mention that he and Postek were also dedicated Communists who met for the first time in a party school in Peekskill, New York. Nor did Postek catch up with the Lincolns by riding in on a supply truck. Postek, who kept a diary of his time in Spain, arrived in June 1938, injured his back in basic training and did not reach the Albacete base camp until early July, where he found himself assigned to the Mackenzie-Papeneau Battalion. By good luck he bumped into Baily while wandering about the encampment. Baily arranged for Postek to be transferred to the Tom Mooney Company in the Lincoln Battalion where he was reunited with his fellow mariners. Postek's June stay in the hospital appears to be the source of Baily's mistaken memory that Postek was returning from medical leave when he was blown up. Postek records that he was with the Lincoln Battalion from the crossing of the Ebro to the retreat from Gandesa. He had gone to the base of Hill 666 to unload a food truck when the vehicle was struck by an artillery shell peppering Postek with shrapnel. Postek only spent a week in a French detention camp before escaping by hiding in the trunk of a car owned by a *Herald Tribune* reporter, hardly time enough for Baily to hear anything, let alone mount a rescue attempt. Baily is not deliberately lying; memories become confused over time and separate events become conflated, but he is guilty of romanticizing his memories to conform to the way he chose to frame his experiences after returning from Spain.[29]

Joe Bianca, the sailor who, according to Bessie, rebuffed Irving Norman, is universally regarded as one of the martyrs of Lincoln Battalion, but there is much more to his story. Bianca arrived in Spain in June 1937, unhappy with the tactics of the Popular Front and struggling with a collection of personal demons, not the least of which was a carefully closeted homosexuality. Bianca was in his midthirties when he joined the Lincolns; he had been a member of the Industrial Workers of the World (IWW) before joining the CPUSA and had a scar along his left cheek that gave him the nickname "the Corsican Cutthroat." He was an effective MWIU organizer, possessed of a deep bass voice and muscular presence that easily dominated a street crowd. Bianca inspired tremendous loyalty in those who knew him. Stanley Postek met him after running away from home, at age 19, and bumming his way to New Orleans, where he intended to become a sailor like his heroes in the Joseph Conrad novels that he read growing up. Postek discovered that it was impossible to get on a ship without seaman's papers and spent several months living in railroad cars and committing petty crimes to keep from starving. Bianca approached him as he sat disconsolately on a bench in Jackson Square, engaged him in conversation, and then took Postek to the MWIU hall for a hot meal and a set of forged seaman's papers.

Postek joined the MWIU and the CPUSA becoming one of Bianca's most loyal supporters calling Bianca and Bianca's close friend, Al Kaufman, his "political godfathers." Close friend might be an understatement. It is highly likely that Kaufman, who also went by the fanciful alias "Oscar K. Everett," and Bianca were homosexual partners. Postek, like most members of the MWIU, chose to pretend otherwise thinking of the two men as "inseparable pals." Postek got into a bar fight in San Pedro with three men who chose a less complimentary term. The widespread acceptance of Bianca and Kaufman's relationship, under the pretense that they were just "pals," is testimony to the careful, and exhausting, balancing act both men performed, and to the value that their comrades placed on their friendship.[30]

Bianca also had a dark side; unlike many other sailors, he drank moderately, but when he did indulge, he became violent. Al Richmond, who got to know

Bianca well when Richmond was assigned as the youth organizer to the MWIU, remembered a night out with Bianca and McCuistion in 1934. The three men attended a party function in Greenwich Village fueled with copious amounts of gin which inspired Bianca's favorite party trick, running a needle through his cheek without flinching, thanks to the loss of feeling in the knife scar. The trio next visited a nearby tavern and nearly got in a brawl over some change Bianca stole off the bar top. The fight was averted by McCuistion's girlfriend. Bianca disliked the young woman intensely for unknown reasons. He terrified the much younger Richmond as they wandered through the Village by playing with a long knife and declaring that he was going to cut her up. Richmond took him seriously, but fortunately McCuistion's companion left the group to return home, leaving the three men on the street trying to decide what to do. Bianca turned abruptly and smashed a restaurant's plate glass window with his bare hand without cutting himself, a trick Richmond hoped he had learned from the cafeteria workers' union, but probably picked up from a sideline as a burglar. Breaking and entering was not Bianca's only crime. At least one offense on his record was so serious that he was refused entry into the International Lenin School in Moscow.[31]

Bianca thrived in combat accustomed to discomfort, comfortable in all-male company and able to channel his darkest impulses into socially sanctioned violence. In other words, he felt free to be himself. The other soldiers admired him as fearless and seemingly indestructible. He treated his comrades kindly, helping them to adapt to the rigors of military life and teaching them little tricks to survive in camp or on the march. He never questioned orders or failed to obey them, but he had a sailor's contempt for the officer class and happily griped about poor food and wet bedding. He spent his leaves in Barcelona with his partner Al Kauffman, until Kaufman was killed in a cavalry attack in the summer of 1938. Bianca fought almost to the end of the war before being killed by shrapnel on Hill 666. Supposedly his last words were, "Well so long boys, see you in Sunday school."[32]

The myth of the "Good Fight" has lasted so long because the returning volunteers internalized the Communist Party line; because VALB institutionalized the narrative and marginalized all dissenters; and because the historians who wrote it all down admired the Lincolns and chose to see them as purely antifascist fighters for democracy. Retiring the myth allows us to see the volunteers as complicated and flawed human beings, not one dimensional, self-sacrificing heroes. The result, as illustrated by Joe Bianca's story, is more compelling, not less.

Notes

1. Carl Nolte, "SF's Memorial to Lincoln Brigade Soldiers Down for Repairs," *San Francisco Chronicle*, August 29, 2018; John Nicholas Twitter, "A Premature Antifascist – and Proudly So," *The Nation*, October 26, 2009.
2. Del Berg was not the last veteran of the Lincolns, that honor belonged to Raphael Buch Brage who died in France at the age of 103. David A. Graham, "The Death of the Last Veteran of the Abraham Lincoln Brigade," *The Atlantic*, March 4, 2016; Dean Burrier Sanchis, "The Last US-born Volunteer: Raphael Buch Barge (1915–2018)," *The Volunteer*, March 4, 2019.
3. The other three memorials are on the campus of the University of Washington, Seattle, the Campus of City University New York, and in Madison, Wisconsin. A short history of the Washington Battalion can be found in Adam Hochschild, *Spain in Our Hearts: Americans in the Spanish Civil War, 1936–1939* (New York: Houghton Mifflin Harcourt, 2016), pp. 135, 229; Lincoln Battalion numbers taken from Alvah Bessie, *Spanish Civil War Notebooks* (Lexington: University Press of Kentucky, 2002), pp. 17, 51.
4. "*The Spanish Earth*: Ernest Hemingway's 1937 Film on the Spanish Civil War," Open Culture, June 28, 2012, http://www.openculture.com/2012/06/ithe_spanish_earthi_written_and_narrated_by_ernest_hemingway.html.
5. Robert A. Rosenstone, "The Men of the Abraham Lincoln Brigade," *Journal of American History* 54, no. 2 (September 1967), p. 327; Bill Baily, *The Kid from Hoboken* (San Francisco: Circus Lithographic Prepress, 1993), pp. 257–67.
6. Alvah Bessie, *Men in Battle* (San Francisco: Chandler and Sharp, 1975), pp. 10–24, 91; Bessie, *Notebooks*, pp. 1, 21; Peter N. Carroll, *The Odyssey of the Abraham Lincoln Brigade: Americans in the Spanish Civil War* (Stanford: Stanford University Press, 1994), pp. 337–9.
7. Company Four was also known as the Tom Mooney Machine Gun Company, formed in 1937 by mariners who were among the first Americans to arrive in Spain. Bessie, *Battle*, pp. 82–5; Bessie, *Notebooks*, p. 17.
8. Bessie, *Notebooks*, pp. 51–2.
9. Bessie, *Battle*, pp. 190–4.
10. Bessie, *Notebooks*, pp. 57–9.
11. Bessie, *Battle*, pp. 140, 57, 89–90, 346–54.
12. Bessie may have been correct in 1975, but today there are close to a dozen International Brigade memorials in America and Canada and hundreds worldwide. The International Brigade Memorial Trust, based in England has a website listing all known memorials, plaques, and other commemorations. http://www.international-brigades.org.uk/content/mapping-memorials; Bessie, *Battle*, pp. xi, xvi; Bernard Knox, "Premature Anti-Fascist," *Modern American Poetry*, http://www.

english.illinois.edu/MAPS/scw/knox.htm. Map of Spanish Civil War Memorials, https://www.google.com/maps/d/u/0/viewer?mid=1lk_fzjGpKKAYZC2dviQa5poOgYg&ll=23.67387664323283%2C-101.52318460000004&z=2.

13 Harvey Klehr, "The Myth of Premature Anti-Fascism," *The New Criterion*, September 16, 2002, http://archive.frontpagemag.com/readArticle.aspx?ARTID=22560.

14 Chris Brooks, "An Analysis of American and Canadian Volunteers Compiled by the International Brigades in Spain," *The Volunteer*, September 26, 2017; Rosenstone, "Abraham Lincoln Brigade," pp. 327–38, quotes from pages 237 and 335.

15 Rosenstone, Abraham Lincoln Brigade , pp. 328, 331–3; Brooks, "Analysis," see sections on age, nationality and profession.

16 Rosenstone, "Abraham Lincoln Brigade," pp. 331–2; Brooks, "Analysis," pp. 21–2.

17 For the difficult transition of the MWIU cadres to the Popular Front see Vernon L. Pedersen, *The Communist Party on the American Waterfront: Revolution, Reform and the Quest for Power* (Lanham, MD: Lexington Books, 2020), chapter 9, The End of the MWIU.

18 The Mackenzie-Papeneau Battalion was named in honor of the Canadians in the International Brigades although it had as many American members as Canadian. Eunice Lipton, *A Distant Heartbeat: A War, a Disappearance and a Family's Secrets* (Albuquerque: University of New Mexico Press, 2016), pp. x, 1–2; Federal Bureau of Investigation (FBI) Summary, Memorandum on the Veterans of the Abraham Lincoln Brigade 1937–1948, FOI release date, June 19, 2008, governmentattic.org, p. 88.

19 Veterans of the Abraham Lincoln Brigade, *Petitioner, v. Subversive Activities Control Board*, Respondent, 331 F.2d 64 (D.C. Cir 1964), https://law.justia.com/cases/federal/appellate-courts/F2/331/64/445906/.

20 Stephen Koch, *The Breaking Point: Hemingway, Dos Passos, and the Murder of Jose Robles* (Berkeley, CA: Counterpoint, 2005), pp. 163–5; Bessie, *Notebooks*, pp. 25, 133; Ernest Hemingway, "Night before Battle," *The Complete Short Stories of Ernest Hemingway: The Finca Vigia Edition* (New York: Scribner Paperback Fiction, 1987), pp. 437–59.

21 Carroll, *Odyssey*, pp. 237–8.

22 Harry Fisher, *Comrades: Tales of a Brigadista in the Spanish Civil War* (Winnipeg: Bison Books, 1997), p. 71; Testimony of William C. McCuistion, Investigation of Un-American Propaganda Activities in the United States, House Committee on Un-American Activities, November 1, 1939, pp. 6717–23; Carroll, *Odyssey*, p. 233.

23 Furr determined that Herrick based his claim on rumors he heard while in hospital recovering from a wound received at Jarma. Wiliam Herrick, *Jumping the Line: The Adventures and Misadventures of an American Radical* (Madison: University

of Wisconsin Press, 1998), pp. 89–91, 171–3, 178–9; Grover Furr, "Anatomy of a Lie: The Death of Oliver Law," *The Volunteer*, June 1, 2010; Carroll, *Odyssey*, pp. 334–7.

24 Ron Radosh, *Spain Betrayed: The Soviet Union and the Spanish Civil War* (New Haven, CT: Yale University Press, 2001), pp. 241–5.
25 Carroll, *Odyssey*, A Note on Sources, after page 380 and footnotes to pages 108 and 182.
26 Hochschild, *Spain in Our Hearts*, pp. 214–16.
27 Baily, *Hobokken*, *Bremann* incident, pp. 257–65; travel to Spain, pp. 322–9.
28 Baily, *Hobokken*, pp. 335–7.
29 Security Appeal Hearing of Ladislaus F. Szeliga (Stanley Postek's real name) Z-177376, Heard before Tilden H. Edwards, Chairman, Chairman, Security Appeals Board, San Francisco, CA, April 6, 1951, TAM 125 Box 4, Folder 10, Tamiment Library, pp. 1–6; Stanley Postek, "Memories of Spain," ALBA 89, Box 1, Tamiment Library/Robert Al Richmond, *A Long View from the Left: Memoirs of an American Revolutionary* (Boston, MA: Houghton-Mifflin, 1972), pp. 189–90. F. Wagner Labor Archives, Elmer Holmes Bobst Library, 70 Washington Square South, New York, NY 10012, New York University Libraries, pp. X–XI, entry of 29/1/1942.
30 Richmond, *Long View*, pp. 189–90; Postek, "Memories," pp. I–X; "Inseparable pals" quote from Joe North and Ernest Hemingway, *Men in the Ranks: The Story of Twelve Americans in Spain* (New York: Friends of the Abraham Lincoln Brigade, 1939), p. 41.
31 Al Richmond worried that Bianca had murdered someone, but the problem could also have been concern over Bianca's homosexuality. Richmond, *Long View*, pp. 193–7.
32 North and Hemingway, *Men in the Ranks*, pp. 43–4; Richmond, *Long View*, pp. 198–201.

Bibliography

Bessie, Alvah. *Men in Battle*. San Francisco: Chandler and Sharp, 1975.
Bessie, Alvah. *Spanish Civil War Notebooks*. Lexington: University Press of Kentucky, 2002.
Carroll, Peter N. *The Odyssey of the Abraham Lincoln Brigade: Americans in the Spanish Civil War*. Stanford: Stanford University Press, 1994.
Eby, Cecil D. *Comrades and Commissars: The Lincoln Battalion in the Spanish Civil War*, 5th edition. University Park: Pennsylvania State University Press, 2007.

Hochschild, Adam. *Spain in Our Hearts: Americans in the Spanish Civil War, 1936–1939*. New York: Houghton Mifflin, 2016.

Koch, Stephen. *The Breaking Point: Hemingway, Dos Passos, and the Murder of Jose Robles*. Berkeley, CA: Counterpoint, 2005.

Payne, Stanley G. *The Spanish Civil War, the Soviet Union, and Communism*. New Haven, CT: Yale University Press, 2004.

Radosh, Ron. *Spain Betrayed: The Soviet Union and the Spanish Civil War*. New Haven, CT: Yale University Press, 2001.

8

"For a New Antifascist, Anti-imperialist People's Coalition": Claudia Jones, Black Left Feminism, and the Politics of Possibility in the Era of Trump

Erik S. McDuffie

Claudia Jones was nervous *and* optimistic. She was convinced that the United States was on the verge of a fascist takeover during the height of anticommunist persecution across the country in the early 1950s.[1] She expressed this sentiment in her 1951 essay "For the Unity of Women in the Cause of Peace" published in *Political Affairs*, Communist Party of the United States of America's (CPUSA) theoretical journal.[2] She pointed to the resurgence of lynching, a sexist backlash, virulent anticommunist persecution, growing Wall Street power at home, which, together with American military involvement in the Korean War (1950–3) and US Cold War foreign policy allegedly intent on crushing the Soviet Union and perpetuating colonialism, as signs that fascism was near. But Jones remained hopeful. The American masses, especially black working-class women, under the leadership of the CPUSA, she confidently declared, would rise up and agitate "[f]or a new anti-fascist, anti-imperialist people's coalition."[3] Her predictions did not come true in the early 1950s. However, her words of warning are arguably more relevant today than they were nearly seventy years ago.

This chapter examines the key innovations of Jones's thought for Marxism and (re)imagining a future world radically different from the one we have inherited through articles on women, race, and peace published in *Political Affairs* during the McCarthy period.[4] A committed Communist and dedicated Marxist-Leninist, she was the highest ranking black woman in the CPUSA and one of its leading theoreticians on the "Negro Question" and "Woman Question" during the Cold War years. Jones's pioneering writings from the late 1940s and early 1950s on "triply oppressed" black women extended and pushed orthodox Marxism-Leninism in a new ideological and political direction. She was also a political prisoner in the United States. Her visibility in the party, outspoken criticism of Jim Crow, colonialism, and US Cold War politics, and social location as a black working-class woman immigrant exposed her to persecution and resulted in her deportation to Great Britain in 1955. In London, where she lived her final years, she carried out some of her most exciting life work. She emerged as a leader of a dynamic community of young African, Caribbean, and Asian radicals. She died on December 25, 1964, at the age of 49. Growing up in severe poverty and living through years of political persecution had a devastating impact on her health. She is buried to the left of Karl Marx's tomb in London's High Gate Cemetery (Figure 8.1).[5]

Until recently, Jones has been, as diasporic feminist literary scholar Carole Boyce Davies asserts, erased from the black radical intellectual tradition.[6] In the last fifteen years, scholars and activists around the world have rediscovered Jones and a dynamic cadre of black women radicals in the CPUSA who forged black left feminism, a pathbreaking brand of feminist politics that centers working-class women by combining black nationalist and CPUSA positions on race, gender, and class with black women radicals' own lived experiences.[7] This politics also anticipated the US women of color feminism of the 1970s advanced by the Third World Women's Alliance and the Combahee River Collective.[8] These organizations have been critical to inspiring contemporary black, feminist of color, and queer formations, most notably Black Lives Matter and #SayHerName.[9] Through imagining the unimaginable—freedom for all people globally from white supremacy, sexism, war, empire, settler colonialism, fascism, capitalism, and imperialism—Jones proffered a politics of possibility for building a new and more democratic world.[10]

As Carole Boyce Davies points out, Jones's thesis on the "superexploitation of black women" constitutes her key contribution to Marxism, black radicalism, and women of color feminism. Derived from Marxist-Leninist thought, superexploitation refers to uniquely severe, persistent, and dehumanizing forms of exploitation critical to the maintenance of the capitalist system.[11] Jones, however, refashioned this concept by accounting for black women. Informed by Marxism-Leninism, black nationalism, and the lived experiences of working-class women of color, Boyce Davies writes that Jones's thesis referred "to the ways in which black women's labor is assumed; the way they are relegated to service work by all sectors of society, with the complicity of progressive and white women's and labor interests (including those on the Left). It related to their low

Figure 8.1 Claudia Jones, circa 1930s. Credit: Esther Cooper Jackson.

salary, compared with the level of work they are asked to give in return."¹² In a powerful move, Jones located "much of this treatment in the superexploitation of black women as mothers." In other words, the capitalist process brutally exploited black women's role as breadwinners and protectors of families by forcing them to work backbreaking, menial service sector jobs, often under the threat of rape, to ensure the survival of their families and black communities.[13] She, however, did not view black women as victims. Given black women's relegation to the lowest rungs of the capitalist workforce and their location at the interstices of multiple oppressions, she forcefully charged that triply oppressed black women across the African diaspora, not white industrial male workers in economically advanced nations, constituted the vanguard for global transformative change. In drawing these conclusions, she sought to rethink Marxism-Leninism and to recenter the party by moving black women from the margins to the center in revolutionary struggles against white supremacy, male chauvinism, fascism, colonialism, capitalism, and war. These were bold positions given the repressive political moment in the United States.[14]

This chapter makes four interrelated arguments about Jones and her broader significance to the study of Marxism, American communism, black radicalism, black feminism, the African diaspora, our contemporary world, and the future. First, Jones's writing during the Cold War challenged and extended Marxism through centering black women and incorporating race and gender into her political critique.[15] Second, her journalism proffered a cutting-edge antifascist politics that was radical, intersectional, and global in perspective. Third, her antifascist writings contain useful insight into current global events, namely, the rise of fascist, Far Right, and white nationalist movements in the United States and around the world. Lastly, an analysis of Jones's life and politics provides a vision for building a future world beyond the "cautious incrementalism" and liberal neoliberalism of US President Barack Obama and the racist white nationalism and the crony capitalism of his successor—Donald J. Trump.[16]

Early Years and Joining the Communist Party

Claudia Jones's entry into the party during the early 1930s provides broad insight into the powerful attraction that communism had for African Americans during the early and mid-twentieth century. She—like thousands of other black people who joined or participated in the Communist Old Left—did so, not because they wanted to enlist in a conspiratorial movement or spy for the Soviet

Union.[17] Rather, they saw the CPUSA as a powerful vehicle for advancing racial equality, social justice, labor rights, decolonization, internationalism, peace, and to varying degrees women's rights. Certainly this was true of the first blacks to join the party in the years immediately after the Russian Revolution and First World War. These included Harlem-based radicals like Otto Huiswoud, Cyril Briggs, Richard B. Moore, and Grace Campbell. The second generation of black Communists in which Jones was a part joined the CPUSA during the Great Depression. The party's commitment to black-white unity, civil rights, jobs, and internationalism brought them into it.[18]

Jones was born Claudia Vera Cumberbatch in 1915 in Belmont, Trinidad. As a youngster, several relatives left the British Caribbean colony for the United States in search of a better future. In 1924, she joined her family in Harlem, where she grew up. Instead of finding a land of milk and honey, she and her family "suffered not only the impoverished lot of working class native families, and its multi-national populace, but early learned the special scourge of indignity stemming from Jim Crow national oppression," as she wrote years later.[19] The tragic death of her mother from overwork and exhaustion from toiling in a Harlem factory constituted a turning point in Jones's life. Looking back, Jones asserted that her mother's passing facilitated her early awareness of black women's triple oppression.[20]

Beyond her family, national and global events facilitated Jones's radical political turn. Like thousands of African Americans across Depression-era United States, the Scottsboro case of the early 1930s was critical to bringing her into the CPUSA. The "Scottsboro Boys," as they came to be known, were nine African American young men aged 12 to 21 who, in March 1931, were falsely accused of raping two white women aboard a freight train on route from Chattanooga to Memphis. Authorities apprehended the youth near Scottsboro, Alabama. Once there, they were tried by an all-white, Jim Crow court. Eight of the young men were sentenced to death. In response, the CPUSA organized a worldwide amnesty movement demanding the freedom of the young men during the height of the Great Depression. Under the leadership of the party, the Scottsboro case came to symbolize Jim Crowism, lynching, imperialism, poverty, and racial oppression on a global scale. Due to the efforts of Communists and their allies, the Scottsboro youth were spared the death penalty.[21] Jones participated in the Scottsboro demonstrations in Harlem as well as in the Communist-led mass protests in New York around the Italo-Ethiopian War (1935–6), which also radicalized her.[22] Equally important, the utopianism and revolutionary promise of the Soviet Union appealed to Jones. As radical historian Eric Hobsbawm observes about Old Left Communists, the Bolshevik Revolution "was the first proletarian revolution, the first regime in history to set about the construction of the socialist order, the proof both of the profundity of the contradictions of capitalism ... and the possibility—the certainty—that socialism revolution would succeed."[23] Jones subscribed to this view of the Soviet Union. Ultimately, she joined the CPUSA in 1936. In the coming years, she immersed herself in Marxist-Leninist literature and CPUSA-affiliated groups during the Popular Front, the period when Communists worldwide, upon the directives from Moscow in 1935, officially jettisoned sectarian calls for class struggle and world revolution and built a left-liberal coalition to stem the spread of fascism.[24] By the late 1940s, she sat on the party's National Committee, making her the highest ranking black women in the CPUSA. She was a close friend and trusted ally of William Z. Foster, General Secretary of the CPUSA. By the early Cold War years, her brilliance, knowledge of Marxism-Leninism, passion for social justice, belief in the revolutionary possibilities of the global Communist Left, and her lived experiences as an Afro-Caribbean working-class female immigrant in the United States positioned Jones as one of the most influential US Communists and black radicals of her day.[25]

War, Peace, and Antifascism in the McCarthy Period

Claudia Jones, like thousands of US Communists in the early 1950s, believed that the United States was on the precipice of fascism. The CPUSA adopted this line as it moved toward the "ultra-left" under the leadership of William Z. Foster in the postwar years. Abandoning the Popular Front, Communists once again called for socialism and world revolution.[26] This new political line was a response to deteriorating US-Soviet relations and emerging Cold War repression in the United States. The Truman administration launched a policy of containment against the Soviet Union. Organized labor drifted toward the Right. The Taft-Hartley Act of 1947 significantly limited the right of workers to unionize and required union officials to sign noncommunist affidavits. The government began rounding up Communists. On the racial front, civil rights groups distanced themselves from Communists immediately after the war. Additionally, many black Americans—radical and liberal—in the postwar years charged the US government with committing "genocide" against and violating the human rights of African Americans as defined by the United Nations.[27] Proponents of this position pointed to the state-sanctioned and extra-legal production of exploitation, terror, and death experienced by black people in Jim Crow America as evidence of human rights violations.[28] The postwar United States witnessed a surge in lynching and state violence against African Americans. A major race "riot" in Columbia, Tennessee, on February 25–26, 1946, triggered by an altercation between a black veteran and a white merchant prompted white police and national guard troops to kill two African Americans, arrest hundreds of black residents, and invade an African American neighborhood. The disturbance made headlines across the country.[29] In the Chicago suburb of Cicero, an enraged white mob numbering in the thousands viciously attacked a small number of African Americans who had moved into a lily-white neighborhood in July 1951. Many of these rioting whites denounced housing desegregation as "Communism."[30]

Overseas, African Americans fought and died in the Korean War at disproportionately higher rates than their white counterparts. Black women encountered virulent racialized sexual violence and state terror during these years, most notably Rosa Lee Ingram, a Georgia widow, mother, and sharecropper, and her sons who faced death for killing a white male would-be rapist. Her high-profile case made Ingram a household name in African American households.[31] Personally, Jones felt the scourge of state persecution. In 1948, authorities arrested her along with ten other CPUSA national leaders for violating the Smith Act of 1940. The law criminalized calls for violently overthrowing the US government. Neither Jones nor her comrades, who came to be known as the CP-11, issued such overtures.[32] But anticommunist hysteria was in full effect, and Jones suffered accordingly. Two years later, authorities arrested her for violating the Internal Security Act of 1950 (McCarran Act), which authorized the deportation of the foreign-born who were deemed as "subversive."[33] In 1951, she was arrested again for violating the Smith Act. Authorities jailed her for nine months in 1955 before deporting her to Great Britain later that same year, with her health suffering immeasurably. That the state used her writings as evidence in its deportation case against her underscores how cold warriors viewed her journalism as subversive. It was within this context that she wrote about the right-wing turn in US life.[34]

Jones's now classic essay "An End to the Neglect of the Problems of the Negro Woman!" published in 1949 in *Political Affairs*, laid out many of the key arguments she proffered a few years later in her articles on the Korean War, gender, race, class, freedom, and peace. She wrote this essay amid rising domestic Cold War repression and tension between the United States and Soviet Union.[35] As historian Ellen Schrecker points out, "McCarthyism can be seen as the home front of the Cold War. As the confrontation with Soviet Communism escalated, so, too, did the campaign against domestic Communism."[36] Arguably, Jones understood these connections, particularly as they affected women of color at home and abroad, better than anyone else. Drawing from her black left feminist perspective, Jones argued: "Negro women as workers, as Negroes, and as women—are the most oppressed stratum of the whole population." She identified black women's low wages and social status as domestics as the "highest manifestation of capitalist exploitation."[37] She tied black women's multiple oppressions and second-class citizenship to the genocidal conditions in which African American communities lived. According to her, US Cold War domestic and foreign policy further immiserated black women, revealing the fallacy of American democracy before a global audience. Jones pointed to the plight of Rosa Lee Ingram to make this point. According to Jones, Ingram's plight exposed the "hypocrisy of the Truman Administration, which boasts about 'exporting democracy throughout the world' while the state of Georgia keeps a widowed Negro mother of twelve children under lock and key." Moreover, her case illuminated "oppressed status of the Negro family" and "the degradation of the Negro women today under American bourgeois democracy moving to fascism and war."[38] Jones was keenly aware that Jim Crowism represented the Achilles' Heel in US efforts to paint the Soviet Union as an authoritarian regime and to win favor with newly emerging nations of color in Asia and Africa.[39] She also castigated her fellow Communists for their racism and sexism. Demanding that the party eradicate male and racial chauvinism within its ranks, she called on Communists to understand that black women's freedom was critical to advancing justice, socialism, and peace.[40] These ideas served as the basis for her writing on women, peace, race, repression, and freedom in relation to the Korean War.

The Korean War was the largest military conflict since the Second World War and one of the deadliest wars of the twentieth century. The conflict was in many respects a civil war rooted in long-standing social and political instability connected in part to colonialism, foreign intervention, and the emerging Cold War.[41] Following the Second World War, the Korean peninsula was divided into two zones with the north occupied by the Soviet Union and the south occupied by the United States. In 1948, reunification talks broke down and two separate governments formed: the pro-capitalist Republic of Korea (South Korea) backed by the United States and the Democratic People's Republic of Korea (North Korea) allied with the newly established People's Republic of China and the Soviet Union. Over the next two years, small-scale armed clashes occurred between the two nation's regular armed forces and guerillas allied with either country. The conflict took a dramatic turn on June 25, 1950, when North Korean military forces crossed the 38th parallel, the boundary between the two nations, and quickly captured South Korea's capital, Seoul. Soon afterwards, the United Nations authorized the creation of a military force to defend South Korea. The United States provided the bulk of military personnel for this force, while China and the Soviet Union came to the aid of North Korea.[42]

In "For the Unity of Women in the Cause of Peace," Jones focused close attention to the connections linking racial terror, growing corporate power, labor unrest, and political repression at home with the Korean War, US anti-Soviet foreign policy, and decolonization abroad. She argued that triply oppressed African American women were keenly aware of the "growth of terrorization" against black women and families in relation to the Korean War. She pointed to the fact that African American women's sons and husbands fighting in the US armed forces in Korea were often wantonly killed by white American US troops. The high number of court martial charges levied against black soldiers, as well as the lynching of African Americans veterans after returning home, she charged, provided further evidence of state-sanctioned racial exploitation and death of black people.[43] Understanding the war within the geopolitical context of global decolonization and the Cold War, she viewed the Korean conflict as an unjust war against a people of color fighting for national liberation and as a shameless attempt by the United States and its allies to suppress the world socialist revolution. Additionally, she argued that the growing US war economy hurt black women exceptionally hard through speedups, automation, and downsizing and the shifting of resources from social needs to war-making. She called special attention to the high civilian death toll of Korean women and children. Given the war's deadly realities, she contended that women around the world, due to their location as mothers and wives, recognized the danger of war to human survival. For this reason, she called on the CPUSA to mobilize women, especially black women and other women of color in the United States, in the cause for peace.[44]

In "The Struggle for Peace in the United States" published in 1952, Jones made an even strong case against war, fascism, sexism, and racial terror. Contending that a pro-Wall Street "bi-partisan war coalition" and the Truman administration were hell-bent on destroying the Soviet Union and preserving European colonial empires across Asia and Africa, she expressed alarm at the US participation in the Korean War and in the possibility of nuclear holocaust.[45] Meanwhile, she emphasized the ways segregation and lynching damaged US efforts in winning the hearts and minds of people color in the emerging Third World. She wrote: "All over the world, especially among the hundreds of millions of darker peoples in Asia, Africa, Latin America, and the West Indies, the U.S. imperialists are finding the Jim Crow system in this country a most serious obstacle in their path of aggression."[46] She added: "U.S. imperialism, faced with ever-rising and growing struggles from the oppressed Negro people within its own borders, must attempt to hide from world view its own genocidal practices, fearful lest exposure further pulverize its shibboleth of a free nation in a free world."[47] Third World people, Jones asserted, were taking notice of US racial terror. For this reason, "the struggle for peace requires a struggle against colonialism and rejection of racist warmongering." Again, she argued that black woman stood at the front lines in building antifascist, anti-imperialist, antiwar movement. She pointed to the Sojourners for the Truth and Justice, a short-lived black left feminist organization that centered black women to struggles for human rights, peace, women's rights, and decolonization. The Rosa Lee Ingram case was a focal point of the group's activism. For the Sojourners and Jones, Ingram's case symbolized black women's superexploitation and the revolutionary potential of black women in the United States allied with women across the African world and beyond.[48] Beyond the United States, she argued that the Soviet Union constituted a model for racial and gender equality and that the Communist world and nascent Third World were beacons for global peace and democracy. These alleged facts prompted her to call on the CPUSA to build a "people's peace coalition … against war and fascism." Ironically, her calls for peace eventually landed her in jail.[49]

Jones's framing of the Korean War was not without its oversights. First, she essentialized women as naturally inclined to peace. This assertion was (and remains) a common belief among thinkers and activists across the ideological spectrum and from different ethnic backgrounds. However, history has showed that women are as often prone as men to hold pro-war views.[50] Second, Jones simplified the political complexities of the Korean War. She framed the United States and its United Nations allies as rogue aggressors against a defenseless North Korea. The social and political causes of the war were far more nuanced than she admitted, and the Communist invasion of June 1950 did mark a major escalation in military conflict between North and South Korea. Belligerents from both sides of the conflict committed war crimes and human rights abuses. The Soviet Union and People's Republic China, like the United States and its UN allies, backed their respective allies to promote their own domestic and global interests. In the end, the war resulted in the emergence of two authoritarian states on the Korean peninsula—one backed by the People's Republic of China and the Soviet Union, and the other supported by the United States and its allies.[51]

Nonetheless, Jones was undeniably correct in acknowledging the disproportionately high death rate of African American soldiers in Korea, the deep-seated racism within the US military, and the resurgence of racial oppression in postwar American society. She was also correct in calling attention to the large-scale suffering of Korean women and children caused by the fighting. (The Korean War saw a higher proportion of civilian deaths than the Second World War or the Vietnam War.)[52] Even more, it is significant that Jones wrote critically about the Korean conflict. By late 1950, the war was not going well militarily for the United States and its UN allies. A massive Chinese offensive forced US and UN troops into a full-scale retreat from recently captured territory above the 38th parallel.[53] In the United States, opposition and ambivalence toward the war grew as it turned into a stalemate and as a deep economic recession set in. The war intensified anticommunist hysteria and repression. Supporters of the war equated criticism of it with Soviet subversion. The US government was rounding up Communists.[54] Given this context, writing critically about the Korean conflict was a bold move—one Jones surely knew would get her into trouble.

Whereas Jones simplified the political causes and realities of the Korean War, she—like other leading African American Communist spokespersons—romanticized the Soviet Union and overlooked its darker side. Black American Communists aligned themselves with a state that under Stalin devolved into authoritarianism and betrayed the utopian possibilities of the Bolshevik Revolution.[55] Additionally, some US Communists spied on behalf of the Soviet Union against the United States.[56] No credible evidence has surfaced indicating or even suggesting Jones engaged in espionage. However, charging her and other black Communists as Soviet "dupes," as some Cold War-era black liberals and ex-Communists, and scholars have done, misses the boat.[57] For Jones and a generation of black radicals, supporting the Soviet Union was a no brainer. While she may have been naïve or willfully blind about Stalinist atrocities, they were hardly naïve about the depth of white supremacist practices in the United States and the widespread misery of African Americans nor about the violent grip of European imperialism on colonized people. The Soviet constitution professed its solidarity with the world's colonized and nationally oppressed peoples, and white Communists treated Jones with respect that was rare among white Americans. So what she saw in the Soviet Union did represent the possibility of a utopian future, and revolutionaries from around the world echoed their observations. In this light, Jones's support for a nation that was the enemy of their enemy makes sense.

Conclusions and the Politics of Possibility in the Era of Trump

I will end this chapter by returning to Jones's essay "The Struggle for Peace in the United States." In its conclusion, she called on Communists "to work to unite all people who understand that our country is in danger of war and fascism." Even though she and several of her close comrades faced imprisonment, deportation, and harassment, Jones was still confident about the future. She charged that "the working class and Negro people" led by the CPUSA would serve as the vanguard in propelling the United States toward "happiness, security, equality, and peace."[58] Scholars might quibble at the fact that the dire picture Jones painted of the United States in the early 1950s did not come true. They might also point out that a progressive, interracial working-class movement with people of color at the forefront has yet to materialize in this country.

However, Jones's prophetic words are arguably coming true today given the ascendance of fascism, white nationalism, and Far Right movements in the United States and globally. Contemporary Far Right-wing movements share common characteristics of fascism: a promotion of hypernationalism; an appeal to a fictive ideal past; disdain for human rights; warmongering and celebration of the military; virulent anticommunism; racism; xenophobia; scapegoating perceived domestic and foreign enemies; promotion of heteropatriarchy; suppression of labor unions; support for corporate power; distortion of facts and history; an obsession with crime and security; the use of religion to promote reactionary state policies; control of the media; and cronyism and kleptocracy.[59] We can see these characteristics in Far Right political parties across Europe, Brexit, and the US alt-right.[60] The presidential elections of Rodrigo Duterte of the Philippines, Jair Bolsonaro of Brazil, and Donald Trump of the United States signal the rise of Far Right leaders as heads of state.[61] President Trump's self-identification as a "nationalist," rants about an "invasion" of Latinx migrants, initial refusal to condemn white nationalists at the deadly alt-right rally in Charlottesville, Virginia, in 2017; characterization of CNN as "fake news" and media critics as "enemies of the people"; racist demonization of immigrants and people of color; calls for militarizing the border and enlarging US armed forces; corporate-friendly policies; rejection of human-caused climate change; muscular foreign policy; boasts of groping women; and references of El Salvador, Haiti, and Nigeria as "shit hole countries" are just a few examples of his fascist-like rhetoric and policies.[62] Trump's policies and divisive rhetoric has created a climate for and inspired deadly white supremacist violence against people of color in the United States and around the world. Mass shootings of Muslim worshipers at a mosque in Christchurch, New Zealand, and Latinx at a Walmart at in El Paso, Texas, are cases in point. Moreover, the possibility of another US-initiated war in the Persian Gulf looms large.[63] Acclaimed African American poet and educator Haki Madhubuti of Chicago makes this claim about the US forty-fifth president: "Trump's nativist rhetoric and overt fascism synched with the durability of white supremacy (i.e. racism), generational poverty, and U.S.-empire building has imposed newer and more serious life-challenges into the lives of Americans across the socioeconomic and sociodemographic spectrum."[64]

At the same time, Claudia Jones's writings on peace and fascism provide a progressive political alternative to the cautious incrementalism, neoliberalism, and militarism of the Obama administration that in multiple ways maintained the US racial status quo and American empire.[65] Obama became the first African American US president as a result of a savvy campaign that tapped into the freedom dreams of millions of Americans from all walks of life. Speaking in cadences reminiscent of and making references to the slain civil rights leader Martin Luther King, Jr., Obama inspired his supporters. They appreciated the historical significance and symbolism of his campaign, believing he would initiate sweeping progressive change to America.[66] This did not happen. Instead, Obama pursued policies that largely maintained the status quo. His response to the financial crisis of 2007 mainly benefitted banks, which received billions of dollars of taxpayer-funded bailouts from the federal government. Black and brown communities were hit especially hard by this economic downturn and the housing crisis. Obama largely avoided addressing racial injustice out of concern of alienating white voters during his first years in office. Massive protests led primarily by African Americans across the country in response to the police killings of young black men like Trayvon Martin and Michael Brown during the second half of his administration forced Obama to speak out about race. Yet, while he spoke sympathetically about the deaths of these black young men, the US Immigration and Customs Enforcement (ICE) deported a record number of undocumented people from the United States.[67]

Beyond the United States, Obama's foreign policy toward Africa was a disaster. Libya is a case in point. Due to Obama's initiative, the United States and North Atlantic Treaty Organization military forces played a decisive role in the death of Libyan leader Colonel Muammar Qaddafi on October 20, 2011, after a popular uprising overthrew him. Charging Qaddafi with violating the human rights of the Libyan people, Obama claimed that the West responded militarily to avert a humanitarian crisis after Qaddafi threatened to violently suppress the rebellion. Placing Qaddafi's death within the larger context of the revolutions across North Africa and the Middle East that came to be known as the Arab Spring, Obama lauded young people across the Arab world for overthrowing dictators. Looking toward the future, Obama acknowledged that Libyans would face challenges as they moved toward democracy and their "liberation." But he expressed confidence that they could now "look forward to the promise of a new day."[68] That day has yet to arrive. The country has been rocked by an ongoing civil war and humanitarian crisis since Qaddafi's death. Additionally, the US response to Qaddafi was critical to triggering the massive migration crisis in which thousands of people have drowned in the Mediterranean Sea en route from Libya to Europe in search of a better life, expanding the American military presence across the continent, and in destabilizing the Sahel.[69]

Where do we go from here? How can we overcome this country's moribund fear of socialism and deep-seated white supremacy in order to chart a path forward as humanity faces innumerable existential crises? What is our role as scholars of American communism, but to ask difficult questions and to think critically about connections between the past, present, and future? What is for sure is that Claudia Jones's life provides a template for countering prevailing historical narratives that normalize empire, capitalism, white supremacy, war, and heteropatriarchy. Her incarceration, deportation, and erasure illustrate what can happen when left-wing radicals, especially women of color, speak out against authoritarianism and social injustice. Through her brilliance, resilience, and oversights, Jones enables us not only to imagine that another world is truly possible, but to chart a path for creating one. This, I would argue, is the most important historical legacy of the African American encounter with American communism.

Notes

1 Ellen Schrecker, *Many are the Crimes: McCarthyism in America* (Princeton, NJ: Princeton University Press, 1998).
2 Claudia Jones, "For the Unity of Women in the Cause of Peace," *Political Affairs* 30 (February 1951), pp. 151–68.
3 Ibid., 168.
4 Claudia Jones, "An End to the Neglect of the Problems of the Negro Woman!" *Political Affairs* 28, no. 6 (June 1949), pp. 51–67; Claudia Jones, "International Women's Day and the Struggle for Peace," *Political Affairs* 29, no. 3 (March

1950): 32–45; Jones, "Unity of Women"; Claudia Jones, "The Struggle for Peace in the United States," *Political Affairs* 31, no. 2 (February 1952), pp. 1–20.

5 Carole Boyce Davies, *Left of Karl Marx: The Political Life of Black Communist Claudia Jones* (Durham: Duke University Press, 2008), pp. 131–233.

6 On the erasure of Claudia Jones from black radical scholarship, see Carole Boyce Davies, "Sisters Outside: Tracing the Caribbean/Black Radical Intellectual Tradition," *Small Axe* 28 (March 2009), pp. 217–28. Boyce Davies's article is a response to and a critique of the apparent masculinist focus of Cedric Robinson's *Black Marxism: The Making of the Black Radical Tradition* (Chapel Hill: University of North Carolina, 2000).

7 For the original definition of "black left feminism," see Margaret Helen Washington, "Alice Childress, Lorraine Hansberry, and Claudia Jones: Black Women Write the Popular Front," in Bill V. Mullen and James Smethurst (eds.), *Left of the Color Line: Race, Radicalism, and Twentieth Century Literature of the United States* (Chapel Hill: University of North Carolina Press, 2003), pp. 183–204. For scholarly inquiries of black women and the US Left, see Erik S. McDuffie, *Sojourning for Freedom: Black Women, American Communism, and the Making of Black Left Feminism* (Durham: Duke University Press, 2011); Keith Gilyard, *Louise Thompson Patterson: A Life of Struggle and Justice* (Durham: Duke University Press, 2017); Barbara Ransby, *Eslanda: The Large and Unconventional Life of Mrs. Paul Robeson* (New Haven, CT: Yale University Press, 2013); Carole Boyce Davies (ed.), *Claudia Jones: Beyond Containment* (Banbury: Ayebia Clarke, 2010); Boyce Davies, *Left of Karl Marx*; Cheryl Higashida, *Black Internationalist Feminism: Women Writers of the Black Left, 1945–1995* (Urbana: University of Illinois Press, 2011); Dayo F. Gore, *Radicalism at the Crossroads: African American Women Activists in the Cold War* (New York: New York University Press, 2011).

8 McDuffie, *Sojourning for Freedom*, pp. 7–9.

9 Keeanga Yamahtta Taylor, *How We Get Free: Black Feminism and the Combahee River Collective* (Chicago: Haymarket Books, 2017), p. 13.

10 My thinking about the "politics of possibility" is informed by the work of transnational feminist scholar Nancy Naples. Nancy A. Naples, "The Challenges and Possibilities of Transnational Feminist Praxis," in Nancy A. Naples and Manisa Desai (eds.), *Women's Activism and Globalization: Linking Local Struggles and Transnational Politics* (New York: Routledge, 2002), pp. 267–81.

11 Karl Marx, *Capital: A Critique of Political Economy*, vol. 1 (New York: Penguin Books, 1990), pp. 188–246, 655–67, 772–802, 3: 958–61, 971–91.

12 Boyce Davies, *Left of Karl Marx*, 42.

13 Ibid., 38, 39.

14 McDuffie, *Sojourning for Freedom*, pp. 4–5, 7–9.

15 My thinking about "freedom dreams" is taken from historian Robin D. G. Kelley who emphasizes the significance of hope and the imagination, not racism and oppression, as the catalyst for drawing African-descended people to social movements committed to building a new world radically different from the status quo. Robin D. G. Kelley, *Freedom Dreams: The Black Radical Imagination* (Boston, MA: Beacon Press, 2002).

16 I borrow the term "cautious incrementalism" from Geoffrey Kabaservice, "Joe Biden Is the Ultimate Centrist Democrat. Is That a Liability or Strength?," *Guardian*, April 25, 2019. See also, Robin D. G. Kelley, "President Obama: Freedom Democrat or Neoliberal," in Charles P. Henry, Robert L. Allen, and Robert Chrisman (eds.), *The Obama Phenomenon: Toward a Multicultural Democracy* (Urbana: University of Illinois Press, 2011), pp. 253–61.

17 Here I am challenging claims by historians Harvey Klehr, John Earl Haynes, and Fridrikh I. Firsov who frame the CPUSA as a conspiratorial organization blindly committed to advancing the Soviet agenda. See Fridrikh I. Firsov, Harvey Klehr, and John Earl Haynes (eds.), *Secret Cables of the Comintern: 1933–1943* (New Haven, CT: Yale University Press, 2014); Harvey Klehr, John Earl Haynes, and Kyrill M. Anderson, *The Soviet World of American Communism* (New Haven, CT: Yale University Press, 1998); Harvey Klehr, John Earl Haynes, and Fridrikh Igorevich Firsov, *The Secret World of American Communism* (New Haven, CT: Yale University Press, 1995).

18 Minkah Makalani, *In the Cause of Freedom: Radical Black Internationalism from Harlem to London, 1917–1936* (Chapel Hill: University of North Carolina Press, 2014); Mark Solomon, *The Cry Was Unity: Communists and African Americans, 1917–1936* (Jackson: University Press of Mississippi, 1998); McDuffie, *Sojourning for Freedom*, pp. 25–57; Robin D. G. Kelley, *Hammer and Hoe: Alabama Communists during the Great Depression* (Chapel Hill: University of North Carolina Press, 1990); Mark Naison, *Communists in Harlem during the Depression* (Urbana: University of Illinois Press, 1983).

19 Claudia Jones to William Z. Foster, December 6, 1955, in Howard "Stretch" Johnson Papers, Tamiment Library, New York.

20 Ibid., McDuffie, *Sojourning for Freedom*, pp. 96–7.

21 For accounts of the Scottsboro case, see Gerald Horne, *Powell v. Alabama: The Scottsboro Boys and American Justice* (New York: Franklin Watts, 1997); James Goodman, *Stories of Scottsboro* (New York: Vintage Books, 1994). The Scottsboro defendants were Charlie Weems, Ozie Powell, Clarence Norris, Olen Montgomery, Willie Roberson, Haywood Patterson, Eugene Williams, Andrew Wright, and Leroy Wright.

22 Jones to Foster.

23 Eric Hobsbawm, *Revolutionaries* (New York: New Press, 2001), p. 1; for additional discussions of the utopian appeal of the Russian Revolution in the Soviet

Union and globally see, Mark D. Steinberg, *The Russian Revolution, 1905–1921* (New York: Oxford University Press, 2016).

24 Michael Denning, *The Cultural Front* (London: Verso, 1997), pp. xviii, 3–50.
25 McDuffie, *Sojourning for Freedom*, pp. 96–100, 167.
26 James R. Barrett, *William Z. Foster and the Tragedy of American Communism* (Urbana: University of Illinois Press, 1999), pp. 226–51.
27 William L. Patterson, *We Charge Genocide* (New York: International, 1951); Gerald Horne, *Black Revolutionary: William Patterson and the Globalization of the African American Struggle* (Urbana: University of Illinois Press, 2013).
28 Patterson, *We Charge Genocide*; Ruth Wilson Gilmore, *Golden Gulag: Prisons: Surplus, Crisis, and Opposition in Globalizing California* (Berkeley: University of California Press, 2007), p. 28.
29 Manning Marable, *Race, Reform, and Rebellion: The Second Reconstruction and Beyond in Black America, 1945–2006* (Jackson: University Press of Mississippi, 2007), pp. 24–6; Carol Anderson, *Eyes off the Prize: The United Nations and the African American Struggle for Human Rights, 1944–1955* (Cambridge: Cambridge University Press, 2003), pp. 58–9.
30 Arnold R. Hirsch, *The Making of the Second Ghetto: Race and Housing in Chicago, 1940–1960* (Chicago: University of Chicago Press, 1998), pp. 68–99; Thomas J. Sugrue, *The Origins of Urban Crisis: Race and Inequality in Postwar Detroit* (Princeton, NJ: Princeton University Press, 1996), pp. 231–58.
31 McDuffie, *Sojourning for Freedom*, pp. 161, 165–6, 169–70, 175–6.
32 Barrett, *William Z. Foster*, pp. 238–42.
33 Boyce Davies, *Left of Karl Marx*, pp. 134–8.
34 McDuffie, *Sojourning for Freedom*, pp. 171, 205–7; Boyce Davies, *Left of Karl Marx*, pp. 167–89.
35 Jones, "Problems of the Negro Woman!" pp. 51–67.
36 Schrecker, *Many Are the Crimes*, p. 159.
37 Jones, "Problems of the Negro Woman!" p. 52.
38 Ibid., pp. 52, 63.
39 Jones was hardly the only black radical who called attention to the ways in which Jim Crowism sullied the view of the United States among Africans and Asians across the nascent Third World. Prominent black radical spokespersons such as W. E. B. Du Bois, Paul Robeson, and William L. Patterson made similar arguments. However, none of them focused specific attention on black women in relation to the US foreign policy like Jones. Erik S. McDuffie, "Black and Red: Black Liberation, the Cold War, and the Horne Thesis," *Journal of African American History* 96, no. 2 (Spring 2011), p. 236.
40 Jones, "Problems of the Negro Woman!" pp. 51–67; McDuffie, *Sojourning for Freedom*, pp. 167–71.

41 Japan occupied the Korean peninsula from 1905 and 1945. The Japanese ruled Korea with an iron fist. Following the surrender of Japanese forces on the Korean peninsula on August 14, 1945, Soviet forces occupied territory to the north of the 38th parallel, while US forces occupied territory to the south of the line. Allan R. Millett, "The Korean People: Missing in Action in the Misunderstood War, 1945–1954," in William Stueck (ed.), *The Korean War in World History* (Lexington: University of Kentucky Press, 2004), pp. 13–19; Bruce Cumings, *The Korean War: A History* (New York: Modern Library, 2010), pp. xv–xvi.

42 Cumings, *The Korean War*, pp. 1–36, 243; I. F. Stone, *The Hidden History of the Korean War* (New York: Monthly Review Press, 1952); Millett, "The Korean People," pp. 13–51.

43 Jones, "Unity of Women," p. 151.

44 Ibid., pp. 151, 152–3, 159–61.

45 Jones, "Struggle for Peace," p. 2.

46 Ibid., 17.

47 Ibid., 8.

48 Erik S. McDuffie, "A 'New Freedom Movement of Negro Women': Sojourning for Truth, Justice, and Human Rights during the Early Cold War," *Radical History Review* 101 (2008), pp. 81–106.

49 Jones, "Struggle for Peace," p. 20.

50 Inger Skjelsbæk, "Is Femininity Inherently Peaceful?," in Inger Skjelsbæk and Dan Smith (eds.), *Gender, Peace, and Conflict* (Oslo: International Peace and Research Institute, 2001), pp. 47–67.

51 Millett, "The Korean People," pp. 50–1; Cumings, *The Korean War*, pp. 139–46, 165–203.

52 Cumings, *The Korean War*, p. 35.

53 Stone, *Hidden History*, pp. 139–74, 335–48.

54 Schrecker, *Many Are the Crimes*, pp. 249, 286, 287.

55 Leon Trotsky, *Revolution Betrayed* (Mineola, NY: Dover, 2004).

56 Steve Usdin, *Engineering Communism: How Two Americans Spied for Stalin and Founded the Soviet Silicon Valley* (New Haven, CT: Yale University Press, 2005).

57 Cold War era interpretations of the black left and their relation to communism and anticolonialism have found renewed interest among some scholars, see especially Carol Anderson, *Bourgeois Radicals: The NAACP and the Struggle for Colonial Liberation, 1941–1960* (Cambridge: Cambridge University Press, 2015). According to Anderson, too many scholars—most notably historian Gerald Horne—have "rendered the anticolonial trail of the [NAACP] and its allies so small that it was almost invisible, while disproportionately magnifying the footprints of the Left." Calling for the "decentering" of black leftists like W. E. B. Du Bois from the narrative of postwar anticolonialism, she rejects charges made by Du Bois at the time and

contemporary scholars like Horne that the NAACP abandoned anticolonialism during the Cold War. Instead, Anderson argues that the NAACP vigorously promoted a principled stance against colonialism across the emerging Third World (5). In contrast to most accounts, she presents Du Bois unflatteringly as a brilliant but disorganized pan-African activist. While she brings useful insight into the NAACP's anticolonial work during the 1950s, her argument nonetheless overlooks the very real ways the organization deliberately exploited anticommunism and redbaiting to isolate its black left critics and to gain favor with US Cold War policy makers. For an insightful review of Anderson's book, see Robert Shaffer, "African American Agency in US Foreign Policy: World War II to the Present," *Journal of African American History* 103, no. 3 (Summer 2018), pp. 418–29.

58 Jones, "Struggle for Peace," p. 20.
59 Lawrence W. Britt, "Fascism Anyone? The 14 Defining Characteristics of Fascism," *Free Inquiry Magazine* 23, no. 2 (2003), https://secularhumanism.org/2003/03/fascism-anyone/ (accessed October 10, 2018).
60 Gary Younge, "Trump and Brexit Are Symptoms of the Same Failure to Reckon with Racism," *Guardian*, March 30, 2018; Justin Welby, "Archbishop of Canterbury Suggests Brexit in 'Fascist Tradition,'" *Guardian*, February 13, 2017, https://www.theguardian.com/uk-news/2017/feb/13/archbishop-suggests-brexit-fascist-tradition; Anastasia Lacina, "Donald Trump, Brexit, and the Rise of New Fascism," *Fordham Political Review*, January 31, 2017, http://fordhampoliticalreview.org/donald-trump-brexit-and-the-rise-of-new-fascism/ (all accessed November 8, 2018).
61 Sholto Byrnes, "Brazil's Bolsonaro Is Tapping into Seething Discontent over Globalization-Just Like Trump and Duterte before Him," *The National*, October 22, 2018, https://www.thenational.ae/opinion/comment/brazil-s-bolsonaro-is-tapping-into-seething-discontent-over-globalisation-just-like-trump-and-duterte-before-him-1.783111 (accessed November 19, 2018).
62 Julie Hirschfeld Davis et al., "Trump Alarms Lawmakers with Disparaging Words for Haiti and Africa," *New York Times*, January 11, 2018, https://www.nytimes.com/2018/01/11/us/politics/trump-shithole-countries.html (accessed November 8, 2018).
63 "'White Power Ideology': Why El Paso Is Part of a Growing Global Threat," *Guardian*, August 5, 2019, https://www.theguardian.com/us-news/2019/aug/04/el-paso-shooting-white-nationalist-supremacy-violence-christchurch (accessed August 10, 2019).
64 Haki R. Madhubuti, "Introduction," in Haki R. Madhubuti and Lasana D. Kazembe (eds.), *Not Our President: New Directions from the Pushed Out, the Others, and the Clear Majority in Trump's Stolen America* (Chicago: Third World Press, 2017), p. xxix.

65 For an insightful discussion of the connections between Obama's neoliberal policies at home and support for war abroad see, Tariq Ali, *The Obama Syndrome: Surrender at Home, War Abroad* (London: Verso, 2011).
66 Jabari Asim, *What Obama Means: … For Our Culture, Our Politics, Our Future* (New York: William Morrow, 2009).
67 Edward Helmore, "More Major US immigration Raids Likely despite Outcry – Report," *Guardian*, https://www.theguardian.com/us-news/2019/aug/10/ice-raids-us-immigration-workplaces?CMP=Share_iOSApp_Other (accessed August 10, 2019).
68 "Obama on Muammar Gaddafi Death: President Obama Addresses Death of Libyan Leader," *Huffington Post*, http://www.huffingtonpost.com/2011/10/20/obama-muammar-gaddafi-dead_n_1022106.html (accessed July 18, 2012).
69 It should be noted that Obama expanded the US war in Afghanistan even after he received the Nobel Peace Prize in 2009. Kelley, "Freedom Democrat or Neoliberal," p. 260.

   Erik S. McDuffie, "Obama, the World, and Africa," *Souls: A Critical Journal of Black Politic, Culture, and Society* 14, nos. 1–2 (2012), pp. 28–37; William Blum, "Bombing Libya: The Origins of Europe's Immigration Crisis," *Counterpunch*, September 25, 2018, https://www.counterpunch.org/2018/09/25/bombing-libya-the-origins-of-europes-immigration-crisis/ (accessed August 12, 2019).

Bibliography

Jones, Claudia. "An End to the Neglect of the Problems of the Negro Woman!" *Political Affairs* 28, no. 6 (June 1949): 51–67.

Jones, Claudia. "For the Unity of Women in the Cause of Peace." *Political Affairs* 30 (February 1951): 151–68.

Jones, Claudia. "The Struggle for Peace in the United States." 31, no. 2 (February 1952): 1–20.

McDuffie, Erik S. *Sojourning for Freedom: Black Women, American Communism, and the Making of Black Left Feminism*. Durham: Duke University Press, 2011.

Washington, Margaret Helen. "Alice Childress, Lorraine Hansberry, and Claudia Jones: Black Women Write the Popular Front." In *Left of the Color Line: Race, Radicalism, and Twentieth Century Literature of the United States*, ed. Bill V. Mullen and James Smethurst, 183–204. Chapel Hill: University of North Carolina Press, 2003.

9

American Communism in a Time of Détente

Beth Slutsky

In February 1972, President Richard Nixon made his historic trip to the People's Republic of China, putting into place what he wanted to be part of his most significant foreign policy legacy: détente, or the cooling of Cold War tensions. In traveling to China and meeting briefly with Chairman Mao and other Chinese Communist dignitaries, he hoped to show the world that the ideological feuds and proxy wars of the past two-and-a-half decades did not have to determine future relations—especially trade and economic policy—with Communists internationally.[1] Yet, that very same week, while Nixon pursued this diplomatic policy abroad, back at home, a domestic trial had captured the attention of Communists everywhere and threatened to derail his vision for the Cold War. In San Rafael, California, Angela Davis, the famed Communist, philosopher, and Black Panther supporter faced trial for murder charges. The world watched with interest as the brilliant, radical, black, beautiful Communist Party member defended herself in court on murder charges. The weapons she purchased had been used in a dramatic courtroom shoot-out in August 1970 that left a judge and two officers dead. Though Davis was not present at the scene of the crime, and of course she did not pull trigger, in the days that followed the shooting, police issued an arrest warrant for her, she fled, had her name placed on the Federal Bureaus of Investigation's (FBI's) ten-most-wanted list, and eventually she was arrested. After months of preparation and negotiation, Davis's team was ready for the courtroom just as Nixon's diplomats were ready to face an international Communist foe. The parallels between Nixon's attempts to ease tensions with Communists abroad and Davis's trial potentially inflaming foreigners' perception of radicals' treatment at home highlights the way that domestic stresses and international relations converged in the Cold War of the 1970s.[2] The trial and the visit also illustrate the tenuous role of American Communists in the last three decades of the twentieth century.

The interplay between Nixon's attempts to change the world's understanding of the Cold War and Davis's famed trial continued for months. By March 1972, national television in Moscow aired a program titled "Problems and Politics in the USA." It focused heavily on two main topics that Soviets viewed as most damaging to the United States: American involvement in Vietnam (especially since bombing there continued alongside Nixon's February visit to Asia) and Davis's trial. Alarmed at the potential damage this could do to the image of the American justice system abroad, embassy officials in Moscow closely monitored how the Soviet press portrayed these topics and sent telegrams to the Department of State explaining that Vietnam and Davis were "the two most useful propaganda themes of the hour" for Soviets.[3] The duality of Davis's publicized trial occurring at the same time that Nixon pursued this policy abroad highlights the changes and continuities of Cold War era struggles on the world stage. More so, the international intrigue surrounding her trial and the eastern bloc tour Davis took in the weeks after her acquittal reveal how the public experienced these 1972 developments as a continuation of Cold War Communist trials. And although the Nixon administration tried to frame it as removed from previous Cold War trials (after all the Communist Party was not illegal, and her membership was not in question in 1972), his administration was quite interested in and concerned about how her American Communist identity might affect his policy of détente.

The context surrounding Davis's trial and the Communist Party of the United States of America's (CPUSA) role in it helps to illustrate the nature of American radicalism in the last decades of the twentieth century. That Davis faced trial, and that the party publicly led and funded her defense, while Nixon worked to negotiate with Communists abroad and continue to demonize them at home illustrates a new dimension of American radicalism in the last third of the twentieth century. American Communists worked to maintain their relevance through noted trials, leaders, and coalitions. And in this era in which membership in the CPUSA no longer constituted a crime, and as US government leaders cautiously worked to open relations with some Communist nations, its treatment of Communists at home came into focus in a new way. Not only was the outside world watching the relationship between American treatment of Communists at home and abroad, the US government felt this tension and seemed more determined to navigate this more consciously than how it had handled Communists two decades earlier. However, keenly aware that the CPUSA structure still existed and financially supported American revolutionaries, leaders decided to stay the course of détente and monitor the situation. The American Communists aimed to seize on these Cold War trials as a way to build back coalitions and receive public support for a party that had been considered latent and certainly outdated with the generation of baby boomers who considered themselves revolutionaries. It was with this group—through Davis's trial—that the party managed to make a comeback of sorts by acquiring newfound relevance, in a way that lasted to the end of the twentieth century.

These last few decades of CPUSA history, epitomized by Davis's trial and the cooling of Cold War tensions, also allows historians to reflect back on the continuities and changes on this revolutionary movement that lasted for nearly the entire twentieth century. The CPUSA's existence offered American leftists a history, a model of how to live as a "professional revolutionary," and a place to call home—ideologically and culturally. All American Communists believed class to be the fundamental source of inequality. Belonging to the CPUSA gave Communists in the final decades of the twentieth century an enduring ideological identity, institutional support, leadership, and an international communist community. While the ultimate dissolution of the party in the 1990s seems predetermined today, its persistent presence in America throughout the last third of the twentieth century has been understudied and underappreciated in connecting an unbroken line of radicalism across the twentieth century. Understanding the distinct continuities in party policy, leadership, and infrastructure is key to appreciating the significance of the party overall, even for it to stake a claim to an authentic American cultural identity. One of the most enduring and remarkable aspects of radicalism in the twentieth century was the longevity and continuity of the infrastructure of the CPUSA. Although, by 1972, the party had shrunk in size considerably from its heyday in earlier decades, its democratic centralist governing structure, ideology, and strategies of coalition building continued to define the Left in important ways that stretched to the end of the century. Indeed, with the exception of a few years in which it was actually criminalized, the CPUSA stands as one of the most enduring continuous leaders of leftist ideology and activism. Its lasting place in American radicalism marks leftism in America in the twentieth century as continuous, wedded to an overarching principle of class consciousness. In its absence, it remains to be seen how leftist ideology can serve as an influence in American political and social movements.

The legacy of the American communism lies in part in the enduring bureaucratic infrastructure that provided the financial and administrative backing for revolutionaries. Nowhere in the 1970s was this more apparent than in its institutional support for trials and campaigns surrounding communists like

Davis. At the height of escalation in Vietnam and anticolonial struggles around the world, Angela Davis became attracted to American communism when she was a philosophy graduate student studying under Herbert Marcuse at the University of California San Diego in 1967. She was drawn to the intersectional approach to class and racial oppression that California Communists discussed. In her autobiography, she recalled attending a workshop on Black Politics and Economics that argued how "power relationships which placed black people at the bottom stemmed from the use of racism as a tool of the economically ascendant class—the capitalists. Racism meant more profits and, insofar as white workers are concerned, division and confusion."[4] As a black Communist living in California in the late 1960s, Davis became deeply involved in the trials of radical black activists, some of whom had been key leaders in the Black Panther Party. Davis' home branch of the CPUSA, the Che-Lumumba Club formed in part to explicitly come to the defense of incarcerated black men. The Che-Lumumba Club (named after Che Guevara and Patrice Lumumba), formed in 1967 as a racially separate club cell, argued that organizing in poverty-stricken segregated neighborhoods was essential in confronting class struggle in Southern California. With an all-black leadership and racially separatist party cell, black Communists in this club argued that racial separatism was the most effective way to organize segregated poverty-stricken neighborhoods.

When the American Party returned to a racially separatist approach in the late 1960s, it seemed to call into question communists' long-standing class-based understanding of the world. Yet, at the time, Che-Lumumba Club leaders argued to the broader Communist Party that black separatism was necessary for recruiting success. In a position paper that Southern California Communist branches circulated, leaders maintained, "The role of the white organizers in the negro community has been, for years, that of the social workers, the 'do-gooder'. This, together with the rise of nationalist tendencies in the negro ghetto, serves to make it virtually impossible for the white organizers to be greeted as other than the stereotype of the social worker."[5] Arguing for pragmatism and efficiency in their attempts to enlist sympathizers in black neighborhoods, its leaders decided that non-white clubs should be permitted in predominantly nonwhite neighborhoods. Eventually, they argued, nonwhite sympathizers would be more likely to join broader Communist organizers and campaigns if they came to the party through nonwhite leaders. This racially conscious strategy especially served to politicize and mobilize African Americans in Southern California who had been victims of police abuse. With a long and deep history of violence and harassment at the hands of the Los Angeles Police Department, California

Communists argued that even in the context of the Cold War, it would be useful to have nonwhite Communists work to recruit more members. Nonwhite Communist Clubs "could serve to build negro/white unity by instructing white communities on the police harassment in the black ghetto, while serving to give the black community some reason for confidence in white folks," thereby serving the long-term class-based interests of the party.[6]

The CPUSA framed and justified its racially separate cells as a response to the broader radicalization of the civil rights movement, marked by Stokeley Carmichael's coining of the phrase "Black Power," and initiated by the Student Non-Violent Coordinating Committee's (SNCC) expulsion of its white members when it radicalized in 1966. Traditional nonviolent civil rights organizations like the Congress on Racial Equality (CORE) initially argued that "Black Power is entirely consistent with our philosophy and our goals," and that it did not have to include the expulsion of white members. Still, even the civil rights groups that resisted the call for Black Nationalism found themselves becoming more radical in response to the calls for Black Power.[7] Upset over the sluggish pace of improvements in racial equality, by 1967 many activists came to believe that forcing integration "by any means necessary" would be the only way to achieve social change.[8] And the party, Du Bois Club, and Che-Lumumba Club in particular, chose to engage in this dialogue about black separatism in order to maintain their relevance on the civil rights and radical fronts in Los Angeles, even in the context of a broader 1960s exodus of many longtime Communist Party members.

Che-Lumumba Club leaders organized meetings on college campuses, in community centers, and among workers alliances. This kind of Communist activism enabled participants to focus on the intersection between race and class inequality. As antithetical as this may seem to a party wedded to developing class consciousness, adopting a Third-World nationalist ideology toward not just poverty and segregation, but also policing, the party reasoned that in the wake of the August, 1965 Watts uprisings (and the dozens of urban uprisings that followed), the root of the struggle was really a colonial struggle within the United States. "Watts is comparable to a colonial area occupied by an invading armed force," the party argued, "subject to the constant pressures of that alien army."[9] Staking claim to an argument used several years later by Third World Left organizations, including the Black Panther Party, the CPUSA compared the oppression of minorities in the United States with colonized peoples in the Third World.[10] This amounted to more than a power struggle and violation of civil liberties, according to the party. Instead, the eruption of violence—and the police and city government response to this violence—signaled a colonial struggle between an oppressed nation and its colonizers. And it was the infrastructure that the Che-Lumumba Club came to be as a club cell within the CPUSA. Davis, and others like her, joined this broader national and international movement that other communists found useful through which to wage their battles.

This ideological and political framework allowed Communists like Davis to not only articulate this critique of 1970s America, but it also provided the very practical defense for her support of perceived class prisoners. For Davis, one of the most crystallizing moments that exposed the intersections of poverty, racism, violence, and policing happened on January 16, 1970. That day, prisoners at the famed Soledad Prison in California's Central Valley murdered a prison guard in retaliation for the murders of three inmates some days earlier. The murder of the prison guard followed a grand jury's determination that the original killing by the prison guard had been legally justified. After eight days of interrogating the 146 inmates of the wing where the murder occurred, prison officials accused George Jackson, Fleeta Drumgo, and John Wesley Clutchette (all serving time for burglary or robbery) of perpetrating the murder. In the midst of these developments, George Jackson began corresponding with Davis, who was working to bring national attention to the case.[11] Davis had helped to establish the Soledad Brothers Defense Committee to offer legal, financial, and publicity related assistance to the accused. Figures as diverse as Jane Fonda, Benjamin Spock, Noam Chomsky, Allen Ginsberg, along with prominent ministers, professors, and governing officials lent their support to the Soldedad Brother. College campuses, black communities, and leftist circles united in distributing "Free the Soledad Brothers" buttons and by publicizing the accusations brought against the three men. Arguing on several points about the legality of charging the three prisoners with the murder, the Soledad Brothers Defense Committee members hinged a large part of their argument on what they determined to be a paradox: "Three black prisoners are dead at Soledad. This is called justifiable homicide. One white guard is dead. This is called murder."[12] Thus, the CPUSA was reestablishing its value as an entity that constructed coalitions of leftists to draw attention to key trials and campaigns.

In the midst of the campaign to raise funds for the defense, Davis developed a close personal relationship with Jackson. For weeks, she commuted between northern and Southern California to attend Jackson's trial. She also made appearances at high-profile events like one in June 1970 at a rally in front of the State Building in Los Angeles. Standing as a bodyguard on one side of Davis, George Jackson's 17-year-old brother, Jonathan Jackson, proudly situated himself as a protector for the brilliant Communist supporter of his brother. Davis had become such a close friend of the Jackson family by this point that she temporarily moved into the family's home in Pasadena. The following month she and Jonathan traveled to Northern California to visit George.[13]

Then, on August 7, 1970, Davis became the centerpiece of her own murder case, a nationwide manhunt, and massively publicized trial. Jonathan Jackson took several weapons into a San Rafael, California, courtroom where James McClain, a friend of George Jackson's, was to be tried for a prison stabbing at San Quentin. Jackson hoped to free his brother by taking hostages in this courtroom. He ended up taking hostages and killing three people, including the judge and two inmates. Police killed Jackson in the shoot-out that ensued. Three of the guns used in the shootout were legally purchased and registered to Angela Davis. Within the next three days, this piece of evidence led the police to seek Davis's arrest for aiding in the murder. They accused her of having bought three of the guns and conspiring to use them in the shootout. In response, Davis fled Los Angeles, was placed on the FBI's ten-most-wanted list, and hid in multiple cities throughout the country for two months. When the FBI found her in New York on October 13, 1970, and extradited her to California, they charged her with murder, conspiracy to commit murder, and kidnapping because of her indirect involvement in the courtroom shoot-out.[14]

The CPUSA immediately came to her aid, which reflects its continued ability to provide the necessary administrative support for radical-construct coalitions with non-Communist leftists. In fact, Davis's imprisonment and trial dominated the party's agenda for nearly two years. Leading black members of Davis's California Communist Party founded and coordinated the National United Committee to Free Angela Davis (NUCFAD) that drew prominent mainstream national and international attention. Across the country, the NUCFAD organized protests, marches and speeches in prominent public areas to attract as much attention as possible to Davis's case. Seeking to connect race, class, and imprisonment, the party's rallies attempted to promote "the direct link between racism and repression, between racism and arrests, and between racism and the prison conditions which create prison rebellions."[15] They did what they do best, provide support and build campaigns for key trials and campaigns. For example, party officials argued that all prisoners were victims of the capitalist system of class exploitation. Furthermore, nonwhites faced the double burden of class exploitation and racism. Remarkably, Communist leaders did not situate gender in this paradigm as a third level of oppression.[16] Instead, they used these race and class-based connections to build bridges. The Southern Christian Leadership

Conference (SCLC), the Black Caucus, student groups, and the Black Panther Party for Self Defense all backed the NUCFAD because they believed Davis to be innocent. Thus, throughout 1971 the CPUSA established a broad coalition domestically around Davis's impending trial that succeeded in crossing civil rights, Black Power, radical, progressive, and liberal boundaries. Such strong alliances over a Communist likely infuriated Nixon. However, as angered as this rhetoric may have made Nixon the Cold War president, he worked to avoid derailing his new foreign policy goals in an attempt to continue to cool Cold War tensions.

On an international scale, people from around the world—especially from Communist nations—showed their support for Davis in many ways. The CPUSA linked radicals throughout the world, which in the final decades of the twentieth century, served as an important way to sustain a global radical movement. American radicals, especially the younger baby boomer generation, found that a network to global Communists lent a different kind of activism to their work. The FBI, and then embassy officials, closely monitored dozens of applications for visas and reported on the reception American Communists received when traveling abroad. And global Communists appeared all too eager to welcome attention from American radicals, especially as it could tarnish the reputation of—or at least cause young radicals around the globe to question—the American justice system. The Secretary of the German Communist Party linked the Davis case with the "terror campaign of the U.S. in Viet Nam and Cambodia, with the insidious activities of the CIA against the national liberation fronts in developing countries and with the murder of 26 Black Power representatives."[17] For the Nixon administration that hoped to ease tensions between capitalist and Communist nations, these sorts of connections—and the support Davis received domestically—could potentially put the American government on the defensive and exacerbate differences. Meanwhile, Davis supporters in Munich visited the American consulate to submit a list of four thousand signatures gathered in that city to support Davis's defense. Across the Mediterranean, a youth group in Syria sent a delegation of twenty-five to thirty to the American embassy to call for Davis's release. The case of this imprisoned African American radical certainly provided the CPUSA with an opportunity to prove its relevance and to potentially complicate the plans of governmental leaders who sought to downplay political radicalism in their effort to unify over shared economic interests.

Seemingly on all continents, officials observed what the US embassy in London reported: that the Davis case is "the sort of humanitarian cause that is appealing. ... The Angela Davis case will receive widespread and increasing coverage in the British media and at least a sector of the public will take a keen interest in the course of American justice."[18] And many foreigners indeed acted on this interest. Petitioning the American government from abroad, Czechoslovakians wrote dozens of letters to the American embassy in Prague to protest Davis's initial imprisonment. Their leading publications followed up with regular updates about the progress of her appeals and trial. Ever careful to portray her trial in the most judicial and transparent light, American officials in Prague claimed to have responded to each individual letter they received.[19]

Some foreigners in eastern bloc nations in fact used Davis's trial to view the criticized American judicial system for themselves. In December 1970, fourteen leading Russian scientists sent a letter to President Nixon pleading for Davis's release. In response, Nixon promptly ordered the American embassy to communicate with the group and extend an invitation to the scientists to personally attend and observe the trial "to see justice in action," which they accepted.[20] In their correspondence, American embassy officials explained to the scientists that Davis "will receive the same impartial treatment under the American judicial system as any other individual charged with a crime," and confirmed the practice that "the proceedings involving Dr. Davis will be heard in open court and will be fully reported by representatives of the American and international press." Thus, much of the American government's response to international concern over Davis's trial focused on portraying it and the judicial process as routine, fair, and thoroughly American.[21] It served Nixon's international goals for Davis's trial to be depicted as simply a murder trial rather than something much larger and relating to her Communist involvement or personal affiliation with radicals.

Imprisoned for sixteen months awaiting trial, Davis finally went before a jury of eleven whites and one Mexican-American on February 27, 1972, the same week when Nixon visited Asia. To mobilize her national and international supporters, the NUCFAD published "FrameUp: A Weekly Trial Bulletin," to present regular updates on the progress of Davis's more than three-month-long trial.[22] The publication chronicled everything from day-to-day details about who was in the courtroom on given days, to witnesses, to additional publicity that the case was garnering, to pleas for additional funds from subscribers. After three months of presiding over Davis's murder trial, on June 4, 1972, after deliberating only thirteen hours, the jury acquitted Davis of all charges.[23] After announcing their verdict, a number of jurors publicly announced their support for her. One juror even came out to celebrate with Davis on the day of her release. Another wrote a book chronicling the ordeal of serving on such a publicized trial of an acclaimed woman.[24] Now it was up to the CPUSA to determine how to propel her trial into something larger that could sustain its place in American radical life.

Maintaining the momentum started by party members during the trial, Davis continued speaking and giving interviews reflecting on her time in prison, and more important to them, attacking the chronic problems of the prison system. Giving voice to condemn mass incarceration long before prison reform activists of the 1990s decried statutes such as the "three strikes" laws, Davis worked to again link class, poverty, racism, and incarceration. In an interview with a Black Panther newspaper, Davis told of repeated injustices that she heard of and became involved in as a prisoner.[25] She and the party took full advantage of the spectators who lingered after the trial and tried to bring these baby boomer radicals into the party. A three-week tour to raise funds for Davis's $250,000 legal expenses, ending in a massive rally at Madison Square Garden, brought this black Communist woman into the national and international spotlight.

From New York City, Davis and her close comrades turned their attention to supporters abroad and traveled to several foreign countries, including the Soviet Union. American officials in each country they visited closely monitored Davis's itinerary, appearances, and reception. She first arrived in Moscow at the end of August 1972, where she recalled being "accorded a heroine's welcome."[26] Davis spent a busy ten days attending factory meetings, visiting with dignitaries, holding rallies, and even receiving a title of honorary professor at Moscow State University. American diplomats informed their Washington counterparts that the Soviet evening news programs broadcast Davis's public appearances in great detail for every day of her trip. Reporting back to the State Department, officials abroad wrote that Davis "put on a thoroughly orthodox Soviet-style performance during her 13-day visit to the USSR ... her big-name appeal was well exploited by her Soviet hosts. She was shown in the company particularly of Soviet women, youth, the university community, the 'developing' minority nationalities of Central Asia, party members, workers, and Third World students in the USSR."[27]

Still, while the tone of American telegrams about Davis's visit in Moscow did not sound alarmed, government officials offered some analysis and context to their reaction behind her visit. This made it apparent that American officials felt they must pay close attention to her tour because they had Nixon's foreign policy to implement and they were somewhat concerned about how Davis's presence as an American Communist deeply critical of American Cold War policy could affect it. Telegrams specifically noted with relief that Davis made no direct attacks on the Nixon administration and that the national leaders of the Soviet Communist Party "maintained its distance during Angela's visit," and went to lengths to be reassured that she was not received as a "prominent political figure" but rather a "communist intellectual." Moreover, one American diplomat analyzed that Davis's visit came at a delicate time for the Soviets given their "hopes for further development of US-USSR trade, and the imminent arrival of Henry Kissinger as an ongoing reminder of the Nixon visit."[28] Thus Davis's Soviet visit served to complicate a delicately developing American-Soviet détente.

After touring the Soviet Union, she moved on to Europe where on September 12, 1972, fifty thousand supporters greeted her at the Berlin airport to commence her five-day-tour of Germany. Just as in Moscow, American embassy officials sent regular updates to the State Department noting the number of her appearances, supporters, and her statements in Germany.[29] On the next leg of Davis's trip, officials in Prague reported her September 17 arrival and then corresponded with the FBI asking for advice on how to respond to the local media about her appearances. They felt they needed to respond strategically to her appearances, one of which was at a crowded theater where three thousand spectators watched as Davis "wowed the crowd by … planting a kiss" on the cheek of a national Communist Party chair for raising his clenched fist to show his support for the iconographic move of the Black Power identity.[30] American officials—ever careful to downplay their public criticism of Communists because of Nixon's foreign policy aims—decided to stay in the background and simply note on classified memos that the whole-hearted reception she experienced might not have been entirely genuine by all ranks of Communists.

These trips were not new, and charting the popularity of American Communists abroad had become a regular part of embassy officials' roles. Perhaps, the careful tone of officials in 1972 had been informed by its experiences in the 1960s when American governmental leaders recorded not only how American radicals moved throughout Communist-aligned nations, but also American officials had to determine how an international Communist movement factored into the Cold War geopolitical situation. Years before Davis's posttrial tour, international Communist events had drawn radicals from nearly all continents, illustrating an important point of significance about American communism serving to connect radicals at home with radicals abroad in a systematic way. In 1968, for example African American baby boomer Communists attended a World Youth Festival in Bulgaria, and then toured the Soviet Union.[31] While belonging to the CPUSA in 1968 meant pledging allegiances to the party's internal democratic centralist structures, which was understandably unappealing and rigidly bureaucratic for a younger generation of radicals, it did provide black radicals with the global Communist movement. Moreover, what some of this generation had started to embrace was the fact that it was precisely the infrastructure and bureaucracy of the CPUSA that had managed to keep the party afloat for decades. Though antidemocratic by definition, and unappealing in governing style to many activists of her era, the party presented this generation of communists an opportunity to relate to an international world of leftists (Figure 9.1).

At the 1968 World Youth Festival, American Communists joined with twenty-thousand young communists from around the world. The American press and embassy officials widely remarked about how this and other festivals would be used as propaganda for anti-Vietnam War and Third World Liberation movements, and the American Communists that attended embraced the opportunity. The *LA Times* reported that "pieces of American planes shot down in Vietnam will be awarded as medals to participants," in this kind of "Marxist Olympics."[32] Some American Communists proudly declared that they donated blood at the conference to be sent to North Vietnamese soldiers and civilians. Intending to form a coalition between young radicals from Communist nations and from non-Communist nations, organizers of this and several other similar events fostered a global Communist movement that was made more possible by the infrastructure of the CPUSA.

The connection to international communism continued to appeal to black Communists, while it also compelled the American government to heighten its surveillance of them. In the summer of 1969, in the midst of the fury of anti-Vietnam protests, American radicals belonged to an infrastructure of global communism. For more than two months, a delegation of American Communists traveled to Cuba, reportedly at the invitation of the Cuban government. FBI records indicate that the National Secretariat of the CPUSA advised its members to steer clear of official Cuban dignitaries, but the members brushed aside this advice and accepted the invitation to spend time in Cuba.[33]

A curious exchange that reflects the continued struggles of the Cold War occurred over Davis's visit to Tanzania the following year. Davis made a trip to African nations to meet supporters there and to attempt to forge relationships with international dignitaries. However, when she tried to visit the president of Tanzania, he refused to set up a meeting with her, reportedly saying he would not waste his time with an American Communist and asked "what did she bring here besides her beauty." American officials in Dar es Salaam were quick to note this cool reception and exchanged several telegrams with those on the ground and

American Communism in a Time of Détente 217

Figure 9.1 Angela Davis urges "Declare your independence: Vote for Hall and Tyner." Credit: Library of Congress, Washington, DC, Reproduction Number: LC-USZC4-6510 (color film copy transparency) LC-USZ62-123084 (b&w film copy neg.)

the State Department about such cracks in Davis's international support.[34] While more of an aberration than representative of the positions of foreign leaders toward Davis's visit, this interaction nevertheless signals the interplay between détente and continued American radicals' efforts to promote communism.

If only temporarily, Davis's case brought widespread attention to the American Communist Party, which radical leaders at home and abroad only hoped would carry over into campaigns to help other political prisoners who they argued had been victimized by the capitalist system. According to one chronicler of Davis's trial, "Communism in America hasn't been as active as it is today for the past forty years. On campuses, on street corners in major cities, and during mass demonstrations, speakers are constantly proclaiming their determination to overthrow the capitalist system." The case mentioned earlier of the Russian scientists' letter to President Nixon and his response is a case in point.[35] Although Davis's case put the spotlight on Cold War-era divisions, Nixon's administration worked to frame it less about foreign communism versus domestic capitalism and more about the ways in which all Americans—even Communists—were tried fairly for crimes they were accused of committing. Government officials at home and abroad (as well as foreign governments) had to respond carefully and coolly so as to avoid confronting political differences. That the American and Communist governments both recognized the challenges posed by Davis, but did not have her case derail détente reflects how, by 1972, differing ideologies did not fuel the Cold War at the highest levels. It also suggests the enduring relevance of the CPUSA in continuing to push forward a radical movement through its money, leadership, structures, and abilities to build coalitions with non-Communist leftists.

CPUSA leaders of course continued to push for leftist radical change domestically and globally throughout the remainder of the 1970s, 1980s, and into the 1990s, albeit on a much different scale than its strategies from the 1930s. The party's path to socialism had changed substantially from what it had embraced in earlier years. For one, it did not seem to be as far left as other Maoist revolutionaries who espoused immediate revolution. Second, by the mid-1970s Gus Hall conceded that his grandchildren most likely would not live under communism. Instead, he and the national party leadership came to embrace a gradual replacement of capitalism by socialism. They claimed "that U.S. socialism will clearly be marked 'made in the USA.'"[36] Most of their publications heralded that while "the future of humanity is socialism," the majority of Americans would have to democratically decide to pursue this end to monopoly capitalism. By the early 1980s, the Communist Party had even fully come to support a left-center alliance, although it continued to run candidates in national elections.[37] Due in part to their strong internal organization, but also to their willingness to participate in the democratic process, the CPUSA—especially particular branches that spoke directly to local issues in California—remained relevant in the 1980s.[38] In the 1980 and 1984 presidential elections, Gus Hall and Angela Davis ran on the CPUSA ticket for president and vice president respectively. These kinds of campaigns required organizers collecting hundreds of thousands of signatures to earn candidates' spots on the ballot. Just as Communists and their sympathizers canvassed for this across California in the 1930s, they continued in this tradition throughout the 1980s.[39]

Beyond running candidates in local elections to maintain the recognition and relevance of communism, throughout the 1980s, a core group of committed revolutionary activists redirected the party's activities to reflect changing problems of the country. Leaders like Kendra and Franklin Alexander, Carl Bloice, and a few other committed Communists in the Bay Area organized for wider ranging programs that focused on labor, peace, antiracism, and local radical electoral politics. Bay Area residents took notice and connected Communist activism in this last decade of the Cold War to a deeply entrenched leftist political climate. Mainstream newspapers like the *San Jose Mercury News* reported in 1987: "In the Bay Area, the Communist Party is working to unionize Silicon Valley workers and works with other groups to urge local governments to provide more affordable housing for the poor."[40] The San Francisco Party focused its activism on homelessness, while in Oakland it devoted its attention on the effects of plant closings on recently unemployed workers. The party also operated Bread and Roses, a bookstore in San Jose, where a substantial amount of party activity occurred. While local campaigns sustained the broader-based leftist activism in the Bay Area, Communists still made broader efforts to connect the local with national and international revolutionary movements. Party leaders encouraged members to support both local causes rooted in labor organizing, as well as more global antiapartheid activism.[41] Regardless of the party's national and internal political battles, a small cohort of Communist leaders took the Northern California party's priorities in an active and public direction. This open strategy allowed party members' involvement to be less threatening and be legitimated in the public realm.

In what turned out to be the final months of the CPUSA, the party had a steady membership base of between four thousand and fifteen thousand.[42] Still, coinciding with such international changes, rifts inside the party in the late 1980s caused a group of Northern California leaders to push the national party to reform its authoritarian ways. In an initial attempt to reform it from within, Charlene Mitchell and Danny Rubin, both National Board members, announced at a famous December 1991, national party conference in Cleveland, Ohio: "We believe that a majority of the Party will agree that substantial alterations from past practice must be made in our method of election of leadership to make it more democratic ... We are convinced that for the membership to have a full voice in policy-making, it needs and has a right to know of major alternatives and differences." Calling for a considerably different democratic structure in the Communist Party, reformers demanded to have direct input to the Central Committee.[43] Naturally, staunch supporters of Hall and the party's traditional democratic centralist structure felt deep betrayal and alarm at what they perceived to be factionalism. Jarvis Tyler, speaking on behalf of the Presiding Committee at the December 1991 conference, denounced eleven members by name, who he claimed were plotting secession in the hospitality room of the conference hotel.

For six months leading up to the reform conference, these eleven members had indeed been formulating their criticisms of the CPUSA's current democratic centralist structure and policies. In "A Message to the National Committee," this group of insurgent reformers condemned the party for straying away from its all-encompassing 1980 goal of attacking the Far Right by adopting, what they believed to be, a more ambitious and divisive goal of creating an anti-monopoly alliance. They feared Hall's continued leadership and directives would alienate labor alliances and African Americans. The insurgent's message went on to criticize the party for failing to give adequate attention to promote disarmament. Furthermore, they charged that Hall refused to allow the party to focus on organizing service industry workers and that he rejected calls to place women's oppression high on their agenda. Using the democratic centralist structure of the party to push Communist priorities in these seemingly unpopular directions, Hall ultimately forced many prominent members, such as Kendra Alexander, Angela Davis, and Charlene Mitchell, to join the initiative sect.[44] Most alarming to Hall, the reformers called upon the party, and Socialist and Communist parties around the world, to turn inward. Members of the insurgent initiative group implored the CPUSA leadership and membership base to realistically examine the weakening and collapse of the Soviet bloc and rely on self-criticism as a path to understand and adapt to a real-world implementation of socialism. The party needed to become more open and democratic, the reformers contended. Alexander and the other separatists decreed, "The existence in our ranks, including in the leadership, of diverse opinions should not be considered harmful or exceptional."[45] But their opinions did not convince Hall to change the party's ways.

At the national party convention in December 1991, Hall and other leaders immediately dismissed from their leadership roles all people associated with the initiative movement.[46] By early spring, 1992 the Northern California branches of the Communist Party voted openly and overwhelmingly to leave the CPUSA.[47]

The policies and tactics of the Central Committee, particularly of Gus Hall, frustrated most members in California to the point of no reconciliation. Those who ultimately decided to leave had a very hard time making the break, but they determined that the best way to enact the social and economic changes they envisioned was through a more democratically oriented organization. While remaining a steadfast devotee of the CPUSA's hierarchy for decades, the eventual criticism and abandonment of the Stalinist style structures led the party to fracture permanently.

Upon resigning from the party, California communists quickly dropped the capital "C" and continued to identify as radicals, albeit through non-CPUSA structures. Especially in Northern California, former Communists moved quickly to establish the Committees of Correspondence (COC), which claimed one thousand members upon its inception—80 percent of the former Northern California membership in the CPUSA. Created in California in the spring of 1992 and nationally the following year, the COC allowed itself a greater degree of internal democracy. The committees claimed that they sought "to create a broad front against reaction and militarism, for expanded democracy, equality, jobs, economic security, peace and solidarity, and radical social reforms."[48] A National Conference on "Perspectives for Democracy and Socialism in [the] 90s" at University of California Berkeley in July of 1992 formally founded the COC as a national left activist organization. Attendees of this conference elected former and seasoned Communist leaders like Kendra Alexander as a member of a five co-chairperson committee that reported to a national structure, akin to the organizing structure of the CPUSA.[49] Their goals paralleled the goals of the local CPUSA, but they could pursue them without accountability to and interference from the Central Committee. Support for the peace movement, fighting racism and sexism, and combating a declining standard of living for working people were their foremost goals.[50]

In the wake of the dissolution of the CPUSA, American radicals still very much identified as communists, just without access and obligation to the formal party structures. In 1990, when longtime California Communist Dorothy Healey published her memoir, the *LA Times* did a feature article interviewing her in light of the ending of the Cold War and the seeming collapse of the Communist bloc nations. Sounding as anticapitalist and revolutionary in her critique of American anticommunist foreign policy as ever, Healey's rhetoric was as intense in 1990 as it was in 1940. According to the interview, "Healey said, it is easy to understand the upheaval in Eastern Europe. What she cannot understand if why Americans have not taken to the streets to protest the savings and loan scandal."[51] Instead of viewing the collapse of the Soviet Union as a "triumph of capitalism," Healey argued instead that end of the Cold War marked "a defeat of Stalinism—the practices and concepts of that version of socialism, of centralized, authoritarian bureaucracy."[52] The following year, Healey was appointed to be the vice-chair of the Democratic Socialists of America.

The end of the CPUSA was tied to a dramatically changing international radical movement, and to dynamics within the party leadership and structure. As this generation of American radicals that had weathered the intense anticommunism of the Cold War, remained devoted through the social protest radical movements of the 1970s, and still decided that the party was the best way to wage their struggles, in some ways it seems an abrupt ending for a decades-old party. For decades, the democratic centralist organizational structure of the party presented a methodical way to go about waging their struggles as professional revolutionaries. But ultimately, the rigid structure helped the party stick together much longer than any other radical organization in the twentieth century. The CPUSA stands as one of the most enduring and significant representations of leftist activism in American history. To its membership base who found it to be a community, a profession, and model to live as revolutionaries, the party was a home to a group who had been demonized by most of America. And within this home, activists worked to build bridges with similarly minded activists, some more successful than others. The CPUSA leadership and campaigns in the final decades of the twentieth century illustrates the effectiveness and the limits of this in the era of détente.

Notes

1 For general background on Nixon's détente policy, see: Lloyd Gardner, *The Great Nixon Turnaround* (New York: New Viewpoints, 1973); Robert Litwak, *Détente and the Nixon Doctrine: American Foreign Policy and the Pursuit of Stability, 1969–1974* (Cambridge: Cambridge University Press, 1974); Joan Hoff, *Nixon Reconsidered* (New York: Basic Books, 1994), pp. 147–207.

2 Some studies that have examined the interplay between international relations and domestic developments in the Cold War include Thomas Borstelmann, *The Cold War and the Color Line: American Race Relations in the Global Arena* (Cambridge: Harvard University Press, 2001); Paul Gordon Lauren, *Power and Prejudice: The Politics and Diplomacy of Racial Discrimination* (Boulder, CO: Westview, 1988); Penny M. Von Eschen, *Race against Empire: Black Americans*

and Anticolonialism, 1937–1957 (Ithaca, NY: Cornell University Press, 1997); Mary L. Dudziak, *Cold War Civil Rights: Race and the Image of American Democracy* (Princeton, NJ: Princeton University Press, 2002).

3   Telegram from American Embassy in Moscow to Department of State, March 1972, General Records of the Department of State RG 59, Box 2682 NWDPH-2 1997, National Archives, College Park, MD.
4   Angela Davis, *Angela Davis: An Autobiography* (New York: International, 1974), p. 160.
5   Los Angeles Community Organizing Committee, Position Paper, 1966–7, folder 3/box 2, W.E.B. Du Bois Club, L.A. and national, Robert Duggan Collection, 1120, UCLA Special Collections, Los Angeles.
6   Ibid.
7   Los Angeles CORE, *Here We Stand*, undated, file 4/box 14, CORE 1959–64, Twentieth Century Organizational Files, SoCalLib.
8   Stokeley Carmichael, *Toward Black Liberation* (Ithaca, NY: Glad Day Press, 1966); William Van Deburg, *New Day in Babylon: The Black Power Movement and American Culture, 1965–1975* (Chicago: University of Chicago Press, 1992); John Dittmer, *Local People: The Struggle for Civil Rights in Mississippi* (Urbana: University of Illinois Press, 1994); Maurice Isserman and Michael Kazin, *America Divided: The Civil War of the 1960s* (New York: Oxford University Press, 2000); Kenneth J. Heineman, *Put Your Bodies upon the Wheels: Student Revolt in the 1960s* (Chicago: Ivan R. Dee, 2001), pp. 106–35.
9   Dorothy Healey, Southern California District Policy, 1966 CPUSA Convention, Los Angeles, 1966: p. 5, folder Alexander, Kendra, Franklin and Kendra Alexander Collection, SoCalLib.
10 This is unique because third world leftist organizations were anti-Soviet Maoist Marxists, which of course countered CPUSA positions. See: Laura Pulido, *Black, Brown, Yellow and Left: Radical Activism in Los Angeles* (Berkeley: University of California Press, 2006), chapter 4.
11 Davis, *Angela Davis*, 256–60; folder Soledad Brothers Defense Committee, Franklin and Kendra Alexander Collection, SoCalLib.
12 Angela Yvonne Davis (1944–), folders 1–3/box 1, Records: UCLA Academic Freedom Case, 1969–71 and Angela Davis Defense Committee, 1969–75, Angela Davis Collection, SoCalLib; Soledad Brothers, and Soledad Brothers Legal Committee, letters of support, folder, Soledad Brothers, Franklin and Kendra Alexander Collection, SoCalLib.
13 The Professor, *Angela: A Revealing Closeup of the Woman and the Trial* (North Hollywood, CA: Leisure Books, 1971), pp. 27–45.
14 The Professor, *Angela*; Marc Olden, *Angela Davis: An Objective Assessment* (New York: Lancer Books, 1973); Davis, *Angela Davis*; Charlene Mitchell, *The Fight*

to Free Angela Davis: Its Importance for the Working Class (New York: New Outlook Publishers, 1972).

15 Charlene Mitchell, *The Fight to Free Angela Davis: its importance for the working class*, 20th National Convention Communist Party, USA, 1972, 6

16 Mitchell, *Fight to Free Angela Davis*, p. 6; un-authored speech, 1970, folder Angela Davis, Niebyl-Proctor Center for Marxist Research, Oakland. See also: "Angela Rally: Massive March Monday," *The Sacramento Observer*, February 10, 1972, p. A1; "Free Angela Office in Fillmore," *Sun Reporter* (San Francisco, CA), February 6, 1971, pp. XXVII, 52, 9; for general clippings folders from *People's World*, policy statements, speeches, and letters see Angela Davis: Defense Committee Collection, folders 1–3/Box 2, and Franklin and Kendra Alexander Collection, SoCalLib.

17 Telegram to Department of State regarding German-language newspapers and Davis trial, November 24, 1970, General Records of the Department of State, Numeric Files, 1970–73 RG 59, Box 2681 NWDPH2-1997, National Archives, College Park, MD.

18 Telegram from American Embassy in Munich to Department of State, March, 1971; Telegram from American Embassy in Beirut to Department of State, May 13, 1971; Telegram from American Embassy in London to Department of State, April 28, 1971, General Records of the Department of State, Numeric Files, 1970–73 RG 59, Box 2681 NWDPH2-1997, National Archives, College Park, MD.

19 Telegram from American Embassy in Prague to Department of State, February 16, 1971, General Records of the Department of State RG 59, Box 2682 NWDPH-2-1997, National Archives, College Park, MD.

20 Telegram from American Embassy in Moscow to Department of State, January 7, 1971, General Records of the Department of State, Numeric Files, 1970–3 RG 59, Box 2681 NWDPH2-1997, National Archives, College Park, MD; The Professor, *Angela*, pp. 154–5, 164–5.

21 "The Professor," *Angela*, pp. 154–5, 164–5.

22 The National United Committee to Free Angela Davis and All Political Prisoners, "FrameUp: A Weekly Trial Bulletin," San Francisco and San Jose, CA; "Soledad Defense Committee," file 11, box 38, Twentieth Century Organizational File, SoCalLib.

23 Earl Caldwell, "Angela Davis Acquitted on All Charges," *New York Times*, June 5, 1972; Angela Yvonne Davis (1944–), file 1–3/box 1, Records: UCLA Academic Freedom Case, 1969–71 and Angela Davis Defense Committee, 1969–75, Angela Davis Collection, SoCalLib.

24 Mary Timothy, *Jury Woman: The Story of the Trial of Angela Y. Davis* (San Francisco, CA: Glide, 1975); Davis, *Angela Davis*, pp. 336–8.

25 Elaine Brown, "Welcome Home, Angela Davis," *The Black Panther Intercommunal News Service*, March 4, 1972.

26 Angela Yvonne Davis (1944–), file 1–3/box 1, Records: UCLA Academic Freedom Case, 1969–71, and Angela Davis Defense Committee, 1969–75, Angela Davis Collection, SoCalLib.
27 Telegram from American Embassy in Moscow to Department of State, September 14, 1972, General Records of the Department of State, Numeric Files, 1970–3 RG 59, Box 282 NWDPH2-1997, National Archives, College Park, MD.
28 Ibid.
29 Telegram from American Embassy in Germany to Department of State, September 12, 1972, General Records of the Department of State, Numeric Files, 1970–3 RG 59, Box 282 NWDPH2-1997, National Archives, College Park, MD.
30 Telegram from American Embassy in Prague to Department of State, September, 1972, General Records of the Department of State, Numeric Files, 1970–3 RG 59, Box 282 NWDPH2-1997, National Archives, College Park, MD.
31 *Daily World*, September 3, 1968. See also: House of Representatives Ninetieth Congress, Second Session, "Subversive Involvement in Disruption of 1968 Democratic National Convention, Part 1," Hearings Before the Committee on Un-American Activities, October 1, 3, and 4, 1968 (Washington, DC: U.S. Government Printing Office), P. 2299. https://books.google.com/books?id=bTkWA AAAIAAJ&lpg=PA2299&ots=ynxr7jnBCl&dq=daily%20world%20september%20 3%2C%201968%20communist&pg=PA2234#v=onepage&q=daily%20world%20 september%203,%201968%20communist&f=false.
32 "Youth Festival to Be Used for Propaganda, Datelined Sofia, Bulgaria," *Los Angeles Times*, May 6, 1968.
33 FBI letter dated August 11, 1969.
34 Telegram from American Embassy in Dar es Salam to Department of State, August 31, 1973, General Records of the Department of State, Numeric Files, 1970–3 RG 59, Box 282 NWDPH2-1997, National Archives, College Park, MD.
35 The Professor, *Angela*, pp. 154–5, 164–5.
36 Ibid., p. 156.
37 "Kendra Alexander, Bay Area activist," *Committees of Corresponder Newsletter*, May–June 1993, p. 4.
38 Roger Smith, "Communists—It's Hard to See Red These Days," *Los Angeles Times*, July 17, 1980, pp. 1, 24–5. The national fracturing leading to the emergence of these two organizations stemmed back to student movements of the 1970s. Major differences stemmed from disagreements over the Soviet Union's aggressive foreign policy.
39 "Communist Ticket Nears Qualification," *Sacramento Bee*, August 8, 1984, Metro A.
40 Dennis Rockstroh, "Communist Leader Capitalizes on 'Regular-People' Image," *San Jose Mercury News*, November 10, 1987, p. 1C.

41 Giuliana Milanese, interview by author, San Francisco, September 24, 2005. She talked about labor activism in 1980s. She also described how committed Alexander was to the Free South African Movement.
42 The lower estimate was referenced by Richard Starr, editor of the Yearbook on International Communist Affairs, while the higher number was supplied by the CPUSA. Carrick Leavitt, "Aghast U.S. Communists Make Lonely Bid to Evolve toward More Democratic Goals," *Deseret News*, October 22, 1990, p. A8.
43 Charlene Mitchell and Danny Rubin, National Board Members, *Democratic Leadership Elections: A Critical Question*, September, 1991, folder CPUSA December 1991, CPUSA Convention Dissent Papers Collection, SoCalLib; Record of motions acted on, National Committee Meeting, CPUSA, September 8, 1991, folder CPUSA December 1991, CPUSA Convention Dissent Papers Collection, SoCalLib.
44 Charlene Mitchell, interview by author, New York, September 20, 2005; Giuliana Milanese, interview by author, San Francisco, September 24, 2005.
45 Most tellingly, the group wrote, "We uncritically defended practices which have proven themselves historically outmoded, at best. Of course, we do not need to apologize for our defense of socialism, but we do need to acknowledge that in defending it, we also voluntarily put on blinders about its weaknesses." Kendra Alexander et al., *Message to the National Committee*, May 18, 1991, pp. 3, 14, folder CPUSA December 1991, CPUSA Convention Dissent Papers Collection, SoCalLib; See also: Charlene Mitchell, "Remarks of Charlene Mitchell to National Committee/National Council," August 5, 1990; Kendra Alexander et al., Letter to "Comrades," October 21, 1991, folder CPUSA December 1991, CPUSA Convention Dissent Papers Collection, SoCalLib; Gus Hall, National Chairman, CPUSA, *The Crisis in Our Party: Report to the National Committee, November 16–17, 1991*, folder CPUSA December 1991, CPUSA Convention Dissent Papers Collection, SoCalLib.
46 "Kendra Alexander, Bay Area Activist," p. 4.
47 Ibid.
48 Committees of Correspondence, "Press Release for Immediate Release," New York, NY, December 23, 1991.
49 "Kendra Alexander, Bay Area Activist," p. 4.
50 Rockstroh, "Communist Leader," p. 1C.
51 Kathleen Hendrix, "Embracing What's Left of the Left," *LA Times*, August 7, 1990, pp. E1–E2.
52 Ibid.

Bibliography

Borstelmann, Thomas. *The Cold War and the Color Line: American Race Relations in the Global Arena*. Cambridge: Harvard University Press, 2001.

Davies, Carol Boyce. *Left of Karl Marx: The Political Life of Black Communist Claudia Jones*. Durham: Duke University Press, 2008.

Davis, Angela. *Angela Davis: An Autobiography*. New York: International, 1974.

McDuffie, Erik S. *Sojourning for Freedom: Black Women, American Communism, and the Making of Black Left Feminism*. Durham: Duke University Press, 2011.

Pulido, Laura. *Black, Brown, Yellow and Left: Radical Activism in Los Angeles*. Berkeley: University of California Press, 2006.

Sides, Josh. *LA City Limits: African American Los Angeles from the Great Depression to the Present*. Berkeley: University of California Press, 2003.

Slutsky, Beth. *Gendering Radicalism: Women and Communism in Twentieth-Century California*. Lincoln: University of Nebraska Press, 2015.

Weigand, Kate. *Red Feminism: American Communism and the Making of Women's Liberation*. Baltimore, MD: Johns Hopkins University Press, 2002.

10

The Party's Over: Former Communist Party Members in the San Francisco Bay Area

Robert W. Cherny

Among the CP's legacies must be counted its long-term influence on the people—more than one hundred thousand—who became party members in the 1930s and 1940s, then left. There exist conflicting images of former party members. One derives from the former Communists who became prominent conservatives. Several parlayed their former party activities into jobs as professional witnesses in the late 1940s and 1950s, as the Justice Department launched trials of Communist Party members for violating the Smith Act and other laws. Some of them wrote books or went on speaking tours. Several books in the 1940s and early 1950s presented former leftists (not all of them party members) who became conservatives, including *I Confess* by Benjamin Gitlow (1940), R. H. S. Crossman *The God That Failed* (a collection of essays, 1949), and Whittaker Chambers's *Witness* (1952). A recent example is Daniel Oppenheimer's *Exit Right* (2017).[1]

A few journalists and historians have challenged that image by examining the experiences of longtime Communist Party members, including some who left the party. The best known is by Vivian Gornick, a journalist, whose *The Romance of American Communism* (1977) presents edited interviews with former Communist Party members, many from New York, identified by pseudonyms. As her title suggests, she organized the book around the concept of *romance*, and her interest in psychoanalysis meant that she was especially interested in the connection between ideology and her subjects' inner life. Sympathetic to her subjects, Gornick focused on their psychological attraction to and subsequent estrangement from the party. She has recently called this an error, ensuring, she says, "that the complexity of my subjects' lives would not be explored."[2]

California in general, and the Bay Area in particular, included significant numbers of Communist Party members throughout the 1930s–1950s. In 1931, the party counted just 409 members statewide, including 171 in the Bay Area and 196 in Los Angeles.[3] By 1945, the California Communist Party claimed some 6,200 members, making it the second largest district (after New York) by a significant margin. Though California accounted for less than 7 percent of the total US population then, California Communist Party members made up about 10 percent of all Communist Party members. of all US residents.[4]

This essay draws upon my research on the Communist Party in the San Francisco Bay Area[5] to present an analysis, based on memoirs, interviews, and oral histories, of twelve men and ten women active in the Communist Party in the 1930s and 1940s who left the party in the 1950s.[6] The group includes all those for whom I could locate sources for their decision to leave the party and their subsequent political activities. None of them became conservatives. I do not assume that these twenty-two are representative—in fact, they are unusual in that they left records of their activities in and out of the party over many years. Nor do I assume the Bay Area is representative, although I suspect patterns in other Pacific Coast cities are likely similar. Nevertheless, as a group, they reveal interesting patterns regarding their participation in the party, their reasons for leaving, and the long-term influence of their life in the party.

All twenty-two subjects were Communist Party members for five years or more; eighteen were members for ten years or more and ten belonged for more than twenty. They came from a range of backgrounds and experiences. Ten were born or grew up in the Bay Area; seven came from the urban northeast. At least half were members of a left-wing union at some point. Bill Bailey and Leo Nitzberg fought in Spain, and Loretta Starvus's first husband, Irving Keith (Kreichmar), died there. Jessica Mitford tried unsuccessfully to get to the front lines in Spain as a reporter. Loretta Starvus attended the International Lenin School in Moscow, and several went to local leadership schools. At least three ran for elective office as Communist Party candidates. Seven held state leadership positions, and four others held local leadership positions.[7] Ten were not in the leadership during most of their time as party members, although two were tapped for leadership during the leadership vacuum of the mid-1950s. Thus, most left the party after many years of membership and at least some participation in leadership.

These twenty-two men and women were more likely than the general population to have had one or both parents who were foreign-born, a pattern similar to the party more generally.[8] More than two-thirds of the group were of foreign parentage; by comparison, some 63 percent of all CPUSA members were affiliated with a foreign language fraction as of 1929.[9] For some, their experience in the party seems to have been, in part, an experience in Americanization.[10] I could find sufficient information for only one person of color, Revels Cayton. (There were more African Americans who took significant roles in the Communist Party in the Bay Area, but I could not find source materials for them.)

For these twenty-two, an understanding of their life within the party and their reasons for leaving are crucial to understanding their lives after leaving. All faced varying degrees of anti-Communist scrutiny during the late 1940s and early 1950s, but none acknowledged it as reason for leaving the party. For most, the events of 1956 seem to have been more of a catalyst than cause for their departure. Instead, for most the decision to leave grew out of their dissatisfaction with the party's sectarianism and political isolation and a sense that the party no longer corresponded to their own commitment to broadly based political and social change. After leaving, most engaged in mainstream politics in ways similar to the Popular Front of the late 1930s and the Second World War.

Life in the Party

Seventeen of the twenty-two subjects were in their teens or early twenties when they first joined the party. Fourteen joined in the 1930s, and seven in the 1940s. Louise Todd, the earliest to affiliate, joined the Young Workers League in 1922 and the party in 1930. The twenty-two subjects show considerable diversity in their education at the time they first affiliated: six had not completed high school, six were high-school graduates, four had some college time, and one, Jessica Mitford, had been educated by private tutors. Five were college graduates when they first joined.[11] That fifteen of the twenty-two had completed high school at the time they joined and nine had some college experience marked them as unusual at a time when, nationwide, fewer than 30 percent of adults had completed high school and fewer than 5 percent had four years of college. This level of education is likely related directly to the tendency of this group to have left records of their party activities and is another clue to their somewhat exceptional backgrounds as party members.

Party schools sometimes supplemented formal schooling. Dave Jenkins left school after the eighth grade and later attributed his real education to party schools and the bohemian-left culture of Greenwich Village. Bailey left school after the fifth grade and later recalled that, after joining the party, he read every night when he did not have a party class or meeting.[12] At the time they joined, nine were blue-collar workers, four held clerical or secretarial jobs, one was a high-school student, four were college students, one was a bank employee, one a journalist, one a lawyer in a federal agency, and one a research economist. Two of the women came from well-to-do families.[13]

A significant majority were party members by 1938, at the height of the Popular Front, when California Communist Party members worked alongside mainstream Democrats to defeat an antiunion proposition and elect New Deal Democrats as governor, lieutenant governor, and US senator. With the Molotov-Ribbentrop Pact, however, the party veered back into the political margins.[14] The Second World War brought a return of the Popular Front and more participation in mainstream politics, mostly alongside the Democratic Party. But Jacques Duclos's article in 1945 (discussed in James Ryan's Chapter 2) sent the Communist Party away from the mainstream and far from meaningful political influence (Figure 10.1).[15]

Figure 10.1 Phyllis "Pele" De Lappe, a staff member for the *People's World*, drew this cartoon of the most prominent members of the California Labor School's faculty and staff, c. 1948. David Jenkins, the director, is in the lower left. Leo Nitzberg, who taught photography, is in the upper right, with a camera. Credit: Courtesy Labor Archives and Research Center, San Francisco State University.

Despite such turbulent oscillations by the party during the late 1930s and the 1940s, San Francisco's vibrant labor-left culture extended well beyond the party. The California Labor School (CLS), founded in 1944, quickly came to occupy the center of that labor-left culture and attracted thousands of students. Dave Jenkins, the director, had a relatively free hand, although the party could veto major decisions.[16] Social science classes were Marxist. Carol Cuénod recalled about her political economy class, "The glories of the Soviet Union were drummed into us ... it was the successful socialist country and socialism, of course, made wonderful sense."[17] Enrollments in psychology, humanities, and art classes, many with little ideological content, often outnumbered those in the social sciences. One could spend nearly every evening and weekend at CLS events. Lecture topics ranged from "How to Read Music" to "How to Combat Discrimination." Lecturers, exhibitors, and performers included Imogene Cunningham, W. E. B. Du Bois, Paul Robeson, Pete Seeger, and Edward Weston, whose photography exhibition at CLS came directly from the New York Museum of Modern Art. Social activities included dinners, programs, and an Artists' Carnival. The school also proved a fertile recruiting ground—Jenkins once signed up forty new Communist Party members during one recruiting drive.[18] The party created labor schools in other cities, notably the Jefferson School in New York City, but none of the others' curricula ranged as widely as that of the CLS.[19]

In addition to Jenkins, at least seventeen others among the twenty-two subjects took part in CLS activities—teaching classes, lecturing, participating in panel discussions, and taking classes. Cuénod enrolled in classes, sang in the chorus, and volunteered to crank the mimeograph, design flyers, and staff the switchboard. "Once I walked into the School," she recalled, "I didn't leave until they locked it up."[20]

This labor-left culture had its own radio and print media. Between 1943 and 1945, Paul Ryan, a Communist Party member and journalist, presented the news on radio station KYA. Sidney Roger then offered a similar program on station KGO. The *People's World* (*PW*), the western counterpart to the *Daily Worker*, carried sports news, women's and children's features, reviews of art, music, literature, and film, and, of course, the party's political perspective. Subscribers significantly outnumbered party members, especially in the Bay Area and Los Angeles. Adam Lapin and four others among the twenty-two edited or contributed articles to the *PW*, and Pat Tobin once directed fund-raising. In the late 1940s and early 1950s, local groups closely linked to the Communist Party, including the Progressive Citizens of America and the Independent Citizens' Committee for the Arts, Sciences, and Professions, sponsored public lectures.[21]

The Bay Area's left-wing unions, notably the International Longshoremen's and Warehousemen's Union (ILWU) and its locals, supported these institutions, channeling funds and students to the CLS, buying *PW* subscriptions, and underwriting radio programs. Two groups, the American Russian Institute and the Russian American Society, received support from *Vsesojuznoe Obschestvo Kul'turnykh Svyzei s zagranitseior* (VOKS) the All-Union Society for Cultural Relations with Foreign Countries, a Soviet government agency.[22]

Party members could live almost entirely within this labor-left culture. Every week they were expected to attend party meetings, take part in other party activities, and otherwise support the party, activities that could include cranking a mimeograph machine, presenting the party's views in public meetings, raising funds, pushing petitions, and preparing the educational component for their club's weekly meeting. (During the 1940s and 1950s, the lowest level of organization was called a club or branch.) Given the potentially all-consuming nature of party membership, the most active members socialized largely with other members and married other members. Leaving meant losing one's friends. Keith Eickman later observed, "the discipline of the party was great because of the fact that after you had been in the party for many years, your whole social life developed around the party … you were almost afraid of being thrown out."[23]

Life within the party could also mean that one's life was directed by the party. Its directives sent members across the country. Bill Bailey was sent to Hawai'i to organize for the party and later to New York to run for port agent for the Marine Firemen's union (MFOW). Party leaders told Dave Jenkins, who excelled at organizing and fund-raising, to return to blue-collar work, so he spent several years working on the docks. Starvus enjoyed her work as an organizer for the United Electrical Workers' union in Los Angeles but agreed when told to move to San Francisco and become state organizational secretary.[24]

Party assignments could take precedence over family. In the late 1940s, Rudie Lambert chaired the committee that expelled his brother Walter, an experience that Louise Todd, Rudie's wife, described as "very traumatic" for both brothers. They didn't speak to each other for ten years. When told to do party organizing in Los Angeles, Tillie Olsen, seemingly without a qualm, left her partner and young daughter. Todd recalled that, when the party was organizing its underground leadership in the early 1950s, one woman was told, "You are to do this, but you must forget … that you have a family." The woman refused. Todd and Adam Lapin did go underground, leaving their families for as long as five years. Lapin left small children.[25]

Women in leadership often asked the state executive board for permission to have a child. In the late 1930s and 1940s, according to Todd, "the atmosphere in the party was that, if you held a position of leadership, you were trying to get out of work if you wanted a child." She characterized her own decision not to have children as an "unnecessary" and even "tragic" sacrifice. For women in the party with children, Todd recalled, "there were great difficulties," especially "for reasons of neglect, leading children to feelings of great resentment toward their parents." Starvus and Tillie Olsen noted that children were not welcome at party meetings.[26]

A few years after Starvus reluctantly agreed to become state organizational secretary, she left that position because she felt she was not effective. She later criticized male party leaders who "shoved" women into clerical and secretarial positions and discouraged them from speaking out. Todd also recalled "many manifestations" of "male supremacy" by party leaders.[27] Eva Lapin Maas reflected:

> It was women who served the coffee and typed and mimeographed the leaflets ... Although women led and carried out neighborhood branch activities, they did not receive much recognition ... A branch might occasionally hold a discussion on male chauvinism, but ... without the vocabulary to conceptualize feminist thinking or a women's movement to empower it, the discussions went nowhere and were not taken seriously.[28]

The frustration expressed by Lapin, Olsen, Starvus, and Todd regarding male chauvinism also appears in accounts by Dorothy Healey, a Communist Party leader in Los Angeles, and Peggy Dennis, the widow of Eugene Dennis, both written after they left the party. Healey noted that female party members sometimes discussed such matters among themselves but did not take them into larger party discussions for fear of losing what status they had within the party.[29] Of course, this situation was not unique to the Communist Party, and, as Beth Slutsky and Lisa Ruben have argued, the California Communist Party may have been more open to women than similar institutions at the time.[30]

All the institutions that structured the Bay Area's labor-Left culture came under attack during the resurgence of anticommunism after the Second World War. Between 1939 and 1955, Harry Bridges, Australian-born president of the ILWU, was repeatedly charged with being a party member and was subject to deportation; Bridges's defense activities siphoned off the energies and funds of many ILWU and Communist Party members, as did other defense committees. After 1949–50, when the Congress of Industrial Organizations (CIO) expelled the ILWU and other left-wing unions, those unions were raided by others, causing some to fight for their continued existence and reducing or eliminating their financial support for Left organizations.[31]

The CLS became a target. The State Federation of Labor (ASFL) told AFL unions to withdraw support. Civic leaders and some CIO unions soon followed. The California Un-American Activities Committee (CUAC) labeled the CLS a Communist Party front. When the attorney general listed the CLS as subversive, it retroactively lost its nonprofit status and was billed for back taxes. The curriculum and other activities dwindled. On May 3, 1957, federal marshals padlocked the school's doors, seized its property, and attached its bank account for payment of back taxes.[32]

Sidney Roger's radio broadcasts ended in 1950. The *PW* lost subscribers, from more than fifteen thousand in 1947 to six thousand by the late 1950s. It shrank from a full-size daily to a tabloid and a weekly by 1957.[33] By the late 1950s, mostly only memories remained of the once thriving and wide-ranging labor-left culture of the late 1940s and early 1950s.

Beginning in 1949, the US government charged Communist Party leaders with violating the Alien Registration Act of 1940—the Smith Act. The party reacted by directing some leaders, including Adam Lapin and Todd, to "go underground," to serve as "reserve" leaders in case those charged under the Smith Act were sent to prison. In 1951, Smith Act prosecutions extended to California Communist Party leaders, including Starvus and Oleta O'Connor Yates. Attendance fell at local Communist Party club meetings. The San Francisco Russian Club, for example, attracted only four or five members, including a Federal Bureau of Investigation (FBI) informant. By 1954, three years had passed since a section leader had visited the Russian Club. A subsection leader explained, "the old, trained leaders are gone, some to jail and some underground," and consequently "the rank and file comrades do not get sufficient leadership."[34]

Some chafed under the party yoke. By the early 1950s, Revels Cayton, the only African American for whom I could locate sources, was at odds with party leaders who criticized his influence on Paul Robeson and disagreed with his arguments for African American caucuses in unions. Lincoln Fairley later described his club, made up of members of ILWU Local 10 (longshore workers), as "a complete farce" with "little influence," and therefore a waste of his time. Told by the party to go underground, Dave Jenkins refused, and some party leaders criticized him for "stepping outside the discipline of the Party." Estolv Ward was among those who grew dissatisfied with the party after the Duclos article.[35]

In 1947, the CP claimed some 70,000–75,000 members nationwide. Under attack from the government and anticommunist groups, and with some internal dissent over the Duclos article, the party shrank by two-thirds within a few short years; by the early 1950s, there were only about twenty-five thousand members. In 1956, a double blow came from abroad: Khrushchev's speech describing Stalin's many atrocities, and the Soviet invasion of Hungary. By 1959, the party lost some 80 percent of its members, shrinking to about three thousand members nationwide.[36]

Leaving the Party

Amid these external attacks, in late 1949, coincident with a Soviet campaign against national chauvinism in Eastern Europe, the Communist Party of the United States of America (CPUSA) launched a campaign against white chauvinism, which it described as the key underlying feature of American capitalism's success in keeping the working class divided.[37] The campaign quickly degenerated. Dorothy Healey reflected, "A legitimate concern turned into an obsession," and became "a ritual act of self-purification that did nothing to strengthen the Party in its fight against racism and was manipulated by some Communist leaders for ends which had nothing to do with the ostensible purpose of the whole campaign." She added, "Once an accusation of white chauvinism was thrown against a white Communist, there was no defense." In Los Angeles, Healey estimated, the party expelled two hundred people, "usually on the most trivial of pretexts." Healey's description was also accurate for San Francisco. Communist Party members who ran afoul of members of the local Control Commission were called before that body, charged with white chauvinism, and purged. Party members were prohibited from associating with those who had been expelled; failure to follow that rule became grounds for expulsion.[38] Thus, under severe external attack, the Communist Party fell to consuming itself. Similar patterns existed elsewhere in the country.[39]

Judy and Leo Nitzberg and Keith Eickman were ousted for white chauvinism. The Nitzbergs went to Los Angeles to see friends; upon arriving, their friend insisted they accompany her to a political meeting at an African American church, although Judy was wearing slacks. For this breach of decorum, the Nitzbergs were expelled from the party. Eickman was expelled because he disagreed with an African American—a good friend of his—in a union stewards' meeting. The white chauvinism campaign was "useful," Eickman reflected, "to some people who wanted to get rid of some of the others." He added, "They probably did me a favor … it would have been difficult for me to voluntarily separate myself from the CP." Judy Nitzberg agreed—expulsion freed her and Leo to do things they would never have had time for as party members.[40]

Four of the twenty-two quit in the early 1950s. Fairley, a Harvard PhD in economics and research director for the ILWU, left around 1950. In addition to finding his club a waste of time, he was highly critical of the CP's theoretical journal, *Political Affairs*. He described its economic articles as "very, very poor" and found its economic analysis "always wrong."[41]

Jack Olsen was educational director in ILWU Local 6 (warehouse workers). Around 1950, Teamster raids on Local 6 included extensive red-baiting, with Olsen a target. Pressured to resign as educational director, he returned to work as a warehouseman but was repeatedly fired shortly after being dispatched to his job assignments. He left Local 6 and the Communist Party in 1951 or 1952. Tillie Olsen, Jack's wife, also left, after she was red-baited from a position in the Parent Teacher Association and criticized for bringing her baby and ironing to party meetings. Jack was likely reflecting on the post-Duclos Communist Party when he explained: "the Party had lost its viability as an American working-class force … It was unable to react properly to events or to provide leadership."[42]

Cayton stopped attending party meetings by 1952 and "drifted out of the Party." "I didn't have any quarrel with them," he said, "It was just that I no longer belonged."[43]

More than a third of the twenty-two subjects attributed their decision to leave to the events of 1956. Edith Jenkins wrote about the Khrushchev revelations, "we who had linked years of humanist struggle to our belief in the USSR were shocked past understanding. We swung between anger at those who had deceived us and at ourselves for our own part in our deception." Dave Jenkins was more explicit, "It was like a rape, a mental and emotional rape because we were involved with hundreds of non-Party people to whom … we had denied the possibility of these 'slave labor' camps, [and] the murder of honorable and fine people." For Bailey, Hungary was "the straw that broke the camel's back." He remembered thinking, "you stupid bastards. Is this socialism at work?" and informed a longtime comrade, "I've had enough of the Party's stupidity and bungling." For Estolv and Angela Ward, too, Hungary was the breaking point. Jenkins guessed that 80 percent of local CP members left following the events of 1956.[44]

For Eva and Adam Lapin, leaving "was a momentous decision," both political and "deeply personal and emotional," but also easier because so many of their friends were leaving. Some left by not attending meetings, but others submitted a formal resignation. Angela and Estolv Ward met with two members of Angela's club and Oleta O'Connor Yates to announce their decision; the other two club members also resigned. O'Connor Yates left soon after. Dave and Edith Jenkins's resignations brought a visit from Bill Schneiderman, longtime state secretary, who tried to dissuade Dave—but completely ignored Edith. Cuénod, who was not attached to a club, could find no one to receive her resignation: "I called Oleta ... before that meeting took place, Oleta left the Party. I remember doing the same thing with Loretta Stack, and the same thing happened. It became almost a comedy."[45]

Mitford was less shocked by the Khrushchev revelations, because, she later wrote, "I had never been as thoroughly convinced as most comrades of Soviet infallibility." She hoped Khrushchev might bring more political and intellectual freedom in the Soviet Union. Elected to the Communist Party's 1957 national convention, Mitford viewed it as a battle between advocates of more internal democracy, autonomy from foreign Communist parties, and an independent road to socialism, on one side, and "the hidebound, orthodox leadership" on the other. Advocates for change dominated the convention, but the "hidebound, orthodox" leaders, led by 76-year-old William Z. Foster, remained in power. Mitford and her husband, Robert Treuhaft, resigned in 1958.[46]

Starvus found the invasion of Hungary "shocking" and considered the party's leadership "bankrupt" and the party itself stagnant and paralyzed. She, O'Connor Yates, and Todd (the latter also a delegate to the 1957 convention) were three of twenty-six Californians who resigned together in March 1958, citing the Communist Party's "deeply rooted dogmatism" and "total isolation" from emerging social movements, as well as the failure of the convention to change the leadership. Todd later cited her "disillusionment with the Soviet Union" and the CPUSA's leadership, adding "the party had become totally irrelevant in the political life of the country" and "so isolated and sectarian nothing could be accomplished by remaining as members."[47]

Thus, many of the twenty-two left the party not solely due to the events of 1956. For them, including some who left before 1956, their decision reflected their understanding that the party had become politically isolated, sectarian, and dogmatic. The aftermath of the 1957 convention produced resignations by others who had hoped for reform from within. CUAC gleefully reported that, as of 1959: "there was very little Party activity conducted openly in California ... [the CP] was unable to attract new recruits and suffered from a dire lack of financial support ... front organizations shriveled, dried up and withered away."[48]

Life outside the Party

Either before or after leaving the party, several of the twenty-two faced problems with employment because of their identification with the Communist Party. Five had belonged to seafaring unions—Bailey in the MFOW; Tobin in the Nation Union of Marine Cooks and Stewards (NUMCS) and later the National Maritime Union; and Jenkins, Cayton, and Don Watson in NUMCS. Jenkins and Cayton stopped going to sea before the Coast Guard began screening Communist Party members off US-flagged ships. Tobin, Watson, and Bailey were screened off, and Tobin and Bailey were expelled by their unions. Starvus was expelled from the Waitresses' Union when she was indicted under the Smith Act. Angela and Estolv Ward had been organizers for left-wing unions that had shrunk or disappeared by the mid-1950s. Jack Olsen was unable to remain in any warehouse job, apparently because the FBI intervened with employers. Cayton had held a salaried position in the National Negro Congress as did Mitford in the Civil Rights Congress, but the party dissolved both organizations in the early 1950s. For Adam Lapin, leaving the party meant leaving his job as associate editor of the *PW*.

For more than half the men, the ILWU became a place of refuge. Eickman and Leo Nitzberg continued in Local 6, and Nitzberg later transferred to Local 10. Cayton joined Local 6 briefly. Jenkins had joined the ILWU's Sacramento local before he left the party and later transferred to Local 10. Tobin joined Local 10 in 1959. Bailey started in another ILWU local, transferred to Local 10 and then to Local 34 (ship clerks). Watson also joined Local 34. Adam Lapin briefly wrote for the ILWU's newspaper. Carol Cuénod found a clerical position at ILWU headquarters and later became librarian and archivist. The Olsens, Caytons, Tobin, and Cuénod all lived in St. Francis Square, a San Francisco housing development created by the ILWU and inhabited by many ILWU members and retirees.[49]

Jack Olsen left Local 6 to become an apprentice in Typographical Local 21, where his brother was an officer. He remained in that union for more than twenty years, then became the first director of the newly organized Labor Studies program at San Francisco City College.[50]

The day he left the party, Bailey told a friend, "I feel that a very heavy weight has been lifted from me … like I have just been handed a whole new set of freedoms." Eva Lapin had a similar reaction, "Once you left the Party, you were free to move in any direction." Allan Yates said of his and Oleta's decision to leave, "we felt truly liberated."[51] Others had similar reactions.

All the women used their new freedom to chart new careers. If the ILWU became a refuge for many of the men, San Francisco State College served that function for several women. Tillie Olsen participated in a summer workshop, then took a class in creative writing. Edith Jenkins earned an MA in English, taught literature at community colleges, and served on the board for San Francisco State's Poetry Center. Judy Nitzberg earned her BA and MA in history and became a high-school teacher. Eva Lapin took a bachelor's degree at San Francisco State and a master's at the University of California, Berkeley, both in social work, then became a social worker. Cuénod was chosen for a National Endowment for the Humanities (NEH) seminar with Herb Gutman, after which she completed a BA at Goddard College. She later became an archivist at San Francisco State.[52]

Todd worked first as a legal secretary, then became a medical secretary. Starvus learned typing and bookkeeping and found a company unconcerned about her past politics. When Cayton became deputy director of the city's Public Housing Authority, he helped Starvus get a job there.[53]

The discipline and accountability expected of party members, as well as the Communist Party's emphasis on "educationals" in party meetings, may have prepared some to become published authors. (However, one woman, not one of the twenty-two, left the party because, she said, its "educationals" were "like a book club where nobody really understood the books."[54]) Adam Lapin published travel books under a pseudonym. Fairley wrote an analysis of the ILWU's pathbreaking Modernization and Mechanization Agreement of 1960 and followed it with a history of Mt. Tamalpais, the dominant topographical feature in Marin County, north of San Francisco. Edith Jenkins published her poetry in journals and three books. She, Eva Lapin Maas (who remarried after the death of Adam), and Bailey published memoirs. Watson wrote articles on the history of California farm labor and contributed papers at meetings of the American Historical Association, Bay Area Labor History Workshop, and Southwest Labor Studies Association, the latter two of which he helped to found and lead. Estolv Ward authored a biography of Tom Mooney, and he and Angela completed several oral histories for the Bancroft Library's Regional Oral History Office.[55]

Mitford was the most prolific author. *Hons and Rebels* was published in Britain in 1960 and in the United States as *Daughters and Rebels*. Other books followed: *The American Way of Death* (1963), an exposé of the funeral industry that made her reputation as a muckraker; *The Trial of Dr. Spock* (1969); *Kind and Usual Punishment: The Prison Business* (1973); *A Fine Old Conflict* (1977); *The Making of a Muckraker* (1979); and *The American Way of Birth* (1992).

Daughters and Rebels, *A Fine Old Conflict*, and *The Making of a Muckraker* were autobiographical. Robert Treuhaft, her husband, shared the research and analysis for *The American Way of Death*, and wrote *The American Way of Death Revisited* (1998).[56] Their penchant for muckraking journalism undoubtedly derived from their Marxist perspective on capitalism.

If Mitford was the most prolific author, Tillie Olsen was the most acclaimed. A short story, "I Stand Here Ironing" (1956), was named one of the year's best. In the years following, she received an NEA fellowship, a Guggenheim, other prestigious awards, appointments as artist-in-residence at prestigious institutions, and nine honorary doctorates. *Tell Me a Riddle,* her best-known work, appeared in 1961, and *Yonnondio*, a long-delayed novel from the 1930s, was published in 1974. Much of her fiction depicted the lives and struggles of working-class people, especially women, a reflection both of her own life and her Marxist views.

Several held union leadership positions. Jack Olsen became a labor council delegate from Typographical Local 21. Judy Nitzberg served on the executive committee of the San Francisco Federation of Teachers, American Federation of Teachers Local 61. In Local 6, Eickman was repeatedly elected as business agent, then secretary-treasurer, and finally president. Bailey was elected vice president of Local 10. Tobin served for nine years as the ILWU's legislative representative in Washington. For twenty-four years, Watson was repeatedly elected to Local 34's executive board and served as its chair for twenty years, overlapping with eleven years as secretary for the ILWU's Northern California District Council, which included lobbying in Sacramento.

Most were Democrats. Watson left the Communist Party just as party leaders were trying to advance him into leadership and instead joined the Young Democrats and the California Democratic Council (CDC), an organization of liberal Democrats. He became deeply involved in supporting the United Farm Workers, eventually volunteering half his working hours, the origin of his interest in agricultural labor history. Eva Lapin Maas joined a militant group of social workers, marched against the war in Vietnam and counseled draft resistors, threw herself into the emerging women's movement, and prepared meals for the homeless. Starvus, after retiring, participated actively in the tenants' organization where she lived and advocated for better public transportation. Tobin spent his retirement working for world peace and nuclear disarmament. Leo Nitzberg and Bailey belonged to the Veterans of the Abraham Lincoln Brigade and joined other veterans in traveling to Spain after the death of the Franco. Most of the twenty-two left records of support for the civil rights movement, the antiwar movement, and the women's movement.

Dave Jenkins became the most involved in Democratic politics. In 1963, he helped to secure endorsements from the ILWU and other unions for the mayoral campaign of John F. Shelley, a liberal Democrat, then advised Shelley, once elected, on appointments. In 1964, Jenkins participated in the city's "freeway revolt," to stop freeway construction from destroying neighborhoods and parks, and in anti-Vietnam War demonstrations in 1966.[57] In 1967, he joined the mayoral campaign of Joseph Alioto, a mainstream Democrat, explaining, "We had a frankly opportunistic line of staying with a guy who we thought could win." Jenkins brought Cayton and two African American ILWU leaders to meet Alioto, who agreed to expand black representation in city government. As mayor, Alioto appointed union members and African Americans—including several former Communists—to nearly every city commission and board. In 1977, the *San Francisco Chronicle* described Jenkins as "one of the canniest operators ever to insinuate himself into the City Hall mainstream" and as "a kind of jack-of-all-liberal trades." Jenkins also took positions that led some to label him an opportunist. He worked against a proposition to restrict the sale of furs because it would damage the Fur Workers Union, and he worked for tobacco companies against a proposition limiting smoking on the grounds that it was aimed at the working class. He also consulted for developers seeking special treatment for particular projects.[58]

In the 1960s, Cayton took a leadership role in the city's civil rights movement. In 1964, Mayor Shelley, likely with advice from Jenkins, appointed Cayton to the city's new Human Rights Commission and then appointed him deputy director of the Public Housing Authority. Mayor Alioto picked him for deputy mayor for social programs. After retiring, Cayton served on the Juvenile Justice Commission.[59]

Eickman was appointed to the city's Recreation and Parks Commission and later to the Bay Conservation and Development Commission, a regional planning body. After retiring, he served on the governing boards for KQED (public radio and TV) and the city zoo. His son Kent observed, "He felt he needed to give back to society."[60]

Treuhaft and Mitford resigned from the Communist Party to use their time more productively in movements for social change. Treuhaft and his law partner, Doris Brin Walker, who remained in the CP, represented clients on the Left in the 1960s and 1970s, including the United Farm Workers, the Black Panthers, Free Speech activists (Treuhaft was among those arrested), Vietnam War draft resisters, and Angela Davis. (Hillary Rodham spent the summer of 1971 as an intern at Treuhaft and Walker, but was apparently not radicalized.[61]) Treuhaft and Mitford participated in the New Politics movement in the mid-1960s, and Treuhaft ran unsuccessfully for district attorney under its auspices.[62]

Some of the group turned to nonpolitical pastimes. Leo Nitzberg worked on photography, became an accomplished potter, and raised tropical fish. Todd renewed a youthful enthusiasm for hiking in the Sierra Nevada and became a volunteer docent at the California Academy of Sciences. O'Connor Yates also enjoyed wilderness hiking, and became what her obituary called "a nature lover and rock hound"; she also participated in the city's Horticultural Society and Bonsai Society. Starvus led efforts to create a community garden at her housing development. Fairley helped organize the San Francisco New School, patterned after the New School for Social Research in New York. Bailey was featured in ten documentary films, two by the BBC, and two feature films.[63]

Reflections on Life in the Party

Few of the twenty-two expressed regret for their time in the party. Eva Lapin Maas reflected that "the Party had shaped our lives, given us a way of viewing the world, framed our family life, and influenced our selection of friends, books, movies, and activities." Bailey concluded his memoir with the commitment that had guided his entire life: "to witness an injustice and do nothing—that is the biggest crime." Though critical of the Communist Party, Eickman did not regret his time as a member. "The Party gave me an understanding of the class relationship of society," he said. "It gave me a political attitude that made me different from any of the others in the union who didn't have that background" and who didn't understand "politics to the same degree."[64]

In their joint resignation letter in 1958, Todd, O'Connor Yates, and Starvus (and twenty-three others) described the party as "the great radical movement of our generation" and explained:

> Had we to choose again, we would identify ourselves with it for the same reasons that caused us to do so then: these include the Party's important role in the unemployed movement, its contributions to organizing workers in basic industry, its effective participation in the fight for Negro rights, its pioneering efforts in the struggle against war and fascism, its solidarity with the socialist sector of the world, its aspirations for a socialist America, and its study of scientific socialism, Marxism-Leninism.

They emphasized that theirs was "not the action of hopeless people retiring from a fruitless cause" but instead "the beginning of an active search for what we are convinced will be a hopeful future," and they advocated efforts "by those who have left the Communist Party, to preserve and develop further what was healthy and valuable in our experience."[65]

For the large majority, leaving the Communist Party did not mean rejecting causes that had motivated them as party members—racial equality, an end to poverty, peace, and varying versions of socialism—but it did mean rejecting Stalinism and the Soviet version of socialism. Todd reflected: "The Party's advocacy of socialism was based on the Soviet example ... I felt that our advocacy of Socialism should be based on American realities." Cuénod was more direct in 1994: "The idea of socialism I accepted, and I still do ... But the glorification [of the Soviet Union] we practiced was dangerous ignorance." Several included democratic centralism in their criticism of Soviet influence.[66]

By leaving the party, the large majority freed themselves to participate in politics on their own terms. Most joined the city's political mainstream as Democrats and did their part to push that mainstream to the left. Shelley's election as mayor in 1963—with Jenkins's assistance—marked the first time that a liberal Democrat held that office. Jenkins, Cayton, and other former Communist Party members who supported first Shelley and then Alioto did not by themselves bring the end of fifty-two years of Republican rule in city hall, but they did play some role in pushing Shelley, Alioto, and subsequent mayors to the left. Former party members did not create the city's volatile politics of the 1960s, 1970s, and 1980s—the 1960 anti- House Un-American Activities Committee (HUAC) demonstration, the civil rights movement, opposition to the war in Vietnam, the women's movement, the LGBTQ movements—but many of them, and sometimes their adult progeny, were there, in person or in spirit.

Notes

Thanks to Bill Issel, Lisa Rubens, Harvey Schwartz, Nora Lapin, and Katherine Sibley for commenting on drafts of this essay.

1 Benjamin Gitlow, *I Confess* (New York: Dutton, 1940); Whittaker Chambers, *Witness* (New York: Random House, 1952); R. H. S. Crossman (ed.), *The God That Failed* (New York: Harper, 1949); Daniel Oppenheimer, *Exit Right: The People Who Left the Left and Reshaped the American Century* (New York: Simon & Schuster, 2017). See also George Packer, "Turned Around: Why Do Leftists Move to the Right?," *New Yorker*, February 15, 2016, https://www.newyorker.com/magazine/2016/02/22/why-leftists-go-right.

2   Vivian Gornick (ed.), *The Romance of American Communism* (New York: Basic Books, 1977); Vivian Gornick, "What Endures of the Romance of American Communism," *NYR Daily*, April 3, 2020, https://www.nybooks.com/daily/2020/04/03/what-endures-of-the-romance-of-american-communism/. See also Sophie Pinkham, "How Vivian Gornick Reinvigorated Political Writing," *New Republic*, May 1, 2020, https://newrepublic.com/article/157527/vivian-gornick-romance-american-communism-reinvigorated-political-writing. See also Kenneth L. Kann, *Comrades and Chicken Ranchers: The Story of a California Jewish Community* (Ithaca, NY: Cornell University Press, 1993); Judy Kaplan and Linn Shapiro (eds.), *Red Diapers: Growing Up in the Communist Left* (Urbana: University of Illinois Press, 1998). Kann, an historian, also used pseudonyms for his edited and conflated interviews with members of a community of Jewish Communist chicken farmers in Petaluma, California; his work focuses on the evolution of the community, especially the relations among community members' politics, Jewish identity, and farming. Kaplan, an editor, and Shapiro, a historian, also presented edited interviews, and much of their focus is on growing up in the party and the implications of that for adult life.

3   District 13 membership materials from 1931, file 2499, opis 1, fond 515 (papers of the CPUSA), Russian State Archives for Social and Political History. I've dealt with some of the history of the party in the San Francisco Bay Area in the 1930s in two articles: "Prelude to the Popular Front: The Communist Party in California, 1931–1935," *American Communist History* 1 (2002), pp. 5–37, and "The Communist Party in California, 1935–1940: From the Political Margins to the Mainstream and Back," *American Communist History* 9 (2010), pp. 3–33.

4   Membership numbers are taken from "Communist Party Membership by Districts," *Mapping American Social Movements Projects*, online at https://depts.washington.edu/moves/CP_map-members.shtml.

5   My larger work-in-progress will survey the CP in the Bay area from its founding to the late 1950s.

6   The twenty-two and sources of information are:

Arnstein, Edith: see Jenkins, David, and Edith Arnstein Jenkins;

Bailey, William "Bill": Bill Bailey with Lynn Damme, *The Kid from Hoboken: An Autobiography* (San Francisco, CA: Circus Lithographic Prepress, 1993); interview by Robert Cherny, 1993; [San Francisco] *The Dispatcher*, April 13, 1995, p. 7;

Cayton, Revels: Richard S. Hobbs, *The Cayton Legacy: An African American Family* (Pullman, WA: Washington State University Press, 2002);

Cuénod, Carol: Carol Cuénod Oral History, Interview by Harvey Schwartz, Labor Archives and Research Center, San Francisco State University (hereinafter LARC), 1994, revised 2014 (hereinafter, Cuénod oral history);

Eickman, Keith: "Keith Eickman: Idealism and Disappointment," in Harvey Schwartz, *Solidarity Stories: An Oral History of the ILWU* (Seattle: University of Washington Press, 2009), pp. 274–80 (hereinafter, Eickman oral history); interview by Robert Cherny, 1993; obituary, *San Francisco Chronicle*, August 20, 2006, p. B-8;

Fairley, Lincoln: Interview by Robert Cherny, 1986;

Fried, Judith: see Nitzberg, Leo, and Judith "Judy" Fried Nitzberg;

Gizzi, Angela: see Ward, Estolv, and Angela Gizzi;

Jenkins, David "Dave," and Edith Arnstein Jenkins: *The Union Movement, the California Labor School, and San Francisco Politics, 1926–1988,* interviews with David Jenkins by Lisa Rubens, 1987 and 1988, University of California, Bancroft Library, Regional Oral History Office (hereinafter, Jenkins oral history); Edith A. Jenkins, *Against a Field Sinister* (San Francisco, CA: City Lights Books, 1991); Cherny interviews, May 8, 1987, December 3, 1992; obituary, Edith Arnstein Jenkins, *San Francisco Chronicle*, October 31, 2005, p. 18;

Krupnick, Eva: see Maas, Eva Krupnick Lapin;

Lapin, Adam: see Maas, Eva Krupnick Lapin Maas;

Lerner, Tillie: See Olsen, Jack, and Tillie Lerner Olsen;

Maas, Eva Krupnick Lapin, and Adam Lapin: Eva Maas, *Looking Back on a Life in the Left: A Personal History* (self-published, 1998);

Mitford, Jessica, and Robert Treuhaft: Jessica Mitford, *A Fine Old Conflict* (New York: Alfred A. Knopf, 1977); Thomas Mallon, "Red Sheep: How Jessica Mitford Found Her Voice," *New Yorker*, October 16, 2006, pp. 176–82; *Left-Wing Political Activist and Progressive Leader in the Berkeley Co-op: Robert E. Treuhaft*, interviewed by Robert G. Larsen, 1988–89 (Berkeley Oral History Project, Berkeley Historical Society, 1990); Treuhaft obituary, *Guardian*, November 19, 2001; Treuhaft obituary, *Los Angeles Times*, November 16, 2001; Treuhaft obituary, *New York Times*, December 2, 2001; Mitford obituary, *London Telegraph*, July 25, 1996;

Nitzberg, Leo, and Judith "Judy" Fried Nitzberg: Interview with Judy Nitzberg by Robert Cherny, March 25, 2018; interview with Judy Nitzberg by Timothy V. Johnson, 1985, https://vimeo.com/246813359/; Jack Withington, "Petaluma Young Men Went to War," *Petaluma Argus-Courier*, http://bill-hammerman.blogs.petaluma360.com/13266/petaluma-young-men-went-to-war/ . Kann's *Comrades and Chicken Ranchers* includes stories of the Nitzberg family, but Kann disguised his subjects with different names and sometimes conflated individuals from different families. Thus, Ben Hochman's story is basically that of Sol Nitzberg, Leo's father; Joe Hochman's story is basically that of Leo; and Betty Epstein Hochman is based on Judy, but Judy is embarrassed that people who figure out the pseudonyms would think that she had said things attributed to "Betty";

O'Connor Yates, Oleta: obituary, *San Francisco Examiner*, March 2, 1964, p. 50; obituary, *San Francisco Chronicle*, March 3, 1964, p. 20; "We Quit Red Party—Yates," *San Francisco Examiner*, March 3, 1964, p. 3;

Olsen, Jack, and Tillie Lerner Olsen: Schwartz, *Solidarity Stories*, pp. 280–8 (hereinafter, Olsen oral history); Jack Olsen obituary, *San Francisco Chronicle*, February 28, 1989, p. B-6; Constance Coiner, *Better Red: The Writing and Resistance of Tillie Olsen and Meridel Le Sueur* (New York: Oxford University Press, 1995); Panthea Reid, *Tillie Olsen: One Woman, Many Riddles* (New Brunswick: Rutgers University Press, 2010); "Tillie Olsen," *Literary Ladies Guide* (https://literaryladiesguide.com); Jesse Hamlin, "Forever Dedicated to the Cause," *San Francisco Chronicle Datebook*, January 10, 2008, pp. E1, E2; Tillie Olsen obituary, *San Francisco Chronicle*, January 3, 2007, p. B4; *Leon Olsen Oral History Transcript*, interview conducted by Adah Bakalinsky, Labor Archives and Research Center, San Francisco State University, 1992, https://archive.org/details/csfst_000013;

Starvus (Stack), Loretta: Loretta Starvus Stack interviews by Lucy Kendall, July 1986–January 1987 (recordings only, no transcript, LARC, https://archive.org/details/csfst_000037/csfst_000037_t02_a_access.mp3, hereinafter Starvus interviews); obituary, *San Francisco Chronicle*, February 9, 2001; "Crags Court Community Garden," https://www.glenparkassociation.org/crags-court-community-garden-a-hidden-gem-in-glen-park/; Molly Martin and Brigid O'Farrell, "The Fort Point Gang May Day Memorial," May 26, 2017, https://nwu.org/the-fort-point-gang-may-day-memorial/;

Tobin, Pat: interviews by Robert Cherny, February 9 and 25, 1987; "Pat Tobin: A 'Working Stiff' Lobbyist for the ILWU," *The Dispatcher*, October 17, 1995, p. 5; Tobin obituary, *San Francisco Chronicle*, September 9, 1995, A18;

Todd (Lambert), Louise: *Oral History: Louise Todd Lambert*, interviewed by Lucy Kendall, May–August, 1976, transcript at California Historical Society (hereinafter Todd oral history);

Treuhaft, Robert: See Mitford, Jessica;

Ward, Estolv, and Angela Gizzi: *Estolv Ward: Organizing and Reporting on Labor in the East Bay, California and the West, 1925–1987*, interviewed by Lisa Rubens, 1987, Regional Oral History Office, Bancroft Library, University of California, Berkeley; Angela Ward obituary, *San Francisco Chronicle*, March 20, 1987, p. A24; Estolv Ward obituary, *San Francisco Chronicle*, March 22, 1993, p. B6.

Watson, Don: Don Watson oral history, interviewed by Harvey Schwartz, 1994, LARC; Schwartz, *Solidarity Stories*, pp. 288–95; interview by Robert Cherny, 1996.

I researched the card files maintained by the California Un-American Activities Committee and looked through all but one of the committee's publications (1945 seems to be unavailable). I found entries for everyone *except* Carol Cuénod and Leo and Judy Nitzberg.

I have referred throughout the essay to Loretta Starvus and Louise Todd because they signed their resignations from the party that way. For the other married women, I have used the names that they commonly used after their marriages.

7   Pat Tobin's positions in the party are not clear from his interview.
8   Seven were of Russian Jewish parentage and one of Austrian Jewish parentage, two had one or both parents Irish Catholic, one was of Italian Catholic parentage, one of Polish Catholic parentage, one of German freethinker parentage, one of English Protestant parentage, one of Scots and German parentage, and two of old-stock Protestant American parentage. One had one parent born in England, and another had a parent born in Switzerland.
9   J. Stachel, "Organization Report to the Sixth Convention of the Communist Party of the U.S.A.," *The Communist* 8 (May 1929), p. 241. I could not find similar data for the 1930s.
10 On this point, see Lisa Rubens, "The Patrician Radical: Charlotte Anita Whitney," *California History*, 65 (1986), pp. 158–71, esp. 71.
11 The three post-baccalaureate degrees were an MA in Slavonic Languages from the University of California, Berkeley (O'Connor Yates), and an LLB (Treuhaft) and a PhD in economics (Fairley), both from Harvard.
12 Jenkins oral history, pp. 20–3; Bailey, *Kid*, p. 211.
13 Edith Arnstein Jenkins's grandparents came to San Francisco during the Gold Rush and established themselves as part of the city's German Jewish elite; Jessica Mitford was the daughter of the second Baron Redesdale, a member of the English nobility.
14 I have dealt with these events at more length in my "Communist Party in California, 1935–1940," pp. 17–27.
15 On the Duclos article, see Harvey Klehr, John Earl Haynes, and Kyrill M. Anderon, *The Soviet World of American Communism* (New Haven, CT: Yale University Press, 1998), pp. 99–106; on the upheaval within the CP in the United States, see Maurice Isserman, *Which Side Were You On? The American Communist Party during the Second World War* (Middletown, CT: Wesleyan University Press, 1982), pp. 216–38.
16 I've described this labor-Left culture in my *Victor Arnautoff and the Politics of Art* (Champaign: University of Illinois Press, 2017), ch. 10. For an overview of the CLS, see John Skovgaard, "The California Labor School" (unpublished paper, 2003, Labor Archive and Research Center, San Francisco State University, hereinafter LARC). Jess M. Rigelhaupt's account of the school, "'Education for Action': The California Labor School, radical unionism, civil rights, and progressive coalition building in the San Francisco Bay Area, 1934–1970" (PhD dissertation, University of Michigan, 2005) was not available as this was written. See also the CLS collections at LARC, and the Urban Archives, California State University, Northridge; interview with Jenkins by Cherny, May 8, 1987; Jenkins oral history; Pele Edises, "The Solid Scholar of Lower Market Street," *People's World*, November 18, 1944, p. 3. For early CP schools in San Francisco, see Lisa Jackson, "Twenty-Four Hour Party People: A Gendered Social History of California Communism" (MA thesis, San Francisco State University, 2015), chapter 2.

17 Cuénod oral history, p. 20.
18 Course catalogs, folders 1–8, box 1; enrollments projected from financial data, folder c, box 4; flyers and announcements, folder 9, box 1, CLS collection, LARC; Holland Roberts memoirs, folder 17, box 1, Holland Roberts Papers, LARC; Cherny interview with Jenkins, May 8, 1987; Jenkins oral history, p. 212.
19 Marvin Gettleman, "The Lost World of United States Labor Education: Curricula at East and West Coast Communist Schools, 1944–1957," in Robert W. Cherny, William Issel, and Keiran Walsh Taylor (eds.), *American Labor and the Cold War: Grassroots Politics and Postwar Political Culture* (New Brunswick: Rutgers University Press, 2004), pp. 205–15, describes similarities between the CLS and the Jefferson School and also the wider curriculum at the CLS.
20 Cuénod oral history, p. 18. I did *not* find evidence of participation by Bailey, Cayton, Starvus, and Todd.
21 The *PW* is available at LARC; for Roger's radio program, see Nathan Godfried, "'Voice of the People': Sidney Roger, the Labor/Left, and Broadcasting in San Francisco, 1945–1950," *American Communist History* 18 (2019), pp. 56–7. Regarding Tobin, see his entry in the CUAC card file.
22 Jenkins oral history, p. 174; California Un-American Activities Committee papers, box 35, California State Archives, hereinafter CUAC papers. Regarding support from VOKS, see V. Semenov, Deputy Head, Hard-currency Financial Office, to V. Kemenov, April 17, 1948, on MID letterhead and marked Top Secret, 5283 s.ch.-22s-82, VOKS Special department, File 23. Correspondence with America, March 8–June 14, 1948, State Archive of the Russian Federation (GARF); Semenov's message included funds for the American Russian Institute (ARI) and the Russian American Society; other sections of the message suggest that some VOKS contributions were on-going; Svetlana Chervonnaya generously provided this citation and translation. For links among VOKS, the KGB, and the ARI, see my *Victor Arnautoff and the Politics of Art*, pp. 137–39, 273, n. 26.
23 These generalizations draw from several of the sources in note 3; Eickman interview.
24 Bailey, *Kid*, pp. 302, 3380; Jenkins interviews; Starvus interviews, side 20.
25 Todd oral history, pp. 133, 149, 195, 214–38; Maas, *Looking Back*, chapter 8; Reid, *Olsen*, pp. 120, 139.
26 Todd oral history, pp. 125–6, 127. 130; Starvus interviews, side 20; Reid, *Olsen*, p. 392, n. 39.
27 Starvus interviews, sides 24, 26; Todd oral history, pp. 124, 127.
28 Maas, *Looking Back*, p. 117.
29 Dorothy Ray Healey and Maurice Isserman, *California Red: A Life in the American Communist Party* (Urbana: University of Illinois Press, [1990] 1993), p. 178; Peggy Dennis, *The Autobiography of an American Communist: A Personal View*

of a Political Life, 1925–1975 (Berkeley, CA: Creative Arts Book; Westport, CT: Lawrence Hill, 1977), p. 56.

30 Rubens, "Patrician Radical"; Beth Slutsky, *Gendering Radicalism: Women and Communism in Twentieth-Century California* (Lincoln: University of Nebraska Press, 2015).

31 For Bridges and the ILWU, see Charles P. Larrowe, *Harry Bridges: The Rise and Fall of Radical Labor in the United States* (New York: Lawrence Hill, 1972); Stanley I. Kutler, *The American Inquisition: Justice and Injustice in the Cold War* (New York: Hill and Wang, 1982), chapter 5; Peter Afrasiabi, *Burning Bridges: America's 20=Year Crusade to Deport Labor Leader Harry Bridges* (Brooklyn: Thielmere Books, 2016). I discuss Bridges's relation with the CP at length in my forthcoming biography of Bridges.

32 California Legislature, *Third Report: Joint Fact-Finding Committee on Un-American Activities in California: 1947*, pp. 77–94; boxes 45 and 52c, CUAC papers; the reduction in course offerings and programs can be traced through folders 1–9, box 1, CLS collection, LARC; see also Skovgaard, "California Labor School," p. 17; Jenkins interviews; Jenkins oral history, esp. pp. 171–2, 174; Holland Roberts memoirs, folder 1/21, box 1, Roberts papers, LARC; flyer, "How to Padlock a School," folder 4, box 5, CLS collection, LARC; report of Max H. Fischer, 10-20-57, Arnautoff FBI file, 4: 26–36, esp. 29.

33 Godfried, "Sidney Roger"; Al Richmond, *A Long View from the Left: Memoirs of an American Revolutionary* (New York: Delta, 1975), esp. pp. 300, 298ff., 382.

34 Reports of William B. Dillon, October 28, 1954, March 1, 1955, Victor Arnautoff FBI file, National Archives, 3:14–27, 54–78, esp. 16, 59–60.

35 Hobbs, *Cayton Legacy*, pp. 172–3; Jenkins interviews; Jenkins oral history, pp. 179, 180; Tobin interview; Fairley interview.

36 Federal Bureau of Investigation, *Membership of the Communist Party, 1919–1954*; the copy on line includes source information, most from the CP itself; at https://archive.org/details/foia_FBI_Monograph-Membership_of_CPUSA_1919-1954; Harvey Klehr and John Earl Haynes, *The American Communist Movement: Storming Heaven Itself* (New York: Twayne, 1992), pp. 108, 137, 147.

37 National Education Department, Communist Party, "The Struggle against White Chauvinism" (September 1949), box 13, folder 57, American Left Ephemera Collection, Archives Service Center, University of Pittsburg, http://digital.library.pitt.edu/u/ulsmanuscripts/pdf/31735051655326.pdf (accessed December 2, 2013).

38 Healey and Isserman, *California Red*, p. 126; Mitford, *A Fine Old Conflict*, pp. 127–8; and below, for the experiences of the Nitzbergs and Keith Eickman.

39 See, e.g., Klehr and Haynes, *American Communist Movement*, p. 125;

40 Interview with Judy Nitzberg and conversations over many years; Eickman interview; Eickman oral history, p. 279.

41 Fairley interview.
42 Olsen oral history, p. 287; Reid, *Olsen*, pp. 181, 189, 392, n. 39; Coiner, *Better Red*, pp. 150–1.
43 Hobbs, *Cayton Legacy*, pp. 173–4.
44 Jenkins, *Field Sinister*, p. 34; Jenkins oral history, pp. 188–9, 194; Bailey, *Kid*, pp. 419–20; [San Francisco] *The Dispatcher*, April 13, 1995, p. 7.
45 Maas, *Looking Back*, pp. 81–2; Jenkins oral history, pp. 190–1; Cuénod oral history, p. 38.
46 Mitford, *A Fine Old Conflict*, pp. 257–8, 273–80.
47 Starvus interviews, side 24; Todd oral history, pp. 256, 269, 271; Bill Sennett et al. to National Committee, March 26, 1958, attached to Todd oral history, following p. 295; *San Francisco Examiner*, March 3, 1964, p. 3.
48 California Legislature, Senate Fact-Finding Committee on Un-American Activities, *Eleventh Report, Un-American Activities in California, 1961* (Sacramento, 1961), pp. 12–13.
49 The ILWU's constitution prohibited discrimination based on race, color, creed, national origin, religion, or political belief. The dispatch systems for Locals 10 and 34 prevented employers from discharging workers for political reasons. Local 6, which also had a dispatch system, was less successful to protecting its members once they were dispatched and became responsible to a particular employer. Keith Eickman, later Local 6 business agent, was able in at least one instance to prevent the discharge of a former CP member from a warehouse job. By the mid-1950s, the ILWU included longshore workers and warehouse and miscellaneous workers in all Pacific Coast states and the Territories of Alaska and Hawaiʻi, including agricultural workers in Hawaiʻi. I would expect similar patterns in other areas with a significant ILWU presence.
50 Olsen oral history; Starvus interviews, side 25.
51 Bailey, *Kid*, p. 421; Maas, *Looking Back*, p. 87; *San Francisco Examiner*, March 3, 1964, p. 3.
52 Reid, *Olsen*, pp. 189, 190, 194, 195; conversations with Judy Nitzberg; Maas, *Looking Back*, pp. 87–9; Jenkins, *Against a Field*, pp. 69, 70; Edith Arnstein Jenkins obituary; Cuénod oral history, pp. 56–7, 62–4.
53 Starvas interviews, side 25; Todd oral history, pp. 267, 272, 282.
54 Nathan Heller, "Private Dreams and Public Ideals in San Francisco," *New Yorker*, August 6 and 13, 2018, https://www.newyorker.com/magazine/2018/08/06/private-dreams-and-public-ideals-in-san-francisco.
55 In addition to the sources listed in note 3, see "Bill Bailey Videos, Films and Books" (mimeographed list in possession of the author).
56 Treuhaft obituaries: *Guardian*, November 19, 2001; *Los Angeles Times*, November 16, 2001; *New York Times*, December 2, 2001.

57 CUAC card file; CUAC annual report for 1966, p. 117. For the "freeway revolt," see William Issel, "'Land Values, Human Values, and the Preservation of the City's Treasured Appearance': Environmentalism, Politics, and the San Francisco Freeway Revolt," *Pacific Historical Review* 68 (1999), pp. 611–46; Katherine M. Johnson, "Captain Blake versus the Highwaymen: Or, How San Francisco Won the Freeway Revolt," *Journal of Planning History* 8 (2009), pp. 56–83.
58 Jenkins interviews; Jenkins oral history, pp. 217–84 esp. 262a; Hobbs, *Cayton Legacy*, pp, 199–200; Jenkins, CUAC file for 1954–68.
59 Hobbs, *Cayton Legacy*, pp. 199–200; Jenkins oral history, 271; Cayton file, CUAC, 1954–68 cards.
60 Eickman oral history; Eickman obituary, *San Francisco Chronicle*, August 20, 2006, p. B-8; Jenkins oral history, 235.
61 Robert Farley, "She's No Red," *Politifact*, February 15, 2008.
62 Robert Treuhaft obituary, *Guardian*, November 19, 2001; Treuhaft obituary, *Los Angeles Times*, November 16, 2001; Treuhaft obituary, *New York Times*, December 2, 2001; Mitford obituary, *London Telegraph*, July 25, 1996; ; interview with Doris Brin Walker by Robert Cherny, June 29, 2007; CUAC annual reports for 1965, pp. 112, 150, and 1966, pp. 65, 71, 101, 194, 120, 126; *San Francisco Chronicle*, December 28, 1966, p. 2, January 20, 1967, p. 2, January 9, 1994, p. 2.
63 Johnson interview with Judy Nitzberg; conversations with Judy and Leo Nitzberg; Todd oral history, pp. 272, 283; O'Connor Yates obituary, *San Francisco Chronicle*, March 3, 1964, p. 20; "Crags Court Community Garden"; Fairley, CUAC card file for 1954–68.
64 Eickman oral history, p. 280.
65 Copy of letter, Bill Sennett et al. to National Committee, March 26, 1958, attached to Todd oral history, following p. 295. Dorothy Healy, who left the party in 1973, also felt that she had moved to the Left; *California Red*, pp. 243–5, and comments at a conference, *c.* 1974. Leah Schneiderman, widow of Bill Schneiderman, joined the party in the early 1920s, left only in the early 1990s, but also expressed her optimism for her new affiliation on the Left; interviews by Robert Cherny, April 14, 1987 and April 26, 1993.
66 Cuénod oral history, p. 66; Todd oral history, p. 120-1.

Bibliography

Bailey, Bill, with Lynn Damme. *The Kid from Hoboken: An Autobiography*. San Francisco, CA: Circus Lithographic Press, 1993.
Cuénod, Carol. *Carol Cuénod Oral History*, interview by Harvey Schwartz, 1994. Labor Archives and Research Center, San Francisco State University.

Hobbs, Richard S. *The Cayton Legacy: An African American Family*. Pullman, WA: Washington State University Press, 2002.
Jenkins, David. *The Union Movement, the California Labor School, and San Francisco Politics, 1926–1988*, interviews by Lisa Rubens, 1987 and 1988. Regional Oral History Office, Bancroft Library, University of California, Berkeley.
Maas, Eva. *Looking Back on a Life in the Left: A Personal History*. Self-published, 1998.
Mitford, Jessica. *A Fine Old Conflict*. New York: Alfred A. Knopf, 1977.
Reid, Panthea. *Tillie Olsen: One Woman, Many Riddles*. New Brunswick: Rutgers University Press, 2010.
Schwartz, Harvey. *Solidarity Stories: An Oral History of the ILWU*. Seattle: University of Washington Press, 2009.
Starvus Stack, Loretta. *Loretta Starvus Stack Oral History*, interviews by Lucy Kendall, 1986 and 1987. Labor Archives and Research Center, San Francisco State University.
Todd Lambert, Louise. *Louise Todd Lambert Oral History*, interviews by Lucy Kendall, 1976. California Historical Society, San Francisco.

Conclusion

Vernon L. Pedersen and Katherine A. S. Sibley

In her keynote speech at the Williams College conference, which marked the centennial of the founding of the Communist Party of the United States of America (CPUSA) and launched this volume, Dr. Randi Storch told the story of a black resident of Chicago, who, when faced with eviction, urged her children to "run quick and find the Reds." Storch used the phrase as a metaphor for the historians' quest, after the opening of the Russian archives in 1991, to "run quick" and do the same. As the essays in this volume demonstrate, there were a lot of "Reds" to find. Due to the shortage of sources, previous studies of American communism were often superficial, lacking in detail, based on single sources and thus missing a good number of these characters. If earlier studies were thin in their coverage, articles and monographs drawing upon the vast resources of the archives tended to be tightly focused and drowning in detail. Exploration of new material required the careful turnover of small pieces of the big canvas, as did the examination of unanswered questions and the careful placing of long missing pieces of evidence. Initially, the exposure of once secret aspects of party history—long overlooked and often denied—dominated popular and academic attention overshadowing other aspects of Communist engagement in US politics and culture. And, as Storch remarked, some used the new sources to vigorously continue "inwardly focused ... partisan battles," countering others who clung to their heroic vision of the party's role in American life. Although the participants in the 2018 conference represented several generations of scholars, Storch despaired of seeing an end to such ideological battles within the life spans of anyone present.

Nevertheless, her talk quickly switched from pessimism to optimism because, in other ways, the future appeared bright. Some questions have been conclusively answered by the party's records, the most important being the existence of a tight relationship between the CPUSA and the Soviet Union. Equally importantly, as

Storch noted, the records laid to rest who was and who was not a Communist revealing the broad swath of the party's influence on a national level and its significant local impact in states like California, New York, and Maryland. For three decades the party played a key role in broad-gauged progressive activism. For too long, that role has been overshadowed by its sudden disgrace in the 1950s. Although Storch, a member of the Executive Committee of the Historians of American Communism, felt that the traditional and revisionist schools of thought still represented the bulk of continuing research on the party, the essays in this volume indicate otherwise. While traditionist scholars may tend to take a top-down approach, focusing on the Soviet role, and revisionists prefer a bottom-up one, highlighting the contributions of Communist activists, in other ways the schools are starting to merge. The chapters in this volume acknowledge the Soviet connection in their analyses and use it to frame their specific subjects. The dual nature of American communism, as a domestic political party and at the same time part of an international movement, makes it a particularly interesting subject in the age of globalization. The CPUSA was always a minority movement in the United States, but it was not an insignificant force, especially during the earlier years of its century in American life. Communists were consumed by their vision of the world and rightly respected as the party of action, standing up for racial justice, for example, in ways that even the National Association for the Advancement of Colored People (NAACP) was reluctant to imitate. Their ideas and members reached into every corner of American life and their disciplined centralized structure gave them influence far beyond their always modest numbers.

The task of the Historians of American Communism (HOAC) and the aim of the authors in this book has been to integrate the history of the party into the history of the United States. Randi Storch put it well in her keynote address:

> In our enthusiasm to "Run Quick and Find the Reds" we have each written a piece of the story, but we have yet to fully ingrate [the pieces] into a broader narrative. ... We have yet to fully engage the larger narrative that drives the survey of US history; and we have yet to fully bring 21stcentury questions to bear on the history of American communism.

The opening of the Russian archives transformed the field of American Communist Studies. Our task in these chapters has been to address Storch's charge, to use those insights from the archives to transform the broader history of the United States as well, and we hope that our book has been a first step in the foundation of a more fully dimensional understanding of the party's role in American life.

Notes on Contributors

Robert W. Cherny, Professor Emeritus at San Francisco State University, received his PhD from Columbia University in 1972. He is the author of three books on US politics, in the period between 1865 and 1925, and thirty-nine published essays; coauthor of two books on San Francisco history, a US survey textbook, and a California history textbook; and coeditor of two anthologies. He has been an NEH fellow, Distinguished Fulbright Lecturer at Moscow State University, Visiting Research Scholar at the University of Melbourne, and Senior Fulbright Lecturer at the University of Heidelberg.

John Earl Haynes held the post of 20th-Century Political Historian in the Manuscript Division of the Library of Congress from 1987 until his retirement in 2012. He received his PhD in 1978 from the University of Minnesota. He is the author or coauthor of twelve books and more than one hundred historical essays. He is a founding member of the Historians of American Communism and is the online editor of H-HOAC.

Edward P. Johanningsmeier teaches at the University of Delaware as adjunct faculty. He is the author of *Forging American Communism: The Life of William Z. Foster* (1994), and has published numerous articles and reviews on the history of the CPUSA.

Harvey Klehr is Andrew Mellon Professor Emeritus of Politics and History and former chairman of the Political Science Department at Emory University, where he taught from 1971 to 2016. He is the author or editor of fifteen books, three of which have been nominated for the Pulitzer Prize. He was the recipient of the Emory Williams Distinguished Teaching Award for Emory College in 1983 and was recognized as the University Scholar-Teacher of the Year by Emory in 1995.

Denise Lynn is Associate Professor of History and Director of Gender Studies at the University of Southern Indiana in Evansville, Indiana. She received her PhD in History in 2006 from Binghamton University, SUNY. Lynn's research focus has been on women in the CPUSA during the Popular Front. She is particularly interested in rank-and-file women in the party who operated outside of the Central Committee. Her articles have appeared in *American*

Communist History, *Women's History Review*, *Journal of Cold War Studies*, *Radical Americas*, and *Journal for the Study of Radicalism*.

Erik S. McDuffie is an associate professor in the Department of African American Studies at the University of Illinois at Urbana-Champaign. His research and teaching interests include the African diaspora, the Midwest, black feminism, black queer theory, black radicalism, urban history, and black masculinity. He is the author of *Sojourning for Freedom: Black Women, American Communism, and the Making of Black Left Feminism* (2011). The book won the 2012 Wesley-Logan Prize from the American Historical Association and the Association for the Study of African American Life and History, as well as the 2011 Letitia Woods Brown Award from the Association of Black Women Historians.

Vernon L. Pedersen is professor of history and the head of the department of International Studies at the American University in Sharjah. He has also served as the chair of the Science and Humanities Division at the University of Providence, a private Catholic college in Great Falls, Montana, and as Dean of Faculty at the American University in Bulgaria. Pedersen is a 1993 graduate of Georgetown University, specializing in the history of American and international communism.

William C. Pratt is Professor Emeritus of History at the University of Nebraska at Omaha (UNO), where he served on the faculty for forty-two years. He also has taught at Philadelphia College of Textiles and Science and Hope College. He holds a BA in history from Ursinus College, a MA in American Studies from the University of Maryland and a PhD in History from Emory University. He was the Distinguished Fulbright Lecturer in American History at Moscow State University (2000) and a Senior Fulbright Lecturer in American Studies at the University of Warsaw (2007).

James G. Ryan is professor of history at Texas A&M University's Galveston campus. He received a BA and MA from the University of Delaware and a PhD in 1981 from the University of Notre Dame. Ryan was promoted to full professor in 2004. He is the author of the only scholarly biography of Earl Browder, the CPUSA's most successful leader. Ryan has served as a Fulbright Specialist in Poland (2006) and Kazakhstan (2009).

Katherine A. S. Sibley is professor of history at Saint Joseph's University in Philadelphia. Her books on Soviet-American relations include *Red Spies in America: Stolen Secrets and the Dawn of the Cold War* (2004), *The Cold War*

(1998), and *Loans and Legitimacy: The Evolution of Soviet-American Relations, 1919–1933* (1996). Her work in first ladies includes a biography, *First Lady Florence Harding: Behind the Tragedy and Controversy* (2009), and two edited books, *A Companion to First Ladies* (2016), and *Southern First Ladies: Culture and Place in White House History* (in press). Sibley received her BA, MA, and PhD from UC Santa Barbara.

Beth Slutsky, PhD, is a historian of modern American women's history and a scholar of history education at UC Davis, with the History Department and the California History Social-Science Project. She published *Gendering Radicalism: Women and Communism in Twentieth Century California* in 2015, which explores the roots of leftist radicalism among California women. Slutsky is a lead author of California's newly revised and adopted History-Social Science Framework, which guides k-12 history education in the state.

Index

Abraham Lincoln Battalion 162, 165
Abraham Lincoln Brigade T-shirts 167
Abramowitz, Esther 68
Africa 194
African Americans 191, 193, 195, 208, 220, 236
Alexander, Kendra 221
Alexander Vassiliev's Notebooks 129
Alien Registration Act of 1940 236
Alioto, Joseph 243
Al Kauffman 179
Alliance for Democracy 112
Al Richmond 8
America First Committee 121
American anticommunism 142
American Civil Liberties Union 116
"American Commission" 76, 79
American Communism and Soviet Russia 8
American Communism in Crisis (1943–1957) 17
American Communist Studies 256
American Federation of Labor (AFL) 36–7, 43, 67
American Federation of Teachers Local 61 242
American Historical Association 241
"Americanization" 70
American labor movement 17
The American masses 185
"American Plan" 71
American progressivism 9
American Russian Institute 234
American Socialist Party (ASP) 44, 65–6, 115
American trade unionists 68
American Way of Birth, The (1992) 241, 242
American Way of Death Revisited, The (1998) 242
American Way of Death, The (1963) 241

American Women's Association Clubhouse 150
anarchists 68
Anderson, Sherwood 77
anti-anticommunism 10
anti-communist liberals 36
antifascism 190–5
anti-House Un-American Activities Committee (HUAC) demonstration 245
anti-Marshall plan agency 35
anti-stalinists 144
anti-Varga campaign 34
anti-Vietnam War 216, 243
Arbenz, Jacobo 129
Armour meatpacking executive (1917) 73
Army's Signals Intelligence Service 119
Axis powers 167
Avrich, Paul 68

Baily, Bill 164, 230, 234
Baldwin Locomotive Works 67
Ball of Fire (movie) 1
Bancroft Library's Regional Oral History Office 241
Barrett, James R. 48–9, 69
Battle of Brunette 173
Battle of Teruel 163
Bay Area Labor History Workshop 241
Bay Conservation and Development Commission 243
Beal, Fred 4
Bedacht, Max 76
Bentley, Elizabeth 123, 129
Berg, Del 161
Bessie, Alvah 164–6, 171, 172, 176
Bianca, Joe 165, 176, 178
 "the Corsican Cutthroat" 178
Biden, Joseph 111, 130
"Big Bill" Haywood 43

the Black Caucus 211–12
Black Panther Party 212
Black Panthers 243
Black Politics and Economics
 workshop 208
"Black Power" 209
"Black Sox" scandal 3
Bois, W. E. B. Du 233
Bolshevik Revolution 18, 70, 112, 114
Bolshevik Russia (1919–20) 114–16
Bolshevism Menace 115
bootlegged passports 119
Boston 116
Bremen 176
Bridges, Harry 235
Briggs, Cyril 188
Britain 20, 22–3, 30, 32
British 170
Brooks, Chris 169
Browder, Earl 19–21, 24–5, 28
 Atlanta Penitentiary 54, 57, 58
 expelled from CPUSA 38
 Groves, Gladys L. 42–3
 history of 42
 Kansas's left-wing miners 44
 Moscow representatives 44
 party's history 66
 public leadership role 66
 Russia's revolutions 43
 skilled office workers 44
 Socialist Party (SP) 42
 Teheran Thesis 25–7
 years of attempting to return to CPUSA
  leadership 32
Brown, John 49
Brown, Michael 197
Buford (transit ship) 115
Buhle, Paul 70
Bukharin, Nikolai 18, 75
*Bulletin of the Information Bureau of the
 CC RCP(b): Issues of Foreign Policy* 27
Burdick, Quentin 97
Burns, William 111

Cahill, John T. 53
California Academy of Sciences 244
California Communist Party 211, 236
California Democratic Council
 (CDC) 242
California Labor School (CLS) 233

California's Central Valley 210
California Un-American Activities
 Committee (CUAC) 236
Campbell, Grace 188
Cannon, James P. 18, 45, 65, 71, 74, 75,
 82, 90–1
Carnegie mines, western Pennsylvania 77
Carpenter, Michael 130
Carroll, Peter 165, 174, 175
Carroll, William 67
Casey, Joseph 120
Castro, Fidel 128
Cayton, Revels 236
Central Co-operative Exchange
 (CCE) 98
Central Intelligence Agency (CIA) 111,
 128, 167
Chair Martin Dies (D-Tex.) 119, 120
Chambers, Whitaker 7, 119, 122, 123, 229
 "revolting cynic" 141
 Stalinist 141
*Changes in the Economics of Capitalism as
 a Result of the Second World War* 31
Charles Ruthenberg group 66
Che-Lumumba Club 208–10
Chicago 115
Chicago trade unionists 91
Childs, Morris 30–4
China 113, 123, 205
Christman, Alvin 96
Church Committee hearings 128
Citizen Genet 113
Civil Rights Congress 240
Clune, Lori 125
Clutchette, John Wesley 210
COINTELPRO investigations 128
Cold War 2, 82, 96, 112, 122–9, 146–7,
 151, 156, 185, 192, 193, 205–7, 209,
 212, 214–16, 218, 221, 222
Cold War academics 130
Cold War Communist trials 206
Combahee River Collective 186
Committees of Correspondence
 (COC) 221
"Communism" 191
Communism in American Life series 7–8
Communist Infiltration of the Radiation
 Laboratories, University of
 California, Berkeley (CINRAD)
 investigation 121

Communist Information Bureau
   (Cominform) 35
Communist International (Comintern) 3,
   66, 91, 117, 169
   Comintern Apparatus (COMRAP)
      probe 122
   Comintern at the Russian State Archive
      for Social and Political History
      (RGASPI) 175
   The Comintern Era 18–24
   Comintern's Executive Committee
      (ECCI) 48
   Comintern survey 170
Communist Labor Party (CLP) 3, 18, 115
Communist Manifesto 20
communist organizers 71, 73, 78
*Communist Party and the Auto Workers
   Union* (1980), 8
Communist Party in Maryland, 1919–1957
   (2001) 9
Communist Party of the Soviet Union
   (CPSU) 9, 24
Communist Party of the United States
   of America (CPUSA) 1, 90, 91, 115,
   120, 141, 161, 185, 206, 237, 255
   American Communism 207–8, 215
   American Communist
      movement 65, 73
   American Communist Party 48, 51, 82,
      83, 217–18
   American communists 19–21, 24, 27,
      37, 65, 66, 91
   Communist Party 188–90
   Communist Party members 230
   "Communism Is Twentieth Century
      Americanism" 20, 50
   Depression Era Party 4
   party assignments 234
   party members 234
   party workers 79
Communist Party Standard Bearers 50
Communist Political Association (CPA) 3,
   6, 26, 95, 115
*Communists in Harlem during the
   Depression* (1983), 8
Communists' Kharkov city
   committee 46–7
communist union organizers 5
Company Four, machine gun
   company 165

*Comrades: Tales of a Brigadista in the
   Spanish Civil War* (1997) 173
Confédération Génerale du Travail
   (CGT) 68
Congressional committees 161
Congress of Industrial Organizations
   (CIO) 5, 17, 30, 36, 41, 73, 97, 235
Congress on Racial Equality (CORE) 209
Conrad, Joseph 178
conspiracy/conspiracy theories 7, 10, 43,
   112–14, 122–3, 127, 130, 151, 211
Contemporary Historians 163
Council of Foreign Ministers 34
counterintelligence apparatus (1930) 119
Coxey's Army 67
CP-11 191
Cravath, Paul D. 117
criminal syndicalism laws 74
Crossman, R. H. S. 229
The Crucible (1953) 8
Crouch, Paul 119
Crow, Jim 186
Cuba 67, 117, 170
Cuénod, Carol 233, 239, 240
Cumberbatch, Claudia Vera 188
Cunningham, Imogene 233
Czolgosz, Leon 114

Daily Worker 1, 17, 21, 22, 30, 34, 49, 51,
   90, 96, 98, 119, 165, 166, 175, 233
Darcy, Samuel Adams 47
Darwinism 69
Daughters and Rebels 241, 242
Davies, Carole Boyce 186
Davis, Angela 243
   American communism 208
   Bancroft Library's Regional Oral
      History Office 241
   British media 213
   California Communist Party 211
   "Declare your independence: Vote for
      Hall and Tyner" 217
   guns 211
   left-wing unions 240
   murder charges 205
   presidential elections 218–19
   "unprecedented attack on American
      democracy" 111
Debs, Eugene 71, 74
"deep state" conspiracy 114

"Defeat [Republican nominee Alfred] Landon At All Costs; Vote for Earl Browder" 51
"Democratic Front" 51
Democratic National Convention (1948) 29
Democratic Party 30, 35, 97
Democratic Party/Republican Party 18
Democratic People's Republic of Korea 192
Denning, William 73
Department of Defense (DOD) 130
deportation method 116
Detroit 116
Dewey, Thomas 36
Dies, Martin 119–21
Dil Pickle Club 68
Dimitrov, Georgi 22, 26, 49, 79–80
A Distant Heartbeat: A War, a Disappearance, and a Family's Secrets 171
Dozenberg, Nicholas 119
Drama Travel Service 145
Draper, Theodore 8, 65, 74
Dreiser, Theodore 77
Drumgo, Fleeta 210
Dubofsky, Melvyn 68, 77
Du Bois Club 209
DuBois, W. E. B., 67
Duclos, Jacques 27–8, 232
Dyson, Lowell K. 89, 95–6, 102n1

the Eastern Division 96
Eastern Europe 2, 32–4, 123
Ebro campaign 177
"eclecticism" 69
Eickman, Keith 234, 237–8
Eisenhower, Dwight D. 124
Eisler, Gerhart 19
El Salvador 196
European syndicalists 68
"the Evil Empire" 128
Executive Committee of the Historians of American Communism 256
Exit Right (2017) 229

Fadiman, Clifton 143
failure of American Communism 65
"Faking of Americans, The" 151

Farmer-Labor Era 90–2
Farmer-Laborism 91
Farmer-Labor Party (FLP) 3, 93
Farmers Holiday 92
Farmers National Committee for Action (FNCA) 93
Farmers National Weekly 94
Farmers Union 96, 97
Farmers Union Grain Terminal Association 97
Farm Revolt (1930s) 92–5
fascism 19
Federal Bureau of Investigation (FBI) 7, 55, 57, 59–60, 89–90, 97, 101, 111, 119, 121–4, 145, 150, 162, 205, 211–12, 215–16, 236, 240
Federated Farmer-Labor Party 3, 91
Fifth Amendment 53
A Fine Old Conflict (1977) 241, 242
Finnish Americans 90, 98–100, 170
Finnish Workers Federation 98
First World War 43, 112, 113, 173, 175–6, 188
Fish Committee 117
Fisher, Harry 172, 173, 176
Fitzpatrick, John 70
Florida 67
Fond 515 9, 10
Ford, James W. 50
Foreign Affairs (2017) 130
the *Foreign Relations of the United States* series 128
"For the Unity of Women in the Cause of Peace" 185
Fort Upton 116
For Whom the Bell Tolls 172
Foster's Chicago-based TUEL 45
Foster, William Z. 26, 43, 45, 47–8, 72
  and Abramowitz, Esther 68
  "the age of industrial violence" 68
  comrades 80–1
  "expert in organization" 75
  funeral in Red Square 83
  Home Colony on Puget Sound 68
  international syndicalist movement 68
  "introduction to the class struggle" 66, 67
  Marxist political outlook 81
  "open drive" 77

Peters's judgment 82
radical syndicalists 67–8
"rotten diplomacy" 76
"Save the Union" 77
Fox, Jay 68
Fraina, Louis 65
"FrameUp: A Weekly Trial Bulletin" 213
France 20, 67, 167, 177
Frankenstein, Richard 80
Franklin D. Roosevelt (FDR) 79, 117, 163
Franklin Roosevelt's administration 5
"fraud and a hoax" 123
Freedom of Information Act (FOIA) 89–90
Free Speech activists 243
French labor movement 67
Fried, Richard 9, 129
Friendship and Fratricide: An Analysis of Whittaker Chambers and Alger Hiss (1967) 10
Fuchs, Klaus 121
Furr, Grover 174
Fur Workers Union 243

Gates, John 166
Gelhorn, Martha 163
General Motors (GM) 78
General Secretary 66
A Generation on Trial: USA vs Alger Hiss (1951), 8
George Washington Battalion 163
Germany 67
Gerstle, Gary 41
"Get Tough with Russia" foreign policy 97
Gitlow, Benjamin 18, 19, 91, 229
God That Failed, The (1949) 229
Gold, Harry 119, 121, 123, 129
Goldman, Emma 115
Gompers, Samuel 68, 73–4
"Good Fight" myth 163, 164, 170–2, 174, 176, 179
Gornick, Vivian 229
Graham, David 162
Graham, Thomas 114
"Grand Alliance" 23
Grand Army of the Republic (GAR) 171
Graubard, Mark 148–9
Great Britain 167, 186
Great Depression 19, 48, 169, 188

Great Lakes region 98
The Great Purge 141, 144
Great Steel Strike (1919) 68, 70
Great Steel Strike and Its Lessons, The (1920) 70
Greenglass, David 121, 129
Greenwich Village 179
Groves, Gladys L. 42–4
Guatemala 129

Hall, Gus 7, 100, 218–19, 221
Hambers, Walter 147
Hammer and Hoe: Alabama Communists during the Great Depression (1990) 11
Hammersmark, Sam 68
Harris, Kitty 47
Harris, Lem 93
Harris, Mary G. (Mother Jones) 72
Haskell, William 117
Hawks, Howard 1
Haynes, John Earl 2, 9, 124, 129, 168
Haywood, William D. 83
Healey, Dorothy 237
Hellman, John 6–7
Hellman, Lillian 163
Hemingway, Ernest 163, 172
Herald Tribune 178
Herrick, William 172–4
Hervé, Gustave 68
Hill 666 177–8
Hiss, Alger 7, 8, 10, 13, 128, 129, 154
Historians of American Communism (HOAC) 2, 256
Historical Advisory Committee (U.S. State Department) 129
Hitler, Adolf 49, 169, 171
Hobsbawm, E. J. 75, 188–9
Hochschild, Adam 115–16, 176
Hofstadter, Richard 113
Hons and Rebels 241
Hoover, Herbert 73
Hoover, J. Edgar 115, 117, 118, 121, 125, 127, 130, 162
House Un-American Activities Committee (HUAC) 5–6, 174
Huiswoud, Otto 188
"Hunger Marches" 4

Ibarruri, Doelores *(La Pasionaria)* 172
I Confess (1940) 229
I Led Three Lives (TV Series) 127
ILWU's Northern California District Council 242
industrial unionism 73
Industrial Workers of the World (IWW) 44, 67, 115, 178
Ingram, Rosa Lee 191, 192, 194
Institute of Politics in Williamstown 117
"intellectual dynamism" 144
Internal Security Act of 1950 191
International Labor Defense 5, 142
international labor radicalism 66
International Ladies Garment Workers Union 142
International Lenin School 20, 230
International Longshoremen's and Warehousemen's Union (ILWU) 234
International Seamen's Union 170
Interwar Years, The 116–20
Invitation to an Inquest (1983) 10
Iowa 96
Iran 129
Italo-Ethiopian War (1935–6) 188
Italy 67
Isserman, Maurice 8, 11, 49
"I Stand Here Ironing" (1956) 242
Ivens, Joris 163

Jackson, George 210
Jackson, Jonathan 211
Jackson, Robert H. 53–4
Jaffe, Philip J. 50–1
Japan 117
Jenkins, Dave 231, 233, 234, 236, 243
Jews 113
Johanningsmeier, Edward P. 48
Johannsen, Anton 68
Jones, Claudia
  accounting for black women
  Achilles' Heel in US 192
  Cold War 188
  CP-11 191
  early 1930s 187, 188–90
  essay in *Political Affairs* (1949) 191
  historical narratives 198
  Korean War 194, 195
  peace and fascism 197
  political prisoner in the United States 186
  Rosa Lee Ingram 192
  "superexploitation of black women" 186, 188
Jones, Jack 68
Journal of American History 169
Jowitt, William 10
Juvenile Justice Commission 243

Kailin, Charlie 161
"Karelian Fever" 99
Kaufman, Irving 125
Kazin, Michael 73
Keeran, Roger 8
Keith, Irving 230
Kelly, Robin 11
Kennedy Assassination 113
Kerr, Clark 8
Khrushchev, Nikita 7, 82
Khrushchev revelations 238, 239
Kid from Hoboken, The 164, 176
Kimmage, Michael 144, 154
Kind and Usual Punishment: The Prison Business (1973) 241
Kissinger, Henry 215
Klehr, Harvey 9, 41, 124, 129, 168, 169
Knights of Labor 67
Korea 123
Korean War 7, 97, 171, 185, 191–4
Kropotkin 69
Kuivinen, Einar 96, 100
Kuomintang (KMT), nationalist party 47
Kutulas, Judy 144

Labor History (1985) 11
LaFollette, Robert 3, 45, 90, 91
Lapin, Adam 233, 240, 241
LA Times 216, 221
Latin America 194
Leavenworth Penitentiary 43
Leninist Communist Party 75
Lenin's Left-Wing Communism: An Infantile Disorder 70
Lenin, V. I. 4, 20, 44, 46, 68, 70, 73–6, 100, 112, 115, 142–3
Lewis, John L. 78
Les Cahiers du Communisme 27
Lewis, John L. 77

Library of Congress 90
Lichtenstein, Nelson 78
Lincoln, Abraham 171
Lincoln veterans 169
Lipton, Eunice 170–1
litmus test 97
"Little Steel," May of 1937 79
A Long View from the Left: Memoirs of an American Revolutionary (1973), 8
London 177
London's High Gate Cemetery 186
Los Angeles Police Department 208–9
Louis Freeland Post 116
Lovestone, Jay 18, 19, 65, 66, 98
Lozovsky, Solomon 31, 45, 47, 71, 75

Mackenzie-Papeneau battalion 171, 177
MacLeish, Archibald 163
"Madison County Plan" 93
Madison Square Garden 54
magnification 122
"Manichean perspective" 156
Manley, Joseph 68
Many are the Crimes: McCarthyism in America 11
Mark, Eduard 23, 32–4
Marine Firemen's union (MFOW) 234
Marine Workers Industrial Union (MWIU) 170
Marshall, George C. 124
Martens, Ludwig 115, 117
Martin, Trayvon 197
Marty, Andre 172
Marxism-Leninism 20, 22, 25–6, 33, 185–6, 188, 190, 244
"Marxist Olympics" 216
Marx, Karl 46, 186
Mason, Noah M. 120
Massachusetts 117
Maas, Eva Lapin 244
Making of a Muckraker, The (1979) 241, 242
McCarran Act 191
McCarthy, Joseph 7–9, 11–12, 113, 123–7, 130, 161, 185, 190–1
McClain, James 211
McCuistion, William C. 172–3, 179
McKinley, William 114
Men in Battle 164, 166, 167, 172

"The Men of the Abraham Lincoln Battalion" 169
the "Mental Comintern" 24–5
Mexico 66
Mikhelson-Manuilov, Solomon 51
Miller, Arthur 8
Mink, George 152
Minnesota (northern) 3, 17, 41, 92, 96, 98, 101
Minnesota Farmer-Labor Party (FLP) 41, 93
Minnesota Farmers Union 98, 100
Mitchell, Charlene 219
Mitford, Jessica 230, 231
Modernization and Mechanization Agreement of 1960 241
Modern School movement 69
Molotov-Ribbentrop Pact 81, 232
Monatte, Pierre 68
Montana (northeastern) 7, 92, 94–6, 98
Mooney, Tom 241
Moore, Richard B. 188
Mormons 113
Mortimer, Wyndham 78
Moscow 2
Moscow Show Trials 141
Mossadegh, Muhammed 129
Mueller, Robert 111
Murphy, Frank 78
Murray, Robert 116
Muslims 113

Naison, Mark 8
Naming Names (1980) 9
National Association for the Advancement of Colored People (NAACP) 122, 162, 256
National Endowment for the Humanities (NEH) 241
National Executive Committee 43
National Front policy 26–7, 32, 33
National Industrial Recovery Act (NRA) 77
National Labor Relations Act 30
National Labor Relations Board 51
National Maritime Union 173, 240
National Origins Act 116, 117
National Recovery Administration 51
National Security Agency (NSA) 111

National Textile Workers Union (NTWU) 4
National United Committee to Free Angela Davis (NUCFAD) 211
Nation, The 161–2
Nation Union of Marine Cooks and Stewards (NUMCS) 240
Nazi Germany 20–2, 25, 52, 54, 170
Nazism 19
Nazi-Soviet pact (1939) 5–6, 52
Navasky, Victor 9
Negro slavery 115
"Negro Question" 185
Nelson, Steve 123
neo-Malthusianism 69
New Deal political coalition 17, 26, 36
New Deal Democrats 232
New Deal program 19
New Jersey egg farmers 98
New Leader 147
New Masses 143
New Politics movement 243
New York 67, 96, 116
New York Museum of Modern Art 233
New York Sun 146, 147
New York Times 21, 53, 115, 165
New York World-Telegram 142
Nightmare in Red: The McCarthy Era in Perspective (1990) 9
Nitzberg, Judy 238, 242
Nitzberg, Leo 230, 240, 242, 244
Nixon, Richard 128, 205
non-aggression pact VALB members 171
non-Communist political formations 33
non-Communist Trade Union Educational League (TUEL) 71
Non-Intervention Committee 166
Norman, Irving 165
North America 25
North American Newspaper Alliance (NANA) 163
North Atlantic Treaty Organization (NATO) 197
North Dakota organization 97
North, Joe 165
NSA method 128

The October Revolution 3
Odyssey of the Abraham Lincoln Brigade: Americans in the Spanish Civil War 175

Office of Strategic Services (OSS) 167, 168
"Old Bolsheviks" 52
Old Left Communists 189
Oliver Law case 174
Olmsted, Kathryn 113
Olsen, Jack 238, 240, 242
Olsen, Tillie 238, 242
1917 Espionage Act 113, 114
1938 Munich pact 51
1948 Election
    CPUSA's activities 31
    Democratic National Convention 28
    Democratic Party 29–30
    European industry 31
    Popular Front strategy 28
    President Truman 28
    Republican controlled Congress 30
1948 Henry Wallace presidential campaign 90
1968 World Youth Festival 216
1982 Executive Order 128
Oppenheimer, Daniel 229
Oregon 67
Ortega, Daniel 171
"Oscar K. Everett" 178
Oval Office 73

Palmer, A. Mitchell 3, 114, 115, 130
Palmer, Bryan 65
Panyushkin, Alexander 31
"paranoid style" 113
Paris Peace Conference 34
Parsons, Albert 68
Passaic Strike of 1926 75
Passos, John Dos 77, 163, 172
Patton, James 96
peace 190–5
Pearl Harbor 113
Pennsylvania Railroad 67
Pennsylvania Sugar company 119
People's Commissariat of Justice 47
People's Republic of China 194
People's World (PW) 232, 233, 236
Pepper, John 45, 75, 91
"Perspectives for Democracy and Socialism in [the] 90s" 221
Philadelphia Negro, the 67
Philadelphia's Lithuanian Socialist Chorus 115–16
Philbrick, Herb 127

Philippines 117
Platte County, Missouri 43
Pogány, Joseph 81
Political Affairs 185, 191, 238
Popular Front 5, 50, 95–8, 169, 170, 178, 189, 190, 232
Portland 67
postal communications 23
Postek, Stanley 177, 178
Poyntz, Juliet Stuart
  alleged liquidation 155
  anti-Nazi opposition work 149
  Bykov, Boris 146
  disappearance of Juliet 142
  with German and Soviet spies 153
  German Nazism and Italian fascism 143
  international students recruitment 148
  member in CPUSA 142
  New York Sun 146
  party leader 147
  reunification 146
  sexist law 148–9
  Solow 145, 147, 148
pre-Communist radicalism 73
"premature antifascism" concept 167, 168
"premature antifascist" 162, 167
President Truman 28–9
Preston, William Jr. 116
"Problems and Politics in the USA" 206
Producers News 94, 99
Progressive Citizens of America 233
Progressive Party 6, 35, 36, 97
Public Housing Authority 243
Puerto Rico 117
Puro, Henry 92
Putna, Viovt 151

Qaddafi, Muammar 197–8
QAnon conspiracy theory 113

Rackley, Mildred 175
Rafalko, Frank J. 119
Ramseyer, C. William 118
Reagan, Ronald 128, 171
Red Chicago: American Communism at Its Grassroots, 1928–35 (2007) 11
Red Guard companies 47
Red Harvest: The Communist Party and American Farmers 89

Red International of Labor Unions (RILU) 19, 44, 68
Red International of Trade Unions (Profintern) 4
Red Scare/Red Scares 5, 8, 112, 115, 116, 119, 122, 126
"Reds Inflaming Blacks" 115
Reed, John 83
Reno, Franklin Victor 119
Reno, Milo 93
Republican-led US Senate Select Committee 111
Reuther, Walter 78, 80
"Rigged Witch Hunt" 111
Robeson, Paul 233
Robinson, Donald 142
Roger, Sidney 236
Romance of American Communism, The (1977) 229
Roosevelt, Franklin D. 19, 25, 51
Roosevelt Recession 78
Roots of American Communism, The 8
Rosenberger, Laura 112
Rosenberg, Ethel 7–8, 10, 125–6
Rosenberg, Julius 7–8, 10, 125–6, 129
Rosenberg Ring 119, 123
Rosenstone, Robert 163–4, 169, 170
Rosenthal, Henry 143
Rossiter, Clinton 7–8
Rossmer, Alfred 68
Roubles, Jose 172
Rubens, A. A. 150–1, 154
Rubin, Danny 219
Rumrich, Gunther 152
Russia 111, 117
Russian American Society 234
Russian-born immigrants 115
Russian Civil War 4, 44
The Russian Revolution 4, 188
Russian State Archive of Socio-Political History (RGASPI) 9, 10, 129, 175, 176
Russo-Finnish War of 1939–40 100
Ruthenberg, Charles 83, 91
Ryan, James 66, 67, 81
Ryan, Paul 233

San Francisco Bay Area 230
San Francisco Chronicle 243
San Francisco Federation of Teachers 242

San Francisco New School 244
San Francisco Russian Club 236
San Francisco Party 219
San Jose Mercury News 219
Schein, G. David 125
Schrecker, Ellen 11, 191–2
Scotland 67
The "Scottsboro Boys" 188
Secretary of the German Communist Party 212
Society of the Cincinnati 171
Second Red Scare 8
Second World War 6, 9, 17, 23, 49, 90, 95, 112, 113, 121–2, 154, 167, 168, 192, 195, 232, 235
"Secret speech" (1956) 123
The Secret World of American Communism (1995) 9
"Security Index" 122
Seeger, Pete 233
Selective Service Act 43
Senator Frank Church (D-Idaho)'s hearings (1975) 128
Senator Tom Cotton (R-AR) 113
Seventh Ward 67
Seventh World Congress of the Comintern (1935) 5
Shelley, John F. 243
Shelley, Mayor 243
Show Trials, The 144
Skittereen 67
Smith Act 6, 37, 191, 229, 236
Smith, Bradley F. 121
Sobell, Morton 129
social fascists 5, 49, 93, 170
Socialist Democratic Party of Germany (SPD) 68
Socialist Party of America (SPA) 3
Socialists 68
  dissenters 79
  soapboxers 67
Soledad Brothers Defense Committee 210
Solow, Herbert 141
Southern Christian Leadership Conference (SCLC) 211–12
Southwest Labor Studies Association 241
Soviet-American agreements 27
Soviets at Work, The 143
Soviet Union 1, 2, 4–9, 11, 20, 23, 25, 28, 41, 46, 47, 65–6, 99, 113, 116, 117, 120, 129, 141, 169, 171, 174, 176, 185, 188, 190–4, 215, 221–2, 233, 239, 245
Soviet Secret Police 151
Soviet spies 121, 123
USSR 21–3, 30, 46–8, 51, 54
The Soviet World of American Communism (1998) 9
Spain 164, 166, 171, 174
Spain Betrayed: The Soviet Union in the Spanish Civil War 174
Spain in Our Hearts: Americans in the Spanish Civil War, 1936–1939 176
Spanish-American War 171
Spanish Civil War 161, 164, 166
Spanish Earth, The 163
Spengler, Oswald 149
Stachel, Jack 49
Stalinism 65
Stalin, Joseph 18–19, 25, 46, 52, 117, 141, 169, 174
"Stalinization" 74
Stalinization of American Communism 73
Stanwyck, Barbara 1
Starobin, Joseph 17, 24
Starvus, Loretta 230, 244
State Department (1991) 129
State Department's liberalization of credit policies 117
State Federation of Labor (ASFL) 236
Steel Strike (1919) 71, 72, 77
Steel Workers' Organizing Committee (SWOC) 79
Stent, Angela 111
Stern, Marvin 174
Storch, Randi 2, 11–12, 255–6
Stover, Fred 97
The Strange Case of Alger Hiss (1953) 10
"The Struggle for Peace in the United States" (1952) 193, 196
"student agitators" 127
Student Non-Violent Coordinating Committee's (SNCC) 209
Subversive Activities Control Act (1950) 125
Subversive Activities Control Board (SACB) 171
Sullivan, Thomas R. 43
supporters 1
Syndicalism (1912) 68–9

Taft-Hartley Act in 1947 30, 190
Talbott, Glenn 97
Taunton, Massachusetts 67
telegrams 214–15
Tell Me a Riddle 242
Texas 67
Thatcher, Bill 97
Third Period 4, 9, 47–9, 98
Third World Left organizations 209
Third World Liberation movements 216
Third World Women's Alliance 186
Thomas, Norman 51
"Three Generations: Historians view American Communism" 11
Thurmond, Strom 36
Thurston, Robert 152
Tilton, Alfred 119
tobacco 166
Todd, Louise 231, 244
Tom Mooney Company 177
Trade Union Educational League (TUEL) 45
Trade Union Unity League 71
Tresca, Carlo 152
Treuhaft, Robert 239, 242
Trial of Dr. Spock, The (1969) 241
Trilling, Lionel 143
Trotskyist dissenters 79
Trotsky, Leon 81, 142
"troll factories" 112
Trump, Donald 13, 111–12, 114, 124, 130, 185, 188, 196–7
Tydings, Millard 123–4, 130
Tyler, Jarvis 220

un-American activities 119
Union of Russian Workers 3
Unions and Union Leaders of their Own Choosing (1960) 8
United Auto Workers (UAW) 78
United Electrical Workers' union 234
United Farmer 92
United Farmers Educational League 91
United Farmers League (UFL) 92–5
United Farm Workers 242, 243
United Mine Workers Union (UMW) 75
United Nations 7
United States 2, 18, 19, 25, 30, 41, 65, 67, 68, 70, 71, 81, 89, 92, 99, 100, 113–17, 121, 129, 143, 144, 149, 154, 163, 165, 167, 169, 173, 174, 185, 186, 188, 190–3, 195–7, 206, 209, 241, 256
Unity Alliance 99
"Unity Caucus" radicals 78
University of California San Diego (1967) 208
Upper Peninsula of Michigan 92, 99
US Cold War foreign policy 185
US electoral system 112
US Immigration and Customs Enforcement (ICE) 197
US Military documents 168
USS President Monroe 177

Varga, Eugene S. 31
VENONA transcripts 11, 129
Veterans of Foreign Wars (VFW) 171
Veterans of the Abraham Lincoln Brigade (VALB) 171
The Vietnam conflict 41
Vietnam War draft resisters 243
Volunteer for Liberty 175
Voorhis Act (1940) 23, 54
Voorhis, Jerry 120
Vronsky, Boris 31
Vsesojuznoe Obschestvo Kul'turnykh Svyzei s zagranitseior (VOKS) 234

Walker, Adelaide 141, 143–4
Wallace, Henry 29, 35, 36, 97
Walsh, Edmund 123
Ward, Estolv 236
"Ware group" 95
Washington, George 113, 171
Weinstone, William W. 47–8, 76, 79
Welch, Joseph 125, 127
West Indies 194
Weston, Edward 233
Which Side Were You On? The American Communist Party during the Second World War (1982) 8
White, G. Edward 128
White, Paul 175
Wiggens, Ella May 4
Williams College conference 2, 11, 255
Wilson, Veronica 127
Wilson, William B. 116
Wilson, Woodrow 73, 116
Wisconsin education system 162
"witch hunt" 123

Witness (book) 142, 154–5, 229
Wobblies 68
Wolff, Milton 167–9, 171, 172, 174
"Woman Question" 185
Workers and Farmers Cooperative Unity Alliance 98
Workers International Relief 5
Workers Party 3, 90–2, 98

XV Brigade Political Commissar 166
XV International Brigade 162

Yale University Press 174
Yates, Allan 240
Yates, O'Connor 239, 244
Yonnondio 242
Young Communist League 169
Young Democrats 242
Yates, O'Connor 239

Zelensky, Vladimir 111
Zeligs, Meyer A. 10
Zhdanov, Andrei 35, 37
Zumoff, Jacob A. 46

www.ingramcontent.com/pod-product-compliance
Lightning Source LLC
Chambersburg PA
CBHW072129290426
44111CB00012B/1836